The Irish Contribution to European Scholastic Thought

To all who taught and studied
Scholastic Philosophy at Queen's University, 1909–2009

The Irish Contribution to European Scholastic Thought

James McEvoy and Michael Dunne

EDITORS

With a foreword by His Eminence Cahal B. Cardinal Daly

FOUR COURTS PRESS
for the IRISH PHILOSOPHICAL SOCIETY

Set in 10.5 on 12.5 Ehrhardt for
FOUR COURTS PRESS LTD
7 Malpas Street, Dublin 8, Ireland
e-mail: info@fourcourtspress.ie
http://www.fourcourtspress.ie
and in North America
FOUR COURTS PRESS
c/o ISBS, 920 N.E. 58th Avenue, Suite 300, Portland, OR 97213.

ISBN 978–1–84682–165–3

Printed in England by
CPI Antony Rowe, Chippenham, Wilts.

Contents

Foreword

CARDINAL CAHAL B. DALY

I feel honoured to have been asked by Professor McEvoy to give the opening address at this important international conference marking the centenary of Queen's University. The distinguished list of speakers itself tells of the international outreach of the University's chair of Scholastic Philosophy. It tells also of the esteem in which Professor McEvoy is held in the world of scholarship, whether across Ireland or in Louvain or in Rome or in the United States. It speaks also of the international dimension of Scholastic Philosophy as an academic discipline.

That dimension was bitterly disputed when our University was being instituted a century ago. Queen's University was founded as a replacement for the Queen's College, Belfast, itself a college within the Royal University of Ireland. When the whole island of Ireland was under British rule, university education was for long the exclusive prerogative of Trinity College, Dublin, a university which saw itself as a sister university of Oxford and Cambridge and which was then, like them, Anglican in ethos and British in its sense of identity. The Royal University through its Colleges in Dublin, Cork (QCC) and Galway (QCG) was designed to offer university education to Catholics. Queen's College, Belfast, was originally intended as a university primarily for Presbyterians, and, as such, it had close links with Scottish universities.

Early in the twentieth century it was felt that the Queen's Colleges needed to be given full university status and prestige and a corresponding constitution. At the end of 1908 a new Irish Universities Act was given the royal assent. Under this Act the Queen's University in Belfast received its present title and university commissioners were named, whose function was to draw up statutes for the new university and to provide for its governance and administration. The new university was formally constituted on 31 October 1909.

Presbyterians, with memories of disadvantage and even discrimination in comparison with the established Church of Ireland, were insistent that the new university was to be non-sectarian. They were, at the same time, anxious that, while Roman Catholics would be accepted as students, they would enjoy no kind of favourable treatment in the new university. The commissioners, however, were conscious that the Catholic population could provide an added supply of students and thus add strength to the new university. The Catholic bishops also

7

favoured the attendance of Catholics at Queen's, since Catholics in the North of Ireland, up to then, had been largely denied the benefits of university education. Some Catholics had attended the Queen's College at Belfast, but these were relatively few in number.

The bishops, however, considered that separate provision should be made for Catholic students in some sensitive areas of learning, particularly in history, in English literature, in medical ethics and in 'mental and moral science'. They asked that separate chairs be set up in these departments to cater for Catholics. The commissioners decided to make special provision for Catholics in two of these departments: medical students were to have part of their training in the (Catholic) Mater Infirmorum Hospital, and a lectureship in Scholastic Philosophy was to be set up in the new University. The last-named lectureship would at that time have required the appointment of a Catholic priest to the academic staff. This, and the very suggestion of a separate department of Scholastic Philosophy, was vigorously opposed by some of the commissioners, who had the strong support of the Protestant public in general. There were notable exceptions, including the doughty Presbyterian minister, the Revd J.B. Armour of Ballymoney, together with the professor of Latin, namely Robert Mitchell Henry, who became my revered teacher of Latin in the 1930s and who was, I am glad to say, a good friend of mine from my student days onwards.

Appeals were launched on behalf of two Presbyterian ministers and of Lord Londonderry against the decision of the commissioners. Their contention was that the establishment of Scholastic Philosophy as a university discipline was a violation of the non-denominational character of the new university, since Scholastic Philosophy was not a proper academic discipline but was instead a branch of Roman Catholic theology. The case was heard before the Irish privy council in October 1909. The commissioners, aided by Fr Thomas Finlay SJ, argued that

> Scholastic Philosophy is not a system of theology but a philosophical system, based on the principles and methods of Aristotle [...]. If it is legit-imate to teach philosophy at all it is as legitimate to teach it from the Scholastic as from any other standpoint.

The hearing lasted three days. The appeals were dismissed. The privy council ruled that Scholastic Philosophy had a rightful place in any academic curriculum. The chief secretary at the time, Augustine Birrell, later referred to one of the judges who heard the case as a man 'of sound Protestant convictions' but open-minded. This judge, according to Birrell, expressed surprise that there had been such a dispute about an author, St Thomas, whose book (and I quote) *The Imitation of Christ*, was read by Protestants as well as by Catholics, and was a book to which nobody could take exception! He was obviously open-minded as between Thomas Aquinas and Thomas à Kempis!

The Presbyterian General Assembly, however, expressed strong disapproval of the setting up of the lectureship. A resolution was moved at the Convocation of the new university, describing the Scholastic Philosophy lectureship as 'tentative and probationary'. Attempts were made at various times to limit the scope of teaching in Scholastic Philosophy at Queen's. Yet Scholastic Philosophy survived and flourished. The present conference is one sign of its healthy state and of its contribution to the repute of this university.

One feature of the teaching of Scholastic Philosophy in Queen's is that, for a great part of the last century, most of the priests of the diocese of Down and Connor have been graduates of this University and of its Department of Scholastic Philosophy. This has been a factor for good will between the university and the Catholic clergy of this whole area, and indeed between Queen's University and the Catholic population of this city and its surrounding area. More recently, the same has been true for seminarians of the diocese of Derry. The importance of this as a contribution to what we are now calling a 'shared future' between Catholics and Protestants, between nationalists and unionists, in Northern Ireland should not be under-estimated.

However, if one were making a case for the teaching of Scholastic Philosophy in a university nowadays, one would not be invoking the rights of Catholics to university teaching in 'their' tradition in philosophy. One would be insisting rather on the intrinsic value of Scholastic Philosophy as a full and equal participant in philosophical thought and debate across the world.

Indeed, one could argue that Scholastic Philosophy has an important role to play in the dialogue between different traditions in modern philosophy and particularly in the necessary dialogue between the British or Anglo-Saxon tradition in philosophy and the European tradition. The British tradition is broadly empiricist, sometimes positivistic, and has little sympathy for metaphysics. It tends to retain the old post-Enlightenment mentality of the so-called 'leap across the Middle Ages', and it tends to regard most modern European philosophical thinkers and writers as dealing with themes which belong rather to the realm of imaginative literature and poetry than to that of philosophy. There are, of course, exceptions, like that of Wittgenstein – although he was sometimes misread as being a founding father of logical positivism. Philosophical dialogue between the British tradition and, say, the French or German tradition in their modern expressions, is rare. Each tends to regard the other as doing something which, whatever its literary quality may be, is simply not philosophy. When I began teaching here, I found very few books in the philosophy section of the library in any language except English. I have to say, however, that I had excellent relationships with my colleagues in the

Department of Philosophy, and helpful dialogue between the two departments was a regular feature of my teaching experience in Queen's.

Debate between the different traditions in philosophy, and especially between what I call the British tradition and the European traditions, is, I believe, more than ever necessary; and I believe that Scholastic Philosophy, which pre-dates all of them, can play an important role in this dialogue. Peter Geach once remarked that Thomistic philosophy can enable us to approach modern philosophers with a truly open and objective mind, because it frees us from the limiting and constricting mindsets of modern culture, which almost a priori excludes the metaphysical and the transcendent.

Finally, I wish to point, if I may, to what I see as one of the dangers facing the modern university, at least in these islands of ours. Depending as they do to an unhealthy degree on the State as their main source of funding, universities are coming under increasing pressure to subserve utilitarian ends rather than the pursuit of knowledge. They are seen as agents of the economy, or instruments of a 'knowledge-based economy', rather than as seekers after truth. Departments of teaching and learning which are not regarded as serving economic development are steadily being phased out. The abandonment of the teaching of classical Latin and Greek by many universities is a case in point. Philosophy departments in general face an uncertain future. Scholastic Philosophy in particular will have to work hard to ensure its survival as a distinct university discipline. A good economy is eminently desirable and even necessary, but it does not of itself serve the still greater cause of the good life. Plato's aphorism remains true: the unexamined life is not worth living. It is still sadly possible '*propter vitam vivendi perdere causas*'. However, I do not wish to end on a negative note. This centenary conference gives hope for the future.

I warmly welcome our distinguished speakers. We look forward eagerly to their contributions.

Post-scriptum

If I may be allowed a *post-scriptum* comment, I should wish to say that my immediate predecessor in the Department of Scholastic Philosophy, Monsignor Arthur Ryan, a distinguished teacher, public lecturer and writer, wrote, in 1940, in a paper delivered at the Maynooth Union, a paragraph of which I was strongly reminded by several of the lectures delivered at this conference. The paper in question had the title: 'Christianity, Nationalism and Race'; I quote:

> Can we imagine today that easy commerce of minds by which a professor of philosophy could teach successively in Italian, French and German universities without noticing anything more than a difference in climate? Could we imagine Dr Peter Coffey holding the chair of Philosophy at Moscow, or Dr Julius Hecker in Maynooth? Yet a great predecessor of Dr

Coffey's did just that. St Thomas Aquinas taught in Naples, Paris and Cologne; and noticed perhaps a difference in scenery and temperature, but was equally at home in the spiritual, cultural and moral sphere in all three. This moral and spiritual unity is clearly an incalculable benefit for human relationships, and its loss is an enormous disaster.[1]

---

1 See Monsignor Ryan's posthumous collection of papers, *Mirroring Christ's splendour*, ed. Ambrose Macaulay (Dublin, 1984).

Notes on contributors

CARDINAL CAHAL B. DALY was born on 1 October 1917 at Loughguile, Co. Antrim, the child of a schoolmaster of Co. Roscommon origin. He studied at St Malachy's College, Belfast, Queen's University, and St Patrick's College, Maynooth, where he was ordained a priest in 1941. He was awarded the degree of DD from the Pontifical University, Maynooth, in 1944. In 1946, he was appointed to a lectureship at the Scholastic Philosophy Department, QUB, where he was subsequently made a reader in 1965. Appointed bishop of Ardagh and Clonmacnois in 1967, he moved to the see of Down and Connor in 1982 and to the archdiocese of Armagh in 1990. He is the author of fourteen books and innumerable other publications, and is an honorary DD of QUB.

CATHERINE KAVANAGH is a graduate of University College, Dublin, and holds a doctorate in Philosophy from Notre Dame University, Indiana, where she has also lectured. She is the author of several articles on Iohannes Scottus Eriugena. Since 2006 she has been a lecturer in Philosophy at Mary Immaculate College, University of Limerick.

BISHOP JOHN FLEMING was born at Ardpatrick, Co. Limerick, in 1948. Educated at St Munchin's College, he is a graduate of NUI (Maynooth, 1968). He was ordained a priest for the diocese of Limerick in 1972. He studied matrimonial law in Rome and London and obtained a doctorate in Canon Law at the Gregorian University, Rome. In 1985 he was appointed director of formation at the Irish College, Rome and became its rector in 1993. He was appointed bishop of Killala in 2002.

MICHAEL DUNNE was born in Dublin in 1962. After graduating from UCD in 1985 he worked in Italy as a research assistant with the Index Thomisticus. While there he embarked upon research into some of Ireland's medieval Scholastic heritage. Beginning with Peter of Ireland (*c.*1200–65), he undertook the edition of the extant works. His research formed the basis of his doctoral thesis, which was later published. This interest continues with his current research project: the edition of the Scholastic works of Richard FitzRalph (1300–60). He lectures in Medieval Philosophy and the Philosophy of Religion at NUI Maynooth. In 2008 he was elected president of the Irish Philosophical Society.

JAMES McEVOY occupies the chair of Scholastic Philosophy in the School of Politics, International Studies and Philosophy at QUB. He was formerly Dean of Philosophy at the National University of Ireland, Maynooth, and before that he was a Professor at the Institut Supérieur de Philosophie at the Université Catholique de Louvain, Louvain-la-Neuve, Belgium. He has written or edited over twenty books. His research strengths are in Medieval Philosophy, Neoplatonism, and the philosophy of friendship and community. He is a priest of the diocese of Down & Connor. In 1982 he was elected to membership of the Royal Irish Academy. He is Doct. Lett. h.c. of Leicester University.

DECLAN LAWELL was born at Glengormley, Co. Antrim, in 1977. After attending St Malachy's College, Belfast, he gained a BA in Scholastic Philosophy and Latin/Greek from Queen's University, Belfast, before obtaining the STB in Theology at the Gregorian University, Rome. He graduated from Queen's University in 2008 with a PhD in Scholastic Philosophy for a thesis on Thomas Gallus (d. 1246) and has published several pieces of his research work.

MICHAEL HAREN edits the Calendar of Papal Registers for the Irish Manuscripts Commission. His other publications include *Medieval Thought: The Western Intellectual Tradition from Antiquity to the Thirteenth Century* (2nd edition, 1992); *Sin and Society in Fourteenth-Century England* (2000); and numerous articles on ecclesiastical history. With Y. de Pontfarcy, he has edited *The Medieval Pilgrimage to St Patrick's Purgatory: Lough Derg and the European Tradition* (1988).

RUAIRÍ Ó hUIGINN graduated with a first-class honours degree in Celtic Studies at University College, Dublin in 1976 and obtained a PhD from Queen's University, Belfast in Celtic in 1989. He has held lectureships at the universities of Uppsala (1978–80), University College, Galway (1980–1), Bonn (1981–5) and Queen's University, Belfast (1985–93). He is currently Professor of Modern Irish at the National University of Ireland, Maynooth. His research interests include Celtic Historical Cycles, Onomastics and the Ulster and Fenian Cycles. He edits *Ainm: Bulletin of the Ulster Place-Name Society* and *Léachtaí Cholm Cille* and is co-editor of *Bliainiris*. He is a member of the Royal Irish Academy.

MARTIN W.F. STONE is Professor of Renaissance and Early Modern Philosophy at the Hoger Instituut voor Wijsbegeerte, Katholieke Universiteit Leuven, Belgium. He is the author of many studies on late medieval and early modern Scholasticism, as well as the Scholastic traditions of early modern Louvain. He has a specific interest in the philosophical thought of the Irish Franciscans in the seventeenth and eighteenth centuries. His two-volume history of late Scholastic ethics, *The Subtle Arts of Casuistry*, will soon be published by Oxford University Press. This will be followed by a monograph, *Scotus Hibernicus*, on the Irish friars.

PADRE ALESSANDRO APOLLONIO is Assistant General of the Franciscan order of the Frati Francescani dell'Immacolata. He is rector of the Seminario Teologico of the Frati where he is professor of Logic and of Franciscan Theology and editor of the magazine *Immaculata Mediatrix*. He is the author of numerous publications on epistemology of Scholastic–Scotist inspiration.

DR LIAM CHAMBERS is a lecturer in the Department of History at Mary Immaculate College, University of Limerick. His publications include *Rebellion in Kildare, 1790–1803* (1998) and *Michael Moore, c.1639–1726: Provost of Trinity, Rector of Paris* (2005). He is currently working on the history of the Irish College in Paris 1578–2000, for which he was awarded an IRCHSS Government of Ireland Research Fellowship in 2005–6.

PHILIPP W. ROSEMANN was born in 1964 in Frankfurt am Main. After studies at the universites of Hamburg, Belfast (QUB) and the Université Catholique de Louvain, he taught at Uganda Martyrs University for a year. He has been with the University of Dallas since 1998. His areas of interest are medieval thought and postmodernism. His most recent books are *Peter Lombard* (2004) and *The Story of a Great Medieval Book: Peter's Lombard's 'Sentences'* (2007). He is currently editing a volume of essays for Brill ('Medieval Commentaries on the Sentences of Peter Lombard', vol. 2) and is working for Eerdmans on a book devoted to the religious meaning of transgression. He is the editor of the 'Dallas Medieval Texts and Translations' series.

GAVAN JENNINGS received an MA from University College, Dublin for his thesis on Berkeley's theory of radical dependence (1992), and in 1998 a PhD from the Pontifical University of the Holy Cross, Rome, for his thesis on the Aristotelian dialectic. He is a priest of the Opus Dei prelature and is the Honorary Secretary of the Irish Philosophical Society.

ÉAMONN GAINES is a native of Dublin, and a graduate of University College, Dublin and NUI Maynooth. He has taught philosophy courses at NUIM, the Pontifical University at Maynooth and the Queen's University of Belfast.

Editors' introduction

The centenary of Scholastic Philosophy at QUB could have been celebrated in more than one academic mode.[1] It would have been perfectly possible to have envisaged a conference on a theme of general philosophical interest, such as action theory, to which Scholastic philosophers have made contributions down the ages. Alternatively, a colloquium could have been planned with Thomistic thought, or some aspect of it, at the centre of its focus. Another possibility would have been to study the historiography of Scholastic Philosophy in some of its medieval and modern manifestations. We believe that the choice at which we arrived has the merit of originality.

Of the many conferences bearing upon Scholastic Philosophy, medieval thought or Thomism (both medieval and modern) down the years, none as yet has focused upon the Irish contribution to European Scholastic thought. We felt the time to be ripe for the historical exploration of this theme, especially since we recognized that a talented team of researchers could be assembled for the purpose. Such a venture could not have been contemplated even as recently as ten years ago, whereas at the present time some historical research is being conducted into each of the major figures and indeed the institutions that merit consideration in the centuries-wide span to be covered. This holds true not only of the medieval centuries but of the modern; numerous Irishmen were active in the forty-six or so Irish Continental Colleges, as well as in various universities in France, the Iberian Peninsula, the German Empire and Italy, from before AD 1600 up until the 1790s, when the French Revolution put a sudden and definitive end to these developments by secularizing the institutions in which these Irish figures were professors. Much of the property, books and goods belonging to these colleges, and even many of the college buildings in various parts of Europe, were diverted by the revolutionaries into the French military effort. It is our hope that the present book gathering together the papers presented at the conference will draw up a balance-sheet of the most recent research on the broad

---

1 The historical background can be found in the following, *inter alia:* Maisie Ward, *Insurrection versus resurrection* (London, 1937), ch. 3, 'The Irish university – an educational question', pp 50–77; id., *The Wilfred Wards and the transition* (London, 1934), ch. XVI, 'The university question', pp 260–76; David Kennedy, *Towards a university: an account of some institutions for higher education in Ireland and elsewhere, and of the attitude of Irish Catholics to them, with particular reference to Queen's College and Queen's University, Belfast* (Belfast, 1946), pp 63–8; Fergal McGrath, *Newman's university: idea and reality* (Dublin, 1951); id., 'The University Question', in *A history of Irish Catholicism*, v, fasc. 6: *Catholic Education* (Dublin, 1971), pp 84–142; T. Moody and J.C. Beckett, *Queen's, Belfast; the history of a university* (London, 1959), 2 vols.

topic, while at the same time stimulating fresh efforts and new inquiries within its ambit. The research emphasis upon Scholastic thought in Europe and the contribution made to it over many centuries by scholars of Irish birth seemed a suitable way of celebrating one hundred years of Scholastic Philosophy at Queen's.

Celebrations of the centenary of the Irish Universities Act (1908) are being held this year in Dublin, Cork and Galway, at the other institutions directly affected by the measure. Queen's University has mounted a series of celebratory events of which the conference of 26–28 June was one. The present collective work should be regarded as a literary *floreat* to the University; an expression of the hope that the services it provides for the community in Northern Ireland may continue to prosper and that its reputation may continue to grow steadily within the wider academic world.

This centenary reminds us that Scholastic Philosophy figured as a degree subject in the Faculty of Arts for almost all of the past hundred years. Former members of staff and students in the Department have fresh memories of the academic personalities, the achievements in teaching and research, and the student attainments, which made up its vital experience. It has been decided to include in the present volume a Prosopography comprising notices of the first four lecturers in the Department of Scholastic Philosophy.

A word deserves to be said here about the fourth of these figures, Cardinal Cahal B. Daly, who has graciously contributed the Foreword to the present work. His more than seventy years of association with Queen's enables him to recall some of the figures who played a part in the transition from college to university status that marked the year 1908; Professor R.M. Henry, for instance, was his teacher in the Latin Department, and a personal friend as well as the supervisor of his MA thesis. Cardinal Daly is indisputably the most distinguished figure to emerge from the former Department of Scholastic Philosophy, and his participation in the centennial conference enhanced the occasion just as his presence over the three days of its duration enlivened it. One of those present later commented that he possessed not only the longest memory but the most accurate one of the whole assembly.

* * *

The sense of nostalgia felt at this centenary is not without an intimation of finality. Several years ago the decision was reached not to make any further staff appointments in Scholastic Philosophy. Something of the subject is still to remain, in the form of continued provision of modules in, for example, Scholastic Ethics and Metaphysics. Acknowledgment should be made here of the integration of Scholastic Philosophy into the fabric of the University throughout the hundred years, ever since the decision was taken to accept the subject as a worthy addition to the university curriculum.

* * *

It is to each of the contributors to the present volume that the thanks of its editors go in the very first place, for having enriched our knowledge of Irish Scholastic history; each one of them has come forward with a unique contribution to knowledge. Most of the chapters making up the present book had their origin in the conference of June 2008. Particular thanks are due on the other hand to Dr Declan Lawell and Mr Éamonn Gaines, each of whom contributed a commissioned chapter, to help complete the mosaic. It has been decided to reprint as an additional chapter the Revd Professor McEvoy's inaugural lecture of 1976, 'Values, Limits and Metaphysics', because of its programmatic character relative to Scholastic Philosophy. The chapter on the Minor Irish Scholastics by Professor McEvoy was also written for the book, as was the Prosopography of the earliest lecturers in Scholastic Philosophy. Fr Gavan Jennings deserves a particular word of acknowledgment for having filled with his lecture (and the resulting chapter) on Peter Coffey the painful gap left in the conference programme by the sudden and untimely death of Professor Thomas Kelly, whose absence was deeply felt at the conference; almost all the participants had known him in life. May he rest in peace.

The thanks of the Conference organizers are offered to the sponsors who made it possible. The QUB School of Politics, International Studies and Philosophy in the person of its Head, Professor Shane O'Neill, encouraged and facilitated the centenary conference, and generous sponsorship was made available from the School funds. The QUB Centenary Fund administered by Pro-Vice-Chancellor Gerry McCormac also made a welcome subvention. Supplementary funding came from the Faculty of Arts, Celtic Studies and Philosophy, NUIM and (very suitably in view of the historical intertwining) the Institute of Philosophy of the Katholieke Universiteit Leuven (Belgium).

The editors acknowledge a particular debt of gratitude to the diocese of Down and Connor which in the person of its now-retired bishop, the Most Revd Patrick Walsh, agreed to cover the costs incurred in the preparation of the present volume for publication; and also to the Taoiseach, Mr Brian Cowan TD, who made a generous grant from the Commemorations Initiatives Fund of his office, in favour of our publication and hospitality costs.

The June 2008 conference was held under the academic auspices of the Royal Irish Academy, the School of Politics, International Studies and Philosophy, QUB and the Irish Philosophical Society. The latter body is the co-publisher of the present work. Its former President, Dr Mette Lebech, was most helpful to the organizers and deserves our sincere thanks. The current President, Dr

Michael Dunne (2008–), has close links with Scholastic Philosophy at QUB. A number of academic colleagues took on Conference roles, and we thank Professor Cynthia Macdonald and Professor Marie-Therese Flanagan (QUB), Dr Kevin O'Reilly (Milltown Institute, Dublin), Dr Mette Lebech (NUIM) and Professor William Desmond (KU, Leuven) for their contributions as chairs of the various sessions. Mr Éamonn Gaines and Mr Gaven Kerr aided the organizers in several ways and both of them deserve our thanks for their efforts on behalf of the conference.

The late Dr Michael Adams, whose loss we deplore, welcomed this book and worked with its editors up to the very week of his death; may he rest in peace. The thanks of the editors are addressed to Mr Martin Fanning of Four Courts Press and his associates, all of whom have been unfailingly courteous and efficient while seeing the present book on its way through the press. Dr Julia Hynes, the capable and welcoming Conference Manager, has also been the editorial assistant responsible for co-ordinating the efforts that have resulted in the present book, whose editors wish to extend their sincere thanks to her for the conscientious and devoted way in which she has carried out her task. Without her painstaking efforts and her assiduous work this publication simply could not have been finalized within the requisite time scale. Mr Hugh O'Neill deserves to be thanked sincerely for his proofreading of the whole text of the present work, as well as for valued advice given on numerous occasions to the editors. Finally, we offer a word of appreciation to Anja Vigouroux and Ruth Dilly, of the School of Politics, International Studies and Philosophy, for their help, and also to Deirdre Wildey of QUB Library.

John Scottus Eriugena and the uses of dialectic

CATHERINE KAVANAGH

Dialectic has traditionally been considered the most important of the liberal arts for Eriugena, both in terms of his philosophy as such, and in terms of the importance attached to it in the tradition that precedes him.[1] It is significant from an ontological as well as a disciplinary point of view, in that the structure of being is itself dialectical, and therefore dialectic as a linguistic art is ontologically grounded: the formal workings of dialectic are not merely logical, but also real. The structure of dialectical discourse is a profound metaphor of the twofold process of procession and return, which is itself dialectical. First, we see procession in the image of the movement of God's endless self-revelation in theophany, an image that comes ultimately from Gregory of Nyssa. This makes possible the return, presented in more purely philosophical terms as the correspondence of the formal structure of discourse to the ontological structure of Being itself; as discourse is intelligible, so being is intelligible, and by working through the intelligible structures of philosophical discourse, the soul can eventually return to God. Thus all of Eriugena's works, whether overtly philosophical in content (for example, the *Periphyseon* or the *De praedestinatione*), or

---

1 For an account of the importance of the liberal arts in late Antiquity and the early Middle Ages, see Marie-Thérèse d'Alverny, 'La sagesse et ses sept filles: Recherches sur les allégories de la philosophie et des arts libéraux du IXe au XIIe siècle' in *Mélanges Félix Grat*, 2 vols (Paris, 1946), i, 245–78; P. Riché, *Éducation et Culture dans l'Occident barbare, VIe–VIIIe siècles*, 3rd ed (Paris, 1972): transl. John Contreni, *Education and culture in the Barbarian West, sixth through eighth centuries* (Columbia, SC, 1976); D.L. Wagner (ed.), *The seven liberal arts in the Middle Ages* (Bloomington, IN, 1983); W.H. Stahl, R. Johnson and E.L. Burge, *Martianus Capella and the Seven Liberal Arts* (New York 1971, 1977); H. Steinthal, *Geschichte der Sprachwissenschaft bei den Griechen und Römern mit besonderer Rücksicht auf die Logik*, 2 vols (Berlin, 1890; reprint Hildesheim/New York, 1971); J. Murphy, *A synoptic history of classical rhetoric* (Davis, CA, 1983); George A. Kennedy, *Classical rhetoric and its Christian and secular tradition from ancient to modern times* (Chapel Hill, NC, 1980); also C.E. Lutz, 'Remigius' ideas on the origin of the seven liberal arts', *Mediaevalia et Humanistica* 10 (1956), 32–79; on grammar, Louis Holtz, 'L'enseignement de la grammaire au temps de Charles le Chauve', in C. Leonardi (ed.), *Giovanni Scoto nel suo tempo: L'organizzazione del sapere in età Carolingia: Atti del XXIV Convegno storico internazionale, Todi, 11–14 Ottobre 1987* (Spoleto, 1989), pp 153–69; A. Luhtala, 'Grammar and Dialectic: a topical issue in the ninth century' in J.J. McEvoy, C. Steel and G. van Riel (eds), *Iohannes Scottus Eriugena, the Bible and hermeneutics: Proceedings of the Ninth International Colloquium of the Society for the Promotion of Eriugenian Studies held at Leuven and Louvain-la-Neuve June 7–10, 1995* (Leuven, 1996), pp 279–301.

tending rather towards the exegetical tradition (for example, his commentary on the Prologue to the Gospel of St. John, *Vox aquilae*), are on some level dialectical (just as they are all, due to their textual base, on some level also commentaries), because dialectic is the very structure and dynamism of reality.[2]

As a philosophical method, therefore, dialectic is absolutely reliable, because it is rooted in the very structure of being itself.[3] We see this at work in all of Eriugena's texts: the *De praedestinatione*, written before his exposure to the Byzantine tradition of Pseudo-Dionysius and Maximus Confessor, uses the method of dialectical analysis to resolve what might appear to be a purely theological problem, dependent only on revealed Scripture and religious tradition for a possible solution, and does so on the basis that both religious tradition and dialectical method – faith and reason – are ultimately concerned with truth (or, as Beierwaltes has it, that dialectic is a form of theophany, whereas faith is revealed), and will eventually come to the same conclusions.[4] Following

2 On the nature and importance of medieval dialectic generally, see G. D'Onofrio, *Fons scientiae: La dialettica nell'Occidente tardo-antico* (Naples, 1986), which also includes an extensive treatment of Eriugenian dialectic, pp 275–321. On Eriugena's dialectic, and of the place it occupies within his methodological scheme, see G. d'Onofrio, 'Über die Natur der Einteilung: Die dialektische Entfaltung von Eriugenas Denken', in W. Beierwaltes (ed.), *Eriugena: Begriff und Metapher: Sprachform des Denkens bei Eriugena. Vortraege des VII. Internationalen Eriugena-Colloquiums, Werner-Reimers-Stiftung, Bad-Homburg, 26.–29. Juli 1989* (Heidelberg, 1990), pp 17–38, also G. d'Onofrio, '"Disputandi disciplina": procédés dialectiques et "Logica vetus" dans le langage philosophique de Jean Scot' in G.–H. Allard (ed.), *Jean Scot écrivain* (Montréal and Paris, 1986), pp 229–63. For a slightly different evaluation of the importance of dialectic in relation to grammar and rhetoric, see C. Kavanagh, 'The philosophical importance of grammar for Eriugena', in J. McEvoy and M. Dunne (eds), *Eschatology and history in Eriugena and his age: Proceedings of the Tenth International Colloquium of the Society for the Promotion of Eriugenian Studies, Maynooth and Dublin, August 16–20, 2000* (Leuven, 2002), pp 61–77 and 'Eriugenian developments of Ciceronian topical theory', in Stephen Gersh and Bert Roest (eds), *Medieval and renaissance humanism: rhetoric, representation, and reform*, Brill's Studies in Intellectual History 115 (Leiden, 2003), pp 1–31. 3 *Periphyseon* IV: 'Ac per hoc intelliguntur quod ars illa, quae diuidit genera in species et species in genera resoluit, quaequae ΔΙΑΛΕΚΤΙΚΑ dicitur, non ab humanis machinationibus sit facta, sed in natura rerum, ab auctore omnium artium, quae uere artes sunt, condita, et a sapientibus inuenta, et ad utilitatem sollertis rerum indagis usitata': *Periphyseon: Books I–V*, ed. Édouard Jeauneau, CCCM 161–5 (Turnhout, 1996–2000), Book IV, CCCM 164, 749A, p.12, ll. 283–8 (Other editions of *Periphyseon*: ed. H.J. Floss, PL 122: 439–1022 (Paris, 1853); Iohannis Scotti Eriugenae, *Periphyseon (De Diuisione Naturae)*, Books I–III, ed. I.P. Sheldon-Williams, Scriptores Latini Hiberniae 7, 9, 11 (Dublin, 1968–81); Book IV, ed. Édouard Jeauneau, Scriptores Latini Hibernae 13 (Dublin, 1995); Translation: I.P. Sheldon-Williams (Books I–V), Books IV–V revised by J.J. O'Meara: *Periphyseon (The Division of Nature)* (Montreal and Washington, 1987). According to Werner Beierwaltes, 'Eriugena is convinced that dialectic is not primarily a human invention, but is grounded in being itself. Being therefore possesses a dialectical structure that can be adequately translated into dialectic as a methodology. Thus the ontological significance of dialectic is no mere epiphenomenon of its formal aspect, but is rather the presupposite and basis of the formal aspect. There is then an essential relation between dialectic and the creator who is manifested as theophany in the

his exposure to Byzantine thought, then, Eriugena does not abandon his Western training, but rather finds there a method which unites the two different Christian traditions: several of his remarks in the *De praedestinatione* arising from dialectical structures prefigure, as it were, what he will find developed to a much greater extent in the *Corpus Dionysiacum*. Throughout the *Periphyseon*, we find not only a synthesis of Greek and Latin Fathers – above all Dionysius and Augustine – but also a synthesis of Latin dialectical method (taken principally from Martianus Capella's teaching on the subject) with Byzantine negative theology, the source of which is clearly Pseudo-Dionysius, but a Dionysius which has already been heavily influenced by the glossing tradition of John of Scythopolis and the interpretation of Maximus the Confessor.[5] This synthesis is itself a triumph of dialectic: it represents a magnificent fulfillment of the final phase – *analutikê* – of dialectical method.

THE ORIGIN AND DEVELOPMENT OF DIALECTIC

The liberal art of dialectic has deep roots within the philosophical tradition.[6] It was developed initially as a Platonic response to the problems caused by the Sophist practice of rhetoric: Sophistic pragmatism did not allow for considerations of truth in dispute, and the Socratic *elenchus* seeks to remedy that.[7] For Plato, dialectic, like the mathematics to which it is closely related, is a method that ultimately yields truth, if correctly pursued, because it is the participation by the human mind in the workings of transcendent wisdom, goodness or beauty. For Aristotle, logic is instrumental; the overall title usually given to his logical works – *Organon* – reflects this: it is the method according to which the

ontological structure of dialectic, i.e. the ontological aspect of dialectic allows us to conceive of and describe God's being as dialectical': Beierwaltes, 'Language and object: reflexions on Eriugena's valuation of the function and capacities of language', in G.-H. Allard (ed.), *Jean Scot écrivain*, pp 209–28.   **4** See W. Beierwaltes, *Duplex Theoria*: Zu einer Denkform Eriugenas' in id (ed.), *Begriff und Metapher*, pp 39–64; also 'Negati affirmatio. Welt als Metapher. Zur Grundlegung einer mittelalterlichen Ästhetik durch Johannes Scotus Eriugena', *Philosophisches Jahrbuch* 83 (1976), 237–65, reprinted in W. Beierwaltes, *Eriugena. Grundzüge seines Denkens* (Frankfurt, 1994).   **5** See É. Jeauneau, 'Jean L'Érigène et les *Ambigua ad Iohannem* de Maxime le Confesseur', in F. Henizer & C. von Schönborn (eds), *Maximus Confessor, Actes du Symposium sur Maxime le Confesseur, Fribourg, 2–5 septembre* (Fribourg, Switzerland, 1982), pp 343–64; reprinted in *Études Érigéniennes* (Paris: Études Augustiniennes, 1987); also, H. Dondaine, *Le corpus dionysien de l'Université de Paris au XIIIe siècle* (Rome, 1953), p. 53; also H.U. von Balthasar, *Kosmische Liturgie*, 2nd ed (Einsiedeln, 1961), pp 644–72.   **6** See G. d'Onofrio, *Fons scientiae*, for a comprehensive account of the origins and development of the late antique and early medieval discipline of dialectic.   **7** See B. Cassin, *L'effet sophistique* (Paris, 1995), for a comprehensive account of Sophist thought, including some important observations concerning the Sophistic acceptance of relativism as a philosophical stance; often the actual philosophical theory underpinning Sophistic practice seems strikingly 'postmodern'.

mind can correctly abstract universal truths from the data given by the mutable and particular senses. For Aristotle, the latter is a purely mental process: the abstraction from sensory data carried on by the mind does not reflect or partic-ipate in a corresponding level of transcendence as it does for Plato: logic remains conventional rather than ontological. The results of abstraction reflect real relations, but logical argument remains a purely mental process. Stoic logic took the Aristotelian systematization and applied it to the workings of the *Logos*, the ordering principle which creates both the world and human thought about it: the fact that the same principle underpins both is the reason we can know anything about the external world.

Late Antiquity systematized and developed this tradition in ways which were to be most important for the early Middle Ages. The *Isagoge* of the Neoplatonist Porphyry is an introduction to the *Organon* of Aristotle, in which Aristotelian logic is assimilated to Platonic dialectic, which is seen throughout the Neoplatonic tradition as the working of the Stoic *Logos*, that is, the overflowing of the ineffable Plotinian One into the creative level of Nous.[8] This assimilation of Aristotelian logic to Platonic transcendence gives dialectic a strongly ontological status: it is ultimately how the One works. Cicero's work on the *Topics* is a re-presentation of Aristotle's, which it seeks to make more accessible.[9] By the fifth century, dialectic was part of the liberal arts curriculum, included in the trivium with grammar and rhetoric, and it was to remain so for centuries. However, it is the rather later work of Martianus Capella, Augustine and Boethius which is most significant for Eriugena, and in particular Martianus Capella, whose teaching is similar to that of Augustine on the subject, and Boethius, whose work on the tradition of the *Topics* gives Eriugena some of his most important sources of argument.[10]

Cassiodorus' work, written for the benefit of his monks at Vivarium, repre-sents a simplification of the traditional doctrine for pedagogical purposes, as does Isidore's and Alcuin's.[11] The early Middle Ages, then, in what became

---

8 Cf. Porphyrii *Isagoge*, trad. Lat. Boethius, ed. L. Minio-Paluello, *Aristoteles Latinus* I, 6–7 (Bruges-Paris, 1966); Boethius, *Anicii Manlii Severini Boetii, In Isagogen Porphyrii commenta, editio prima*, PL 64, col. 9–70; *editio secunda*, ibid., cols. 71–158; *editio duplex*, S. Brandt, CSEL 48 (Vienna, 1906). 9 M. Tulli Ciceronis, *Ad Trebatium Topica*, ed. H. Bornecque (Paris, 1960). 10 Martiani Capellae, *De nuptiis Philologiae et Mercurii libri VIIII*, ed. A. Dick & J. Preaux (Stuttgart, 1969), libri IV *De arte dialectica*, et V *De rhetorica*; [Augustine], *De dialectica vel principia dialecticae*, ed. B.D. Jackson & J. Pinborg (Dordrecht & Boston, 1975) and PL 32, cols. 1409–20; Boethius, *Anicii Manlii Severini Boetii, In Isagogen Porphyrii commenta, editio prima*, PL 64, cols. 9–70; *editio secunda*, ibid. cols. 71–158; *editio duplex* S. Brandt, Vienna, 1906; *In categorias Aristotelis libri quattuor*, PL 64, cols. 159–294; *Commentarium in librum Aristotelis Periermeneias vel de interpretatione*, ed. prima, PL 64 cols. 293–392; *ed. secunda*, ibid., cols. 393–640; ed. C. Meiser (Leipzig, *Pars prior*, 1879; *Pars posterior*, 1880); *In Topica Ciceronis Commentariorum libri sex*, PL 64, cols. 1039–174; *De differentiis topicis libri quattuor* PL 64, cols. 1173–216. 11 Cassiodorus, *Cassiodori Senatoris Institutiones, edited from the MSS*, ed. R.A.B. Mynors (Oxford, 1937); Isidore,

known as the *logica vetus*, had most of Aristotle's logical works and various paraphrases of these, Cicero's *Topics*, Boethius' work on these, Martianus Capella, the Pseudo-Augustinian *De dialectica* and the anonymous *Categoriae decem*, a paraphrase of Aristotle's *Categories*. The Carolingian era saw a flowering of new texts composed on the Liberal Arts in general, of which dialectic was still considered the most important. Alcuin is crucially important, in that he set the parameters of study for the Carolingian era as a whole; it would appear that we owe the rediscovery of the *Dicta Carolini* and the importance attached to it to Alcuin's interest in the text; dialectic also served Alcuin well in his controversies with the Adoptionists. Another source of dialectical study, strangely enough, perhaps, lay in the grammatical tradition: Priscian's work on grammar included a lot of dialectical material, and it would appear that the Irish scholars on the Continent had a particular interest in Priscian – arguably more so than other groups.[12]

In the tradition prior to Eriugena, following the teaching of Cassiodorus and Martianus Capella, dialectic is presented as the *ars artium* and *disciplina disciplinarum*: the figure of dialectic in the *De nuptiis* claims that rhetoric and grammar are but aspects of her discipline. Indeed, she goes much further than that, claiming that her discipline underpins all possible *scientia*, suggesting that all disciplines leading to rational knowledge ultimately depend on the structures of thought identified as dialectical.[13] Here we see the basis of Eriugena's emphasis on dialectic as the ultimate *sine qua non* of wisdom: without dialectic, intellectual process or participation in the *Logos* simply is not possible. According to Eriugena, the liberal arts arise from the dialectic inherent in nature. Therefore, they must be inherent in the soul, and this leads him to his highly creative mistranslation of Pseudo-Dionysius' ΑΤΕΧΝΩΣ as *valde artificialiter*.[14] Even in the tradition that preceded Eriugena, then, grammar and rhetoric appear as propaedeutic to dialectic.[15] Another characteristic of the Carolingian develop-

Isidori Hispalensis episcopi Etymologiarum siue Originum libri XX, ed. W.M. Lindsay, 2 vols (Oxford, 1911); Alcuin, *Dialogus de Octo Partibus Orationis*, PL 101, cols. 854–902. 12 For further discussion on this point, see: P. Dutton, 'Evidence that Dubthach's Priscian Codex once belonged to Eriugena', in H. Westra (ed.), *From Athens to Chartres: Neoplatonism and medieval thought: studies in honour of Édouard Jeauneau*, pp 41–2; also A. Luhtala and P. Dutton, 'Eriugena in Priscianum', *Mediaeval Studies* 56 (1994), 153–63; see also R. Hoffmann, "Glosses in a ninth-century Priscian MS probably attributable to Heiric of Auxerre (+ ca 876) and their connections" in *Studi Medievali*, 3a Serie 29 (1988), 805–37. 13 See *De nuptiis* IV, p. 155: Ac prius illud compertum uolo [...] mei prorsum iuris esse, quicquid Artes ceterae proloquuntur. Also G. D'Onofrio, *Fons scientiae*, pp 24–9. 14 See R. Roques, '*Valde artificialiter*: Le sens d'un contresens', *Annuaire de l'École Pratique des Hautes Études V[e] section* (Paris, 1970), 31–72, reprinted in R. Roques, *Libres sentiers vers l'érigénisme*, Lessico Intellettuale Europeo IX (Rome, 1975), pp 45–98. 15 G. d'Onofrio, writing about the presentation of dialectic in the *De Nuptiis*, observes: 'Jean Scot apprit [...] à connaître le pouvoir merveilleux de la dialectique: l'art qui donne au discours humain, fabriqué par la grammaire, et dignement habillé par la rhétorique, la force vitale

ments within the liberal arts is a great deal of overlap: grammar and dialectic overlap in the area of definition, whereas rhetoric and dialectic overlap in the area of topical theory, or the theory of commmonplaces, initially springboards for convincing-seeming arguments in rhetorical theory, but by the Carolingian era, almost completely absorbed into dialectical theory. Grammar provides the basic building blocks of discourse; rhetoric 'dresses it decently' – makes it beautiful – and dialectic provides a vital force of movement, a participation in the dynamism of reality itself, which makes the discourse dynamic.

THE THEORETICAL STRUCTURE OF DIALECTIC

The fundamental elements of dialectical theory as Eriugena conceives of it are taken, as has been said, principally from Martianus Capella's synthesis of the late antique tradition, supplemented by Boethian topical theory. According to Martianus (whose doctrine is substantially Varro's, as is Augustine's), the principal elements of dialectic are four: *de loquendo, de eloquendo, de proloquendo*, and *de proloquiorum summa*. What does each of these terms mean, and what elements do we find there?

(1) *De loquendo*, or the definition of terms: this is where we find the teaching on signification as applied in dialectic. This is the most fundamental operation of dialectic, the definition of the term, and the establishment of the significant divisions between each term. Every term is a *vox*, or utterance, which has a mental content corresponding to a *res*, or reality; according to the *De dialectica* (often attributed to Augustine), to speak means 'to give a sign with the voice' (*articulata voce signum dare*), and this is why this first part is called *De loquendo*: it deals with how we attribute meaning to those mental terms which we utter. The *De dialectica* tells us that a word is a sign of something, which can be understood by the hearer, pronounced by the speaker. A thing, on the other hand, is something which is perceived or understood or present in some way. A sign is what shows the mind both itself and something that lies beyond it; to speak is to give voice to a sign.[16]

In fact, this teaching on the relationship of utterance to signs and signs to things underpins Augustine's work in *De doctrina christiana*, normally considered a work of Christian rhetoric: we see here how the Trivium disciplines had already begun to overlap and interfere with each other, so to speak. This also

---

du mouvement coordonné au moyen de règles certaines et efficaces.' See G. d'Onofrio, '"Disputandi Disciplina"', in Allard (ed.), *Jean Scot écrivain*, pp 229–63 at p. 230.
16 Verbum est uniuscuiusque rei signum, quod ab audiente possit intelligi, a loquente prolatum. Res est quidquid vel sentitur vel intelligitur vel latet. Signum est quod et se ipsum sensui et praeter se aliquid animo ostendet. Loqui est articulata voce signum dare. Articulata autem dico quae comprehendi litteris potest (*De dial.*, 5, col. 1410, p. 86).

shows the fundamental nature of dialectic in regard to the other arts. The fundamental characteristic of the *vox* is that it represents a single idea – so it may be one word, or a group of words: it is not to be identified purely with the noun, which is a grammatical category. Everything else that we find in this section – the five predicables, the ten categories and the three kinds of predication (univocal, equivocal and denominative) is ultimately concerned with definition, of which there are fifteen kinds; in fact, in Book I of the *Periphyseon*, Eriugena uses the distinctions between the different kinds of definition to make important metaphysical points. This is also where we find, in relation to the Categories, the analysis of substance and accident.

(2) The second part is *De eloquendo*, or the teaching on the nature of discourse in general: how do the various significant terms come together to make intelligible utterance? Martianus Capella tells us that here we need to deal with the nature of discourse as such, before going on to examine questions of truth or falsity in discourse.[17] Here is where we find dialectical definitions of *nomen* and *verbum*, and of the relations between them, which is *oratio*. *Nomen* and *verbum* here do not correspond exactly to grammatical nouns and verbs: the emphasis here is on how they signify and relate to each other, in the formation of an utterance capable of transmitting more complex, but unified, mental content.

(3) When we come to *De proloquendo*, we arrive at the teaching on utterance which can be judged to be true or false: this is where we find the teaching on the nature of propositions. All assertions are either positive or negative: a *res* is judged either to be or not to be *x*. Assertion, here, is seen to depend on the verb, but of course we can be talking about a present or an absent thing, making a positive statement about a thing which is, or a positive statement about a thing which is not, or a negative statement about a thing which is not, or a negative statement about a thing which is, giving us four basic types of proposition in all. We also find here the square of opposition, and the teaching on the conversion of propositions.

(4) Finally, in *De proloquiorum summa*, we come to the teaching on the nature of demonstration and inference: how it is we put propositions together to demonstrate the truth or falsity of various situations. This is where we find an exhaustive analysis of the various types of syllogism, and it is only when we get to this part of the discipline of dialectic that we are in a position to develop the kind of discourse which will give us *scientia*: *scientia* depends on the previous processes of definition, signification, assertion and demonstration having been carried out correctly. We have to have a clear idea of what we are talking about,

---

17 In hac igitur parte illud dicimus, quemadmodum iuncta sint nec tamen possint plenam facere sententiam; et si faciunt, quemadmodum falsitati et veritati non sint obnoxiae sententiae, quamvis sint plenae, et quemadmodum ad id perveniatur, ut iam non solum plena sententia sit, sed etiam necessario vera aut falsa, quod est proloquium (*De nuptiis*, IV, 395, p. 189, ll. 15–21)

and we have to be using the correct methodology in our discussion of it, in order for any kind of development of knowledge to take place. Up to this point, dialectic has largely functioned as a process of division: defining terms, defining types of utterance, defining different types of proposition, but here, we come to the turning point, at which dialectic begins to operate synthetically, putting different kinds of proposition together in the various types of syllogism to permit valid inferences, which demonstrate the truths to be found in the various sciences: as demonstrative, dialectic is synthetic.

TOPICAL THEORY: AN ASPECT OF DIALECTIC?

The analysis of the different kinds of syllogism ultimately leads to the consideration of what it is that really distinguishes one kind of argument from another. This is what we find in the theory of topics, explored by Cicero and developed with great force by Boethius in his commentaries on the subject; the theory of topics represents, in fact, a kind of distillation of dialectical doctrine, and it is characteristic of Eriugena that the aspects of dialectic most important for him are the theory of topics and the most dynamic of the different kinds of syllogism, the hypothetical syllogism. The topics were initially an aspect of rhetorical theory, in that they dealt with the construction of convincing argument. The kind of topic depended on the kind of argument and the degree of conviction required; whether a topic was rhetorical or dialectical depended on the kind of argument and conviction needed. Consequently the theory of topics had become very definitely an area of overlap between rhetoric and dialectic; in fact, by the time Eriugena encountered it, it was considered almost entirely dialectical. In Boethius' systematisation of topical theory, the topics are reduced to a small number of *differentiae*, and thus become extremely dynamic, since the *differentia* is the 'bone of contention' so to speak, the element that makes the difference. These *differentiae* – e.g. 'from contraries,' 'from similars,' 'from causes' – established by Boethius turn out to be the foundation of Eriugena's argument in regard to some of his most important ideas – as, for example, when he demonstrates the metaphysical importance of the Categories.

Boethius' topical theory is found mainly in two works: *De topicis differentiis* and *In Ciceronis topica*, which are among his final works.[18] In thus systematizing topical theory, Boethius also develops it: the collection of commonplaces which in the Aristotelian and Ciceronian schools had been practical devices for constructing legal and political arguments became at least *potential* metaphysical structures.[19] There is a considerable amount of philosophical discussion in the

---

18 Works fully cited above in note 10. For the chronology of Boethius' works, see L. Obertello, *Severino Boezio* (Genoa, 1974), pp 329–33 and the table on p. 340. 19 For a succinct and thorough account of the philosophical implications of the Boethian topics, see S. Gersh,

rather more expanded treatment of topical theory, *In Ciceronis topica*, notably in Book V. In the shorter, more basic treatment of topics, *De topicis differentiis*, Book I is devoted to the laying down of basic terminology for the purposes of this discussion; in so doing, Boethius shows an acute awareness of the problems raised by this kind of discourse. In order to make any kind of dialectical or logical argument clear, it is necessary to establish unambiguous terminology for the purposes of discussion; the usual polysemy of language in a 'state of nature' would make nonsense of this kind of division. However, the careful definitions of the negative proposition, the affirmative proposition, the predicative and conditional proposition, the question, the argument, and so on, create a framework for discourse which can only guarantee clarity within a particular sphere and under particular conditions: that is, this discourse needs a foundation of clear, unambiguous concepts in the mind of the philosopher, the dialectician or the orator. This discussion is intended very deliberately to establish a method of approach for the kind of discourse which makes for persuasive argument in rhetoric and seeks to investigate the truth in philosophy:

> So the usefulness and purpose of the Topics have both been made clear, for they aid both competence in speech and the investigation of truth. Insofar as knowledge of the Topics serves dialecticians and orators, it provides an abundance [of materials] for speech (*oratio*) by means of the discovery [of arguments]; on the other hand, insofar as it teaches philosophers about the topics of necessary [arguments], it points out in a certain way the path of truth [...].
>
> For study of the Topics promises something great, namely, the paths of discovery, which those who are ignorant of this account impute altogether to natural talent alone; they do not understand how much by means of this study one acquires that which brings force to art and power to nature.[20]

In this passage, Boethius establishes the fundamental link between the orator, the dialectician, and the philosopher: they all need clear arguments; he also establishes the fundamental difference between them: the philosopher seeks the 'path of truth', whereas the other two are content with 'abundance of materials for speech'. He also highlights the gymnastic nature of topical study: it sharpens the

'Dialectical and rhetorical space: the Boethian theory of Topics and its influence during the Early Middle Ages', *Miscellanea Mediaevalia* 25 (1998), 391–401. The table on p. 393, setting out the relationships between the various types of topic is very useful; although the reduction of the Boethian classification to Poryphyrian trees by E. Stump, *De topicis differentiis* (Ithaca, NY, 1978) has the advantage that it presents the material in a format which would have been familiar to Boethius, and is therefore historically consistent, Gersh's point is well taken that Boethius was dealing with a very complex textual tradition which could only be accommodated by the devising of a more complex structure akin to contemporary semantic models. **20** *De topicis differentiis*, PL 64, col. 1182C–D, trans. Stump, op. cit., p. 42

mind, something which, depending on the point of view, can be seen as either a pragmatic exercise in manipulation or a serious development of the intellectual capacity to understand and appreciate the dynamic of reality.

In Books II and III of *De topicis differentiis*, Boethius carefully outlines and collates the various divisions of the Topics; dialectic is a discipline which is fundamentally a means of finding arguments; the refining of conceptual structures by means of language which is involved in the identifying and distinguishing of the *loci* or 'places', the *topica* or points on which a disputed issue will turn, becomes in itself a division and redefinition of perceived reality which will lead to further disputation, or argument. In Book II, having discussed syllogism and induction, and the incomplete and particular varieties of these (enthymeme and example), and having come to the conclusion that 'all of these are drawn from the syllogism, and obtain their force from the syllogism', and thus concluded that the syllogism is 'principal and inclusive of the other species of argumentation', Boethius goes on to define the *dialectical* topics:

> A Topic, as Cicero would have it, is the foundation of an argument [...]. The foundation of an argument can be understood partly as a maximal proposition, partly as the Differentia of a maximal proposition [...] those maximal [propositions] known per se so that they need no proof from without must impart belief to all arguments ... So in one way a Topic, as was said, is a maximal, universal, principal, indemonstrable and known per se proposition, which in argumentations gives force to arguments and to propositions, being itself either among the propositions themselves or posited outside them. And as a place (*locus*) contains within itself the quantity of a body, so these propositions which are maximal contain within themselves the whole force of secondary propositions and the deriving of the conclusion itself.
>
> In one way a Topic, that is, the foundation of an argument, is said to be a maximal and principal proposition furnishing belief for other [propositions]. But in another way the Differentiae of maximal propositions are called Topics, and they are drawn from the terms that make up the question [...]. There are many propositions which are called maximal, and these differ among themselves; and all the Differentiae by which they differ among themselves we call Topics [...] the substance of anything consists of its characteristic Differentiae [...]. The Topics which are the Differentiae of [maximal] propositions are more universal than those propositions [...] and therefore the Topics which are Differentiae are found to be fewer than the propositions of which they are the Differentiae, for it happens that all things which are more universal are always fewer [...].[21]

21 Ibid., pp 46–8; PL 64, cols. 1185A–86B.

Two kinds of topics can clearly be seen here: one based on maximal propositions, the other based on the *differentiae*.[22] A maximal proposition is a self-evident proposition, but there are hundreds of these, and rather than wasting time learning them by heart, one can identify characteristic *differentiae* of groups of maximal propositions, for example, 'from genus', 'from parts' and learn those: this will in turn recall the relevant maximal propositions, as, for example, 'whatever is present to the genus is present to the species', 'whatever inheres in the individual parts must also inhere in the whole'. Dialectic aims to produce belief; rather than establishing absolute, incontrovertible, logical proofs, which is demonstration, it produces conviction, and for this reason is applicable to a far wider range of arguments than demonstration alone. Boethius therefore brings dialectic very close to rhetoric, which deals with the probable and the particular rather than the demonstrable and universal. Thus maximal propositions, so essential to demonstration, are important to dialectic mainly insofar as they give validity to arguments. Of course, this is of the utmost importance, but the most effective instrument of dialectic is the *differentia* between maximal propositions – that is the middle term in a syllogism, since this is what gives dynamic force to the argument. Thus the 'place' of the argument is actually that which gives force to it: place has become a very dynamic category, and is the springboard for both rhetoric and dialectic. The maximal proposition establishes validity beyond all doubt, but the *differentia* provides for a conclusion that leads to conviction. It is the emphasis on the establishment of conviction rather than on the strictly logical proof which makes dialectic the partner of rhetoric. In the circumstances of a law court or a political discussion, the production of conviction is the most important aspect of argumentation; absolute proof is frequently impossible. For Boethius, it is the practical realities of rhetoric as a means of persuasion in public oratory which establish the differences between the rhetorician and dialectician.

---

22 See E. Stump, *De Topicis,* p. 193: According to Stump, Boethius has given rise to a particular development of the Aristotelian topics in his relocation of the topics within the area of 'Differentiae'; in her view, Aristotle's topics 'are principles similar to Boethius's maximal propositions or strategies for argument or both'; but she claims that 'Boethius seems to think of Aristotle's method as such an unwieldy instrument [i.e. 'a boxful of recipes for arguments to be memorized'], involving the memorization of prefabricated Topics; and his own method for using maximal propositions seems to be much the same: rote-learning of certain self-evident generalizations useful for dialectical arguments'. However, because of the very nature of dialectic, the maximal proposition – that which is known *in se* and incapable of any further demonstration – cannot be the real 'instrument of finding arguments'; the maximal proposition is essential to demonstration, and gives validity to dialectical argument, but demonstration, or the establishment of proofs, is not dialectic; the aim of dialectic, again according to Stump, is psychological rather than logical: 'an argument is what produces belief regarding what was in doubt [...]. The aim of a questioner in a dialectical disputation is to get the answerer to agree to the questioner's thesis; both the questioner and the answerer work at producing conviction for their positions': ibid., pp 198–9.

Boethius' reduction of a very complex tradition of topical theory to a small number of *differentiae* revealed the crucial elements in that tradition – that is, the *differentiae* – and such is the firmness and consistency of his development of this theory that it begins to appear that that these *differentiae* may also be metaphysical categories. Eriugena takes them to be such: together with the Aristotelian Categories, the Boethian theory of topics provides the foundation of all that he considers rational thought. It is, in fact, the cornerstone of his much-vaunted rationality – which, as d'Onofrio points out, is no more than a profound conviction that truth is one, and that both religious doctrine and philosophical speculation will ultimately arrive at the same answers. Thus, the famous Eriugenian reduction of place to definition, which we will now examine, depends on the maximal propositions and the *differentiae* of topical theory.

THE ERIUGENIAN APPLICATION OF TOPICAL THEORY

The category of place as Eriugena describes it has a number of fundamental characteristics: it is definition, it is identified with the dialectical topic, it is at rest, it is always found with time, it is fundamental to all created things, and finally, there is a sense in which it is the final end and perfection of things. He begins his discussion by asserting that [474B] 'place is constituted in the definitions of things that can be defined. For place is nothing else but the boundary by which each is enclosed within fixed terms. But of places there are many kinds: for there are as many places as there are things which can be bounded, whether these be corporeal or incorporeal.'[23] Therefore, from the start, place is seen as an intellectual quality, and the usual significance of place will be explained as a kind of metonymy. In fact, the usual sense of 'place' is really a kind of body: human beings at a certain point on the earth are, materially speaking, bodies within bodies: [478B] 'place is nothing else but the boundary and enclosures of things which are contained within a fixed limit [...] this world with its parts is not a place, but is contained within place, that is, within the fixed limit of its definition [...] bodies are contained within their places, therefore body is one thing and place another, just as the quantity of parts is one thing, their definition another.' Body belongs to the category of quantity, which is utterly different from the category of place, so place cannot be identified with body,[24] and therefore any

23 Jeauneau, *Periphyseon* I, p. 47, 474B, ll. 1375–9: Locus sequitur, qui, ut paulo ante diximus, in definitionibus rerum, quae definiri possunt, constituitur. Nil enim aliud est locus, nisi ambitus, quo unumquodque certis terminis concluditur. Locorum autem multae species sunt; tot enim loca sunt, quot res, quae circumscribi possunt, sive corporales, sive incorporales sint. 24 Ibid., p. 51, 478A, ll. 1530–2: Nam corpora in kategoria quantitatis continentur; kategoria quantitatis a kategoria loci longe naturaliter distat; non est igitur corpus locus, quia localitas non est quantitas [...]. (For bodies are included in the category of quantity, but the category of quantity differs

given body – earth, air, and so on — cannot in itself be a place.[25] The definition of a body is also itself intellectual, since matter is totally formless – for Eriugena here, matter seems only to be a kind of substrate, a purely negative quality:

> How [...] can the matter of a body be the place of a body which is made from it, when even matter is not, in itself, circumscribed by any certain place or mode or form [and] is not defined in any definite way save by negation?[26]

'Place,' then, is whatever is characteristic of something, and indeed some sense of Eriugena's understanding of the true significance of place can be found, for example, in our recognition that French Canada and English Canada are very different, even when they occupy the same space. One might describe the concise statement of such qualities as a definition, and this definition is the place of a thing. Eriugena re-affirms this at 479D–480A: 'true reason teaches that all these things, sensible as well as intelligible, are contained within their proper places, that is, in their natural definitions',[27] and goes on to observe that our usual sense of place comes from a kind of metonymy, where the thing contained (the body), is called from its container (the place, or definition of it). Thus the parts of the world which we normally describe as places – France, Ireland, the Himalayas – are not materially but intellectually places: 'these aforementioned general parts of the world and the parts of those parts down to the smallest divisions are not places but are enclosed within places [...]'.[28] As a result we can say that place is purely intellectual, and being intellectual, it will naturally be affiliated with the Arts: 'place exists in the mind alone. For if every definition is in art and every art is in mind, every place, since place is definition, will necessarily be nowhere else but in the mind.'[29]

Given that place is definition, and definition is intellectual, the question remains as to which of the arts is most closely linked with it. Eriugena says that the art of definition belongs to dialectic. There are two reasons for this statement: in the first place, dialectic is the art of division, and of making things

widely by nature from the category of place. Therefore body is not place, since locality is not quantity [...]). **25** Ibid., p. 49, 475C, ll. 1432–4: Nam si aliud est corpus et aliud locus, sequitur ut locus non sit corpus. Aer [...] igitur locus non est [...] (If body is a different thing from place, it follows that place is not body. Air [...] therefore is not a place [...].) **26** Ibid., p. 64, 488B, ll. 1964–7: Quomodo igitur materia corporis locus corporis, quod ex ea conficitur, potest esse, cum et ipsa in seipsa nullo certo loco, seu modo, seu forma circumscribatur, nulla certa ratione definitur, nisi per negationem? **27** Ibid., p. 53, ll. 1603–5: Haec enim omnia sensibilia, sicut etiam intelligibilia, suis propriis locis, id est, naturalibus definitionibus contineri vera ratio edocet. **28** Ibid., p. 55, 481B, ll. 1661–5: ... has praedictas mundi generales partes, earumque partium partes, usque ad minutissimas pervenientes partitiones, non esse loca, sed locis circumscriptas ... **29** Ibid., p. 48, 475B, ll. 1422 ff.: ... non esse locum nisi in animo. Si enim definitio omnis in disciplina est, et omnis disciplina in animo, necessario locus omnis, quia definitio est, non alibi nisi in animo erit.

precise: dialectic is the art which diligently investigates the rational concepts of the mind. In the second place, of all the arts, dialectic is widest in extension: as we have seen, Eriugena believes that the dialectical structure of the universe – of everything that is – is indicated in Genesis. Thus he writes: (474C–D):

> Among the liberal arts also very many definitions are found: for there is no art without its definitions, as there are the dialectical definitions from genus, from species, from name, a priori, a posteriori, from contraries, and other definitions of this kind, which there is no time to discuss now. For the dialectical definitions extend over so wide a field that from wherever in the nature of things the dialectical mind finds an argument which establishes a doubtful matter it describes the *esse* of the argument [or the seat of the argument] as a place. You will find the same thing in other arts (which are bounded by their places, that is, by their proper definitions …).[30]

Dialectic, in the early medieval sense, covers everything that is; the definitions of dialectic, as he notes here, are based on concepts that, in effect, are the same as the *differentiae* established by Boethius: genus, species, from contraries, and many others, leaving nothing out. These definitions, in effect, are the 'arguments' that establish – that is, clarify, or define – doubtful matters. The nub of this argument, or definition, will be genus, or species, or contraries – in fact, it will be a *differentia*, which makes the 'arguments' Eriugena is discussing look very like maximal propositions; and this *differentia* is a place. Thus the 'argument' is a place, the *esse* of the argument is a place; in fact, the places are topics. That this is indeed what Eriugena means here seems to be borne out by his practice of dialectical argument, which, as we have seen from the examples given above, is based on the interaction of various topics. The question remains as to what constitutes the rhetorical topic. Rhetoric is the art which deals acutely and fully with a topic defined by its seven circumstances, that is, it the art which deals with particular cases.[31] However, if we remember that dialectic deals with 'most general genera and the most special species', it becomes apparent that the rhetorical topic is a subdivision of the dialectical one, exactly as it was for Boethius.

CONCLUSION

One very important thing to note about this conception of dialectic as a whole is that it is linguistic, semantic and symbolic: it is an analysis of the relations between words, but words insofar as they really do convey the realities of things:

30 Ibid.   31 Ibid., 475A, ll. 1403–6.

it is not merely formal. For Eriugena in particular, both words and things participate in the Logos, and thus are mutually symbolic of realities beyond themselves: things, as such, are not opaque – Foucault did have a point in his presentation of pre-modern linguistic sensibility. The Logos continually maintains all things in being, so the relation of speech/grammar to Nature/dialectic is one of the priority of Divine creativity in a simultaneous act of creation that is textual in nature. Therefore human language is neither a straightforward imitation of Nature nor the creator of Nature in some kind of subjective sense, but both speech and Nature owe their existence to the same primordial principle of intelligibility, the Logos. The world created by the Primordial Causes through the Logos is an intelligible world, a kind of text, which can be scrutinized by means of dialectic. Dialectic is therefore a human discovery rather than a human creation.

Thus dialectic is also conceived of, and very strongly, as metaphysical. Dialectical process is not for Eriugena, as it had been for Aristotle, a process of abstraction, still less some kind of postmodern process of construction, but a real participation by the human mind in the cosmic workings of the Logos – as we see in the examination of his topical arguments. Insofar as it is linguistic, it is very closely related to grammar and rhetoric: elements that are grammatical, rhetorical and dialectical can all be seen in Eriugena's hermeneutics. The overlap between rhetoric, dialectic and grammar is no doubt the basis for Eriugena's claim that grammar and rhetoric are branches of dialectic, but whereas dialectic is universal in scope, grammar and rhetoric deal with the particular. Rhetoric in particular has traditionally been identified with the relational, the figurative and the particular (as opposed to the non-relational, non-figurative and universal character of dialectic) – this is Boethian (*De topiciis differentiis*) – but as Stephen Gersh points out, since the relational and the figurative (as the analogical) play such an important part in Eriugenian thought, and since Maximus' theology of the Incarnation, crucial to Eriugena, tends, on a philosophical level, to unite the universal and the particular, 'there is a tendency to assign to rhetoric a status normally reserved for dialectic alone.'[32]

The Maximian union of the universal and the particular within the theology of the Incarnation, and the reflection of this at the linguistic level in the elevated importance of rhetoric, leads also to another conclusion, supported by evidence from contemporary texts: that the relation between rhetoric and dialectic is not one of absolute difference, with rhetoric ultimately ceding place to dialectic, but one of proportion, with rhetoric and dialectic being complementary aspects of the linguistic representation of reality. Eriugenian dialectic, under the influence of Byzantine theology, reverses universal and particular characteristics: *Verbum caro est* [...] *caro verbum est*;[33] thus the particulars with which rhetoric works can

---

32 S. Gersh, 'Eriugena's *Ars rhetorica*', p. 32.   33 D'Onofrio, "'Disputandi disciplina'", p. 230.

assume the status of universals, and likewise, universals can become particulars; given the movement of negative theology towards the transcendent beyond-being, both particulars and universals are, in any case, theophanies.

Given the Eriugenian emphasis on negative theology, even dialectical discourse, which deals with things that are, is analogical in the end; Eriugenian essence – the essence of anything whatever – can never be captured[34] and thus, although dialectical discourse is true, and does indeed reflect the metaphysical structure of reality, in the end it is precisely a reflection, and as such has something of the characteristic absence of reality – of fullness of meaning – which normally characterizes the figurative. Within Eriugenian thought, the figurative does, in fact, contain or conceal, or contain by concealing, some part of reality; real and figurative are relative terms. This is a development of the Dionysian notion of symbol. Insofar as a figure manifests a reality without itself being that reality, a certain tension of presence and absence is felt: the indicated reality is clearly present in some form, but insofar as a figure is a figure, the thing indicated is absent. For Eriugena, reality is ultimately theophany; a thing is insofar as it is a manifestation of God, and thus one might say that a thing is never fully itself, insofar as it is not God – but of course it is itself insofar as God created it so. Thus a similar tension of presence and absence is present in what would initially appear to be the stable categories of real things as opposed to figures; for Eriugena, everything that is, is ultimately a kind of figure.

This recalls the philosophical problem of sameness and otherness that Plato presented in the *Sophist;* for Eriugena, things are both identified with themselves insofar as they are, and other than themselves insofar as they are theophanies. If dialectical discourse represents the structure of things as they are, then rhetorical discourse points to their inherently figurative nature in that they signify – they show, but are not, God. The difference between a figure and a reality, then, emerges as one of degree: a figure contains a higher proportion of dissimilarity than a reality, but both are at once similar and dissimilar. Thus the overlap between grammar and rhetoric, and between rhetoric – which deals with the figurative, and is identified with the particular, or concrete – and dialectic, which reflects the metaphysical structure of reality, and is identified with the abstract and universal – is not an intellectual failure to differentiate sufficiently between different disciplines, but a reflection of the problem of similarity and dissimilarity as a whole. For Eriugena being is itself referred beyond itself, and thus is itself partly figurative.

---

34 Werner Beierwaltes, 'Language and object: reflections on Eriugena's valuation of the function and capacities of language', in Allard (ed.), *Jean Scot écrivain*, p. 221.

Gille of Limerick (*c*.1072–1145), an Irish canonist

BISHOP JOHN FLEMING

Despite the uncertainty which surrounds the life and ministry of Gille of Limerick, documentary evidence shows that in the autumn of 1106, Anselm, archbishop of Canterbury, wrote to him, having been informed of his consecration as bishop of Limerick.[1] History records that nine years later he went to London, where he attended at the royal palace at Westminster the consecration of Bernard, the new bishop of St David's in Wales.[2] In 1132 he urged St Malachy to accept the archbishopric of Armagh. The oath taken in 1139 by Patrick, Gille's successor as bishop of Limerick, can still be seen in the archive of Canterbury cathedral.[3] This indicates that, in all probability, Gille resigned his bishopric in 1138. Finally, the *Chronicon Scotorum* records that he died at Bangor, Co. Down, in the year 1145.[4]

St Bernard, in his Life of St Malachy, written around the same year, says that Gille was papal legate in Ireland.[5] The *Acta* of the Synod of Rathbreasail, as recorded in the Book of Clonenagh, note that he presided at the synod, probably held in the year 1111, in his capacity as legate.[6] However, apart from these scant details and the writings which he left, there is no further definite information on his life.

A great deal of mystery, therefore, surrounds the person of Gille. Nothing definite is known of the place and date of his birth, his studies for the priesthood, his career before 1106 or the precise date and place of his consecration as bishop. Even the form of his name itself has given rise to debate.

Ever since Bernard wrote the Life of Malachy, his friend and Gille's successor as papal legate, the Europeanized form of Gille's name, namely Gilbert, has been used. There is, however, substantial historical evidence to suggest that this form of his name may not have been used by his contemporaries. *Chronicon Scotorum*, when recording his death in 1145, refers to him as 'Gilli'. The manuscripts which copied his writings, *De usu ecclesiastico* and *De statu Ecclesiae,* name him 'Gille' and 'Gilebertus'. Since his family roots are probably to be found in the Norse city of Limerick,[7] it seems reasonable to look to this source for an

1 J. Ussher, *Sylloge*, ed. C. Erlington, pp 62–3. 2 D. Whitelock, M. Brett & C. Brooke, *Councils and synods, with other documents relating to the English Church* (Oxford, 1981), 2 vols, i, 709, 715. 3 N. Ker, *English manuscripts* (Oxford, 1960), p. 40. 4 *Chronicon Scotorum*, ed. W.M. Hennessy (London, 1886). 5 St Bernard, *Vita Sancti Malachiae*, PL 182, 1086. 6 *Keating's History of Ireland*, ed. D. Comyn & P. Dineen (Dublin, 1908). 7 Some suggestions have been made that

indication of what his name might be. 'Gilla' crops up now and then in Scottish Norse names. Most importantly of all in *Brjans saga*, the Old Norse account of the battle of Clontarf, 'Gilla' is often mentioned as a surname, with reference to Jarl Gilla of the Sudreyjar.

The manuscript sources do not use the traditional monastic title Giolla or Gilla, together with Críost, Muire, na Naoimh, Pádráig etc. This is significant, given that his role as bishop of the Norse-Irish city of Limerick was to help introduce the twelfth century reform of the structure of the Church in Ireland. Three forms of his name suggest themselves, therefore, from the earliest sources, 'Gilli', 'Gilla' and 'Gille'. Since the manuscript sources, which were copied around 1186, within forty years of his death, name him Gille, I have suggested that Gille is the form of his name which was probably used by him and his contemporaries.

Three manuscripts, dating from the late twelfth century, contain his writings.[8] These works come under the two titles *De usu ecclesiastico* and *De statu Ecclesiae*. He is also noted for his Diagram and, in particular, for his representation of the hierarchical structure of the Church in terms of a series of pyramids placed within a pyramid. While historians in general acknowledge the existence and importance of his writings, they are often unclear as to their nature, origin and precise contents.

However, despite the uncertainty which surrounds Gille's life and his writings, it is generally agreed that he made a major contribution to the reform of the Church in Ireland during the twelfth century and, in particular, that he was the person mainly responsible for the re-organisation of the Irish Church along the diocesan lines which prevail to this day.[9] His writings, which outline the reasons for undertaking this task, the method he proposed to use to effect it and the directives laid down by him, give us the right to claim him as an important medieval Irish canonist.

In my book on Gille,[10] I looked at Gille in his own time and in his own words. I did so with the hope of shedding some light on Gille as an Irish canonist and, in particular, I tried to situate his thinking within the philosophical and canonical tradition which he inherited, thereby showing the influences which formed his thought. In looking at him in his own words, I entered the world of medieval Latin abbreviations and compared the manuscripts in Durham and Cambridge with the editions of his works published by Ussher, Migne and Erlington. I

his origins lie in present-day Co. Down, since he died there in Bangor abbey. 8 Durham Cathedral Library, MS B.II.35, fols. 36v–38r; Cambridge University Library, MS Ff.i.27, p. 239–42 and Corpus Christi College, Cambridge, MS 66. 9 J. Watt, *The Church and the two nations in medieval Ireland* (Cambridge, 1970), pp 1–34; J. Watt, *The Church in medieval Ireland* (Dublin, 1972); H. Lawlor, 'The Reformation of the Irish Church in the twelfth century', in *Irish Church History*, 4 (1911), 216–18; A. Gwynn, 'The twelfth century reform' in *A History of Irish Catholicism*, 2.1, pp 1–68; D. Gleeson & A. Gwynn, *A history of the diocese of Killaloe* (Dublin, 1962), pp 90–127. 10 J. Fleming, *Gille of Limerick (c.1070–1145), architect of a medieval Church* (Dublin 2001).

derived considerable pleasure from gaining access to the written notes of M.R. James in Cambridge University Library. There, while looking at his handwriting, the two sides of James, on the one hand the expert on medieval manuscripts, provost of King's College, Cambridge, as well as, eventually, Eton College, and, on the other, the ghost story writer in the classic Victorian vein, whose works are regarded as among the finest of their kind in English literature, came together.

THE BACKGROUND TO MEDIEVAL CANON LAW

The most important watershed in the history of the development of canon law was the publication in 1148 by Gratian, an Italian Camaldolese monk, of *Concordia discordantium canonum* or, to give it a title in English, *A harmony of conflicting canons*. This single work brought together all existing canonical texts and laid the foundation for the development of canon law as we know it. Since Gille wrote his two works, *De usu ecclesiastico* and *De statu Ecclesiae*, around the year 1111, he can be placed at the point where the preparation for this monumental work had begun in earnest but its completion was still a generation away. In short, Gille wrote his tracts over thirty years before Gratian published his text, and he must be placed among those who prepared the way for this defining moment in the history of the sources of canon law. I propose, therefore, to examine briefly the background to Gille's formation as a canonist.

During the first half of the twelfth century the main lines of Scholastic thought were laid down. A new outlook on the world of nature and of organized Christian society was defined and the desire for a sense of unity in life and ideals finally took root. In a Continent united by the Christian faith, this ideal won ready acceptance. The early twelfth century, therefore, saw the introduction of systematic order into the mass of material which it inherited in a largely uncoordinated form from the ancient world and from more recent centuries. The practical aim of the reform was to present a clear, unified vision of an ordered world which had its origins in God and its destiny directed towards salvation in him. During the first fifty years of the twelfth century, therefore, scholars attempted to analyse and reconcile ancient texts, establish truth and create a method of practical application which would flow from this truth and result in appropriate rules of conduct. In short, their aim, as R.W. Southern has proposed in his writings,[11] was to define doctrine and turn this into law.

Turning theory into practice and doctrine into law had been an aspect of life in Europe from the time of the conversion of the barbarian rulers. When, for example, a ruler was converted his subjects, whether they liked it or not, were

---

11 R.W. Southern, *Scholastic humanism and the unification of Europe* (Oxford, 1995), i, 237ff.

baptized and brought under the discipline of his new faith. The attempt to conform to the new faith and practice then gave rise to a multitude of decisions by emperors and kings, popes and bishops, general as well as local councils, all of them attempting to implement the Christian faith within their own area of competence. The task which the reformers undertook in the first half of the twelfth century was, therefore, not only to collect and reconcile the various texts promulgated but to establish which authority would then implement defined doctrine. At this time, at almost every level of power, all those perceived to be in authority, whether in Church or State, were claiming an increase in their authority, and to further this all were prepared to comment on heresy, condemn unbelief and establish the truth as they saw it. In the midst of this, while the pope was the recognized authority in matters of doctrine and religious practice, doubts existed about the extent of his power and, in particular, a failure at this time on his part to communicate decisions taken resulted in a limited use of his authority. Outlining clear lines of authority was, therefore, the first step to be taken in the creation of an ordered Christian society in Europe at that time.

While the Church in Western Europe in general was ready for the reform, the Church in Ireland was acutely in need of reformation. The monastic Church, established soon after the death of Patrick, had by the twelfth century outlived its purpose. The glory of its monastic past and its missionary zeal had become a golden memory, and its organisation on the ground no longer served the purpose of pastoral care. Scotland, under Queen Margaret (d.1093), had already begun to restructure a similar monastic organization along diocesan lines and it was inevitable that, with time, Ireland would follow. Ceallach in Armagh had taken the first tentative steps in this, and the emergence of a bishop in Limerick who had been educated at the heart of Europe and lived in a city of the new order provided the much-needed second step in this movement towards reorganization. Having been asked and encouraged to undertake this task by many of the bishops and priests working in Ireland at that time, as he says at the begining of his text *De usu ecclesiastico*, Gille then outlined for them his vision of the Irish Church in a new order.

Copies of the text in which Gille outlined his vision for the Church in Ireland are to be found in three places. MS B.II.35 fols. 36v–38r is to be found in Durham Cathedral Library. It contains two parts of Gille's work, a simple graphic illustration of his vision of the pyramidal structure of the Church together with the text of *De statu Ecclesiae*. It does not have a text of what is often called the Prologue, *De usu ecclesiastico*. Cambridge University Library has the complete works of Gille in its manuscript collection under MS Ff.i.27 fols. 239–42. The illustration of his Diagram in this text is very ornate and is a wonderful item in its own right. MS 66 in the collection of Corpus Christi College, Cambridge, has a copy of *De usu ecclesiastico* but lacks both the Diagram and *De Statu Ecclesiae*.

GILLE'S FORMATION

From the point of view of his role as an Irish canonist it is important to identify both the place of Gille's formation and his location in the Irish canonical tradition. First of all, therefore, the influences which formed his canonical thought must be examined.

Two letters, probably written in the autumn of 1106, provide the basic clue to the place where Gille received his education and in which he worked before returning to Ireland.[12] They are the correspondence between Anselm of Canterbury and Gille. These letters show that the two men met in Normandy. In his letter Anselm wrote, 'We have known each other and delighted in friendship since our time in Normandy.'[13] This reference could indicate a long friendship based on a student relationship from the time when Anselm was abbot of Bec, or a shorter one when the two men met in 1106. This later meeting probably took place at a synod in Rouen, when Anselm had been given permission to return to England and Gille was going back to Ireland. The phrase 'our time' might indicate a longer rather than a shorter acquaintance. It may even suggest that Gille was one of Anselm's last pupils prior to his appointment to Canterbury in 1093. The second clue which confirms that northeastern France was the area in which Gille was educated lies within his treatise *De statu Ecclesiae* itself where he categorizes the laity into three groups, those who plough, those who fight and those who pray. This classification is associated with northeastern France, where it was formulated by Adelbero of Laon and Gerald of Cambrai during the eleventh century. It was adopted without comment by Gille in his text. Based on these two references from within his writings, and without going into a detailed argument about them, it seems fair to say that Gille's canonical formation can be located broadly within the area of northeastern France around Bec, Rouen, Laon and Cambrai.

Laon, in particular, is significant. An important ecclesiastical centre in the late eleventh century, it had an ancient and renowned cathedral school which was the forerunner of the University of Paris.[14] Indeed, during the time when Gille may have studied there, in all probability under Master Anselm and his brother Ralph, Laon attracted more students from all over Europe than any other centre of learning at the time and, according to Southern, it left a deep mark on the future of Scholastic Theology.[15]

Laon was the capital of the old Frankish kingdom and the early Carolingian kings. Under their guidance many scholars from Ireland sought positions in their cathedral schools. From the seventh century onwards the quality of the

12 Migne, *Epistola XXXI, Epistola XXXII*, PL 159, 244. 13 Fleming, *Gille of Limerick*, p. 167. 14 Southern, *Scholastic humanism*, i, 199–200; Fleming, *Gille of Limerick*, pp 99–100; J. Contreni, *The cathedral school of Laon, its manuscripts and masters* (Munich, 1978). 15 Southern, op. cit., p. 199.

education received in monasteries in Ireland began to gain its due recognition in Europe and this development reached its high point in the ninth century with the emergence of men such as Sedulius Scottus and Iohannes Scottus Eriugena. During these centuries scholars travelled abroad on a regular basis and gravitated towards this general area.[16] In the *armarium* or library of the school of Laon, for example, were to be found the works of many Irishmen such as Eriugena, Rabanus Maurus, Sedulius Scottus and many others, and the Irish connection with this area, and with this school in particular, is highly significant. The extent of their learning was truly remarkable. Ó Cróinín, for example, notes that 'Sedulius produced a grammar, a *collectaneum* of rare Greek and Latin words and a commentary on Matthew, as well as glittering verse.'[17] With the advent of Eriugena the Irish intellectual influence on this area reached its zenith. By the eleventh century it began to drift towards the lands of Lotharingia, especially Cologne and Metz, and then into the newer areas of imperial power. From the point of view of this study, the important issue is that Irish scholars had for centuries studied and taught at the heart of the Frankish kingdom, and the thought of this area had been deeply influenced by them from the seventh century onwards.[18]

Clear echoes of the school at Laon are to be found in the writings of Gille: the earthly and heavenly hierarchies of Eriugena; the tripartite division of the role of the laity put forward by Adelbero and his cousin, Gerald of Cambrai; and, in particular, a preocupation with heresy, which had disrupted the schools of this area right through the eleventh century. The Irish influence on the cathedral school in Laon shows, therefore, the cyclic influence of Ireland and the Irish on this area of Europe from the seventh century onwards and, in turn, its influence on the reform of the Church in Ireland in the twelfth century.

It should also be noted that Laon was significant because of the reputation for diplomacy as well as scholarship of its master, Anselm. From about 1080 until about 1120, the time frame within which Gille (in all probability) studied there, this school had a reputation in Europe which was second to none. Anselm was the outstanding master of the school, and he was recognised and respected all over the Continent as reliable, immensely industrious and prudent, even cautious. One of his great achievements was that in a school which attracted students from all over Europe he was known for his ability to encourage debate without provoking the hostility of scholars, with the one notable exception of Rupert of Deutz. Indisputably orthodox in belief and practice, in particular, Anselm's school at Laon became the conduit for those destined to become members of the hierarchy in various countries. Gille's return to Ireland in 1106 from this school therefore almost inevitably led to his consecration as bishop in the Norse-Irish city of

---

16 D. Ó Cróinín (ed.), *A new history of Ireland*, i: *Prehistoric and early Ireland* (Oxford, 2005), pp 396–9.   17 Ó Cróinín, op. cit., p. 399.   18 Ó Cróinín, op. cit., pp 371ff.

Limerick and, eventually, to his being the recipient of a request from priests and bishops in Ireland to outline his theory of ecclesiastical organization.

GILLE, A CANONIST

Broadly speaking, the foundations of Scholasticism rest on the two poles of Paris and Bologna. In Paris a succession of masters systematized a whole corpus of doctrine, and in Bologna a similar group of academics prepared a legal system which was designed to govern the life and organization of the Church in Western Europe. The tradition which Paris inherited in the area of canon law was that of law based on custom, while that of Bologna was founded on compilations of written texts. Gratian, therefore, was rooted in the latter and Gille in the former. In examining the work of Gille from a canonical point of view this fundamental distinction must be borne in mind.

The legal tradition of northern Europe was founded on the law of custom. It was unwritten, and its origin was based on the unity of outlook which formed the basis of the Frankish kingdom and the Carolingian empire. For as long as that unity of understanding remained the binding force of the law of custom was ensured. Councils and courts, therefore, were able to enforce rules which were not the less binding for being unwritten. The mind set of a canonist whose profession was founded on the law of custom was quite different from one who took down a rule book, pointed to the law and then enforced it. Once the former had established the understanding on which the organisation, whether of Church or Empire, was founded he then formulated his policy, painting with broad brush strokes. Thus, for example, Gille, in his Diagram and in the text which accompanied it, could outline his ideas in a free-flowing text, illustrate it with a diagram and then expect that it would be accepted with the same force as a legal text drawn up in Bologna. In this way he could place the pope at the apex of his pyramid, evenly balanced with the emperor and Noah on either side of him. In the descending order of hierarchy, he placed the king beside the primate, the duke with the archbishop, the count with the bishop and the soldier with the priest. Didactic in tone, his writings are entirely free from what we normally associate with a legal text. They are simply an explanation which is based on an understanding of the way things are. They have a gentleness about them which is often lacking in the rigidity of a written legal text, but in the long run he would have considered them as equally binding.

From a canonical point of view, therefore, the tone of Gille's writings is quite different from that of a modern day canonist, or indeed that of Gratian and the school of Bologna in the twelfth century. They are exhortatory rather than prescriptive, encouraging rather than demanding. They are rooted in the tradition of works like the *Decretum* of Burchard of Worms, which has been described as simply a well organised guide to a complicated mixture of ancient wisdom, patristic doctrine and decisions of local councils, with occasional interventions from the distant authority of popes and general councils.[19] However, unlike works such as the *Decretum* of Burchard or the *Panormia* of Ivo of Chartres, Gille's writings are a simple presentation of a theoretical plan which lacks all reference to the sources from which he draws his thought. On the other hand, in common with the practice in northern Europe at the time, they were pastoral handbooks which refer to the ordering of the Church, its sacramental praxis and its pastoral care, and as such they were of immense value to local bishops. Only in the broadest sense could they be looked on as a legal text in the sense in which we understand it today, but this does not exclude them from a tradition which was an essential element in the formation of canon law.

GILLE AND THE IRISH CANONICAL TRADITION

The acknowledged experts on the history of the sources of canon law pay little attention to the Irish contribution to their science. Stickler,[20] for example, gives a short account of what he calls the Penitentials of the Celtic Church in Ireland, and he also acknowledges and describes the *Collectio Hibernensis*. However he places them within what he calls *Ecclesiae insulares*, namely Britain and Ireland, and relegates them to the bottom of the second division, if one may use terminology in current use. He does, however, recognize that the canonical tradition of these islands was very influential in mainland Europe during the first millennium and that it formed the basis for collections such as Dionysiana, Hispana and Hadriana. Needless to say, he does not mention Gille and his writings when he outlines the sources which contributed to Gratian's *Concordia discordantium canonum*. Erdo and the other historians of the sources of canon law follow a similar line.[21]

Ireland can claim its place in the history of the sources of canon law with a number of significant contributions, the Penitentials, the *Collectio Hibernensis*, the writings of Gille and later, in the thirteenth century, William of Drogheda[22] and Johannes de Fyntona.[23] It is possible that, even more importantly, Ireland played a significant role in the formulation of the material which ultimately made up the various canonical collections, such as the Dionysiana. However,

---

19 Southern, *Scholastic humanism*, i, p. 246. **20** A. Stickler, *Historia Iuris Canonici Latini, Institutiones Academicae, Historia Fontium* (Rome, 1974), pp 84–95. **21** P. Erdo, *Introductio in historiam scientiae canonicae* (Rome, 1990). **22** F. de Zulueta, 'William of Drogheda', in *Mélanges de droit romain dédiés à G. Cornil*, 2 vols (Paris, 1926), ii, 639–65; A. Scott, 'Latin learning and literature in Ireland, 1169–1500', in *A new history of Ireland*, i, 965–9. **23** F. Gillmann, 'Johannes von Phintona ein vergessener Kanonist des 13 Jahrhunderts', *Archiv für katholisches Kirchenrecht* cxxvi (1936), 446–84; A. Scott, op. cit., 968–9.

until such time as this aspect of the sources of the history of canon law is analysed the definitive picture of Ireland's role in the canonical tradition cannot be painted with any degree of accuracy.

Each of the acknowledged sources has left a distinctive mark on the tradition. At the level of popular devotion the Penitentials have contributed towards a somewhat rigid and legalistic view of role of canon law in the Church. The *Collectio Hibernensis* has shown that canon law was an important aspect of the Church in Ireland during the first millennium and, in particular, it has reminded canonists of its role in pastoral care. Gille, in his writings, has made a significant contribution to the canonical tradition by his use of the law of custom in order to formulate his theory. William of Drogheda, in his *Summa aurea*, has excited much scholarly comment by following in this Irish tradition. Scott comments on his work by saying, 'No legal principles are enunciated, but many tips and artful dodges well calculated to win a case are imparted.'[24]

The strength of Gille's input into the canonical tradition lies in the clear understanding which he has of the philosophical foundations which underlie the canonical prescription. To date no in-depth examination of the foundation of Gille's thought, and in particular the philosophical presuppositions which support his canonical stance, has been undertaken. But on the surface, his Diagram and his writings clearly outline a philosophical view of world order which is rooted in Christ and which expresses itself in hierarchy. His cosmology is, therefore, Christocentric and his Christology reflects his philosophical outlook. All are summed up in his view of Christ as the One Bishop. Both aspects of this notion, Christ as the One and Christ as the Bishop, deserve closer examination, and they could reveal a valuable insight into the neo–Platonist foundation of his thought. Reference to the notion of Christ as the One and as the Bishop are to be found in his text *De usu ecclesiastico*.[25]

His neo–Platonism is evident, therefore, in his ecclesiology and in particular in his concept of the hierarchical structure of the Church. However, in order to understand the formative influences on Gille's canonical thought it is necessary to identify the roots of his philosophy and in particular to explore his mind as a neo–Platonist. In all probability, two of the sources which influenced his thought were Irish, John Scottus Eriugena and a school of theology which was based in Salzburg, where the cathedral was established by the Irishman, St Fergal. From these sources it could be argued that in the introduction of the notion of Christ as the One and as the Bishop into twelfth-century Ireland, Gille was in fact re-echoing a line of thought which may have prevailed in the philosophical tradition of Ireland in the era of the Celtic Church and which was then introduced into European thought through the influence of the Irish, in the Frankish kingdom in particular.

24 A. Scott, op. cit., p. 965.   25 See edition in Fleming, *Gille of Limerick*, pp 144–5.

At heart, Gille is a philosopher whose philosophical thinking forms the basis of his canon law. In him is seen a canonist who has integrated philosophy and canon law and used both to reform a particular situation. He is also an Irish-European thinker who marries his knowledge of mainstream European thought with his awareness of an Irish tradition and uses both to give effect to his work for the Irish Church. Spanning centuries and distances in Europe he draws on a rich intellectual tradition to compose his treatise for the introduction of the twelfth-century reform in Ireland.

The second strength which he brings to the understanding of canon law is his formation in a tradition where the law of custom prevailed. Based on an accepted understanding between peoples the law of custom avoids, to a great extent, the legalism which the written text tends to promote. Thus for a text whose purpose could be described as canonical, namely the creation of an established order in the Irish Church, Gille's writings are at the same time philosophical, spiritual and pastoral. They lack any trace of the legalism which emerged after the publication of Gratian's work. In a real sense they attempted to do for canon law in the twelfth century what Pope Paul VI tried to do in the wake of the Second Vatican Council, namely to introduce into canonical thinking elements which were philosophical, theological and spiritual. By doing this they show the richness and depth which lies behind the law.

The third aspect of his work which should be highlighted is the contribution he made to a genre of canonical literature known as *libelli de lite*.[26] This format has its origins in the Merovingian and Carolingian worlds and it was used mainly between the mid-eighth century and the twelfth century as a forum for debate on the nature of government, church and society in general. Through this medium ecclesiology and political philosophy developed a particularly practical aspect to their nature. It also helped to bring to the formulation of the canonical collections of the twelfth century a richness of thought which went beyond what we often regard as purely canonical. In short, *libelli de lite* drew on a rich intellectual tradition and translated this into pastoral praxis on the ground. It should be noted that the Irishman, Sedulius Scottus, made a significant contribution to this genre.

While the depth of his contribution has yet to be fully examined and presented, clearly Gille's writings transformed the structure of the Irish Church at the beginning of the second millennium, and perhaps they can still contribute a valuable insight into the role of canon law in the Church of the third millennium.

---

26 D. Luscombe, 'The formation of political thought in the west', in J. Burns (ed.), *The Cambridge history of medieval political thought, c.350–c.450* (Cambridge, 1988); Fleming, *Gille of Limerick*, p. 107.

CONCLUSION

Historians agree that at the beginning of the twelfth century the organisation of the Church in Ireland stood in need of radical reform, and thus the opportunity lay open for a canonist of the calibre of Gille to outline why this should take place and how it ought to be effected. In a real sense, therefore, he had what most successful people have, the good luck to be the right man in the right place at the right time.

The writings of Gille of Limerick are multi-faceted. They may be studied for their philosophical insights and their theological reflections. One may analyse the contribution they made to the transition of the Irish Church from the monastic to the diocesan system of organization. One can examine the original manuscripts in Durham and Cambridge, become an expert in medieval Latin abbreviations and then comment on his style of writing. A liturgist may gain insights into the liturgical life of the Church at the turn of the second millennium, and a bishop gain an insight into what Gille considered important in diocesan life and, in particular, its relationship with the monastic. However, above all, in the pages of his text a picture of Gille emerges as a truly Christian man, a spiritual and unassuming human being, a committed priest and a dedicated bishop. Nine hundred years since his consecration as bishop in Limerick, his true worth and the value of the contribution which he made still remain to be fully appreciated.

CHRONOLOGY

1101	The Synod of Cashel. Papal legate, Máol Muire ua Dunain.
1105	Ceallach, abbot of Armagh, is ordained priest.
1106	Ceallach, abbot of Armagh, is consecrated bishop of Armagh.
1106	Gille is consecrated the first bishop of Limerick.
1106	Gille writes as bishop of Limerick to Anselm, archbishop of Canterbury.
1106	Anselm, archbishop of Canterbury, replies to Gille's letter.
1109	Anselm of Canterbury dies.
1111	Synod of Rathbreasail is held. Gille presides as papal legate.
	He presents *De usu ecclesiastico* and *De statu Ecclesiae* to the synod.
1115	Gille attends the consecration of Bernard, bishop of St David's, Wales, in Westminster, London.
1132	Gille persuades Malachy to accept the archbishopric of Armagh.
1138	Gille resigns the bishopric of Limerick and retires to Bangor Abbey, Co. Down.
1139	Patrick is consecrated bishop of Limerick at Canterbury.

1145   Gille dies at Bangor, Co. Down, and is, presumably, buried there.
1152   The Synod of Kells is held and the diocesan system is finalized.
1181–8   *De usu ecclesiastico* and *De statu Ecclesiae* copied at Sawley Abbey,
          Yorkshire.

Peter of Ireland and Aristotelianism in southern Italy

MICHAEL DUNNE

Peter of Ireland (de Hibernia, de Ybernia) was active as a teacher and writer at the University of Naples from the 1240s to the late 1260s. As is the case with many medieval authors, we know nothing about his early life, other than that he must have been born in Ireland sometime towards the beginning of the thirteenth century. It is a matter of speculation as to whether Peter was of Gaelic or Norman birth. Although he would have begun his basic studies in Ireland, the absence of a University meant that, like Richard FitzRalph a century later, he left Ireland at around fifteen years of age to pursue his studies abroad. Although we know that he graduated as a Master in Arts (there is no evidence that he ever studied theology), we do not know from which university he did so. His interest in medical and scientific questions would suggest Oxford where such matters were held in particular estimation, probably thanks to the influence of its first chancellor, Robert Grosseteste. On the other hand, his approach to logic would suggest a Parisian influence. It may well be the case that, like many Oxford students, he studied for a time at both universities. In any case by the 1240s he found himself as professor of Logic and Natural Philosophy at the world's first state university at Naples. Because of family ties among Norman families, there was a good deal of contact between southern Italy, England and Ireland. This may have been a factor in Peter's having obtained a quite prestigious position at Naples.

Peter is perhaps one of the best known Irish thinkers on the continent owing to the fact that he was the teacher of the young Thomas Aquinas at Naples University from 1239 to 1244. If so, in all likelihood it was he who first introduced Thomas to the study of Aristotle and perhaps also to the commentaries of Avicenna and Averroës. The result of this may have been to point Thomas in the direction of a more naturalistic approach to philosophical questions than that of his later teacher, Albert the Great, or indeed many of his contemporaries.

The original interest in Peter's extant works was that they might shed light on what Peter taught to the young Thomas Aquinas. However, based upon internal evidence, the surviving works would seem to date from at least a decade later, and to relate to lectures given in the 1250s and 1260s. Although some continuity is to be supposed with the lectures Aquinas would have heard, Peter is now considered in a more independent light, rather than simply in glory reflected from his famous pupil.

The three surviving texts, each witnessed in a single manuscript, give us but a glimpse of what must have been a distinguished and productive career.[1] The texts are all *reportationes*, or records of Peter's lectures. If the text of his commentary on Aristotle's *Peri Hermeneias* survives, it seems reasonable to think that he lectured on the complete *ars vetus*. His commentary on *De longitudine et brevitate vitae* indicates that he probably lectured on other books of the *Parva naturalia*, after having lectured on the *De anima*. His frequent references to Aristotle's works on biology indicate that he probably taught those works which were gathered together under the title *De animalibus*. Frequent references to medical sources indicate an acquaintance with the nearby medical school of Salerno. Finally, the extent to which he was held in respect by his contemporaries is to be seen in the disputed question on the origin of the design of an animal's body which was debated in public before King Manfred by various professors of the University of Naples, while the honour of giving the definitive answer was accorded to Peter. It was, perhaps, the crowning point of a long career.

That Peter had an open and enquiring mind is not open to doubt. He was aware of contemporary developments and was to the forefront of those who welcomed the new learning which had arrived with the translations of Aristotle's works and his Arabic commentators, as well as the work of Maimonides and the translations of medical works by Constantine the African and Isaac Israeli.[2] Nor was he slavish in his attitude to this new thinking. For instance, although much indebted to the thought of Averroës, he criticised the latter's notion of a single passive intellect for all human beings. He rejected determinism as well as the contemporary dualism between good and evil found among the Cathars of

---

1 Magistri Petri de Ybernia, *Expositio et Quaestiones in Aristotelis librum De longitudine et brevitate vitae*, edited with an introduction by Michael Dunne, *Philosophes Médiévaux*, Tome XXX (Louvain & Paris, 1993); *Expositio et Quaestiones in Peryermenias Aristotelis*, ed. Michael Dunne, *Philosophes Médiévaux*, Tome XXXIV (Louvain & Paris, 1996).   2 At the instigation of the Emperor Frederick II Hohenstaufen, the work of the great Jewish thinker Moses Maimonides was translated into Latin in the 1240s, a result of Jewish-Christian co-operation. This co-operation continued, since we know from Rabbi Moses ben Solomon of Salerno that he met with Peter of Ireland, whom he called 'that wise Christian', and some others in the 1250s to discuss the leading doctrines of Maimonides. Some evidence of the discussion has been preserved in Hebrew, and in view of recent developments in philosophy and theology, Peter's views sound quite modern: 'Master Peter of Ireland recognises that Christians, in believing that the Divinity became incarnate, accept the necessary conclusion that God has undergone emotion, movement and change.' See Giuseppe Sermoneta, *Un glossario filosofico ebraico italiano del XIII secolo* (Florence, 1969), p. 45n: 'Ecco quanto mi ha spiegato il Sapiente cristiano, Maestro Petri de Bernia. Dise che 'possibile' potrà essere predicato in due sensi. Il primo: ogni cosa *può* essere e *può non* essere. Possibile è che nel mese di Ševàt [gennaio-febbraio] cada la pioggia, ma è anche possible che non piova. L'altro possible consegue dalla necessità. Ad esempio: il Filosofo dice che il mondo, in quanto c'è, *era possible* e non impossibile. *Essendo* è possibile, in quanto se fosse stato impossibile, non ci sarebbe stato.'

southern Italy. In logic, he was well aware of contemporary modist approaches at Paris regarding the distinction between the *modus significandi* and *modus intelligendi*, that is, the difference between the way words signify things and the way in which things are understood (or sense and reference). In the introduction to his commentary on the *Peri Hermeneias* he defines philosophy in the following terms: 'The goal of philosophy is the knowledge of the truth of all things insofar as this is possible for human beings to grasp. Now one part of philosophy considers the truth of all things which do not derive from anything we do, and this is called theory. The other part considers those things which derive from what we do, and this is called praxis. Both parts of philosophy, namely theory and praxis, are the object of science [...]. The goal of theory is truth, that of praxis is action.' The Aristotelian influence is unmistakable. The influence is also clear in the manner in which he did philosophy, where, like his student Thomas Aquinas, a clear distinction between philosophy and theology is maintained and the task of each defended and respected. Peter regards himself as part of a philosophical tradition which is wider than his own culture. His devotion to Peripatetic philosophy is wide enough to include the philosophical cultures of Islam and Judaism. His philosophical method is devoted to the search for the truth in a way which is independent of theology or personal belief. Although there are a few brief allusions which identify him as a Christian, in his writings there are no references to Scripture or to the Church Fathers. Boethius is mentioned but, remarkably, Augustine is not. The whole Christian Neoplatonic tradition is absent. Peter's admiration for Aristotle is clear, as when he suddenly states in the course of expounding a text of Aristotle: 'Will anyone ever exist who will be able to fully comprehend the depths of that spirit who is Aristotle?'

It is hard in terms of our times to assess his 'originality' and 'influence'. The medieval respect for authority meant that any thinker holding a professional qualification or function was expected to relate positively to the Western tradition. While this aspect of Scholasticism is often criticized, its strengths are rarely acknowledged. Peter belongs to a time in medieval and Western thought which was devoted to the recovery of a correct understanding of Aristotle's thought. For example, of all of the extant medieval commentaries on the *De longitudine et brevitate vitae*, it is clear that Peter's is by far the most comprehensive and extended treatment of Aristotle's philosophy of biology as presented in that work. We also know that when Thomas Aquinas was preparing his own commentary on the *Peri Hermeneias* he had a copy of Peter's text, to which he made frequent references. Although Peter at times is somewhat eclectic in his choice of material, he represents those thinkers who brought about a necessary stage in the recovery of Greek philosophy. In doing so they served to provide a foundation for later thinkers, who were thus enabled to pursue philosophical thought in quite innovative ways.

AQUINAS' TEACHER? THE DEBATE WITH ROBIGLIO

In 2002 Andrea Robiglio put forward the provocative thesis that when he was a student at Naples Thomas Aquinas did not have the philosopher Peter of Ireland as professor.[3] This is despite the fact that, as the author notes, many writers, including most recently J.-P. Torrell, accept the historiographical tradition according to which Peter of Ireland was the teacher of Thomas Aquinas in the 1240s. Robiglio quite correctly points out that we have very little evidence concerning Thomas' studies and teachers in the years 1239–44 when he was a student at the *studium generale* of Naples. Indeed much of what we can say has to be surmised from other sources regarding what would have been normal at the time, namely, that as part of his studies as a student *in artibus* he would have attended lectures in philosophy. Such studies would, as a matter of course, have included logic and the philosophy of nature. Nothing strange here. What the content of his lectures was we shall probably never know. We can speak of the possibility that Thomas may have studied Aristotle together with the Arabic commentators (including Averroës) at Naples at a time when these were banned at Paris. It is unlikely that the founder of the University of Naples, the Emperor Frederick II, would have respected a papal ban.

I have argued against Robiglio that the testimony of William of Tocco and Peter Calo is to be trusted.[4] The evidence is that Peter of Ireland was active in the Naples-Salerno region *c.*1250–65. His surviving works are on logic and the philosophy of nature, which agrees with what Peter Calo said. We also know, which in a sense is a more important point, that when Thomas was preparing his commentary on the *Peri Hermeneias* he had a copy of Peter's commentary on the same text *prae oculis*. It is not impossible that Peter was a teacher in the 1240s. There seems no good reason to reject the documented historical sources.

Tocco was certainly in a position to have gained his information from a reliable source. To say that Tocco is wrong and to state that Thomas never had the philosopher Peter of Ireland as professor is something which Robiglio does without putting forward convincing arguments.

3 M. Dunne, '"Neapolitan gold": a note on William of Tocco and Peter of Ireland', *Bulletin de la Société internationale pour l'étude de la philosophie médiévale* 44 (2002), 107–11 at 110.   4 See M. Dunne, 'Concerning "Neapolitan gold": William of Tocco and Peter of Ireland', *Bulletin de la Société internationale pour l'étude de la philosophie médiévale* 45 (2003), 61–5; id., 'Peter of Ireland, the University of Naples and Thomas Aquinas' early education', *Yearbook of the Irish Philosophical Society* (2006), 84–96.

THE 'DETERMINATIO MAGISTRALIS'

Perhaps the most accessible text of Peter's is the first to have been printed, the *Determinatio magistralis* edited by Clemens Baeumker in 1920.[5] This text shows that Peter was at the centre of the cultural life at the court of King Manfred of Sicily (1258–66) and was a notable proponent of Aristotelianism in southern Italy. Manfred, like his father Frederick II, encouraged the study of new ideas in his kingdom. For example, Bartholomew of Messina, one of the thirteenth-century translators of the *Aristoteles Latinus*, was present at court where he might have been the 'headmaster' of a circle of translators in the service of the king. He translated not only several Pseudo-Aristotelian treatises (among which the *Problemata physica*), but also works by Hippocrates and Hierocles. He was active at the court of King Manfred of Sicily. Manfred himself before he became king had made a contribution to scholarship when he had translated an important work, the *De pomo* (also known as *De morte Aristotelis*). In the Prologue he gives the reason why he translated the work:

> Wherefore we, Manfred, son of the divine and august emperor Frederick, by the grace of God prince of Taranto, lord of the mountain of honour, Sant' Angelo, and governor general of the illustrious Conrad, second king of Sicily, were laid low by the misfortunes of humanity, the result of a discord of the concordant elements of which we like others are constituted. When a grave illness weakened our body to the point that no one thought we could continue to live in the flesh, great anxiety tortured those present, since they thought that we were frightened at the imminence of our death. But a group of venerable teachers at the court of the imperial, divine, august, and most serene emperor, our lord and father, had presented theological and philosophical documents about the nature of the world, the flux of bodies, the creation of souls, their eternity and perfection, and the instability of material things and the stability of forms, which are not affected by disaster or deficiency in their matter. Bearing these teachings firmly in mind, we were not so saddened at our dissolution as they thought, even though we could not in justice rely on our own merits for possessing the perfection which is our reward, but solely on the Creator's mercy.
>
> Among these was a book called *The Apple*, produced by Aristotle, the prince of philosophers, at the end of his life. In it he shows that wise men do not sorrow over the death of their vile lodging, but joyfully run to the

5 Reprinted in *Expositio et Quaestiones in Peryermenias Aristotelis*, ed. Michael Dunne, *Philosophes Médiévaux*, Tome XXXIV (Louvain & Paris, 1996), pp 246–50. The text has recently been studied by O. Weijers in *La 'disputatio' dans les Facultés des arts au moyen âge* (Turnhout, 2002), pp 216–217, and has been examined and partially translated into French by R. Imbach in *Dante, la philosophie et les laïcs* (Fribourg, 1996), pp 106–9.

reward of perfection; for its sake they did not hesitate in the least to spend their time and their life in the supreme labours of studies, inwardly fleeing the hindrances of the world. We told those present that they should read this book, since from it they would gather that this kind of passing away is of little moment. Since this book was not to be found among Christians, and since we read it in Hebrew, translated from the Arabic into Hebrew; once our health had been restored, we translated it from the Hebrew tongue into Latin, for the instruction of many. In it certain remarks by a compiler have been included. For Aristotle did not write the book, but it is extant as written by others – those who wished to find out the cause of his joy at his death, as is contained in detail in the book.[6]

After Manfred's preface, the text proper begins as follows:

When the way of truth had been closed to the wise and the way of right understanding was blocked, some wise men came together into one house and, with one heart, tried to explain and understand the path of rectitude, by which men should be able to live. They found no path except one, which was that a man should wish for his neighbour what he wishes for himself; that he should withdraw himself from shameful behaviour, confess the truth, inflict judgment upon himself, and fear his Creator.[7]

The Aristotle depicted in the text is not the historical Aristotle but a philosophical ideal, a vision of the Philosopher saint, someone better than Socrates, seen from a Neoplatonic perspective, an 'anonymous Christian' who already knows and accepts the Old Testament. Here is how philosophy and the philosopher are depicted by Manfred – a vision which cannot but have influenced Peter as well:

I have already shown you that a man cannot comprehend the noble sciences except through the stages of the soul, when it is purged, perfected, and cleansed of its impurities; when it departs from the uncleanness which is imprisoned with it – which is produced out of earth, and pursues the pleasures of eating, drinking and amusements, as do the other animals, which lack the wise soul that makes a man restrain his impulses and desires. Because through these stages a man rises above his equal when he dominates his passions and restrains his nature, out of horror at the delights of the body, which defile him; when he seeks instead the delights of the soul in learning the sciences of God, Who created His world by His

---

6 *The Apple or Aristotle's Death (De Pomo sive De morte Aristotelis)*, translated from the Latin with an introduction by Mary F. Rousseau (Milwaukee, WI, 1968), p. 48.   7 Ibid., p. 50.

own wisdom; and when he investigates His ways and understands His secrets. Then the eyes of his soul are opened, they greatly rejoice, and they are delighted by a pleasure which is different from bodily pleasures. For all the allurements of the body are limited; they end in nothing, destroy its substance, and cause it to descend to death. But the delights of the soul are to understand its Creator, to consider His wisdom in the works of the heavens, the courses of the spheres, their forms, and the fact that all things are established and rooted in wisdom. And if he is not able to comprehend profundities of this kind, let a man look at himself and the subtlety of his limbs, each one of the muscles serving to move him, drawing his body to rest and to motion; and powers located in each member for the service of the body, in which nothing is defective or superfluous. Through this he can recognise his Creator and will know that the study of man as he is in this life is despicable; but a soul which desires to know those other sciences is perfect and upright. This soul is not saddened or disturbed when it departs from the body, which opposes the fulfilment of its desire and its quest.

Furthermore, do you not know that a pure and perfect philosopher mortifies all his desires in this world, for eating, drinking, dress, and other pleasures, for treasures of gold and silver? That he despises all pleasures which lead to the destruction of both body and soul?[8]

It is an ideal which is put forward by Boethius of Dacia in his *De summo bono* and is close to the position of the radical Aristotelians; Boethius proclaims, 'Whoever does not live the life of the philosopher does not live rightly.'

This one might say is the cultural context in which Peter appears around 1260 when we are told that King Manfred pondered a problem (*dubitavit*) about the activities of an animal and the organs with which it carries these out. He turned the matter over to the professors or masters at his court, many of them no doubt drawn from the Arts Faculty at the University, and posed them the following question: Are the limbs and organs of animals given to them to enable them to carry out their activities, or are their activities determined by the kind of organs and limbs which they have at their disposal? The question is both an old one and a contemporary one since it addresses the notion of design in nature. In effect, King Manfred was setting up a traditional Scholastic *disputatio* partially to encourage scholarly debate and also (why not?) as a form of entertainment at a court renowned for its culture. We are told that the arguments were given both for and against, but the honour of giving the formal solution, the *determinatio* of a Master, was given to Magister Petrus de Ybernia, who is described as a *gemma magistrorum* and *laurea morum*. The debate itself has not survived but somebody thought it important to write down a copy (*reportatio*) of the solution which

8 Ibid., p. 53.

Peter gave on that day in southern Italy before King Manfred, the last of the Hohenstaufen, then aged around 30 and destined to meet his fate a few years later, in 1266 at the battle of Benevento, where he was defeated by Charles of Anjou.

This disputation was therefore one for a special occasion and was not part of ordinary teaching, given that the problem for discussion had been put forward by the King himself. It may well be that the special occasion was the transfer of the *studium generale* back from Salerno to Naples, where it had been founded by his father, the Emperor Frederick II.

The choice of Peter to determine was question was motivated presumably by his seniority (he had taught Aquinas some twenty years earlier) and by his area of competence (he was professor of Logic and Natural Philosophy), since the question would appear to be a problem in natural philosophy: here we are talking about animals and their organs. Peter, however, begins by noting:

> I say therefore that this problem is one which is metaphysical rather than natural and that its solution is to be found at the end of Book XII of the *Metaphysics* in chapter 10, and that it refers to the question of the care which the First Cause has for those things which are in the universe; for it would not be the act of the One who is Wise and Omnipotent to allow evil, nor to do anything which is unjust, but He disposes all things in the best way possible so that all will be preserved in respect of the eternal permanency of the universe.[9]

We have here a statement of a topic which, a few years later, would also occupy the mind of his great student Thomas Aquinas, namely, the question regarding the eternity of the world.

Peter rather concisely refers to Aristotle's doctrine of a natural providence, not perhaps the survival of the individual but rather the eternal survival of the species. However, does not the problem of natural evil contradict the notion of a providential *ordo*? This evil would seem to be manifested by the fact that in order to live

9 See C. Baeumker, 'Petrus de Hibernia. Der Jugendlehrer des Thomas von Aquino und seine Disputation vor König Manfred', *Sitzungsberichte der Bayerischen Akademie der Wissenschaften*, philos.-philolog. und hist. Klasse, Heft 8 (1920), 41–9 at 41; reprinted in Magistri Petri de Ybernia, *Expositio et Quaestiones in Peryermenias Aristotelis*, ed. Michael Dunne, *Philosophes Médiévaux*, Tome XXXIV (Louvain & Paris, 1996), pp 246–50: 'Dubitauit Rex Manfridus et quesiuit a magistris utrum menbra essent facta propter operaciones uel operaciones essent facte propter menbra. Et fuerunt raciones ducte pro et contra, sed determinauit Petrus de Ybernia, gemma magistrorum et laurea morum. Dixit ergo quod questio ista esset metaphisicalis pocius quam naturalis, et esset determinatum in fine undecimi *Prime Phylosophie*; et quod esset questio de sollicitudine cause prime circa res que sunt in uniuerso, quia non est sapientis et omnipotentis relinquere malum nec facere aliquid iniuste, sed omnia meliori modo quo possunt saluari ad permanenciam eternam uniuersitatis.'

some animals kill and eat other animals. Peter remarks that the difficulty of the problem led some people to posit two principles in things, a principle of good and a principle of evil. It is interesting to note that his source is, as Baeumker pointed out, the commentary of Averroës, which he uses continually throughout his text. The works of Averroës had been translated in southern Italy by Michael Scotus some twenty years previously under the patronage of the Emperor Frederick II, and the version was one of the most important events in the reception of Aristotelian philosophy in the Middle Ages. Incidentally, Averroës' text has the following: '[...] and this problem led some to say that there are two gods, one of whom makes the good things, and the other the not good.' As Baeumker again notes, such dualism was not merely theoretical; the Dominicans had been founded to combat the Albigensian heresy, and Peter would have been well aware of them through his contacts with members of the order. There is also evidence of the presence of Cathars in the region of Campania in the thirteenth century. In any case, Peter rejects dualism on both theological and philosophical grounds, as at once heretical and absurd; absurd because evil cannot exist on its own, since it is a privation and, as Peter concludes, it is not possible for evil to be separated from the good but it must be found with it, since 'everything which is, insofar as it is, is good' – a famous quotation from Boethius whose writings he knew particularly well as a teacher of logic.

The solution which Peter proposes is again taken from the *Metaphysics*, Book XII, ch. 10 and he quotes Aristotle with an eye on the commentary of Averroës as well. I paraphrase the argument as follows:

> We must consider also in which of two ways the nature of the universe contains the good, and the highest good, whether as something separate and by itself, or as the order of the parts. Probably in both ways, as an army does; for its good is found both in its order and in its leader, and more in the latter; for he does not depend on the order but it depends on him. And all things are ordered together somehow, but not all alike, both fishes and fowls and plants; and the world is not such that one thing has nothing to do with another, but they are connected. For all are ordered together to one end, but it is as in a house, where the freemen are least at liberty to act at random, but all things or most things are already ordained for them, while the slaves and the animals do little for the common good, and for the most part live at random; for this is the sort of principle that constitutes the nature of each. I mean, for instance, that all must at least come to be dissolved into their elements, and there are other functions similarly in which all share, for the good of the whole.

In other words, the solution to the problem is to be found in the fact that different beings have different states or functions within the universe of things and as such contribute to the good and perfection of the universe. As regards the heavenly bodies, Peter states that they move freely and without error and so contribute to the greater good. However, the activities of corruptible things are less well disposed and arranged, since some occupy different levels than others, such as wolves and other preying animals. However, nothing is to be found in the universe which is not ordered, and all activities are directed towards one thing; all agents follow order because of one thing and that is the First Cause. Peter continues that in the universe some things exist for the sake of others, even to be the food of others, as plants for animals, and animals for other animals. This, he comments, is the reason why animals fight among themselves. He writes that animals which have curved claws and which eat raw meat fight with all other animals because their life is sustained by eating other animals. Thus, the universal nature arranges everything to offer assistance, and especially to assist and sustain humanity. And so, Peter writes, if an individual of one species is sustained by means of another individual of another species or genus, this is not against the order of nature, but everything has been established because of the good of order and out of the care of the One who orders. Nor is there anything wrong if the benevolence in nature is greater towards one species rather than another. Although nature is the same to all in terms of its influence, the things themselves are not equal in the manner in which they receive this influence. The good of the order of the universe is found according to a greater or lesser extent, inasmuch as the lesser exists for the more perfect, *vilius propter nobilius, imperfectius propter perfectius, materia propter formam et propter motorem.*

Peter knew what he was doing when he began to give examples of animals that live by preying upon others and spoke about birds of prey, mentioning the falcon, eagle and sparrow hawk. We know that at that time Manfred was engaged in editing and completing his father's work, the *Art of Hunting with Birds*.[10] In putting questions to experts, in this case about the preying of one animal upon another, Manfred was following the example of his father who did the same with Michael Scotus, and who corresponded on philosophical matters with experts in the Islamic world. Peter explains the matter in terms of the body-soul relationship in animals: the body exists for the soul; therefore the nature of the soul determines its activities, and these activities determine the kind of body which it must have to carry out those activities. The lion has an *anima gulosa* (a greedy soul) and so has a large mouth and sharp claws; the bird of prey has an angry soul and has a hooked beak and claws to grasp its prey. Nature has given to each creature the appropriate body and bodily activities in accordance with its soul. Take the example of human beings, who among all other creatures have the most perfect soul of all and so have the most versatile and adaptable limb of all, the hand, which can become a hammer, a sword or a pen.

10 Frederick II, *De arte venandi cum avibus*, ed. Carl A. Willemsen (Leipzig, 1942).

Peter concludes that it is clear therefore that 'the limbs and organs of an animal are in function of their activities'; an organ without a function is only called an organ in an equivocal manner. That a bird of prey has a sharp beak and claws is not something which arises out of any material necessity or by chance, but they have these in virtue of a determinate end of their activities. He finishes with these words:

> Thus it is clear, my King, that the organs and powers are for the sake of the activities and not the other way around. Thus, the solution is clear to the problem, as it seems in my judgment.

Martin Grabmann considered Peter's *disputatio* to be of capital importance for the history of the Scholastic method, as it is one of the best examples which has come down to us of a *disputatio* in the philosophy of nature; I see no reason to revise that estimation.[11]

CONCLUSION

The position of Peter of Ireland is now well established within the history of thought and his contribution is acknowledged in terms of the development of Aristotelianism in southern Italy and beyond. His extant works have been edited and published, but they still remain the preserve of the specialist, as do all Latin editions nowadays. This is because we now live in a cultural situation which would have been unthinkable up to a few decades ago. In other words, most people do not now have a knowledge of Latin. Students of medieval philosophy, especially undergraduates, are unable to read texts in the original language and are in need not only of introductions to medieval thought in general, but increasingly of translations of medieval philosophical texts. Series such as the *Dallas medieval latin texts in translation* under the general editorship of Professor Philipp Rosemann are valiantly trying to remedy the situation. It would be a major aid to the public understanding of the Irish contribution to European Scholastic thought if the works of an author such as Peter of Ireland were to be translated, or indeed if substantial selections from him and other medieval Irish thinkers could be translated and made available.

---

11 See M. Grabmann, 'Magister Petrus de Hibernia, der Jugendlehrer des Heiligen Thomas von Aquin. Seine Disputation vor König Manfred und seine Aristoteles-Kommentare', *Mittelalterliches Geistesleben*, I (Munich, 1926), pp 249–65.

Flowers from ancient gardens: the lemma 'amicitia' in the *Manipulus florum* of Thomas of Ireland

JAMES McEVOY

THOMAS DE HIBERNIA

Thomas Hibernicus (or *de Hibernia*) became a fellow of the Sorbonne before 1295; accordingly he must have been born (in Ireland) at least twenty years before then.[1] The little that is known of his life can be recalled briefly. The sparse information recorded about him points to Paris as the place of his studies and of his later residence. Thomas belonged to the secular clergy and was a Master of Arts and a Bachelor of Theology. He published the *Manipulus florum*, his best known work, in the year 1306.[2] He was the author of three other books, or rather booklets, all of which attest to his concern for the pastoral care. The *Manipulus* is primarily a 'manual' or handbook. It may be described as a compilation destined essentially for spiritual reading. Seven copies of books actually owned by Thomas survive as a bequest left by him to the library of the Collège de Sorbonne; one of these books carries notes in his own hand.[3]

The genre of the anthology might not strike one as being Scholastic at all, or at least not in the strict academic sense of the word. When regarded with a neutral eye, is the author of the *Manipulus florum* not a rather unlikely candidate for the appellation 'Scholastic'? When one thinks of the typical productions of the faculties of arts, theology and law in the medieval universities it is the genres of the *summa*, the various kinds of *quaestiones*, the glosses and commentaries on

---

1 'Hibernicus, Thomas', *Oxford DNB* (James G. Clark), 26.997–8. A.B. Scott has summarized the achievement of Thomas in 'Latin learning and literature in Ireland, 1169–1500', in D. Ó Crónín (ed.), *A new history of Ireland*, i: *Prehistoric and early Ireland* (Oxford, 2005), ch. XXVII pp 934–95; in particular pp 957–9.   2 The edition we have employed is that of Antwerp, 1575, printed by Ioannes Bellerus: *Flores Doctorum Insignium, tam Graecorum quam Latinorum, Qui in Theologia ac Philosophia claruerunt, sedulo per Thomam Hybernicum collecti et postrema hac editione a mendis quam plurimis uindicati*. Antverpiae, 1575. A copy is conserved in the Russell Library for Research, Maynooth.   3 A comprehensive study of all aspects of the *Manipulus* has been made by Richard H. Rouse & Mary A. Rouse in a work to which our debt is great: *Preachers, florilegia and sermons: studies on the 'Manipulus florum' of Thomas of Ireland* (Toronto, 1979), (hereafter Rouse & Rouse, 1979). Among the Rouses' other achievements is their edition of Henry of Kirkestede, *Catalogus de libris autenticis et apocrifis*, British Academy, Corpus of British Medieval Library Catalogues, ccxiv, London. See, Rouse & Rouse, p. 161.

ancient philosophical texts, the treatises, dialogues and letters that come sponta-
neously to mind, rather than the anthology. Even today one could undoubtedly
study Scholastic Philosophy in its leading medieval exponents without ever
dipping into any anthology contemporary with them. The present-day student
of medieval theology likewise could well dedicate months or years of study to the
summae and the *quaestiones disputatae*, without feeling that he or she was missing
out by neglecting the florilegia.[4]

My research interest in the *Manipulus florum* goes back some years. The late,
regretted Professor Jacques Follon and I edited an anthology of patristic and
medieval writings on friendship which appeared in 2003 as a successor to our
volume on classical friendship-writings.[5] In a sense we were late imitators of
Thomas of Ireland himself. Thomas occupied a chapter in our anthology,
appearing in a French translation prepared by my late colleague.[6] But my interest
in Thomas has continued to grow, in fact it can now be placed within my wider
research pursuit of the medieval and early modern Irish Scholastic thinkers and
writers.

SURVIVING WORKS

The three minor treatises
Rouse & Rouse list the MSS of three minor works that are firmly attributable to
Thomas' pen. The most widely diffused of these was *De tribus punctis Christiane
religionis*, composed with a readership of secular clergy in mind. The three
points are the Apostles' Creed, the Decalogue and the Seven Deadly Sins. The
second writing, *De tribus ordinibus hierarchie angelice et ecclesiastice*, is devoted to
the hierarchies of heaven and earth; most of its attention is given over to the
structure of the Church Militant. In *De tribus sensibus sacre scripture* Thomas
studies the mystical or spiritual senses of the Bible.[7] These three short writings
are informative concerning their author's views about Church and society. They
reveal a conventional cast of mind, and are suggestive of their author's pastoral
interests; for example, in the role of the priest in the sacrament of penance.

The inauthentic Flores Bibliorum
Among the works wrongly attributed to Thomas of Ireland is a biblical compilation known as the *Flores Bibliae* or *Bibliorum*. In early modern times it was

---

4 The same does not hold true of the *Sentences* of Peter Lombard, which was one of the most
elaborate anthologies of its time; see Philipp W. Rosemann, *Peter Lombard*, Great Christian
Thinkers (Oxford, 2004).   5 J. Follon & J. McEvoy, *Sagesses de l'amitié*, ii, *Anthologie de textes
philosophiques patristiques, médiévaux et renaissants*, Vestigia 29 (Fribourg & Paris, 2003).   6 Follon
& McEvoy, *Sagesses de l'amitié*, pp 443–61.   7 All three are discussed in an article in the present
volume by Dr Declan Lawell.

commonly attributed to Thomas, but no manuscript of the work exists.[8] It was first printed by Guillaume Rouillé at Lyons in 1554, and may have been commissioned by him to accompany in print the *Manipulus florum* of Thomas, which the same printer had published the previous year. This Lyons edition was reproduced at Antwerp in 1555, 1557 and 1567 by the heirs of Jan Steel. We have examined the edition of 1567, the first to attribute the work to Thomas.[9] In many subsequent editions the *Flores* appeared in association with the *Manipulus*, carrying the mistaken attribution.

The biblical anthology arranged quotations from the Old and New Testaments in alphabetical order under two hundred and seventy topics. In form and purpose it continued the extremely popular medieval genre of *florilegia*. The *Flores Bibliorum* is still perfectly usable as a digest of biblical material on friendship.[10] The entry on *amicitia* occupies over five pages in the Antwerp edition. It is subdivided by fifteen internal headings, which group the quotations under notions such as the origin [of friendship], its fruit, gratuity and honesty; its expression in word and deed, followed naturally enough by false friendship and hypocrisy. Like the vast majority of its medieval predecessors this anthology was aimed at facilitating the preparation of sermons, as indeed was, to some extent at least, the piece to which it served as a companion, the *Manipulus* of Thomas.

The Manipulus florum *in an electronic edition*
A new edition of the masterpiece of Thomas has begun to appear. The editor, the Canadian Chris L. Nighman, describes the electronic critical edition he is progressively making available on the Internet as an effort to extend into the electronic age Thomas' own intention 'statim invenire' ('to find at once').[11] The aim of the project is to produce a critical edition of Thomas' original collection of excerpts, the text of these being collated against several printed editions from the late fifteenth and the sixteenth centuries. The edition is providing a practical resource for editors of late medieval and early modern Latin texts, and for students of sermon literature in a particular way. The frequent use of the *Manipulus* by preachers was noted by the Rouses, who considered the work to be primarily a preacher's handbook. Nighman has altered the way we look at

8 Rouse & Rouse (1979), pp 110–11. 9 *Flores Bibliorum, sive loci communes omnium fere materiarum ex ueteri ac nouo testamento excerpti, atque alphabetico ordine digesti, a F. Thoma Hybernico, nuncque demum castigati*, Antverpiae, Apud Viduam et Haeredes Ioannis Steelsij, 1567. The copy we have consulted is to be found in the Russell Library for Research, Maynooth. 10 The lemma on *amicitia* is translated in Follon & McEvoy, *Sagesses de l'amitié*, pp 461–9. 11 See <www.manipulusflorum.com>. Dr Nighman lectures at Wilfrid Laurier University, Canada. I am indebted to him for bringing forward his edition of the lemmata *amicitia* and *inimicitia* for my benefit, and I wish to acknowledge his intellectual generosity in doing so. Between a fifth and a quarter of the *Manipulus* has already been made available, and the editor is developing a search engine for his online edition.

Thomas' compilation, arguing that it was intended to serve as a resource for self-formation by university students, especially those preparing for a career involving pastoral care.[12] One could extend this thought a little: the compilation may have been intended principally for private spiritual reading and the continuing religious formation of priests and student clerics. This aim could help to account for example for the prominence given to *amicitia* through the wealth and the extent of the material in the lemma, whereas *coniugium* (marriage) is given much less prominence by comparison.

THE GENRE OF THE ANTHOLOGY

'Florilegium' is the most common medieval name for a book of extracts or anthology. Thomas outlines his project in the prologue. He chooses two images, one biblical and one classical, to characterize his own literary activity as a compiler. The first of these recalls Ruth (Ruth 2) gleaning in the field after the harvesters – a reference often employed by medieval writers to illustrate the nature of their own relationship to the Fathers of the Church. Thomas, like Ruth, is a pauper: he has nothing of his own, and so is justified in gleaning *auctoritates* from the books of the saints, the doctors and the philosophers. As Ruth gleaned in the field of the 'strong man' (Hebrew: 'Boaz') he, Thomas, works over the fields (that is, the library) of Robert (de Sorbon) 'robustus'. In the succeeding image Thomas compares himself to the widow at the Temple gate (Lk 21: 2–3). It is from his favourite pre-Christian author, Seneca (*Epistulae morales* 88), that Thomas draws the third image of himself as compiler: the Roman philosopher describes the gathering of ideas in terms of bees collecting honey from the flowers and distributing it in their combs. This idea also became a commonplace in prologues to medieval compilations. Thomas' purpose as a compiler is clearly suggested by these two metaphors: he is to be a thoughtful and careful gleaner and an orderly bee. He regards his work as a service by which every reader will be enabled to locate what he needs for his own purpose.[13]

The word 'anthology' is derived from the Greek for a gathering of flowers. The Latin word *florilegium* means the same; it was coined early in the seventeenth century. In medieval Latin, *flores* was in common use, as were such synonyms as *excerpta, liber florum, liber deflorationum* ('plucked flowers'), *flores paradysi, floretum* (garland), and *florarium* (flower garden). According to one authority these words connote 'a collection of chosen but unrelated excerpts from texts, mostly of various authors, put together on non-literary principles

12 Chris L. Nighman, 'Commonplaces on preaching among commonplaces for preaching? The topic *Predicacio* in Thomas of Ireland's *Manipulus florum*', *Medieval Sermon Studies* 49 (2005), 37–57 (see p. 41). 13 'He', or 'she': Christine de Pisan (1364–1430) made use of the *Manipulus* in her vernacular writings; see Rouse & Rouse (1979), pp 213–15.

with the original linguistic expression being retained; sometimes bearing upon the work of a single author.'[14] The Rouses, who are surely well entitled to an opinion on this matter, suggest that 'A *florilegium* is a collection of extracts taken by one person from the writings of others; it is a new arrangement of second-hand material.'[15] The same authors point out that the popularity of the anthology as a genre was naturally great during the Middle Ages, when respect for traditional wisdom was something like a cultural norm and when the production of books by hand made it expensive for most literate people to possess large libraries of their own. It is illuminating to think of the *Manipulus florum* as having functioned as the library of many a clerk or priest who could not afford a whole collection of books, but who had what he had safely between the covers of a single volume.

The florilegium should be distinguished from some associated genres such as the catena ('chain') and the epitome ('summary'). The former was much favoured in the Greek Church; frequently it concentrated upon the Gospels or the Epistles of St Paul, while the latter was common in the Latin schools (*summula*). The medieval anthology had precedents in Latin patristic literature and even in antiquity.[16] Isidore of Seville in his *Sentences* selected propositions from the writings of the Fathers and grouped by problems, so becoming the progenitor of the early Scholastic Sentences collections. Perhaps the real forerunner is Defensor de Ligugé (seventh century) with his *Liber scintillarum*: the record total of 360 surviving MSS attests to its huge success.

In ninth-century Liège the well-known Irish poet Sedulius Scottus made a poetic compilation for his own use. Eric of Auxerre, the admirer of John Scottus Eriugena, showed wide acquaintance with the profane literature of antiquity when assembling the *Dicta philosophorum*. With these anthologies there opens the series of medieval florilegia that rely on ancient authors for the provision of moral counsel. Thomas of Ireland's work fits partly into this schema.

The florilegium was appreciated in the schools of the twelfth century as an aid to learning. In this sense it was fully a product of Scholasticism. Especially when governed by an ordering principle, it met the growing appreciation of mental order and systematization that marked the newly-dawned Scholastic age.[17] The profane literature of antiquity occupied a large place in such gatherings of material as the *Florilegium Gallicum* and the *Angelicum*. The coming of Aristotle through massive injections of translated material gave rise to the *Auctoritates Aristotelis* which picked out the most essential propositions from a wide range of

14 Art. 'Florilegium' in *Lexikon des Mittelalters*, 4.566–76 (E. Rauner and others). 15 M.A. Rouse and R.H. Rouse, 'Florilegia of Patristic Texts', in *Les genres littéraires dans les sources théologiques et philosophiques médiévales: définition, critique et exploitation* (Louvain-La-Neuve, 1982). 16 B. Munk Olsen, 'Les florilèges d'auteurs classiques', in *Les genres littéraires* (1982), 151–64. 17 Jacqueline Hamesse, 'Les florilèges philosophiques du XIIIe au XVe siècle', in *Les genres littéraires* (1982), pp 181–91.

the Latin Aristotle, especially, and other authors in lesser measure.[18] The conjunction of extracts from the saints with some from pagan philosophers, in particular the moralists (we should not forget that Seneca was *moralista* already for Abelard) became widespread as a means of ethical learning and moral formation. Of this variant of the genre the *Manipulus* of Thomas was perhaps the most successful example, with over 180 surviving MSS. Thomas was himself a keen student of the genre in which he chose to excel; he drew upon two little-known florilegia, and in turn his *Manipulus* was to be employed by other compilers after him.[19] (We shall come back to Thomas after completing our survey.) Florilegia were produced from the thirteenth century onwards for important books, not least the Bible, and Robert Kilwardby OP compiled the still-unedited *Tabulae super originalia patrum*. Needless to say, Byzantine and Slavic literatures also had their florilegia. The appetite for florilegia did not fail to make the transition to Renaissance humanism: Albrecht von Eyb's *Margarita poetica* offered exemplary material for the poet and writer; Jakob Wimpfeling's *Adolescentia* was filled with the newer humanistic literature, while the *Adagia* of Erasmus was a commented collection of the ancient proverbs on many topics. In the humanists the preoccupation with moral formation and character exemplarity continued the earlier practice.

CONTENT AND STRUCTURE OF THE 'MANIPULUS FLORUM'

The *Manipulus* consists of about six thousand extracts from works of the Fathers, the ecclesiastical writers, and chosen ancient authorities. Two hundred and sixty-six alphabetically-arranged topics serve to classify these quotations. The compilation is brought to a close with a bibliography of 366 writings which are referenced by title, incipit and explicit. All in all, Thomas produced a very substantial and well-rounded gathering. The arrangement of the topics is the key to the truly extraordinary popularity which the work of Thomas was to enjoy; in its genre it had no real rival in late medieval or Renaissance times, and its popularity was to last into the seventeenth century. No less than 47 printings of the work have been recorded. Thomas used the method of complete or 'absolute' alphabetization to order his themes, and he frequently added cross-references to parallel entries (for example, '*Amicitia: vide etiam in titulo. Acceptio. 7....; Societas. 6.; Inimicitia*'). These references enabled topical searches to be undertaken within the entire book. The number of extracts included in the anthology differs greatly from one topic to another; some merit only three or four entries, while the longest have almost 100; *amicitia* has 95, and *mors*, the longest, 99. The compiler identified each extract in the margin with a letter of

18 J. Hamesse, *Les Auctoritates Aristotelis, Un florilège médiéval: étude historique et édition critique* (Louvain & Paris, 1974). 19 Rouse & Rouse (1979), pp 197ff.

the alphabet, resorting to the double alphabet where necessary. Thomas kept regularly to an order of precedence among the authors he cited; when, for instance, the four Latin Doctors of the Church are quoted they invariably come as a group in the first place, always in the order: Augustine, Ambrose, Jerome and Gregory. Seneca always brings up the rear. The general ordering falls into the categories of patristic, ecclesiastical and ancient, in the descending sequence of their authority for Christians.

The success of Thomas' work is largely due to the way in which it succeeded in combining the use of an alphabetically-organized index with topical arrangement and cross-indexing. The result has aptly been characterized as 'an honest artisan's eminently practical invention'.[20]

SOURCES

Thomas tells us in his prologue that he worked in the library of the Collège de Sorbonne, and in fact the order of the books he cites for a given author reflects with exactitude what is found in the Sorbonne catalogue of 1338, comprising well over a thousand volumes. Good detective work by Richard and Mary Rouse has thrown much light on Thomas' use of sources. He relied chiefly on the *Flores paradisi* and the *Liber exceptionum*, both of Cistercian origin. (Of these two works the actual copies which Thomas used still survive.) Their compilers provided clear references to their own sources, which is no doubt a large part of the reason why Thomas chose to follow them. In addition to the *Glossa* on the Bible and to his own surviving copies of Alain de Lille (*Planctus naturae*) and Pierre de Blois (*Epistolae*), Thomas employed a collection of proverbs known as *Proverbia philosophorum*, which may have been an ancient Latin translation of a Greek collection of sayings concerning friendship and other topics, with some additions made for instance from Seneca. With regard to *amicitia* he took twenty-two extracts from this work, including the four attributed to Theophrastus. Aside from these major collections Thomas had all the *armaria* (bookcases) of the Sorbonne library to draw upon for the *originalia* (or unexcerpted books) of his authors. The bibliography of the *Manipulus florum*, an unusual feature in a medieval work, places under each of the twenty-four authors a list of his works which are its sources. Augustine dominates here, with 148 titles. Some authors (such as Pliny, Macrobius and Maimonides) have only one book-title under their name. It has been established that the vast majority of the titles listed were taken from the books making up the rich bequest to the library by Gérard d'Abbeville, who had in his possession many of the codices belonging originally to Richard de Fournival. Some of these manuscript works can still be consulted at the *Bibliothèque nationale*.

20 Rouse & Rouse (1979), p. 161.

THE CONSTRUCTION OF THE TOPIC 'AMICITIA'

What does Thomas of Ireland's selection of quotations tell us concerning his own approach to the topic of *amicitia*? In the first place, the entry faithfully reflects his own general predilections. The four Latin Doctors of the Church are accorded precedence. St Augustine is first, with ten quotations (as we shall see); St Ambrose follows with five extracts (*De officiis* is quoted three times and *De officiis monachorum* once); St Jerome has also five (from letters, and his commentary on Micah); finally, Gregory the Great occurs once (the *Pastorale*). St John Chrysostom's commentary on Matthew was much frequented by the Latins from the early Middle Ages onwards; Thomas draws a single idea from it, and adds three quotations taken from the Greek saint, quotations which he found in John of Salisbury's *Polycraticus*. Isidore of Seville is drawn on five times (*De summo bono*). John Cassian is quoted seven times (commentary on the Psalms, once, and *Epistolae*, six times). Thomas may have missed some authors (Paulinus of Nola, for instance), but it can be said that his selection from the Doctors and the ecclesiastical writers is judicious; he manages to reflect in small compass almost all the highpoints of earlier Christian thought on the subject of *amicitia*, including friendship with God.

It would be quite unfair to leave the reader without some direct acquaintance, however limited, with Thomas' selection from his authorities. To reproduce in translation the entire lemma *amicitia* cannot be done here, for lack of space. What we can attempt is a survey of the first set of ten entries, all of which are taken from St Augustine, and we can sample them in order to experience the cumulative effect they produce.[21]

The Augustinian passages
(a) 'Augustine in a letter to Jerome: I do not know whether friendships are to be considered Christian which are more to be characterized by the popular proverb, "Flattery makes friends but truth makes enemies", than by the ecclesiastical one, "Better the wounds inflicted by a friend than the fraudulent kisses of an enemy".'[22]

Thomas succeeds at once in focusing his reader's mind upon Christian friendship. The 'popular proverb' came in fact from the playwright Terence (*Andria*, 68); it expresses an apparently cynical judgment on the power of flattery. Augustine finds an altogether higher order of truth in Proverbs 27:6 concerning the requirement of truth in friendship and the debasing effect of flattery.

---

21 Our own translations, unless stated otherwise. For a general study of the place of *amicitia* in Augustine's thought and its relation to *caritas* see J. McEvoy, *'Anima una et cor unum*: friendship and spiritual unity in Augustine', *Recherches de Théologie ancienne et médiévale* 53 (1986), 49–92.
22 St Augustine, *Epistulae*, 82, 4, 31 (CSEL 34, ed. A. Goldbacher, p. 382.14–18).

(b) 'Augustine, *Against the Manichees*, bk 1: Should someone wish to learn the will of God, let him become the friend of God. For if someone wished to know the will of a man without being his friend everyone would deride his impudence. But no one becomes a friend of God unless through a most pure way of life.'[23] Augustine insisted that no one is known unless through friendship. What impudence it would be to claim to know the will of God unless one were (in the biblical expression) 'amicus Dei' (Jud 8:22)!

(c) 'Augustine in a sermon: Be like a doctor; the doctor does not love the sick unless he hates the sickness – he attacks the fever to set the sick person free from it. Do not love the vices of your friends, if you love your friends.'[24]

(d) 'Augustine, *On the True Religion*: This is perfect friendship which makes us love more what is better and less what is lesser. Love a wise and perfect soul just as you see it, but a foolish soul, not for its folly but because it is capable of perfection and wisdom. For one is not to love oneself for one's foolishness; whoever loves himself in this way will not move forward to wisdom. No one will become what he desires to be, unless he hates himself as he is.'[25] The link between friendship for others and the discernment of the good, both for ourselves and for them, is made clear by reference to what justice requires, as well as to the judgment of character that is required for true friendship to be joined.

(e) 'We must never refuse the friendship of anyone who approaches us with a view to friendship; not that we should welcome him in at once, but that we may hope to welcome him, and he should be treated in such a way that he can be welcomed. For we ought to receive in friendship one to whom we may dare to disclose all our intimate thoughts.'[26]

It would be difficult to find a statement closer to the core of Augustine's thought concerning *amicitia* and *caritas* than this one. It is taken from his lengthy discussion of the meaning of 'bearing one another's burdens' (Gal 6:2). It is a far cry from the classical cult of friendship between great men who are equals in virtue and dignity; Augustine insists that friendship is due in some way or degree to all to whom charity is owed. Friendship consists in the constant will for the good of the other for that other's own sake, hence it should play some part in every interpersonal relationship.

(f) 'There is nothing that tests a friend so much as the carrying of his friend's burden. No one is known save through friendship, and the reason why we unflinchingly carry the faults of a friend is because their qualities delight us and captivate us.'[27]

---

23 St Augustine, *De Genesi contra Manichaeos*, 1, 2, 4 (CSEL 91, ed. D. Weber, p. 71.27–34).
24 St Augustine, *Sermones*, 49, 6 (CCSL 41, ed. C. Lambot, p. 619.161–4).   25 St Augustine, *De uera religione*, 48 (CCSL 32, ed. K.D. Daur, p. 248.4–10).   26 St Augustine, *De diuersis quaestionibus*, 71, 6 (CCSL 44A, ed. A. Mutzenbecher, p. 205.108–12).   27 St Augustine, *De diuersis quaestionibus*, 71, 5 (CCSL 44A, ed. A. Mutzenbecher, p. 205.104–7).

Thomas has coupled two quotations coming from the same work. The first forms part of Augustine's interpretation of the Pauline advice about how to 'fulfill the law of Christ' (Gal 6:2). In the second Augustine is once again the realist who advocates that friendship be based upon reality and not upon illusion; it should take account of human frailty without any slackening of good will.

(g) 'Just as the flattery of a friend can pervert, so the insult of an enemy can sometimes correct.'[28]

(h) 'Not everyone who is indulgent is a friend, nor is everyone who beats you an enemy. Better it is to love with severity than to deceive with gentleness.'[29] Friendship and truth combine in what one might call the justice of love – tough love, in the modern expression.

(i) The lengthiest of the quotations, ostensibly taken from a sermon of Augustine, comes in fact from Caesarius of Arles.[30] Three kinds of friendship are distinguished: of bad conscience; according to the flesh; of reason (reciprocal and trusting).

(j) 'You ought not to love your friend so as to get something from him, such as money or some temporal gain; it is not him you love but what he gives you. A friend is to be loved gratis, for his own sake, not for something else. If, however, the rule that you should love a friend gratuitously is a constraint upon you, how gratuitously is God to be loved – who commands that you should love your fellow-man! Nothing is more loveable than God.'[31] This teaching about disinterestedness and gratuity in friendship, and the primacy of the love of God, are indeed Augustinian; however it is once again Caesarius of Arles who is actually writing.

In spite of the imperfections to which we have alluded, Thomas succeeded admirably in sampling Augustine's theory of friendship, the main components of which are genuinely represented through the discerning quotations made. Clearly, Thomas knew where to look in the Augustinian *œuvre*; he had an instinct for what he should take and what he must leave. He doubtless knew, for instance, the moving account of the sudden death of the youthful Augustine's friend (*Confessions*, IV, 4), but the narrative and the reflection on it was simply too long to warrant inclusion in his 'Handful'. He appears to have missed Letter 258, and with that the Ciceronian influence on Augustine.[32] He had nothing like the contemporary sense of Augustine's development, or of the chronological order of his writings. But Thomas did indeed have great learning combined with an

---

28 St Augustine, *Confessionum libri XIII*, 9, 8, 9 (CCSL 27, 3, ed. L. Verheijen, p. 144.57–8). (Trans. Frank Sheed.) 29 St Augustine, *Epistulae*, 93, 2 (CCSL 34. 2, ed. A. Goldbacher, p. 448.23–6). 30 Caesarius Arelatensis, *Sermones*, 21, 3 (CCSL 103, ed. G. Morin, pp 95–6). Such misattributions were no more common in the *Manipulus florum* than generally at the time. 31 Caesarius Arelatensis, *Sermones*, 21, 4 (CCSL 103, ed. G. Morin, p. 96). 32 J. McEvoy, '*Anima una et cor unum ...*', (1986), pp 76–80 (with translation of *Ep.* 258).

expert sense of extraction, and these qualities enabled him to identify passages that were manageable, quotable, numerous, and above all relevant to the topic of *amicitia*.

The lemma inimicitia *(enmity)*

We should not forget that lemmata occur in the *Manipulus* which are addressed to partial synonyms and antonyms of *amicitia*. Among other things, Thomas devoted a brief article to *inimicitia* (enmity). We can learn something from it about how he worked.

There are six entries (a–f). St Augustine's definition of *elemosyna* (mercy) is taken from the *Enchiridion*. From the saint's *De verbis Domini sermo* comes the admonition that as long as you are an enemy to yourself you are at enmity with the Word of God, whereas entering into harmony with yourself will mean finding again one who was as though dead. In *Super Beati immaculati* (Ps 118 [119]) St Ambrose of Milan comments that the worst enemies are generally former friends; nevertheless love of God does indeed mean loving your enemies. St Gregory (the *Pastoral Letter*) reminds his reader that ordinary human virtue requires that one tolerate one's enemies, whereas in God's sight it is actually to love them that is virtue. Following a quotation from one of Gregory's sermons, Thomas passes on to that established classic of the same author, the *Moralia in Job*: 'The humane outlook should tolerate each one who is an enemy, even when it considers him impious and a wrongdoer.'

The selection of pre-Christian writers

Thomas showed no hesitation regarding the adoption of pre-Christian philosophical ideas and motifs regarding friendship, and many other topics also. The literary figures of non-Christian antiquity had in quantitative terms written much more on the subject of friendship than had the Christians of the fourth and fifth centuries; it was perceptive on Thomas' part to rely upon the classical authors for about three-fifths of his material. Beginning with Valerius Maximus, he drew heavily on Cicero (19), as might be anticipated (*De amicitia*, 16; *Ars rhetorica*, 2; *De officiis*, 1). Seneca, as we might expect, yielded the largest number of quotations of any of Thomas' sources (22). Of these five came from the anthology of classical proverbs which Thomas had at his disposal in the library of the Collège de Sorbonne, while seventeen were drawn from the *Letters to Lucilius*. Theophrastus, the successor of Aristotle at the head of the Lycaeum, makes a spectacular entry on the scene: the now-lost digest of the proverbs and sayings of antiquity which Thomas had to hand allowed him to use four quotations from an author whose three-volume work on *philia* (known to St Jerome at first hand) had disappeared for good at the close of antiquity. Of Diogenes Laertius, Thomas found quotations in the same source and used three of them.

The only medieval author in the list (Thomas would have thought of him as a 'modernus') comes in the last place; the compiler had a copy of the letters of Pierre de Blois, but it was from the same writer's *Liber de amicitia* that he selected out nine quotations. In this writing Pierre plagiarized the *De spirituali amicitia* of St Aelred of Rievaulx; his adaptation of the latter work went commonly under the name of St Augustine, right down to the nineteenth century.[33] Through this final group of quotations a Cistercian influence crept anonymously into the *Manipulus* article on friendship.

All in all, it was a rich selection of Christian and classical experience that Thomas placed before his readership. His compilation was judicious and it can still be read with pleasure and profit by the contemporary reader. But it is for the witness it bears to the literary habits and the moral and religious taste of his time that this entry is of value for the historical inquiry into the theory of friendship. The lemma *amicitia* reflects the currency of the theme itself – in colleges and religious fraternities, friendship was an essential aspect of life with a communitarian basis, in times when the isolated individual was considered an anomaly.[34]

THE ACHIEVEMENT OF THOMAS AS AN ANTHOLOGIST

The thirteenth century saw a rapid growth and development in the use of indexes, the systematic ordering of libraries, and the compilation of concordances and other devices for locating and retrieving information of a literary kind. The *Manipulus* is a product of this cultural phenomenon, which it brings to a new high point by means of its systematic ordering and its use of apparatus. The purpose of its arrangement, as we have seen, was to permit its reader to find rapidly what he was looking for. The increasing employment of quotations was a feature of thirteenth-century sermons, especially of those preached before university audiences. Evidence of the employment of the *Manipulus* in the later Middle Ages can be found in other compilations, in Latin and vernacular writers, and in the sermon literature and bibliographies of the period.

In assessing the nature of Thomas' achievement attention must be paid not only to what he included in the lemma *amicitia* but what he omitted. What do his omissions tell us about his project and its execution?

His silence regarding Aristotle, the most significant ancient philosopher of friendship, suggests that Thomas found little in the Peripatetic view of friendship with which to nurture his own intended readership. On the other hand this omission may be a reflection of the intellectual situation at Paris in the

---

33 For a recent estimate of Pierre see R.W. Southern, *Scholastic humanism and the unification of Europe*, ii, *The heroic age* (Oxford, 2001), pp 178–218. 34 On collegiate friendship see J. McEvoy, 'The theory of friendship in the Latin Middle Ages: hermeneutics, contextualisation and the transmission and reception of ancient texts and ideas from *c.*AD 350 to *c.*1500', in J. Haseldine (ed.), *Friendship in medieval Europe* (Stroud, 1999), pp 3–44 at pp 22–3.

aftermath of the condemnation by Bishop Tempier in 1277 of over two hundred philosophical propositions; following that there was a tendency to emphasize the paganism of the Greek thinker. No such fate befell Cicero on the other hand; Thomas welcomed Tully into his pages and pillaged his *De amicitia*, much as Henry of Ghent had done twenty years beforehand in his own *quaestio disputata* on the subject of friendship.[35] Aristotle had threatened to displace Cicero altogether as the philosopher of friendship, in the eyes at least of the more speculative spirits in the heyday of Aquinas and Albert the Great, but following 1277 one can detect a re-evaluation, not to speak of a restoration, of Cicero. Thomas was not keen to favour Platonist or Epicurean influences: he may not have known of the latter, and Neoplatonism was to say the least sparse of doctrine regarding *philia* (as distinct from Eros). Nor did Thomas include Greek Cappadocian or Byzantine material, despite its availability; Gregory of Nazianzen, for instance, had written of his lifelong friendship with Basil, and Michael of Ephesus had commented on Book IX of the *Nicomachean Ethics*. One supposes that Thomas' practical, pastoral and spiritual concerns, when combined with his own conception of his desired readership, focused his vision and rendered certain exclusions almost instinctive. Yet it is striking that he made no room for the *Conferences* of John Cassian, which contained a well-thought-out and practical doctrine on friendship in the monastic community. Thomas was a secular cleric, and he showed upon occasion that he had only a limited sympathy with the monastic order, while with regard to the mendicants his attitude was at best rather cool.

Despite his limitations Thomas merits admiration. He was a Christian humanist *avant la lettre* who put to work the resources of an excellent college library in order to nourish, form, educate, instruct, encourage, ennoble and ultimately purify his readership. His work met with undreamt-of success. Enough is known about the contents of the Sorbonne College Library for us to imagine the scene of Thomas' daily toil over many years. He laboured within the context of a very orderly arrangement of authors in the bookcases.[36] One wonders how his vast project first came to form in Thomas' quite conventional mind. Was the activity of anthologizing in the case of Thomas something of a substitute for higher theological aspirations, for which he felt his mind to be altogether too conventional? It is difficult to imagine Thomas leaving the library to attend regularly at the school jousting-exercises. On the other hand not

35 J. McEvoy, 'The sources and the significance of Henry of Ghent's disputed question, 'Is friendship a virtue?'', in W. Vanhamel (ed.), *Henry of Ghent: proceedings of the International Colloquium on the occasion of the seven hundredth anniversary of his death (1293)*, Ancient and Medieval Philosophy, Series 1. 15 (Leuven, 1996), pp 121–38. **36** Rouse & Rouse, in a Table (pp 122–3), demonstrate that the bibliography of the *Manipulus* and the order in which authors are quoted both reflect with precision the sequence in which the book titles appear in the Sorbonne Catalogue of 1338.

everyone is made for the speculative heights of dialectic or disputation, and as a preacher well-formed and sincerely believing, and likewise as a confessor eager for the betterment of his (mostly clerical?) penitents, the figure of Thomas takes on a quite plausible and reliable shape.

Within the framework of Irish-born Scholastics (taken in the broad sense) working in Continental Europe, Thomas of Ireland can be seen to have occupied a unique niche. His excellence lay in erudition. He proved to be by far the most learned scholar of Irish provenance during the period between 1100 and 1500. He found a place in academic life at Paris as a fellow of the Collège de Sorbonne, acquiring bachelor's degrees in Philosophy and Theology. This suggests that he came to Paris already beneficed, or at least well connected; perhaps he was of Hiberno-Norman stock. He did not specialize as a theologian, preferring for himself the humbler role of anthologist. Yet his achievement in his chosen domain won him fame far beyond anything accorded to any of the other Irish figures who preceded him, and surely far beyond anything that Thomas himself, evidently a humble man, had anticipated. His only boast was that he had put the results of a lot of hard work within easy reach of a readership.[37]

The name of Thomas of Ireland was not forgotten in his own college. For one thing the books he bequeathed to the library carried it. As a mark of honour he was accorded a memorial day, 28 July. When the library building in which he had worked was torn down, *c.*1481, to make way for a new one Thomas was one of the thirty-eight illustrious fellows each of whom was commemorated by a window. That construction was in turn pulled down in the seventeenth century to make way for the present building, but luckily a first-hand description of the old windows survives; it recounts that Thomas' window was placed between those of Godfrey of Fontaines and Henry of Hassia.[38]

37 Prologue, ed. Rouse & Rouse (1979), p. 233.   38 Rouse & Rouse (1979), p. 99.

Thomas of Ireland, the Pseudo–Dionysius and the ecclesiastical hierarchy: a study of the three *opuscula*

DECLAN LAWELL

INTRODUCTION: DATE AND OCCASION

Thomas of Ireland,[1] famed author of the *Manipulus florum*, also wrote three less well-known *opuscula* which have not yet received a critical edition. Only a scant secondary literature exists on the three short works. The opuscula are: *De tribus punctis Christiane religionis* (On the Three Points of the Christian Religion), *De tribus sensibus sacre scripture* (On the Three Levels of Meaning in Sacred Scripture), and *De triplici hierarchia* (On the Threefold Hierarchy), also referred to as *De tribus hierarchiis* (On the Three Hierarchies). This is the order in which the opuscula are presented in the main Parisian manuscripts[2] which witness these texts. It is hence reasonable to assume that the order of treatises reflects their chronological composition. Is there any textual evidence to confirm this proposed chronology?

It is known for certain that the *De tribus punctis* was written in 1316, since Thomas himself provides us with this date: 'Hii sunt tres puncti religionis Christiane collecti per magistrum Thomam Ybernicum anno domini MCCCXVI.'[3] This date is a firm anchor. It is interesting to note how this sentence describes the three points as having being 'collected'. A little further on, Thomas refers to himself as a *collector* and as the *collectionis auctor* ('the author of the collection'). A colophon at the end of the Paris MS 16397 of the *De tribus sensibus* asks of the reader: 'Et tu lector ora pro collectore' ('And you, reader, pray

---

1 For information on the life and works of Thomas of Ireland, consult Richard Rouse & Mary Rouse, *Preachers, florilegia and sermons: studies on the* Manipulus florum *of Thomas of Ireland*, Studies and Texts 47 (Toronto, 1979), especially ch. 4. See also B. Hauréau, 'Thomas d'Irlande' in *Histoire littéraire de la France* 30 (Paris, 1888), 398–408.   2 Paris, Bibliothèque Nationale, MS lat. 16397 (although the *De triplici hierarchia* has been lost from this MS), and MS lat. 15966 which alone contains all three works. I have examined reproductions of both these MSS and have completed a transcription based primarily on MS lat. 15966. I have also examined MS lat. 16536 which contains a copy of the *De triplici hierarchia*. It is to be hoped that a fully critical edition of these texts can be produced in due course. For an exhaustive list of the manuscripts containing the opuscula, see Rouse & Rouse, *Preachers*, pp 246–50.   3 'These are the three points of the Christian religion collected by Master Thomas of Ireland in the year of our Lord 1316.' Medieval orthography has been preserved in the selections from Thomas' writings.

74

for the collector'). The designation of Thomas as a collector is apt because the reader will find little original thought in these treatises. Both in his own estimation and in the view of the author of the colophon (a scribe), Thomas of Ireland was a gatherer of information and not primarily an original thinker.

The *De triplici hierarchia* must have been written after the *De tribus punctis* since in that treatise Thomas refers back to the first treatise, *De tribus punctis*. For example, at the end of the *De triplici hierarchia* Thomas writes: 'Istis autem tribus ierarchiis correspondere debent uel possunt tres puncti religionis Christiane, de quibus supra diximus.'[4] Here, Thomas explicitly states that he has already spoken of these three points above (*supra*). Also in the *De triplici hierarchia*, Thomas states: 'sicut plenius dixi de hoc in tractatu De Tribus Punctis' ('just as I have spoken more fully about this in the treatise *On the Three Points*'). Hence, the *De triplici hierarchia* must have been written after *De tribus punctis* was written in 1316. The *De tribus sensibus* was probably written after the *De tribus punctis* but before the *De triplici hierarchia* since that is the order in which the manuscripts present the treatises.

What was the occasion for the production of these opuscula? It cannot be known for certain, but a tantalising phrase in the *De tribus sensibus* suggests that this treatise at least was delivered as a lecture or reflection before the brothers in some religious house. Thomas refers to a homily written by Gregory, 'quam modo fratres audistis', 'which you, brothers, have listened to just now'.

CHARACTER AND SUMMARY OF THE OPUSCULA

Although each of the treatises can be read independently, the reader is entitled to view the three opuscula as to some extent a complete set which can be examined as a whole. This is so not just because Thomas refers back to, for example, the *De tribus punctis* when writing the *De triplici hierarchia*, nor simply because the number three offers a unifying framework for the structure of the opuscula, but also because of other thematic parallels that Thomas draws. For example, in the conclusion of the *De triplici hierarchia*, Thomas describes how the three hierarchies can be linked with the three points of the Christian religion (for example, point one, the articles of the faith which concern Christ, can be linked to the divine hierarchy of which Christ, truly God and truly man, is a member). Also, at the end of the *De tribus sensibus*, Thomas links each of the ways of interpreting Scripture to each of the hierarchies: the anagogical sense to the divine hierarchy, the allegorical to the angelic, and the moral or tropological to the ecclesiastical hierarchy. The idea of hierarchy then is what unites the three

4 'The three points of the Christian religion, which I dealt with above, should be or at least are able to be aligned with those three hierarchies.'

treatises, and this entitles the reader to consider the three opuscula together and to draw conclusions from such a synoptic overview.

Furthermore, it is the figure of the Pseudo-Dionysius which also unites the three treatises. In the *De tribus sensibus*, for instance, Thomas recalls Dionysius' conversion upon seeing an eclipse on the day of Christ's passion and death (as related in Hilduin's *Vita*), and explains how Dionysius (confused with another St Dionysius) brought the twin flowers of philosophy and military might into France, joining them to the Christian faith, the three then represented by the three leaves of the *fleur-de-lis*. Also, Thomas mentions Eriugena as the 'fourth commentator' (*quartus commentator*) on the books of Dionysius (alongside Maximus, Hugh of St Victor and John Sarrazen).[5] It is very surprising that Thomas, writing in the fourteenth century, seems utterly ignorant of two of the most voluminous Dionysian commentators in the thirteenth century, Robert Grosseteste and Thomas Gallus. Writing after 1316 in *De tribus sensibus*, Thomas of Ireland knows only four commentators on the Pseudo-Dionysius: 'Quatuor enim commentatores fuerunt librorum beati Dionysii, scilicet Iohannes Scotus, Iohannes Sarracenus, Maximus, et Hugo de Sancto Victore.'[6]

Beyond such personal references to Dionysius and his commentators, however, it is Thomas' constant reference to the hierarchical view of the universe learned from the Pseudo-Dionysius which unites the three opuscula. The *regula beati Dionysii* ('the rule of blessed Dionysius'), namely that the lower orders are led back to the highest by means of the middle ones, is repeated mantra-like throughout the *De triplici hierarchia*. Again, in the *De tribus punctis*, Thomas parallels the Neoplatonic exit from unity into multiplicity with the need for a multiplication of ministries in the Church the further one is removed from the unity of the pope:

> Secundum autem beatum Dionysium, et in angelica et in ecclesiastica ierarchia, quanto magis aliqua potestas descendit, tanto magis diuiditur et diminuitur, et per consequens ad sui ministerii executionem plures ministros requirit.[7]

5 The commentary by Iohannes Sarracenus on the *Celestial Hierarchy* (around 1140) remains unedited. For a discussion of this commentary and a list of manuscripts containing it, see Gabriel Théry, 'Existe-t-il un commentaire sur la "Hiérarchie Céleste" du Pseudo-Denys?', *Revue des sciences philosophiques et théologiques* 11 (1922), 72–82. 6 'For there were four commentators on the books of blessed Dionysius, namely, John Scotus, John the Saracen, Maximus and Hugh of St Victor'. In the preceding sentences, Thomas (surely with some national pride) introduced his fellow countryman, Eriugena, as one of the four founders of the *studium Parisiense*, 'scilicet Rabanus, Cladius, Alquinus magister Karoli, et Iohannes dictus Scotus, natione tamen Hybernicus (nam Hybernia dicitur magna Scotia)' ('that is, Rabanus, Cladius, Alcuin the teacher of Charles, and John called the Scot, but he is from the Irish nation (because Ireland is called Great Scotia)'). 7 'Now according to blessed Dionysius, in both the angelic and the ecclesiastical hierarchies, the more any power descends, the more it is divided and diminished, and thus

Thomas imbibed this hierarchical worldview from the Pseudo-Dionysius and was at pains to apply it to the Church and society: everything has its allotted place and should remain in it, receiving from what is superior and ministering to what is inferior. As he wrote in *De tribus punctis*: 'Sed quamdiu homines sunt de foro ecclesie, oportet obseruare ordinem ecclesiastice ierarchie que est ordinata ad instar et similitudinem angelice ierarchie.'[8]

Before proceeding to examine this central Dionysian theme of hierarchy in the three opuscula, it will be helpful to give a very brief summary of the nature of each of them. *De tribus punctis* deals with what Thomas considers to be the three main points of the Christian religion. 'Primus ergo punctus nostre religionis est credere articulos fidei qui sunt quatuordecim et continentur in Symbolo Apostolorum, scilicet *Credo* [...].'[9] Thomas then proceeds to discuss the articles of the faith. 'Secundus punctus nostre religionis est seruare decem mandata decalogi que ponuntur Ex. 20 [...].'[10] Thomas then gives an outline of the ten commandments. 'Tertius punctus nostre religionis est euitare septem peccata mortalia.'[11] Again, Thomas goes on to offer an account of these sins. What is interesting, however, is the digressions that Thomas makes, for the bulk of this treatise is preoccupied with questions arising from the seventh mortal sin, *luxuria*. It is these digressions, I suggest, which betray almost subconsciously the real preoccupations of Thomas of Ireland, as shall be seen.

The *De tribus sensibus* is an account of the four traditional senses or levels of interpretation of the sacred texts in medieval exegesis: the literal, the allegorical, the tropological/moral, and the anagogical. Thomas, however, with his penchant for thinking in threes,[12] deals briskly with the literal meaning and devotes the greater part of the treatise to the three spiritual senses, hence the *tres sensus* of the title. Again, what is interesting in this text is the wanderings that Thomas makes, digressions which interrupt the tight structure that Thomas perhaps intended to make when delineating these three meanings. The treatise is largely centred around various interpretations of the text from Proverbs 1:9: 'Wisdom

requires more ministers for it to be carried out.' 8 'But as long as people remain within the Church, it is necessary to observe the order of the ecclesiastical hierarchy which is arranged in the pattern and likeness of the angelic hierarchy.' Cf. the opening of *De triplici hierarchia*: 'ecclesiastica ierarchia ordinata est ad instar et similitudinem angelice ierarchie'. 9 'The first point then of our religion is to believe the articles of faith, of which there are fourteen and which are contained in the Apostles' Creed, that is the *Credo*.' 10 'The second point of our religion is to keep the Ten Commandments of the Decalogue which are laid down in Exodus 20 ...'. 11 'The third point of our religion is to avoid the seven mortal sins.' 12 Cf. the remarks made of the *Manipulus florum* by Gabriel Théry in 'Catalogue des mss dionysiens des bibliothèques d'Autriche', *Archives d'histoire doctrinale et littéraire du moyen âge* 10 (1936), 163–224 and 11 (1938), 87–130: 'Son *manipulus florum* est insipide, le socius de Sorbonne ne pensant qu'en trilogie' (vol. 10, p. 209: 'His *Manipulus florum* is banal, the fellow of the Sorbonne only thinking in threes')! Théry intended to produce an edition of the *De triplici hierarchia* but never succeeded in doing so.

hath built herself a house, she hath hewn her out seven pillars,' yet it will be interesting to note the departures from strict exegesis made by Thomas which reveal the intentions close to his heart.

Finally, the treatise *De triplici hierarchia* is a description of the three hierarchies[13] and is heavily influenced by the Pseudo-Dionysius. Thomas lists the three hierarchies as follows:

> Est enim secundum ipsum [sc. Dionysium] totius entis siue uniuersi triplex ierarchia: suprema, media et infima. Suprema est supercelestis et diuina, media celestis siue angelica, infima subcelestis siue ecclesiastica.[14]

The quantity of space devoted to each of these hierarchies is revealing about Thomas' mentality since the divine and angelic hierarchies receive only a few pages of attention before Thomas approaches what really captivates him: discussing the ecclesiastical hierarchy. It is this ecclesial emphasis in fact that stands out above all else upon an overview of all three treatises. It is to highlighting this emphasis that I now turn.

THE ECCLESIASTICAL HIERARCHY

The Pseudo-Dionysius[15] was a mysterious Neoplatonic, Christian writer of the late fifth or early sixth centuries. Passing himself off as the Dionysius converted by St Paul at the Areopagus in Athens (Acts 17:34), he was able to assume almost apostolic authority during the Middle Ages until the fraud was uncovered by Lorenzo Valla (d. 1457) during the Renaissance. His writings included the *Celestial Hierarchy, Ecclesiastical Hierarchy, Divine Names, Mystical Theology* and the ten *Letters*. When the Latins of Western Europe began to examine the corpus of writings under Dionysius' name, the treatise called *On the Celestial* (or *Angelic*) *Hierarchy* exercised a particular fascination for the commentators. John

13 It is worth noting that Thomas, and indeed all those inspired by the Pseudo-Dionysius, understood the word 'hierarchy' (coined by Dionysius) to refer not simply to the pope and bishops as we might think today. Rather, hierarchy was 'a sacred order, a state of understanding and an activity approximating as closely as possible to the divine' (Pseudo-Dionysius, *The Celestial Hierarchy*, ch. 3 in Pseudo-Dionysius, *The complete works*, trans. Colm Luibheid, The Classics of Western Spirituality (New York, 1987), p. 153). Hierarchy thus contains the notions of order, understanding and activity – all of which are directed to God – rather than just the clerical state. On this view, God, the angels and lay people as much as the bishops are members of a hierarchy.   14 'According to Dionysius, there is a three-fold hierarchy in the whole of being or the universe: the highest, the middle and the lowest. The highest is supercelestial and divine, the middle is celestial or angelic, the lowest is subcelestial or ecclesiastical.'   15 For a general introduction, see Andrew Louth, *Denys the Areopagite*, Outstanding Christian Thinkers Series (London, 1989).

Scottus Eriugena translated from the Greek the entire corpus of writings, but it was the *Celestial Hierarchy* he selected for his commentary, *Expositiones in hierarchiam coelestem*. Hugh of St Victor (d. 1141) in the twelfth century likewise wrote a commentary on the *Celestial Hierarchy*, as did his fellow Victorine, John Sarrazen (Iohannes Sarracenus, who also translated the works of the Pseudo-Dionysius into Latin around 1167). It was similarly with his *Glosses on the Angelic Hierarchy* (1224) that the abbot of Vercelli, Thomas Gallus (d. 1246) began his project of understanding all the works of the Pseudo-Dionysius. Robert Grosseteste too began his series of commentaries with the *Celestial Hierarchy* (around 1239–41). What interested these commentators was not speculation on the angelic and heavenly spirits considered in themselves, though of course this was part of their concern. Rather, it was the task of applying the lessons learned from the angelic hierarchy to the ecclesiastical hierarchy that was of utmost concern. Hence for Thomas Gallus, for example, the fact that the Seraphim were the highest rank of angels, located in closest proximity to the Godhead in a continual motion of love directed to God, was interpreted allegorically as signifying that the human faculty of love (as opposed to the intellect) was highest in the soul that journeyed towards God. Indeed, Gallus even wrote a short sermon on *How the life of prelates ought to conform to the angelic life*.[16]

It is against this backdrop that Thomas of Ireland's three opuscula need to be situated, that is to say, in light of the method of comparing the hierarchy of the angels with the hierarchy of the Church. What is witnessed, however, in Thomas of Ireland is a sharp switching of interest away from any prolonged exploration of the angelic species in order to focus attention on the ecclesiastical ranks.

DE TRIPLICI HIERARCHIA

The gravitational pull exerted by the ecclesiastical hierarchy on Thomas is manifest above all in his treatise *On the Threefold Hierarchy*. The treatise begins with Thomas' *clavis interpretum*, the hermeneutical key which guides the entire discussion:

> Secundum beatum Dionysium, ecclesiastica ierarchia ordinata est ad instar et similitudinem angelice ierarchie.[17]

The ecclesiastical hierarchy, then, is ordered after the pattern of the angelic hierarchy. Dionysius is invoked by Thomas here as an authority in the first lines

---

16 See Declan Lawell, '*Qualiter vita prelatorum conformari debet vite angelice*: a sermon (1244–1246?) attributed to Thomas Gallus', *Recherches de théologie et philosophie médiévales* (forthcoming).   17 'According to blessed Dionysius, the ecclesiastical hierarchy is arranged in the pattern and likeness of the angelic hierarchy'.

of his treatise, and it is the same Dionysius that Thomas immediately proceeds to quote in order to substantiate his interpretative key:

> Beatus autem Dionysius ibidem de ecclesiastica ierarchia ponit istam regulam: Lex sacratissima diuinitatis est ultima per media ad suprema reducere.[18]

This 'most holy law of divinity', or what Thomas refers to as the *regula beati Dionysii* ('the rule of blessed Dionysius'), or indeed the *lex hierarchica* ('the law of hierarchy') as Dionysius himself frequently calls it, is repeated as a refrain throughout Thomas' entire text. The quotation for Thomas summed up the structured and hierarchical order that must exist throughout the entire cosmos, namely that what is lower is constantly brought back (Greek: *anagesthai*, hence the 'anagogical' ascent of the law of hierarchy) to what is supreme by means of what is in the middle.

This law cannot be subverted, says Thomas, especially when it comes to Church affairs. Is there a danger in Thomas' thought that the Pseudo-Dionysius is being invoked solely for his authority and that his writings are mined only to assert the rights of the ecclesiastical hierarchy? In other words, does Thomas witness to a certain decadence of interpretation that sunders the connections between Church life and its roots in the angelic and divine life, and that sees the law of hierarchy as a way of asserting Church control rather than as providing the theological and angelic template which the ecclesiastical hierarchy must continually seek to imitate? To answer this question, the way Thomas reflects on each of the hierarchies must be examined in turn.

The supercelestial (the prefix *super* designating what is 'above' the celestial/angelic hierarchy) or divine hierarchy is the Trinity. Thomas devotes only a couple of pages to the Trinity, reflecting on the triangle as an image of the three divine persons. Just as the triangle has three angles, each of which covers the entire surface of the shape, so too there are three persons in the Trinity who equally share in the divine essence. Thomas however prefers the Augustinian human and psychological model of the Trinity where the memory, intelligence and will are seen as vestiges of the three persons of the Trinity. In other words,

---

18 'Blessed Dionysius lays down that rule about the ecclesiastical hierarchy in the same place: The most holy law of divinity is to lead what is lowest back to what is highest through what is in the middle.' Cf. Pseudo-Dionysius, *De ecclesiastica hierarchia*, ch. 5: 'Lex quidem haec est Divinitatis sacratissima: per prima secunda ad divinissimam suam reducere lucem' (Eriugena's translation in P. Chevallier (ed.), *Dionysiaca: Recueil donnant l'ensemble des traductions latines des ouvrages attribués au Denys de l'Aréopage*, 2 vols (Bruges, 1937–50), ii, 1330[1–2]). Thomas is here giving a paraphrase of the *lex hierarchica* rather than an exact quotation from the Pseudo-Dionysius. He seems to have Eriugena's translation in mind which he must have preferred to Sarrazen's at this particular juncture.

in the most abstract thoughts on the divine life, Thomas' proclivity is towards the human and to what he can understand by examining his own experience. Thomas abruptly ends his musings on the Trinity with the remark: 'de qua [sc. suprema ierarchia] ista ad presens sufficiant [...]' ('these comments about the highest hierarchy should be enough for now [...]'). These brief comments should suffice for the consideration of the Trinity, says Thomas, perhaps fearing to get lost in speculative muddles, perhaps impatient to get on to considering the ecclesiastical hierarchy. He ends with a quotation from St Bernard (who undoubtedly had Peter Abelard in mind), warning about the twisted curiosity ('peruersa curiositas') that inquires about the Trinity, and recommending the security found in believing what the Church holds: 'credere et tenere sicut sancta ecclesia tenet, fides et securitas est' ('to believe and hold what the Church holds is faith and safety').

Turning to the celestial or angelic hierarchy, Thomas offers a brief description of the nine orders of angels. As if afraid to offer any statement of his own accord, Thomas invokes St Bernard as an authority for what each order specifically accomplishes. Then he immediately brings the reader back down to earth by proffering an example of the three threefold orders of angels in the case of earthly rulers: 'Exemplum huius ponitur in terrenis principatibus [...]' Just as the three orders of angels have varying degrees of proximity to the divine, so too there are different degrees of access to the king in any society: chamberlains and advisors who have direct access, then officers and courtiers appointed to look after large regions, and finally the bailiffs and viscounts given control of particular areas.

None of the orders of angels is given any extended treatment except for two telling exceptions: the Archangels and the Angels. The reason for this is that these are the two orders which have the most direct intervention in the ecclesiastical hierarchy which is Thomas' real concern and where he feels at ease. He is interested in the fact that each nation receives an Archangel as its special protector. The Angels also get a long paragraph because of their role in protecting individual people. He recalls the great *dignitas animarum* ('the dignity of souls') in that each soul has a guardian Angel appointed at birth. Thomas also notes that the angels in general work to bring humans into their company:

> Retrahunt enim a peccato futuro, increpant de preterito, et eruunt a presenti, ut sic homines ad eorum societatem adducantur, quia homines non secundum gradus naturalium, sed iuxta dona uirtutum et gratiarum ad omnes ordines angelorum assumuntur.[19]

---

19 'They [sc. the angels] ward people off from future sin, they reprimand them for past sin and they snatch them away from present sin, so that people may thus be brought into their company. The reason for this is that people are taken up into all the ranks of the angels in accordance with

After only one quarter of the treatise *De triplici hierarchia*, Thomas of Ireland has concluded his reflections on the divine and angelic hierarchies, thus leaving the remaining three quarters of the text to be devoted to the subcelestial or ecclesiastical hierarchy. Such a consideration of the amount of space given to each hierarchy is further evidence of Thomas' attraction towards the church's hierarchy.

Within the church's hierarchy, the highest state belongs to the leaders or prelates, the middle rank to the religious, while the laity comprises the lowest order. Bearing in mind that Thomas further breaks the lay order down into the three ranks of kings, the military and ordinary civilians, it can be noted that Thomas rigidly subjects all orders, sacred and secular, to the control of the church, itself led by the pope. For example, when discussing the 'royal priesthood' in relation to the papacy, Thomas observes:

> dixit beatus Petrus (I Petr. 2): *Vos autem genus electum, regale sacerdotium* etc. Sacerdotium ponit in substantiuo et regnum in adiectiuo. Vnde dicit 'regale sacerdotium', non 'sacerdotale regnum'. Adiectum autem adiacet substantiuo et dependet ab ipso, non econuerso, ad denotandum quod omne regnum debet adiacere sacerdotio et dependere ab ipso.[20]

All power, temporal and spiritual, Thomas explains, must reside in the pope, for just as there is one principle or source ruling over the hierarchy of the universe, namely God, so too in the hierarchy of the church militant it is right that there be one ruler in control. Yet the ecclesiastical hierarchy must continually strive to conform to the celestial or angelic hierarchy: 'Et secundum hoc debentur eis [i.e. to the three orders in the church: the pope, the bishops, the presbyters] tres actus ierarchici ad modum illorum qui sunt in angelica ierarchia, scilicet purgare, illuminare et perficere'.[21] The nexus between the angelic and ecclesial actions is clearly affirmed by Thomas: just as the hierarchical actions of purgation, illumination and perfection are carried out among the angelic ranks, so too in the Church the priests can perfect spiritual creation by baptising souls and nourishing them in the Eucharist; teachers and doctors can illuminate and enlighten others by word and deed; judges or confessors can purge through correction, judgment and punishment.

The middle order of the ecclesiastical hierarchy is also divided into three,

their gifts of virtue and grace, and not in accordance with their natural states.'   20 '... blessed Peter said (1 Pet 2): *You are a chosen race, a royal priesthood* etc. He puts 'priesthood' as the substantive and 'kingship' as the adjective. An adjective is attached to its substantive and is dependent upon it, not the other way about, in order to show that all kingship must be attached to the priesthood and be dependent upon it.'   21 'In accordance with this there are three hierarchical actions due to them in the same way as those in the angelic hierarchy, namely, to purge, to illuminate and to perfect.'

though Thomas is not as clear on these divisions as he is concerning the first and last orders. It is only at the end of this section that he mentions ministers general, (Dominican) priors in particular religious houses, and then (Franciscan) guardians, as an example of this middle order of the religious. Most of the discussion centres around the debate on poverty, perhaps mindful of the disputes among the mendicant orders about these issues in the previous century. As a secular, and perhaps with a dissenting nod in the direction of the mendicants, Thomas patently prefers obedience to any form of poverty, because in poverty one only renounces exterior goods, while in obedience one renounces one's very own will:

> Nam uotum continentie preeminet uoto paupertatis, et uotum obedientie prefertur utrique, cuius ratio est quia inter uirtutes tanto uirtus aliqua est potentior quanto maius bonum contempnit propter Deum.[22]

Although the order of the laity is the last in the sequence of all the orders, it by no means receives less attention from Thomas, who shows not just his inclination to the church hierarchy, but also a fierce concern for proper order in society and for the excellence of the military. Thomas states that justice must be the central concern of kings and rulers in their administration. He cites with approval Plato's opinion that justice combined with wisdom is best: 'Sententia enim Platonis est beatas fore res publicas si eas uel studiosi sapientie regerent, uel earum rectores studere sapientie contigisset [...]'.[23]

Thomas then turns his attention from secular rulers to the soldiers who constitute the second order. He offers a lengthy discussion of the military virtues: courage and hardiness are listed first, and secondly, faithfulness and respect for one's superiors, especially the clergy. Indeed, Thomas says, that is why soldiers receive their swords from the altar, that is, in order to profess themselves sons of the church. Finally, soldiers require humility. Thomas was also a firm supporter of the crusades (*assumptio crucis transmarine*) as is evident in *De tribus punctis* where he states that those who die on crusade will ascend immediately into heaven without enduring any suffering in purgatory. The lay order is concluded with a single paragraph concerning individual lay people: they must live soberly, justly and piously, thus conquering the flesh, the world and the devil respectively.

What kind of man is Thomas portrayed as in these texts? Preoccupied with order in society and with the provision of sufficient soldiers, one is inclined to

22 'For the vow of chastity is superior to the vow of poverty, and the vow of obedience is preferable to both. The reason for this is that among the virtues, any virtue is more powerful the more it despises a greater good for God's sake.' 23 'Plato's opinion is that states would be successful if it happened that students of wisdom ruled over them, or if their rulers applied themselves to the study of wisdom [...]'.

think of Thomas as being not of native Irish, Gaelic stock, but rather of Norman extraction. While a Gael would certainly have been interested in the order and unity of his community, it is easier to envisage a man of Norman descent exhibiting Thomas' particular emphasis on military excellence. Perhaps too it was the Norman Thomas' proficiency in European languages and possible (family) connections in France or even England which offered him ease of passage from Ireland to his place of his study in Paris.

'DE TRIBUS PUNCTIS'

Just under half of this treatise deals with the first two points of the Christian religion, namely belief in the articles of faith and the observance of the Ten Commandments. The articles of the faith are expounded without much elaboration. Most of the commandments are dealt with in a cursory manner, except for the fourth commandment: *Honour thy father and mother*. After recommending obedience to one's natural parents, Thomas goes on to elaborate on the respect and obedience due to one's spiritual parentage, that is, the prelates and mother church. Thomas is particularly interested in insisting on the payment of tithes, which he justifies through another method of linking the angelic and ecclesiastical hierarchies:

> Decima enim pars angelorum cecidit per peccatum. Ista autem ruina debet ex hominibus restaurari. Ideo Dominus precepit hominibus ut ipsi decimam partem bonorum suorum Deo offerant si uelint uenire ad ordines unde decima pars angelorum cecidit.[24]

Just as humans are assumed into the angelic ranks 'iuxta dona uirtutum et gratiarum', as Thomas mentioned in *De triplici hierarchia*, so too can humans ascend to the angels by paying a tenth of their income in restitution for the tenth of the angels that fell from grace.

Thomas then devotes the remainder (over half) of the entire treatise to the consideration of the avoidance of the seven deadly or mortal sins: *superbia, invidia, ira, accidia/pigritia, avaritia, gula* and *luxuria*. *Luxuria* receives the most attention: Thomas presents his views on the various species of sexual sin and shows his pastoral concern to advise the clergy on when they should abstain from celebrating the sacraments or not.

Once these sins are delineated, the remainder of the section deals with the

---

24 'A tenth of the angels fell because of sin. That devastation must be repaired by humans. Hence, the Lord commanded people to offer a tenth of their goods to God if they wish to come to those ranks from which a tenth of the angels fell.'

remedies for the deadly sins: the administration of penance in confession, the practice of the opposite virtues, indulgences, the power of the keys, issues surrounding reserved sins, and so on. In fact, the last third of the *De tribus punctis* is best seen as a confessional manual interspersed with mnemonic verses to help readers remember the points explained. The weight of the *De tribus punctis* thus leans towards the moral issues of sin and the administration of the sacrament of penance.

'DE TRIBUS SENSIBUS'

This treatise[25] is of least concern to the study of Thomas of Ireland's thoughts on the Pseudo-Dionysius and the ecclesiastical hierarchy, dealing as it does with the spiritual senses of scripture. Yet at least one extended meditation gives an insight into Thomas' mind and witnesses to his proud loyalty to Paris and its university. One of the tropological or moral expositions of Proverbs 1:9 (*Sapientia aedificavit sibi domum*) given by Thomas concerns the University of Paris. The Faculty of Arts is the foundation of the university, Law and Medicine being the supporting walls. The roof is Theology and the seven columns of Proverbs are the seven liberal arts. Continuing the traditional idea of the transfer of power (*translatio imperii*) and learning (*translatio studiorum*) from the ancient world, Thomas sees Paris as the successor of Athens. Just as Athens was divided into three sectors, the zone of Mercury (for the merchants and civilians), the zone of Mars (for the chieftains and nobles) and the zone of the Sun (for the philosophers and the schools), so too Paris is divided into the *magna villa* (for merchants and tradesmen), the *civitas* (for the royal court and the cathedral church) and the *universitas* (for the students and colleges). Thomas is not keen simply to trace the Scholastic lineage of the University of Paris back to Athens and Rome; he also wants to point out how wisdom and study are necessary for military success: 'Militie enim uictoria et philosophia et gloria quasi simul concurrerunt, et merito quia philosophia uera docet iuste et recte regnare.'[26] Moreover, Thomas openly supports Plato's idea of the philosopher-king: 'Tunc enim felix erat res publica quando philosophi regnabant et reges philosophabantur' ('Successful indeed was that state when philosophers held power and kings were engaged in philosophy'). Thomas' military preoccupations frequently arise in these treatises, and they reflect his concern for due order in the state as much as in the church.

25 For a short study of *De tribus sensibus*, see Édouard Jeauneau, 'Thomas of Ireland and his *De tribus sensibus sacrae scripturae*' in J. McAuliffe, B. Walfish & J. Goering (eds), *With reverence for the Word: medieval scriptural exegesis in Judaism, Christianity and Islam* (Oxford, 2003), pp 284–91.
26 'Victory in warfare and philosophy and glory have accompanied each other at the same time, so to speak, and rightly so, because true philosophy teaches how to rule justly and rightly.'

CONCLUSION

The concern of this study has been to try to approach Thomas of Ireland's three opuscula as a unified whole and to discern the themes which are of interest to Thomas. Noting that the Pseudo-Dionysius is common to all three treatises, I have singled out the idea of hierarchy as the unifying thread tying together these three varied collections. In particular, it is the hierarchy of the Church which appeals above all else to Thomas, as manifested especially in the material composition of the treatises, where much more space is given to ecclesial organization than to any other considerations.

Thomas of Ireland is therefore an early fourteenth-century witness to the Latin reception of the Pseudo-Dionysius which began in the ninth century with Hilduin and Eriugena and reached its apogee with the great commentaries of Grosseteste, Gallus, Aquinas and Albert the Great in the thirteenth century. Primarily the works of a *collector* and compiler, the opuscula reveal no great originality nor are they aimed at plumbing the depths of the mysterious writings of the Pseudo-Dionysius. Rather, they reveal an author who has thoroughly absorbed the hierarchical vision of the cosmos embodied in the *lex hierarchica* and has sought to apply this rule to the ecclesiastical hierarchy. While paying heed to the spiritual principles of all earthly life and ecclesial government, and to the celestial, angelic hierarchy as the blueprint for the subcelestial, ecclesiastical hierarchy, it is most assuredly on the earth that Thomas fixes his gaze and attention. The paying of tithes, respect for the clergy, the crusades, the papacy, the proper administration of the sacraments and guidance to confessors: these are the practical issues that animate Thomas of Ireland rather than any more theological and speculative matters. Just as some generations of students have found greater inspiration in the Pseudo-Dionysius' *Divine names*, with its focus on analogy, causality, and on what can be known about God from what is more familiar to humans, than in the conceptual and intellectual asceticism of the *Mystical theology*, in a similar way Thomas is more concerned with the *Ecclesiastical hierarchy* than with the *Celestial hierarchy*, without however totally sundering the connection between the two hierarchies.

The modern reader might find much that is distasteful in Thomas' theology and ecclesiology: a belligerent concern with military prowess, support for the crusades, a rigid Church hierarchy that leaves the laity with little to do but obey the clergy, pay tithes and live a holy life. Philosophically speaking, Thomas' confidence in the primacy of unity and identity at the peak of a hierarchical universe does not sit easily in the postmodern climate that seeks to question the hierarchical valorisation of identity and order over plurality and dispersing *différance*. Yet Thomas was a man of his times and is to be evaluated accordingly. He was a lover of his mother, the church, and a zealous pastor concerned with producing these opuscula to help other pastors with preaching (i.e. by using the

three ways of interpreting sacred scripture in *De tribus sensibus*), with confession
(i.e. the confessional aid given in the *De tribus punctis*), all of which was grounded
in the hierarchical worldview learned from Dionysius (that is, *De triplici
hierarchia*). By imbibing the lessons of the Pseudo-Dionysius, Greek
Neoplatonism and eastern mysticism thus came to inform and shape Latin ecclesiology and sacramental practice. Hence, in all of these matters, Thomas never
forgot the spiritual nature of hierarchy – the Church exists not in itself nor for
itself alone, but it exists in order to rise up to union with the Trinity through the
companionship or mediation of the angels. As Thomas remarks succinctly in the
conclusion of *De triplici hierarchia*:

> In quibus habet locum regula beati Dionysii, quia ecclesiastica ierarchia per
> angelicam reducitur ad diuinam.[27]

---

27 'In all these matters the rule of blessed Dionysius applies: for the ecclesiastical hierarchy is
led back to the divine hierarchy by means of the angelic hierarchy.'

Richard FitzRalph of Dundalk, Oxford and Armagh: scholar, prelate and controversialist

MICHAEL HAREN

FIGURE IN A LANDSCAPE

A native of Dundalk (as his pioneering biographer, Fr Aubrey Gwynn, established convincingly from a convergence of the evidence), who in 1346 became archbishop of his native ecclesiastical province, Richard FitzRalph was for some two decades before his death in 1360 a figure of first-rank significance within western Christendom. By no means all of his reputation derived from the intrinsic power of his thought, though in central subjects treated by him he made a notable contribution and on the topic of dominion gave impetus to a reworking which would prove nothing short of revolutionary in its potential. Some part of his reputation was a well-earned notoriety. He was a formidable intellectual pugilist. My song – I should signal frankly – is of arms as well as of the man and the thinker.

The route by which Richard Rauf, from virtually the periphery of the known world, came to such theological prominence reveals a cultural milieu whose level of integration is impressive even in the New Europe of our own day. Certainly, were we at all still, as Aubrey Gwynn put it, 'apt [...] to forget the wide horizons of mediaeval life and thought',[1] FitzRalph's career would be an effective reminder. The integration is the more striking when account is taken of the peculiarity of the local context. Though it is anachronistic to term FitzRalph a 'Palesman', the Dundalk into which he was born, probably just before 1300, was near-frontier territory, in the borderland between the English lordship and Gaelic Ireland. Relations across the racial divide of medieval Ireland were more varied and complex than superficially appears. For this, the defensive quality of the best-known provisions of the Statutes of Kilkenny (1366) are one ready point of reference: the fact that they were felt to be necessary on several counts speaks volumes. Moreover, any proportionate evaluation must begin from the perception that medieval society at large was violent by our standards – preoccupied though we be with the manifestations of social malaise. That said, the contemporary Irish scene was indeed chronically turbulent. The level of feeling

---

1 A. Gwynn, 'Richard FitzRalph at Avignon', *Studies* 22 (1933), 591–607 at 604.

at its most heated is dramatically expressed by the accusation included in the Remonstrance of Donal O'Neill, lodged in 1318 in the course of the Bruce invasion, that among the colonists 'not only their laymen and secular clergy but also some of their regular clergy dogmatically assert the heresy that it is no more a sin to kill an Irishman than a dog or other animal'. Specifically, a Franciscan friar, Simon (perhaps Simon Mercer of the Drogheda house)[2] was alleged to have maintained before Bruce that to kill an Irishman was no sin and that if he had done so himself he would notwithstanding celebrate Mass.[3] The course of the Bruce invasion itself points up the social catastrophe inseparable from such political and cultural cleavage. Whether provoked by Friar Simon's vehemence (as surmised by Fr Gwynn) or in an independent act of mayhem, the Dundalk convent of his order was burnt in the town's sack in 1315 and the guardian and twenty-two friars massacred.[4] The reality was an acute problem for a pastoral archbishop, as FitzRalph evinced in his sermon to the people of Drogheda on Lady Day, 1349 in the town's Carmelite church, reflecting on the text of Revelation (8.13) *Ve, Ve, Ve habitantibus terram* ('Woe, woe, woe to the inhabitants of the land'):

> The second 'woe to the inhabitants of the land' is the woe of guilty dealing in their way through life, which woe those given over to earthly things incur often through their crass ignorance and especially in this land, in two cases. The first case is that when there is endemic warfare between Irish and English – from whose fault soever it springs – they believe that it is permitted them not only to plunder and despoil but to kill their adversaries, deceived as they are by crass ignorance – since it is permitted to no one to kill anyone unless in self-defence or in his capacity as servant of the law enacting its authority, which they are not if they do that by their own authority. And if you should say that they are in this servants of the law because the royal law condones that, I reply: 'They are not in this case ministers of the law, since the law condones but does not prescribe their acting so.' Moreover, although they should be in this servants of a legal law, yet they are not in this servants of the law of God, because it does not condone but punishes such deeds, inasmuch as wilful homicide is counted among the mortal sins – theft too and rapine – and now love of one's enemy is universally a precept of such force that no one shall of his own accord inflict evil on his enemy. Therefore such violators of human beings are without excuse in the sight of God and by the same token those who take property until they make satisfaction in accordance with their ability. For

---

2 As suggested by A. Gwynn, 'Richard FitzRalph, archbishop of Armagh', *Studies* 22 (1933), 389–405 at 396.   3 *Scotichronicon by Walter Bower*, ed. N.F. Shead, W.B. Stevenson and D.E.R. Watt, vi (Aberdeen, 1991), pp 394–7.   4 *Materials for the history of the Franciscan province of Ireland*, coll. and ed. E.B. FitzMaurice and A.G. Little (Manchester, 1920), p. 95.

the sin is never demitted unless what is taken away is restored if there be capacity to restore. The reason for this is obvious. The sin is never remitted without true penitence for the sin and no one ever truly repents that he has deprived another of that which he deliberately holds from him. For the fault is not only the theft of another's property but the retention of it. And on this account, in that there has been misappropriation, no one ever truly repents that he has stolen those things belonging to another which he deliberately strives to retain. Let him fast, let him give alms, let him pray assiduously and it will profit him nothing as regards [eternal] life, while he deliberately retains another's property unjustly – for he does not repent.

There is another case in which men often sin, namely, when by judgment of earthly law, against the law of conscience or the law of God, they occupy lands or say that they justly possess other goods, in that they possess according to such and such a law – damning themselves, because no earthly law can judge concerning what is hidden but it judges only of what is evidential. It can therefore be the case that the truth is hidden and one party knows this – on what ground [sc. he possesses] – although the evidenced colour is false, which is the colour that the jury perhaps follows, thinking that it is giving true verdict, in which case the holder accordingly possesses the property of another, not his own, because a false judgment never truly transfers dominion.[5]

---

5 Secundum ve habitantibus terram est ve conversacionis culpabilis in processu, quod ve terrenis dediti per ignoranciam crassam sepe incurrunt et specialiter in hac terra in duobus casibus. Primus casus est quod, cum est guerra communis inter Hybernicos et Anglicos, cuiuscumque culpa provenit, credunt quod liceat eis non tantum rapere <et> spoliare sed adversarios occidere, ignorancia crassa decepti, quoniam nemini licet quemquam occidere nisi se tuendo aut fuerit legis minister auctoritatem legis agens, inter quales isti non sunt si propria auctoritate illud agunt. Et si dixeris eos esse in hoc legis ministros quia lex regia id concedat, respondeo (fo. 38vb) non sunt in hoc casu ministri legis, lege solum concedente, non precipiente, <ut> hoc ag<a>nt. Item quamvis essent in hoc legalis legis ministri non tamen sunt in hoc ministri legis Dei, quia talia non concedit sed punit, <in> quantum homicidium voluntarium inter peccata mortalia computatur, furtum eciam et rapina, et modo inimici dileccio secundum omnes in tantum precipitur quod nullus suo inimico inferat gratis malum. Ideo tales invasores hominum sunt inexcusabiles apud Deum et similiter raptores, donec satisfecerint iuxta posse. Numquam enim dimittitur peccatum nisi restituatur ablatum si assit restituendi facultas. <Cuius> racio est in promptu: numquam sine vera peccati penitencia relaxatur peccatum nec quisquam unquam vere penitet se rapuisse alienum quod sponte detinet. Non enim culpa sola est raptus set ipsa rei aliene retencio. Et ob hoc, quia sunt annexa, numquam vere quis penitet se rapuisse male aliena que sponte nititur retinere. Ieiunet, det elemosinas, oret assidue et nichil sibi proderit ad vitam dum sponte retinet alienum iniuste, quia non penitet. Est casus alius in quo homines sepe peccant, videlicet cum per iudicium legis terrene, contra legem consciencie sive contra legem Dei, terras occupant aut alia bona dicunt se iuste possidere ex quo secundum talem legem possident, seipsos dampnantes, quia nulla lex terrena iudicare potest de occultis set solum iudicat de manifestis. Potest igitur esse quod veritas in casu latet et pars hoc novit, pro quo <sc. (?) possidet>, color licet falsus est patens, quem colorem sequitur forsitan inquisicio iuratorum estimant<ium> se

There will be occasion to return to the theme of dominion. The pastoral implications of the first theme noticed here was the subject of FitzRalph's outburst in the papal consistory in 1357, during his final onslaught on the friars' privileges.

> For I have in my diocese of Armagh, as I suppose, two thousand subjects who every year are involved in sentences of excommunication on account of the sentences passed against wilful homicides, public robbers, incendiaries and the like; of whom scarcely forty in a year come to me or to my penitentiaries; and all such men receive the sacraments like other men and are absolved – or are said to be absolved; nor are they believed to be absolved by any others except by the friars, without doubt, for no others absolve them.[6]

These two passages encapsulate FitzRalph the pastor. They manifest his urgent preoccupation with justice both in the abstract and in the concrete. They demonstrate that the campaign against the friars' privileges, as conceived and pursued by him, was no mere protectionism of the economic interest of the secular clergy – though this interest, concretely in the receipt of tithes and offerings, was trenchantly maintained as a divinely grounded right. It was the convictions-based defence of a regime of moral authority whose efficacy was seen as radically contingent on the maintenance of homogeneity and exclusivity. How those convictions relate to FitzRalph's wider thought and the influences upon him is an important part of his intellectual biography.

HISTORIOGRAPHICAL INTRODUCTION

I have already been drawn to introduce the scholar whose work more than that of any other laid the foundation for our understanding of FitzRalph in the round. Commencing with a series of articles published between 1933 and 1936 in the Jesuit journal, *Studies* – whose contribution to the country's intellectual life in that period merits specifically recalling – Fr Aubrey Gwynn provided a meticulous outline of the biography and writings. Gwynn sketched, with a confidence which no contemporary Irish historian could have rivalled, his protagonist's Irish, English and continental profile. For all the elaboration that has followed, those pioneering pieces continue to be worth reading, both for the

---

dicere veritatem, in quo casu sic optinens rem possidet alienam non suam, quia falsum iudicium numquam transfert vere dominium. Oxford, St John's College, MS 65, fo. 38v. The sermon, of date 25 March 1349, is no. 33 in Gwynn's listing: cf. below, n. 7. **6** *Facsiculus rerum expetendarum et fugiendarum*, ed. E. Brown (2 vols, London, 1690), ii, 468. Cf. W.A. Pantin, *The English church in the fourteenth century* (Cambridge, 1955), p. 156.

sobriety with which they evaluate the fundamental evidence and for the acuity with which they interpret it. Where subsequent research has made new discoveries, these have, as in a jigsaw nearing completion, slipped readily into place within the framework that Gwynn established. One other publication by him remains – regrettably, I have to say – a fundamental tool for work on its subject. This is Fr Gwynn's analysis of the Sermon-Diary, which appeared in the *Proceedings of the Royal Irish Academy* for 1937.[7] There, besides a description of the composition of the diary and a catalogue of the manuscripts, is contained a detailed listing of the contents, with modernized datings, and datings or suggested occasions of sermons' delivery when such is not explicit in the manuscript tradition. FitzRalph was a regular, committed preacher – a function that he viewed as a specific 'office'[8] – and his activity in the role is documented, though certainly not comprehensively, from July 1335 (when on his first visit to Avignon he preached on the feast of St Thomas of Canterbury) to the Epiphany of 1359. I say 'regrettably' with reference to Gwynn's fundamental aid because, although individual sermons have been published and expounded, this collection of ninety-two sermons of rarely paralleled pastoral vigour and of peculiar historical interest urgently needs critically editing as a whole. Fr Gwynn, both in print and in several conversations which I was privileged to have with him while he was still at the peak of his intellectual powers (I speak of a time when he was a few years on either side of eighty!) opined that the Oxford, St John's College 65 manuscript of the sermon-diary was to be preferred. This is a judgement which my own, as yet sporadic, work on the text has convinced me is correct. I adopted the manuscript accordingly as the base when editing Sermon 40, that delivered in 1352 to the layfolk of Drogheda on the subject of tithing, on a number of counts one of the most interesting of the pastoral sermons,[9] and I follow it for the extract from Sermon 33 presented here. What is required urgently, however, is a complete collation – which in addition to its establishment of text would assist address to some of the contextual problems still unresolved.

The second scholar claiming notice at this point is the Danish historian, L.L. Hammerich. He approached FitzRalph by way of an interest in a facet which, while it may appear at first encounter merely incidental, is of major continental literary concern. Hammerich took up the remarkable and seminal account of a pilgrimage made in late autumn 1353 to St Patrick's Purgatory by the figure known in central Europe as Ritter Georg. George Grissaphan was a young man of some twenty-four years who had been on campaign in southern Italy enforcing the claims of King Louis I of Hungary to the kingdom of Naples,

---

7 A. Gwynn, 'The sermon-diary of Richard FitzRalph archbishop of Armagh', *Proceedings of the Royal Irish Academy* 44: C 1 (1937), 1–57.   8 See ibid., 30.   9 M. Haren, 'Montaillou and Drogheda – a medieval twinning' in A. Meyer, C. Rendtel and M. Wittmer-Butsch (eds), *Päpste, Pilger, Pönitentiarie: Festschrift für Ludwig Schmugge zum 65. Geburtstag* (Tübingen, 2004), pp 435–56 at pp 452–6.

disputed (1347–52) with a rival branch of the Angevin dynasty. In the course of his captaincy in Apulia, George had committed what we would recognize as war-crimes, in remorse for which he abandoned knighthood, sought absolution from the papal penitentiary and made the pilgrimage to Compostela. There he learned of St Patrick's Purgatory and with one servant in tow journeyed on foot through France and England until he arrived at Lough Derg. It is Archbishop FitzRalph who definitively retrieves this episode from the realm of fairy-tale – who indeed, in all probability, was responsible for its being known at all. The lengthy narration of George's pilgrimage was compiled by an anonymous Provençal-speaking Augustinian friar, putatively engaged by FitzRalph himself, through the agency of his nephew and namesake, then at the papal curia. The narration is preceded by the text of six precisely dated letters, referring to George's pilgrimage. Two of these are by FitzRalph. The intellectual significance of his involvement I leave for the moment in order to return to Hammerich's contri-bution. Having previously published a short article[10] Hammerich followed with the magnificent edition of the *Visiones Georgii*.[11] From the fourteenth to the sixteenth century, this narrative, both in its Latin and vernacular versions, was responsible for a burst of continental attention to St Patrick's Purgatory that has never quite dissipated. I was much struck when contributing on the subject at a conference in Budapest several years ago[12] at how familiar the continental partic-ipants in general were with the Purgatory's medieval reputation. Among Hungarians, the fifteenth-century nobleman, Tar Lörins, who, inspired by George's example, made the pilgrimage in the grand style in 1411, is both as pilgrim and for his general historical profile as familiar a name in his native Hungary as Brian Boru's in Ireland.

From this introduction to him as George's referee, Hammerich went on to study FitzRalph's involvement in the anti-mendicant quarrel. Hammerich's tracing of the stages of this involvement hang on an argument for the dating of certain of FitzRalph's sermons which I have argued to be unsafe[13] – though I

---

10 L.L. Hammerich, 'Eine Pilgerfahrt des XIV. Jahrhunderts nach dem Fegfeuer des hl. Patrizius', *Zeitschrift für deutsche Philologie* 53 (1928), 25–40. 11 *Visiones Georgii: visiones quas in purgatorio sancti Patricii vidit Georgius miles de Ungaria A.D. MCCCLIII*, ed. L.L. Hammerich, Det kgl. Danske videnskabernes selskab. Historisk-filogiske meddelelser, 18: 2 (Copenhagen, 1930). 12 European Catholic Bishops' Conference: fifth annual COMECE summer university, Leányfalu, Budapest, Hungary, 13–17 September 2003. M. Haren, 'European cultural unity in the Middle Ages: the case of the Hungarian pilgrims to St Patrick's Purgatory'. 13 I first presented the argument at the conference, 'The Irish in medieval England', University of London, Queen Mary and Westfield College, 11–12 April 1995, and published it subsequently in M. J. Haren, 'Richard FitzRalph and the friars: the intellectual itinerary of a curial controversialist', in J. Hamesse (ed.), *Roma, magistra mundi. Itineraria culturae medievalis: mélanges offerts au Père L. E. Boyle à l'occasion de son 75e anniversaire*, Fédération internationale des instituts d'études médiévales, Textes et Etudes du Moyen Age 10 (3 vols, Louvain-la-Neuve, 1998), i, 349–67.

remain close to Hammerich as regards his reading of FitzRalph's mind on the central issue. However, the enduring product of his interest in this aspect is, again, the edition of a fundamental text: the archbishop's *Propositio* 'Unusquisque', delivered before the consistory of Clement VI in 1350, which marks definitively the inception of his public anti-mendicant stance.[14] This *Propositio* Hammerich prefaced with an edition of the long autobiographical prayer which stands as an epilogue, though perhaps written much later than the rest of the work,[15] to the *Summa de questionibus Armenorum* ('Treatise on the questions of the Armenians'), (Book 19, c. 35). Besides its circumstantial detail, the prayer has the fascination of revealing in intensely short space the private spiritual fervour of a figure who – though several of his sermons point firmly in the same direction – presents to us otherwise as a public and university man, abstract thinker and, sometimes quite brutal, controversialist. The autobiographical prayer is suggestive of the quality that so impressed the folk of FitzRalph's immediate context as to engender the odour of sanctity. Witness the ditty of indeterminate dating recorded by a seventeenth-century Irish exile in the folio of the manuscript containing the *Martyrologium Dungallense*:[16]

> Many a mile have I gone
> And many did I walk
> But never saw a holier man
> Than Richard of Dundalk.

The last scholarly contribution that I record at this stage of my preliminary review of the state of the question is by far the most comprehensive – Katherine Walsh's intellectual biography of FitzRalph, published in 1981.[17] It will long remain as the foundation and essential point of reference for all further endeavour. I frankly and gratefully acknowledge as much precisely because I have found myself pushed in regard to a central thesis of Professor Walsh's book to quite a different conclusion from that for which she has so vigorously argued in it. The campaign against the pastoral privileges of the four mendicant orders – Franciscans, Dominicans, Augustinians and Carmelites – dominated the last decade of FitzRalph's life from its opening by the *Propositio* 'Unusquisque' of 1350 until his death *c*.November 1360. Its explanation is of first-rank concern in understanding the protagonist's development and outlook. Katherine Walsh saw his preoccupation as the product of those turbulent Irish conditions on which I

---

14 L.L. Hammerich, *The beginning of the strife between Richard FitzRalph and the mendicants with an edition of his autobiographical prayer and his proposition 'Unusquisque'*, Det kgl. Danske videnskabernes selskab. Historisk-filogiske meddelelser, 26: 3 (Copenhagen, 1938). 15 Cf. below, n. 16 [p. 11]. 16 Bruxelles, Bibliothèque nationale, MS 506, fo. 115r. See Hammerich, *Strife*, p. 11. 17 K. Walsh, *A fourteenth-century scholar and primate: Richard FitzRalph in Oxford, Avignon and Armagh* (Oxford, 1981).

have deliberately dwelt. It is fair to put the case in her own terms: 'The most likely explanation for FitzRalph's sudden and total opposition to the friars is that on acquiring a large diocese to administer he was faced in an acute form with the problem of enforcing episcopal authority. The problem of the exempt religious who exercised a pastoral ministry was made more difficult by the tensions of a racially divided community and FitzRalph showed an intense awareness of this situation. It can be argued that his previous experience of the mendicant orders had been limited to the atypical situations of the schools at Oxford and the cosmopolitan convents at the papal curia, whereas in the course of his duties as archbishop he encountered the practical problems caused by exempt religious in general, linked with the specific issues which arose when mendicant confessors might abuse the confessional in excessive support for one "nation" or the other.'[18]

Eloquently as this case is argued, I have never found it convincing. As regards the 'two nations' aspect, an a priori objection is why FitzRalph should have regarded the friars as having a monopoly of partisan attachment. It is worth noting that the Remonstrance of Donal O'Neill, while specifically attacking the Franciscan Friar Simon, the Cistercian monks of Granard and Inch[19] and condemning all religious, friars preacher and minor, monks, canons and other such of the English nation,[20] accuses their layfolk and their seculars [sc. secular clergy] and regulars jointly of promoting the 'heresy' complained of, particularly mentioning the zeal of the monks (perhaps again the Cistercians) in this regard.[21] It need hardly be laboured that the Remonstrance is not the source to which one should look for an indictment of the Gaelic clergy on this count – though it does assert that the Irish have, under English tutelage and by the association, been corrupted from 'their holy and dove-like simplicity'.[22] My demurral from the thesis that FitzRalph's anti-mendicant campaign is a product of the peculiar conditions encountered by him as archbishop is not however principally founded on this a priori objection. It is based primarily on a reading of his sermon-diary and the hints that that contains, as noted by Hammerich and – despite the direction which her own thought took – by Katherine Walsh herself, that even before FitzRalph's appointment to Armagh (indeed before he would have had direct pastoral experience of the cure of souls in his own right, while still dean of Lichfield, to which dignity he was appointed in 1335) he had begun to evince concerns which became a driving force of the campaign against mendicant privileges. These were above all the absolute obligation of restitution of ill-gotten gains as a prerequisite for absolution in the confessional regime and the friars' alleged shortcomings in failing to enforce it. As long ago as 1955, in the published text of his Birkbeck Lectures in the University of Cambridge, one

---

18 Walsh, *Scholar and primate*, p. 363.   19 *Scotichronicon*, ed. Shead et al., vi, 396–7.   20 Ibid., pp 392–3.   21 Ibid., pp 396–7.   22 Ibid., pp 390–1.

of the foremost scholars in the field, Dr W.A. Pantin of Oriel College, Oxford, had drawn attention to how an anonymous pastoral treatise of English production, the *Memoriale presbiterorum* ('Handbook of parish priests'), anticipated just by a year or two the first articulation of FitzRalph's views on these counts and, from a connection between the treatise and Avignon, suggested that there might have been an influence. When I came, as Pantin's penultimate doctoral student forty years ago, to study the *Memoriale presbiterorum*, I was thus forced to confront the development of FitzRalph's own positions. I owe my subsequent interest in him to this introduction. On the basis of my research, I have been led to the perception that FitzRalph's polemical campaign is not essentially a product of Irish conditions, that, rather, he came to his archbishopric already highly sensitized and that he found there – as so often is the case with intellectual voyaging – what he had been heavily influenced to seek out. In the Augustinian world-view, which the character equally of his thought and associations suggest that he had thoroughly absorbed, the deficiencies that he encountered were those of people at large: the mass of self-seeking, morally anarchic, reprobates, their post-lapsarian degradation unrelieved in its social consquences by an admixture of the elect. This was markedly the outlook of his patron, Bishop Grandisson of Exeter,[23] whose preoccupations and those of his circle go far to explain what Katherine Walsh identified as a conundrum of FitzRalph's development.[24] If Katherine Walsh's study at the time of its writing was at all influenced by prevailing conditions in emphasizing so forcefully the peculiar moral problems thrown up by chronic intercommunity violence and pillage, I in my turn – since history is not written in cultural abstraction – may well perhaps be influenced by the contemporary context in my emphasis on the vitality, complexity and ease of passage of influence between medieval England and Ireland. 'In my emphasis', I would stress. That FitzRalph is to be seen as heavily indebted in his pastoral – including his polemically pastoral – stance to an orientation absorbed from English associations is a position which the evidence, on my reading, forces one to adopt. In that sense, his distinctive pastoral stance – applied and responding to the turbulent conditions of his archdiocese – is of a piece with those other wide-ranging intellectual influences to which, so far as our evidence carries, he first came to be exposed in an English context, as student and master in arts and subsequently as master of theology at the university of Oxford.

23 See M. Haren, *Sin and society in fourteenth-century England: a study of the Memoriale Presbiterorum* (Oxford, 2000), pp 44–65.   **24** See Walsh, *Scholar and primate*, p. 349.

ACADEMIC PROGRESSION

Along with the papal curia of Avignon, the University of Oxford is one of the major institutional contexts of FitzRalph's intellectual development. An attempt on the part of archbishops Lech and Bicknor in the second decade of the fourteenth century to establish a university in Dublin foundered and for the rest of the Middle Ages Ireland (in marked contrast to Scotland) remained without a university. FitzRalph's Sermon 33 contains a lament over the fact that 'we are remote from every centre of higher study.'[25] Nevertheless theology certainly, and therefore the necessary arts preparation for it, is likely to have been maintained in the friars' schools. It has been surmised that FitzRalph may have benefited from such teaching among the Franciscans of Dundalk.[26] From such a background, the transition to Oxford would have represented an intellectual continuum. Certainly, for Irishmen (both Gaelic and of the lordship) in search of university training throughout the late Middle Ages, Oxford was an obvious choice of destination. In the middle of the fourteenth century we are provided with a valuable snapshot of attendance. Of the twenty-seven university casualties in the great riot of St Scholastica's Day, 10–12 February 1355, just over a quarter are evidently Irish – judged either by surname or by their having the Christian name 'Malachy': witness, for example, Gilbertus Offerir, Patricius Magbradaid, Karolus Ogormuly, Dionisius Ohagagan.[27] These members of the category of being still alive but their lives despaired of may have met the cry of 'Havoc, Havoc, Smite fast, give gode knocks' as a heavily Ulster contingent.[28] Of the two organizational divisions – so-called nations – into which the university was divided, the Irish were grouped with the 'southerners'. As I have commented elsewhere, this makes the more surprising that when FitzRalph emerges into the university records in 1325 it is as a member of Balliol – whose associations were northern. By then he was master of arts and already studying theology: he was probably in his mid-twenties. His subsequent association with Mickle university hall, the future University College, founded by William of Durham with a particular focus on supporting theology, is in keeping with this 'northern' colour.[29] By now he had adopted the form 'Fitz' as an addition to the plain 'Rauf' which is the form of the family name occurring in the Dowdall deeds and patent and close rolls.[30] It was a piece of social climbing, certainly, but of a type current: we have a striking, near-contemporary, counterpart in the theologian Thomas Brightwell who, as his will reveals, was the scion of a family

---

25 'qui remoti sumus ab omni studio generali': Oxford, St John's College, MS 65, fo. 37rb. **26** Walsh, *Scholar and primate*, p. 12. **27** Lincoln Archives Office, Register 8 ('Memoranda of Bishop John Gynwell, 1350–62'), fos. 66r–67r. **28** The surnames quoted here suggest as much. **29** See Haren, 'Richard FitzRalph and the friars', pp 349–50. **30** See Gwynn, 'Richard FitzRalph, archbishop of Armagh', pp 393–5.

with the manorial name Attewell, evidently considered incompatible with its bearer's advance in status.[31]

FitzRalph's new *persona* was mocked in a satirical poem addressed to him as chancellor of the university by an adherent of the attempted secession to Stamford by a section of the academic body (in the period 1333–5). It appears that the chancellor, perhaps with a dash of that impetuosity which impelled him as a future polemicist,[32] had wagered his head that the move to this minor but promising Scholastic town (it had a Carmelite and perhaps a Dominican *studium* to render it plausible as a base) would be over in six months, for the satirist twits him with the inconvenience which follows his misjudgement. FitzRalph's chancellorship lasted from May 1332 to May 1334. The basic qualification for office was provided by his doctorate in the higher faculty of theology, in which he had incepted probably in mid-1331 and in which Bishop Burghersh in his letter of appointment described him as 'now actually regent'.[33] However, his accession is a sign of standing and in keeping with an earlier encomium by Bishop Grandisson, dating to 1329, to introduce him as guardian and tutor of the bishop's nephew to the Parisian university scene where the latter was going to study. There FitzRalph is 'distinguished among all students and teachers of the university of Oxford as outstandingly acute and discriminating'.[34] Grandisson was a careful talent-spotter and a prelate of rigorously high standards and conviction, whose patronage was a crucial factor in FitzRalph's rise. Formerly archdeacon of Nottingham, he may be the explanation for that 'northern' bias to FitzRalph's early academic career already commented on. Grandisson himself had studied at Paris under Jacques Fournier, the future Benedict XII and before that the bishop of Pamiers at the centre of the inquisition into Catharism made famous by Le Roy Ladurie's study of life in the sub-Pyreneean village of Montaillou. Fournier's espousal of St Augustine's analysis of the human condition emerges clearly from his *Postill on Matthew*, a product in part of his Parisian teaching.[35] His Augustinian outlook, bringing with it a rigorous commitment to disciplinary order, and his career as a markedly reforming pope must be thought a major influence on his pupil, as upon his pupil's protégés and episcopal circle. Among that circle was the author – as now identified – of the pastoral treatise which I have already mentioned as a putative influence on FitzRalph, the *Memoriale presbiterorum*.

The exercises required of a late-medieval theologian both in his progress to the degree of master and in his regency (or formal commitment as a teacher

---

31 See Haren, 'Richard FitzRalph and the friars', pp 351–2. 32 Cf. Gwynn, 'Richard FitzRalph, archbishop of Armagh', 404. 33 *The registers of Henry Burghersh 1320–1342*, ed. N. Bennett, Lincoln Record Society 90, ii (2003), p. 83, no. 1828; *Snappe's formulary*, ed. H.E. Salter, Oxford Historical Society 79 (Oxford, 1923), p. 75. 34 *The register of John de Grandisson, bishop of Exeter (AD 1327–1369)*, ed. F.C. Hingeston-Randolph, i (London, 1894), p. 233. 35 See Haren, 'Montaillou and Drogheda', pp 445–7.

following inception as master) conformed to a standard pattern. They produced FitzRalph's earliest work, his *Lectura* or Commentary on the *Sentences* of Peter Lombard. As understood to date, its interest derives mainly from the commentator's later importance which is so large as to warrant subjecting all his writings to close scrutiny, when similar commentaries by other figures of the late Middle Ages remain as yet unread. That was not the judgement of contemporaries, for the manuscript circulation (with the notable exception of Oxford, Oriel College, MS 15)[36] testifies to early reading, before its author became known as *Armachanus*, and certainly quite independently of his raised profile as controversialist.[37] FitzRalph's Commentary has in its own right been the subject of a monograph by the distinguished historian of late medieval thought, Gordon Leff. It has been reviewed from the perspective of Wyclif's development in the Oxford of a generation later.[38] In its own time it attracted notice of significance from FitzRalph's younger contemporary at Oxford, the Franciscan, Adam Wodeham, and at Paris from the Augustinian friar, Gregory of Rimini.

The university of Oxford in the first half of the fourteenth century was in intellectual ferment. Under the impetus of masters of such marked originality as Walter Burley (engaged in theology at Oxford for approximately the first decade of the century), William of Ockham (active at Oxford until *c.*1320), whose nominalist logic Burley opposed, and FitzRalph's slightly older contemporaries, Thomas Bradwardine and Thomas Buckingham, the burning questions were a complex of interrelated issues. In logic, psychology (a branch of natural philosophy) and theology respectively, they were: the status of the universal concepts by which the mind engaged with the world of sense experience; the relationship between intellect and will; the role of grace in merit; the compatibility of divine foreknowledge and contingency at large and in relation to human freedom in particular. These and related cosmological questions such as infinity and eternity were to dominate late medieval thought. The resulting trends in theology, when eventually through the first medium of mass communication they burst from the confines of the schools to the attention of a wider intellectual public, split Europe in the sixteenth century into mutually uncomprehending camps. Already in FitzRalph's time they were beginning to divide the academic community. As a commentator on the *Sentences* in this early phase of discussion, FitzRalph had to pick his way carefully through terrain in which the landmarks were shifting. His path is only now being mapped out in detail – a principal cartographer being Dr Michael Dunne, who is engaged on the much-needed edition of the *Sentences* Commentary. FitzRalph himself seems never to have approved a final version. In view of the revision which (as I

---

36 A fifteenth-century manuscript, it uniquely designates FitzRalph as 'Armachanus'. See G. Leff, *Richard FitzRalph commentator of the Sentences* (Manchester, 1963), p. 186.   37 See Walsh, *Scholar and primate*, p. 38.   38 J. A. Robson, *Wyclif and the Oxford schools* (2nd edn. Cambridge, 1966).

will note later) we can follow taking place in the case of FitzRalph's later work, the *De pauperie Salvatoris* ('On the Saviour's poverty'), understanding the evolution of the Commentary will be of interest beyond its considerable significance for the latter text. Of the seven principal manuscripts and several fragments in which the work is preserved, Gordon Leff remarked: 'They have frequently defied all efforts at elucidation.'[39] We look forward all the more keenly to Dr Dunne's conclusions. Leff, in general, emphasized the conservatism of FitzRalph's approach as commentator. The resulting impression that he was a fence-sitter I suspect may be exaggerated. FitzRalph himself, looking back on his preoccupations during this period, saw it as one in which he had engaged variously with the positions of Ockham and Burley.[40] Evidently, however, evaluation of the work is premature in advance of the progress which will be possible when the text is critically edited. Leff mused that FitzRalph 'resisted any temptation he may have felt to be drawn very far from the traditional highway of Augustinianism.'[41] In view of the committed Augustinianism of those close to him, it would be surprising if that temptation were much in evidence. Neither need it to have been, classically, as regards the central issues identified. Augustine's doctrine of the grace of election is best understood as an effect on the will which is the counterpart of illumination on the mind, the grant of an understanding of the nature of the good such as efficaciously to elicit free actions directed to its attainment, an interplay in which the tensions of the intellectualist and voluntarist perspectives are reconciled. However, the issues were now being given a new, acute, edge and the theologians of FitzRalph's generation were faced with the challenge of finding a new *modus vivendi* between the approaches. 'Future contingents' are the subject of FitzRalph's *Quaestio biblica* ('Biblical question') – with which, following his reading of the *Sentences*, he opened his reading of the Bible – as identified by Jean-François Genest, from a close scrutiny of critical citations in Adam Wodeham's lectures on the *Sentences*, and edited by him from the two manuscripts of FitzRalph's Commentary which carry it: Worcester Cathedral Library MS Q. 71 (fos. 137–141v) and Paris, Bibliothèque nationale, MS 15853 (fos. 98va–102va).[42]

There is an interesting hint of the extra-academic topicality of these debates and, one supposes, of concern to be abreast of them on the part of a pastorally-engaged bishop, in the evidence that a specific, related issue was the subject of a set-piece debate at Exeter. We know from an apologetic letter to the king in 1349[43] that Grandisson was keen to preserve the old tradition – antedating the

39 Leff, *Commentator*, p. vii.   **40** Cf. Walsh, *Scholar and primate*, p 42. The evidence is a letter to Giovanni Marignola, bishop of Bisignano, printed in Gelasius Dobner, *Monumenta historica Bohemiae nusquam antehac edita*, ii (Prague, 1768), pp 73–4.   **41** Leff, *Commentator*, p. 173.   **42** J-F. Genest, 'Contingence et révélation des futurs: la *Quaestio biblica* de Richard FitzRalph', in J. Jolivet, Z. Kaluza, A. de Libera (eds), *Lectionum varietates: hommage à Paul Vignaux (1904–1987)* (Paris, 1991), pp 199–246 at pp 215–46.   **43** Pantin, *Church*, pp 115–16; *The*

primacy of the universities and the friars' schools – in which a cathedral might aspire to be a centre of higher learning. Though Lincoln's glorious heyday under William de Montibus was long gone, lectures were continuing there in the mid-fourteenth century[44] and from Wells in the early fifteenth century survive John Orum's lectures on the Apocalypse.[45] Grandisson's own Augustinianism would have ensured that the question debated at Exeter between Thomas Buckingham (who had formally a local link, being chancellor of the cathedral until 1349) and an unknown 'reverend doctor', 'Whether all adults and children who died before Christ died in mortal sin and without the grace of present justification and remission, being bound to perpetual loss of the vision of God', commanded at least one pair of closely attentive ears. The account of what took place is contained in the text of Thomas Buckingham's *Quaestiones* preserved in Oxford, New College, MS 134, where he is described as 'showing the finding of a Catholic middle way between the errors of Pelagius, Cicero[46] and Scotus, [and] that predestination, preordinance, eternal forewilling and the unfolding course of God stand with free-will and merit of the creature'.[47] In that delineation, we have much of late-medieval theology. About two decades later (*c*.1366–8), the Benedictine monk-theologian, Uthred of Boldon (who incepted as master of theology in 1357), in disputations centred equally on these topics of grace and justification, was to maintain controversially a doctrine of the 'clear vision' of God given everyone in their last moment, whereby they chose definitively between good and evil. His position – the object of determined attack by the friars, whom he had otherwise antagonized – though not he himself, was condemned by Archbishop Whittlesey (1369).[48] 'Uthred's argument', commented Dr Pantin, 'springs from a generous and charitable motive, a desire to demonstrate that everyone is given a fair chance, but the doctrine as he works it out is a dangerous one, for it would seem to reduce all the moral and spiritual life of a man, before the instant of death, to a triviality.'[49] Though medieval thinkers are rarely overtly sentimental, the preoccupation with 'a fair chance' is likely to have had force. The specific mention of children in the formulation of the debate at Exeter is noteworthy. Uthred's response seems to owe something to the mystical currents of the century. More specifically, however, it may be rescued from all implication of trivializing. Viewed against 'the Aristotelian

---

register of John Grandisson, ed. Hingeston-Randolph, i, 307–8. **44** *Calendar of entries in the papal registers relating to Great Britain and Ireland. Petitions to the pope*, ed. W.H. Bliss, i (London,1896), p. 230. **45** Oxford, Bodleian Library, MS Bodley 859, fos. 261–289v. **46** On the model of Thomas Bradwardine's *De causa Dei contra Pelagianos*, Pelagius must be taken to represent the Ockhamist position, Cicero a generally naturalistic, humanistic one. **47** Oxford, New College, MS 134, fo. 324r, as edited in Pantin, *Church*, pp 263–6. **48** M.D. Knowles, 'The censured opinions of Uthred of Bolton', *Proceedings of the British Academy* 37 (1951), 305–42; repr. in idem, *The historian and character and other essays* (Cambridge, 1963), pp 129–70. **49** Pantin, *Church*, p. 169.

revival' by which Pantin otherwise found him to be heavily influenced,[50] Uthred's solution can be readily accommodated within that philosophy of the training in virtue which so moulds the personality as to make the choice of the good almost a reflex action. Uthred himself is known to have prized the regularity of monastic discipline and regarded its institution as in peculiar sympathy with man's nature.[51] It is in this context that his 'clear vision' may be seen as representing not moral asyndeton but radical conjunction with what precedes. Neither Buckingham nor his disputant on what was essentially the same underlying issue is likely to have quarrelled with the premiss of continuity but it is evident from Buckingham's report that his disputant took a rigorously high Augustinian position. Pantin suggested that the unnamed disputant might have been FitzRalph. Given what I see as FitzRalph's general bent, this seems in principle altogether plausible and it is one more point that may perhaps be elucidated by detailed study of the text of the *Sentences* Commentary, and perhaps of the magisterial determinations which accompany it in one of the manuscripts,[52] several of which have meriting as their focus. In turn, close work may indicate whether FitzRalph's authorship – which has been tentatively established – of four disputed questions in Vienna, Österreichische Nationalbibliothek CVP 5076, is more or less tenable.

THE PAPAL CURIA

The second major institutional context for FitzRalph's thought is the papal curia at Avignon. Shortly after his term as chancellor of Oxford, FitzRalph made a brief sojourn at the curia, evidently on university business. That initial stay ended with his provision by Benedict XII to the deanery of Lichfield cathedral in December 1335. There were three subsequent visits during FitzRalph's career. The lengthiest was a period from 1337 to 1344, spent there as a litigant on behalf of his cathedral. He returned in 1350, for the first time since his provision as archbishop, when, on 5 July, he preached the *Propositio* 'Unusquisque' against the friars' privileges, as I have already noted. He remained at the curia until approximately the middle of the following year. Finally, in the early summer of 1357, when he had already been engaged intermittently for a year in close combat with the friars on the English scene over the twin themes of poverty and pastoral rights, he transferred or was forced to transfer the contest to the curia of Innocent VI, where he pursued it doggedly until his death in November 1360.

50 W.A. Pantin, 'Two treatises of Uthred of Bolton on the monastic life', in R.W. Hunt, W.A. Pantin, R.W. Southern (eds), *Studies in medieval history presented to Frederick Maurice Powicke* (Oxford, 1948), pp 363–85 at pp 384–5. Cf. Pantin, *Church*, p. 174.   51 Ibid.   52 Florence, Biblioteca nazionale, MS A III 508, fos. 109vb–129vb.

Since its mordant denunciation as the 'Babylonian Captivity' by Petrarch, the papal residence at Avignon (1309–77) has had an image problem – so serious a matter is it to have a wit as foe. Organizationally, however, Clement V's temporary move, prompted by political problems with King Philip IV of France, to what was not the French kingdom but a papal enclave independent of it, was a major success. Situated at a point of relatively easy river-valley recourse from the north and having both coastal and sea access from the mediterranean world, the Avignon popes built on the foundations of thirteenth-century canonistic developments a governmental machine wide and complex in its remit and efficient in its functioning.[53] Culturally too, Avignon came to be a flourishing centre. Petrarch, critic though he might be, serves as one ready point of reference. But the popes and their entourage were a major source of patronage across the range, as visitors to the papal palace complex may see to this day.

For FitzRalph, his long second visit was not only a success in terms of enhanced profile and career advancement, and, incidentally, in terms eventually of the specific issue that had brought him there, but of notable intellectual development. His *Summa de questionibus Armenorum* is the product of a particular stimulus within the vibrant, cosmopolitan milieu. Islamic pressure on Eastern Christianity prompted contacts from both Armenians and Greeks in the pontificate of John XXII aimed at securing military assistance from the west. Within Armenian Christianity itself there was established under Dominican influence a Latinizing wing of which representatives were present at the curia during FitzRalph's second sojourn.[54] Perhaps because of his interest – embodied in a sermon that he preached in the Dominican church at Avignon on the feast of the translation of St Thomas of Canterbury (7 July) 1335 – in the question of the beatific vision, the subject of controversial views propounded by the recently deceased John XXII and a topic on which Benedict XII considered the Armenians aberrant, FitzRalph was accorded a role in contacts with the Armenian party. The *Summa* – which is addressed to two members of it, Nerses Balientz, whom Benedict XII in 1338 appointed archbishop of Manazgard, and the monk, John Kernatzi – was certainly inspired by these contacts (though as it developed it did not confine itself to the issues from which it derives its title). In all probability, it was thus at least partly written in the period 1339–44 – even though its formal dedication is to Pope Clement VI (d.1352), under whom discussions with oriental Christianity were continuing, and post-dates FitzRalph's elevation as archbishop. In fact, here too there may have been long-continued tinkering, for the concluding autobiographical prayer is best judged on content to date from FitzRalph's final, fourth period at the curia post-1357.[55]

53 The classic study is B. Guillemain., *La cour pontificale d'Avignon. Etude d'une société* (Paris, 1962).   54 The context is ably depicted in Walsh, *Scholar and primate*, pp 137–46.   55 For the relevant argument, see ibid., pp 132–6.

Written in the form of a dialogue between 'Ricardus' and his interlocutor 'Johannes' (perhaps Kernatzi), the *Summa* consists of nineteen books. The earlier are those most directly focused on issues of concern in the Armenian context specifically (including, notably, treatment of the two natures of Christ) but there are matters – especially the primacy of the Roman church, the *Filioque* in the Creed, and Purgatory – which concerned also relations between Latins and Greeks. FitzRalph's need to expound the doctrine of Purgatory in this context must be thought a plausible explanation for the interest which he took in the case of George Grissaphan and – on the hypothesis that he was an agent in securing a redaction of George's account of his experiences – the lengths to which he went in pursuing it. The final books, XVIII–XIX, address issues between Christianity and Islam, based on Robert of Ketton's twelfth-century version of the Koran, and Judaism. No doubt as dictated by his perception of the requirements of presentation variously as regards Eastern Christianity and Judaism but also from a new focus evidenced in his autobiographical prayer, in which he represents himself as a convert from the logico-philosophical approach to theology, FitzRalph's avowed method in the bulk of the *Summa* is an adherence to the literal sense of the Bible.[56] In Books XV–XVII, however, he reverted to several of the preoccupations of his academic phase to address again free will and divine foreknowledge, this time with the arguments in mind of a younger generation, evidently of university theologians but unidentified and whom FitzRalph viewed unsympathetically. Among those influenced by his treatment in this context was Wyclif, who used the *De questionibus Armenorum* in his teaching in the arts faculty at Oxford during the 1360s, as documented in his own treatises collected as the *Summa de ente* ('On Being').[57] Finally may be noted a theme of considerable significance for FitzRalph's later work. In Book X, chapter 4, of the *Summa*, is adumbrated the doctrine that no-one in a state of mortal sin has true dominion. There has been a hint in the sermon passage that I quoted at the beginning of my paper of how 'dominion' began to play a part in FitzRalph's pastoral direction. The abstract elaboration of the theme soon assumed major dimensions, as the central concept of his treatise, *De pauperie Salvatoris*.

The prologue to the *De pauperie Salvatoris* traces the work's inception to a commission given by Clement VI in the eighth year of his pontificate (that is, 7 May 1349–6 May 1350, coinciding with FitzRalph's third sojourn at the curia but preceding his delivery of the *Propositio* 'Unusquisque') to FitzRalph and two other, unidentified, doctors of theology. Their brief was to investigate disputed

---

56 FitzRalph's exegetical principles have received important theoretical consideration in A.J. Minnis, '"Authorial intention" and "literal sense" in the exegetical theories of Richard FitzRalph and John Wyclif: an essay in the medieval history of biblical hermeneutics', *Proceedings of the Royal Irish Academy* 75 C (1975), pp 1–30.   57 Robson, *Wyclif and the Oxford schools*, pp 71, 96, 155, 188, 199, 205, 207, 216.

matters concerning 'proprietorship or the lordship, possession and right of use of things such as our Saviour and Lord Jesus Christ held and as do the friars minor and their order, imitating (as they maintain) the poverty of our Saviour'.[58] The investigation was to include review of the various papal rulings on the subject. It is implicit that there was at least one participant representative of or at least sympathetic to the mendicant position. The initial description in FitzRalph's treatise of the business at issue is that it 'had been shredded during many years among the the the two principal orders of mendicants'.[59] In fact, the 'shredding' had been mainly a Franciscan affair. The reference to the Dominicans here may indicate that the 'committee' consisted of FitzRalph (his views, soon to be published, no doubt already well known at the curia), a Franciscan (from the order most diametrically opposed) and a Dominican (as occupying the closest approximation achievable to a middle position). The deliberations had proceeded 'protractedly and diffusely' (one may well imagine that this is no hyperbole) before Cardinal Etienne Aubert, to whom, as Innocent VI, the prologue is addressed. In FitzRalph's judgment the parties were 'dissecting – with stings of serpents rather than knives or blades – the bark, well up from the roots'.[60] 'Stings of serpents' leaves no room for doubt: there was less than unanimity on this committee. It was time to take axe in hand. 'Fired with the zeal of elucidating the truth', and, vitally, with a claim to curial support for the initiative ('spurred on by the encouragements of certain of my lords cardinals'),[61] FitzRalph tackled the roots himself. The task thus begun in the curia was continued in Ireland 'in snatched intervals between the waves of the pastoral office breaking unceasingly'.[62] It was not as he wished nor how it ought to be and was too long – an effect of the spread of those roots and the material's difficulty.

Again, the work is a dialogue: Richard and a John, who impresses by his confidence and probing. Could he be Grandisson? Certainly, we have evidence both from the Exeter register and from the *Memoriale presbiterorum* – considered as a product of the bishop's *familia* – of an early and urgent concern on Grandisson's part with the ethical dimensions of the exercise of office and a firm insistence that lack of integrity in office constitutes moral turpitude.[63] The *De pauperie Salvatoris* is, under cover of its overt subject matter, a wide-ranging analysis of the relationship between right and moral integrity. As such, it can readily be seen as representing a continuum of investigation in which Grandisson himself with his strongly Augustinian impress could not fail to be interested – even if, no more than FitzRalph or, indeed, Augustine himself, he cannot be thought a likely advocate of the result's general application in practice. In the ecclesiastical context specifically, Grandisson had a high concept of the dignity and inviolability of the clerical order and prelacy. The two strands in Grandisson's own

58 John Wyclif, *De dominio divino*, ed. R.L. Poole (London, 1890), p. 273. **59** Ibid. **60** Ibid. 61 Ibid. **62** Ibid. **63** See Haren, *Sin and society*, pp 51–5; cf. ibid., pp 59–61.

world-view point to a paradox much commented on in relation to the thesis
central to the *De pauperie Salvatoris* – that of dominion by grace. As Aubrey
Gwynn showed, this doctrine, though present in thirteenth-century canonist
thought, received its major elaboration within the Augustinian order, especially
from Giles of Rome, during the contest between Boniface VIII and Philip IV of
France. It was a justification of the hierocratic thesis, the subordination of
temporal to spiritual power.[64] During the pontificate of John XXII, William of
Cremona, prior-general of the Augustinians from 1326 to 1342, deployed it
against the *Defensor pacis* ('Defender of the Peace') of Marsiglio of Padua, whose
argument accorded to the temporal power a regulatory authority over the
church.[65] Gwynn suggested, convincingly, that as a theologian in curial circles
William may have had contact with FitzRalph during the latter's second,
extended, stay in Avignon. For FitzRalph the analysis bore against the friars on
a double count. It overturned their primitive (now in practice outmoded)
ideology – adherence to a concept of apostolic poverty incompatible with his
thesis of the common lordship of the just. It advanced the principle, already
present in the *Propositio* 'Unusquisque',[66] that their lack of integrity in alleged
abuse of privileges constituted a ground of the privileges' removal, as the fall of
Adam led to his expulsion from paradise (a fundamental theme of *De pauperie
Salvatoris*). Though this was a new direction indeed, the doctrine was still being
pressed to hierarchical service – the rationale of prelacy and the divinely instituted prerogatives of the secular clergy. It was, however, as the event
demonstrated, capable of being enlisted under another banner – that of
rendering corrigible a delinquent ecclesiastical establishment. The latter proposition would have been anathema to Grandisson and to FitzRalph. Accordingly,
while it is evident that Wyclif – whose citations makes his debt, on the level of
recognizance, indisputable – was a keen student of FitzRalph's analysis, he is
incapable of classification as disciple in any but a superficial sense.[67]

The *De pauperie Salvatoris* as it originally stood consisted of seven books. The
first five range over the concepts of dominion or lordship, possession, title,
proprietorship and use. These no doubt represent that engagement with the

64 A. Gwynn, *The English Austin friars in the time of Wyclif* (Oxford, 1940), pp 35–73. 65 See
Guillelmi de Villana Cremonensis Tractatus cuius titulus Reprobatio Errorum, ed. Daragh
MacFhionnbhair, Corpus Scriptorum Augustinianorum 2 (Rome, 1977). 66 Ed. Hammerich,
Strife, p. 72. 67 The matter is judiciously considered by J.I. Catto, 'Wyclif and Wycliffism at
Oxford 1356–1430', in J.I Catto and R. Evans (eds), *The history of Oxford university*, ii (Oxford,
1992), pp 175–261 at pp 203–4, 211–12. The latest analysis of Wyclif's position and examination
of FitzRalph's theory as a source for it neatly characterizes the latter in these terms: 'It [sc.
FitzRalph's theory] exhibits neither the papalist hierarchic claims of the earlier Augustinian
friars nor the revolutionary spirit of its immediate successor': S.E. Lahey, *Philosophy and politics
in the thought of John Wyclif* (Cambridge, 2003), p. 62. Relative to the trenchancy of these applications, FitzRalph's handling may indeed seem 'disappointing' (ibid.). A large part of its interest
is the very hesitancy, betokening genuine exploration, with which the issues are pursued.

roots on which the author had found the committee work so deficient. Books VI and VII examine respectively the concept of apostolic poverty and the principles of the evangelical life, together with the history of papal constitutions bearing on regular mendicancy (predominantly those of Nicholas III and John XXII), especially as pertinent to the Franciscan ideal. Evidently a draft at least of the treatise as originally planned existed by late 1356 for in a sermon of 18 December preached in the hall of the bishop of London, Michael Northburgh, FitzRalph referred to the seven books as having been directed for approval, discussion and, if necessary, correction to pope and cardinals and as having been 'given over for communication' to interested parties in Oxford.[68] In the course of his subsequent and final residence at Avignon, litigating against the friars, FitzRalph added an eighth book specifically on the subject of mendicancy – though with adversions on the friars' pastoral privileges – intended to summarize the controversy as it had developed since the writing of the original work, in the course of and arising from his series of London sermons – that of 18 December, just mentioned, and the three following preached at St Paul's Cross – and also in his *Defensorium curatorum* ('Defence of the Curates'), preached at Avignon.

ASPECTS OF THE TRADITION AND SCHOLARLY AGENDA

The manuscript tradition of the *De pauperie Salvatoris* reflects the two-stage genesis that I have outlined. The eighth book is transmitted both alone[69] and conjoined with the preceding seven.[70] Paris, Bibliothèque nationale, MS lat. 3222 (which belonged to William Cecil, Lord Burleigh, and subsequently to Colbert) is on palaeographical grounds to be judged contemporary with the date of writing. It is by a professional scribe. My use of it to date suggests that while its text is good it has defects. The text of the eighth book of the *De pauperie Salvatoris* is there followed by a collection of other items relating to FitzRalph's cause and the controversy (including, fos. 117–158, the *Defensio mendicantium*, 'Defence of the Mendicants', of Roger Conway OFM, composed in 1359 as a riposte to a tract by FitzRalph, *De audientia confessionis*, 'On the hearing of confession', written at Avignon) – on the papal decree *Vas electionis*, issued in condemnation of Jean de Pouilly. With Cambridge, Sidney Sussex College, MS 64, this manuscript evidently brings us in close proximity to the course of the proceedings at the papal curia.

Requiring special notice, as remarkable in conveying more than – outside of a repeated lecture course – is normally known of the process of medieval compo-

---

68 For the suggested significance, see Haren, 'Richard FitzRalph and the friars', pp 363–4.
69 Paris, Bibliothèque nationale, MS lat. 3222. Berlin, Deutsche Staatsbibliothek, MS Magdeburg Domgymnasium 47. 70 Cambridge, Corpus Christi College, MS 180; London, Lambeth Palace, MS 121.

sition, is the manuscript of the first seven books of the *De pauperie Salvatoris* preserved in Vienna, Österreichische Nationalbibliothek CVP 1430. It carries an inscription of ownership by the Bohemian master Adalbert Rankonis, doctor of theology and one-time rector of Paris university.[71] This provides the information: 'Fuit reverendi domini Ricardi primatis Ybernie [...] quem ipsemet dominus Ricardus composuit contra fratres mendicantes in curia Romana [...]' (literally, for the moment: 'It was of the reverend Lord Richard, primate of Ireland, which the same Lord Richard composed against the mendicant friars in the Roman curia').[72] Adalbert is known to have studied at Oxford,[73] where he might, just, have been present at the time of the work's circulation there. He subsequently spent a period at Avignon (1363–4 and perhaps earlier).[74] The fact that the manuscript lacks the eighth book probably cannot be taken as indicative of the point of its acquisition by him.[75] That might be a relic of the text's genesis.Whether he acquired it at Oxford or Avignon, however, Adalbert, by his evident interest, can hardly but represent a crucial point of junction. In currents of debate on matters which – as transformed by Wyclif's redirection – came to have revolutionary application, he links pre-Wyclifite Oxford and pre-Hussite Bohemia, later to be so heavily indebted to Wyclifite thought. This dimension of the *De pauperie Salvatoris* awaits the thorough evaluation which its importance deserves.

As already noted, CVP 1430 witnesses to a text in evolution. It carries extensive revisions and interpolations of a character that can only be authorial and that entered the published tradition. One obvious hypothesis is that its revisions, being authorial in substance, might be authorial also in execution.[76] Initial promptings of my review of them to date as preliminary to the more comprehensive study that I project within a critical edition of the *De pauperie Salvatoris* are to caution. Some, despite evidently having authorial sanction, are to be judged non-authorial in rendering.[77] It seems that CVP 1430, having

71 See J. Kadlec, *Leben und Schriften des Prager Magisters Adalbert Rankonis de Ericinio*, Beiträge zur Geschichte der Philosophie und Theologie des Mittelalters, neue Folge 4 (Münster, 1971). 72 Vienna, Österreichische Nationalbibliothek CVP 1430, fo. 1r. See K. Walsh, 'The manuscripts of Archbishop Richard FitzRalph in the Österreichische Nationalbibliothek, Vienna', *Römische historische Mitteilungen* 18 (1976), 67–75 at 67.   73 See A.B. Emden, *A biographical register of the university of Oxford*, 3 vols (Oxford, 1959), iii, 1547.   74 Kadlec, *Leben und Schriften*, p. 11; Walsh, 'The manuscripts', 71.   75 As suggested by Walsh, 'The manuscripts', 71.   76 See Walsh, *Scholar and primate*, p. 475.   77 An omission as against the published text, putatively by homoeoteleuton, in an addition by *cedula* to the text as it originally stood at CVP 1430, fo. 41r, of a passage that is necessary to the sense of the argument effectively deters the hypothesis that the addition was physically written by the author: it was evidently copied from an exemplar by a copyist not quite following the drift. By the same token, an initial error in the elaboration 'aliud est enim causam propriam quam proprium ius habere' (cf. Poole, ed. cit., p. 404, ll. 15–16) which appears as an addition at the foot of CVP 1430, fo. 40vb, is revelatory. There, the words, 'quam proprium' were at first omitted from the phrasing. Since the effect of the omission is syntactically impossible the elaboration is incompatible with a hypothesis of

received a good deal of internal correction and revision,[78] in some measure at least represents a text that was further economically updated by the transfer on to it of elaborations and amendments that are authorial but not all, certainly, executed by the author himself.

The history of editing *De pauperie Salvatoris* to date has been complicated and unsatisfactory. R.L Poole printed the first four books from one Oxford manuscript read in the light of another[79] as an appendix to his edition of Wyclif's *De dominio divino* (*On divine dominion*).[80] Two unpublished doctoral theses independently edited Books V–VII.[81] Evidently, in the critical edition of the treatise as originally conceived, Books I–VII, the revisions of CVP 1430 need careful distinction and presentation. Book VIII, which could in principle be approached editorially – as it was generated authorially – as a separate entity, remains wholly unedited and has accordingly an urgent claim to attention.

Beyond the need for editions – and preceding them in the case of the individual sermons especially – a major desideratum is a comprehensive census of the manuscript circulation of the corpus of FitzRalph's writings. Katherine Walsh has announced this as a project in hand[82] and there is no-one so well-placed and qualified to bring it to fruition. At that point, she had located 182 codices. A few summary indications may be given, for general information, of the tradition's configuration. Interest in the anti-mendicant strand seems to have been heavily a northern and central European affair.[83] The *Summa de questionibus Armenorum*, with some forty-five manuscripts, had a European-wide circulation of which Avignon and Paris were principal centres of dissemination,[84] and – as might be expected – had a special interest during the deliberations between

---

authorial composition but exhibits, rather, a copying error. 78 A notable example of fluidity is at CVP 1430, fo. 51r, where a lengthy exchange between the interlocutors which does not seem to have survived to the published version was written and cancelled. It must be considered highly improbable that a passage which had already been cancelled in an exemplar would be copied in order to be (silently) marked as cancelled. There are lesser examples of the same phenomenon. 79 Oxford, Bodleian Library, MS Auct. F. infra I.2, used as the basis of the edition. Oxford, Merton College, MS. 113, used in a supplementary fashion. 80 Wyclif, *De dominio divino*, ed. Poole. 81 Helen Hughes, '*De pauperie Salvatoris of Richard FitzRalph of Armagh*' (University of Manchester, PhD thesis, 1927), using the same two manuscripts as Poole but having the Merton manuscript as the base with alternative readings given from the Bodleian manuscript; Richard O. Brock, 'An edition of Richard FitzRalph's *De pauperie Salvatoris*, Books V, VI and VII' (University of Colorado, PhD thesis, 1954), editing from the same Bodleian manuscript collated with the Merton manuscript, and on certain points using Paris, Bibliothèque nationale, MS lat. 15375 and Cambridge, Corpus Christi College, MS 180. 82 Walsh, *Scholar and primate*, p. 469. 83 See Gwynn, 'The sermon diary', 45–7, containing, at p. 46, a list of manuscripts with present locations as follows: Paris, Vatican City, Prague, Cracow, Wolfenbüttel, Danzig, Berlin, Leipzig, Munich, Bruges and England. Present location, of course, is a fallacious guide: as Gwynn remarks there, the three Vatican manuscripts of the *Defensorium curatorum* are of German origin. Cf. Walsh, *Scholar and primate*, pp 469–71. 84 See Walsh, *Scholar and primate*, p. 130.

eastern and western churches at the council of Ferrara-Florence in the mid-fifteenth century.[85] Its single, sixteenth-century, printed edition[86] is unsatisfactory: could theological preoccupations of our own time prompt new critical effort? It is on such trends that scholarly endeavour of lasting value so often depends – witness the magnificent, continuing, consequences in editorial achievement of Pope Leo XIII's patronage of the thought of St Thomas Aquinas. Among the manuscripts, including fragments, of the *Commentary on the Sentences* may be noted especially Paris, Bibliothèque nationale, MS lat. 15853, bequeathed to the library of the Sorbonne in 1360 by the Paris master Jean Gorre, whose text is accompanied by annotations in a hand which Leff suggested might be FitzRalph's own.[87] Since it is reported as differing from that of annotations in Vienna, CVP 1430,[88] the possibility should be considered on its substantive merit, pending ultimate discrimination and judgement regarding the revisions in the latter. Worcester Cathedral Library, MS Q. 71, identifies the Commentator as 'Ricardus Hybernicus' which suggests that it dates from before his elevation to dignity. The early date of circulation to which these manuscripts and others of the Sentences-Commentary tradition attest has an implication for evaluating FitzRalph's perceived importance. As already observed, interest in him as commentator was independent of his reputation as established by his mature works or by his polemics. So high was the profile which these earned for him that the youthful thinker has tended in historical evaluation to be obscured. Rectification of that distortion will no doubt be yet another of the fruits to be gathered from Dr Michael Dunne's work, to whose completion we look forward with eager anticipation. Daunting as may be the tally of *desiderata*, it is perhaps the ultimate tribute to the subject's range and depth of interest that, three-quarters of a century after Aubrey Gwynn's first address to FitzRalph's intellectual biography and despite the substantial progress in understanding that intervening research has contributed, so much remains to engage and reward scholarship.

85 See ibid., p. 131.   86 Ricardus Radulphi, *Summa de questionibus Armenorum* (Paris, 1511). 87 Leff, *Commentator,* p. 179.   88 See Walsh, *Scholar and primate,* p. 475.

Minor Scholastics of Irish origin up to 1500

JAMES McEVOY

Five figures, all born in Ireland (Iohannes Scottus Eriugena, Gille of Limerick, Peter of Ireland, Thomas of Ireland and Richard FitzRalph) have each been deemed worthy of a chapter in the present volume. In addition to these, four comparatively minor figures (William of Drogheda, Geoffrey of Waterford OP, Malachy of Limerick and Mauritius Hibernicus a Portu OFM) deserve to be taken into account. Eriugena (d. *c.*870) is the obligatory starting point from which to begin considering Irish links with European philosophy and theology in the course of the Middle Ages. His stature is such that his place in the history of European thought is an assured one. He was not a Scholastic, however, for that designation is conventionally applied to authors and works after *c.*1100, though with a run-up period of two or three generations. Each of the major figures has been granted commensurate attention whereas the minor ones will be discussed in the following pages.[1]

Our account may fittingly begin with a brief survey of the four leading contemporary scholarly sources of knowledge and information regarding medieval Irish Scholastics and the writings some of them produced.

The earliest of these (1958) is A.B. Emden's list of Oxford students and masters.[2] The University of Oxford attracted many young scholars of Irish provenance from *c.*1230 to 1250, and continued to do so until just after 1500. In the earlier part of the period most of those whose names have come down to us were of Anglo-Norman parentage, and it is only after *c.*1350 that more and more Gaelic Irish names occur. Few scholars from Ireland distinguished themselves in medicine or law, the great majority of graduates and doctors being products of the faculties of arts, theology and canon law; some naturally combined theology and canon law in their course of study.[3] In 1540 the canon law faculty was closed by Henry VIII as part of the Reformation. This date marked effectively the end of widespread Irish attendance at the University and the beginning of the long connection between Irish Catholics and the universities of Spain, the Spanish

---

1 I am grateful to Dr John Flood for supplying bibliographical references and to Mr Hugh O'Neill for his comments on a draft of this article. 2 A.B. Emden, *A biographical register of the University of Oxford to AD 1500* (Oxford, 1958), 3 vols. 3 The *Lectura Hostiensis* was the textbook in canon law; students from Ireland quite frequently used their copy as a pledge on a loan, their names thus finding their way into Emden's register because the loan was placed on record.

Low Countries and Italy, including Rome. For the historian of Oxford the suppression of 1540 clearly marks the end of the medieval period, as Emden observed.[4] There can be no doubt that unknown numbers of students from Ireland attended the universities of Paris, Padua and others during the medieval period, but the low rate of survival of matriculation and college documents from these institutions leaves Oxford by contrast in a very strong highlight. So far as the known attendance there on the part of Irish-born students and masters is concerned, the Oxford of the later Middle Ages is a case apart from all others. The two islands of Britain and Ireland formed part of Europe and shared in the European experience up to the sixteenth century, and hence the Irish partici-pation in university education at Oxford forms an important aspect of the general theme of the present book and one that is uniquely well documented.

Relying principally upon the records of coroners, the royal courts and what survives of college and matriculation rolls, Emden listed all known names of Oxford students and masters up to 1500, indicating which of them were authors of Scholastic material. The value for our present purposes of his thorough compendium lies in his identification of the names of numerous scholars who came from Ireland, or were at least associated with the country (for example, through holding a benefice in an Irish diocese, though born in England or in some cases elsewhere). The Register can be searched by means of its index of names, which includes a total of 76 O's and Mac's. Emden devoted a similar study to the University of Cambridge but very few names with Irish associations are to be found in it.[5] To the numerical value of the information extractable from Emden's volumes we will return presently; in the meantime we turn our attention to the second contemporary source of relevant information for our study.

In 1997 the American scholar Mary Hayes Somers published her alphabetical list of the known Irish university scholars between 1200 and 1500 or so.[6] She based her work on that of Emden but extended the research net to the University of Paris. She incorporated all the available information into the mini-biographies of individuals which she drew up, referring in particular to career and (where appropriate) publications. The result is extremely useful for our purposes. She found that university records at Paris for the thirteenth and fourteenth centuries identify twenty individuals as coming from Ireland whereas none can be found in the records of the fifteenth century. Though it is not always possible to make a neat separation between Irish and Scottish names, those who were definitely of Irish provenance were a mixture of secular clergymen, regulars and some laymen. Three of the regulars were masters of theology at the Dominican priory of St Jacques and a Franciscan was a master of theology at the

---

4 Emden, *Biographical register*, i, Introduction. 5 Only two clearly Gaelic names occur: Cornelius O'Mullaly, subsequently bishop of Clonfert, then Emly and finally Elphin; and Malachy O'Quirk, *c*.1440. 6 'A prosopography of Irish scholars', *Medieval Prosopography* 18 (1997), 139–87.

Cordeliers in Paris. The most famous of the seculars was the author Thomas of Ireland. Many of these Irish figures eventually secured appointments in the Church in Ireland. Hayes Somers warns that the small numbers of Irish names in the surviving records cannot by any means be taken as an exhaustive reflection of the total Irish presence at Paris during the period.

Hayes Somers' exploration of the Oxford records, supplemented by all the ecclesiastical and civil registers available, reveals that 190 names associated with Ireland can be identified between the thirteenth and the fifteenth century: 52 in the thirteenth, 58 in the fourteenth and 80 in the fifteenth century. Anglo-Norman names predominate in the record. The appellation *Hibernicus* or *de Hibernia* was common, but of course of itself it provides no evidence as to whether an individual was of Anglo-Norman or native origin. Secular clergy made up the largest group, with only 21 of those named coming from the mendicant, Augustinian and Cistercian orders. It is worth recalling that the names in Emden's list are those that happened to find their way onto some document or other; his total of 15,000 covering three centuries may represent as little as 20 per cent of all students. Thus there were undoubtedly many more Irish at the university than can be actually named. Most of the scholars returned to their country of origin to serve in the Church, often rising to high office; five Oxford graduates became archbishops of Armagh, four of Cashel and four of Dublin. According to Anthony Wood, the seventeenth-century historian of the University of Oxford, a street in the medieval town came to be known as 'Irishman Street' from the number of Irish lodging there. Hayes Somers concluded her pioneering study with the reminder to the reader that around 150 Irishmen can be named, men who during the same period studied at various universities on the continent but who cannot be definitely attached to a particular institution. She implies that some further evidence can be expected to turn up as research cuts deeper into the surviving, fragmentary records.

The third of the scholarly works that must be taken into account is Professor Richard Sharpe's list of medieval British and Irish authors.[7] Building upon a long bibliographical tradition but surpassing it in scope, scholarly exactitude and completeness, Sharpe has compiled entries on the 2283 individuals from Britain and Ireland who from St Patrick down to AD 1540 were authors in any literary genre (letter, poem, annals, hagiographical life, treatise, Scholastic exercise or *summa*). He takes in all known writers, including those whose work is now untraceable and those whose output survives only in manuscript form, being as yet unedited. In every case full bibliographical information is supplied. In Sharpe's expert opinion 106 writers can be identified who came from Ireland, or at least were related to it in some way that justifies their inclusion in his list.[8]

---

7 Richard Sharpe, *A handlist of the Latin writers of Great Britain and Ireland before 1540, with additions and corrections*, Publications of the Journal of Medieval Latin, 1 (Turnhout, 2001).
8 Professor Sharpe deserves thanks for communicating his list to me and permitting me to

Upon closer inspection some surviving writing or writings of a broadly
Scholastic kind can be attached to about forty of these names. With a few notable
exceptions the writings are minor or unedited compositions. The names in
question are reproduced here, the reference to Sharpe's *Handlist* being given as
a number within brackets. (Addenda nos. are indicated by asterisk.)

Adam Payne OESA (d. after 1429, bishop of Cloyne), author of a *quaestio* (34).

David O'Bugey O.Carm. (d. after 1324) (226).

Gilbert of Limerick (d. 1145) (373): see the chapter by J. Fleming in the present
volume.

Henry Crumpe O.Cist. (d. after 1401), *Quaestiones* (446).

Hugo de Scotia (date unknown), surviving unedited *Sermo de otiositate hominis*
(528).

John Allen (1476–1534, archbishop of Dublin), several Latin writings (45*).

John Colton (d. 1404, archbishop of Armagh), several writings, including lost
Tractatus pro sedatione schismatis (647).

John of Darlington OP (d. 1284, archbishop of Dublin), *Concordantiae
Anglicanae*, the second verbal concordance to the Bible (659).

John of Fintona (latter half of the 13th century), glosses (unedited) and a
commentary (of which a single quotation survives) on the *Decretum* of
Gratian (691).[9]

John Foxholes OFM (Iohannes Anglicus), (d. 1475, archbishop of Armagh):
prolific author of numerous surviving Scholastic works including a
commentary on Book 1 of the *Opus Oxoniense* of Duns Scotus (702).[10]

Malachias of Limerick (fl. 1270), *Tractatus de septem venenis* (1028).

Mauritius Hibernicus O'Fihely OFM Conv. (d. 1513, archbishop of Tuam),
editor of writings by Duns Scotus and others and author of *Enchyridion fidei*
(1053).

Michael Tregury (d. 1471, archbishop of Dublin), writings recorded by bibliographers (1062).

Patrick of Ireland (late 13th century), Sophisma: 'Homo est animal' (5 MSS, ed.)
(1159).

Peter of Ireland (mid-13th century) (1182): see chapter by M. Dunne in the
present volume.

Richard FitzRalph (d. 1360) (1329): see chapter by M. Haren in the present
volume.

---

reproduce it and refer to it in print.   **9** See the informative paragraphs on John, who came from
the modest locality of Fintona in Co. Tyrone, in Scott, 'Latin learning', pp 968–9.   **10** Foxholes
was nominated to the see of Armagh but renounced his claim when it was contested; he never
lived in Ireland but did exercise an influence upon Maurice O'Fihely through his edition of
works by Duns Scotus. Maurice O'Fihely took cognizance of Foxholes' edition while working on
his own (see the chapter by Martin Stone in this volume).

Robert Worksop OESA (d. 1324, bishop of Connor), a *quaestio*, uned. (1540).

Stephen of Lexington O.Cist. (d. 1260), *Speculum confessionis* (uned.) (1670).

Thomas of Ireland (d. after 1329) (1767): see chapters by J. McEvoy and D. Lawell in the present volume.

Thomas Kelly (d. after 1374), *Repetitiones* on Justinian (in 1 MS, unedited), (1770).

William of Drogheda (d. 1245), *Summa aurea*, ed. (2041).

William of Hotham OP (d. 1298, archbishop of Dublin), *Quodlibet* (uned.); Sermons (uned.); Commentary on *De anima* (?), (2086).

William of Montoriel (13th century), lost *Summa libri praedicamentorum* (2130).

William of Paull O.Carm. (d. 1349, bishop of Meath), lost *De ente rationis formaliter* (2142).

We owe the most recent scholarly contribution to the study of the Scholastics of Irish origin in medieval times to the pen of Brian Scott, formerly professor of Medieval Latin at Queen's University.[11] His searching and well documented account of the Latin writing stemming from Ireland during the later medieval centuries discusses each of the Irish Scholastic authors, as well as of course the writers in other genres. Wide reading in unedited sources and early editions characterize this work, as does sensitivity to the historical, cultural and linguistic background of the various authors. Reference will be made to it regarding the individual writers we discuss.

THREE FIGURES OF THE THIRTEENTH CENTURY: WILLIAM OF DROGHEDA, GEOFFREY OF WATERFORD AND MALACHIAS HIBERNICUS OFM

William of Drogheda is linked by his name to the small trading town at the mouth of the Boyne River (Droichead Atha, 'ford bridge'), a settlement which attracted Anglo-Norman traders from *c*.1200 onwards.[12] On several occasions he referred to himself as 'W. De Drokeda'. William was regent (that is, a teaching master) in civil law at Oxford by 1239, indeed he is the first known doctor of civil law of the University. In a writ of Henry III (which William, evidently a good self-publicist, preserved) he is addressed as *regens in legibus* ('professor of law'). The Drogheda man was an active advocate; he records, for instance, that he

11 A.B. Scott, 'Latin learning and literature in Ireland, 1169–1500', in Dáibhí Ó Cróinín (ed.), *A new history of Ireland*, i: *Prehistoric and early Ireland* (Oxford, 2005), pp 934–35. 12 On William, see Hayes Somers, 'A prosopography', pp. 164–5; Scott, 965–8. Jane E. Sayers argues that William had no connection with Drogheda; see her article on William in the *Oxford DNB* and her study 'William of Drogheda and the English canonists', in P. Linehan (ed.), *Seventh international congress of medieval canon law* (Cambridge: 1984), pp 205–22. H. Zapp has written a brief entry on William in the *Lexikon des Mittelalters* 9. 170–1.

appeared in the chancellor's court of the university 'on behalf of one of my students against an important party of Oxford.'

William composed a legal treatise with the title *Summa aurea* ('the Golden Summary'). The work made his name as a legist and remained in use for several generations, in some parts of Italy as well as in England. The complete silence of the faculty of canon law at Oxford up to the early fourteenth century, along with that of his own colleagues in civil law, means that William of Drogheda is the only published lawyer of the university known to us from the entire first century of its existence. His book is the only literary (as distinct from documentary) evidence for the shape of contemporary legal teaching at Oxford. Indeed, the authority on the whole subject, the late Fr Leonard Boyle OP, described William as 'the first and the only literary light of the faculty of civil law [at Oxford] in the Middle Ages'.[13] His sole surviving writing was deemed worthy of a modern edition.[14]

In the words of its author, the *Summa* was devoted expressly to 'the manner of pleading, opposing, replying, reflecting, and distinguishing truth from falsehood'. It was in other words conceived Scholastically as a guide to legal procedure, and the constant use made of the *quaestio* identifies its method as that of the schools generally. Sometimes criticized for its apparent disorderliness, William's treatise has found a defender in Brian Scott.[15] The opening chapter suggests a rather practical intention: to discuss how to compose petitions to the Roman curia and to employ the *stilus curiae,* or correct curial style (Boyle, p. 539). The section on papal rescripts and their verification would have given useful instruction to budding lawyers. The chapters on citation and writs are really a formulary, with many documents included as examples. As a Scholastic lawyer William was thoroughly conversant with canon law, to which Roman civil law served in his eyes as an *ancilla*. In the *Summa* the view is defended that rectors as well as other priests and clerics may legitimately devote themselves to the study of civil law. William's opinion in this matter ran counter to the influential decree *Super specula* of Pope Honorius III (1219), which so far as England was concerned was reinforced c. 1239 by the authority of Robert Grosseteste, bishop of Lincoln, along with some of his episcopal colleagues. William was clearly not afraid to defend a minority view. One is inclined to wonder whether in taking up the stance he did he was in effect defending his own standing (he was rector of two parishes and presumably a priest), or whether on the other

---

13 L.E. Boyle OP, 'Canon law before 1380', in J.I. Catto (ed.), *The history of the University of Oxford,* i: *The early Oxford schools* (Oxford, 1984), p. 539. 14 William of Drogheda, *Summa aurea,* ed. L. Wahrmund (Quellen zur Geschichte des römisch-kanonischen Prozesses im Mittelalter), vol. II p. 2 (Innsbruck, 1914). 15 A.B. Scott, 'Latin literature', p. 966–7: 'If one allows for the way in which the methods or argument used in theological and philosophical teaching, and writings derived from that teaching, invaded the more practical fields of medicine and law, then the work is less disordered than Kantorowicz or de Zulueta make out.'

hand he was promoting open access to his subject with the hope of a resulting gain in student numbers.

The St Albans chronicler, Matthew Paris, who respected William highly, described him as dying in miserable circumstances (*lugubriter*) in the year 1245 while engaged on a case; he was murdered in his home by his servant, one Ralph de Boklande, described as *armiger* (squire). The site where the tragedy occurred is still known: William's house was known as Drawda Hall till 1985, when the bookshop it housed was turned into a unisex hairdressing salon.[16]

The name Jofroi (Geoffrey, Ir. Shafraí) came to Ireland with the Normans. **Geoffrey of Waterford**, a Dominican priest who died *c*.1300, attained a modest celebrity as a translator of Latin works into his native Anglo-Norman dialect.[17] He lived at the Dominican convent of St Jacques at Paris before setting off for the Holy Land as a missionary. Dates are hard to establish regarding his activities. He is to be found later at Rome where he became a papal penitentiary. From there he wrote to the prior of the Paris convent to inform the community that the General of the order, Jordan of Saxony (elected 1222), had drowned off the coast of Anatolia on 13 February 1237.

This priest-scholar and missionary was considered a very good linguist, speaking *Gallica* (French), being skilled as a matter of course in Latin and learned besides in Greek and Arabic. It is for his translations that he is remembered. The following Latin-French versions are attributed to him.

> Dares the Phrygian, *De excidio Trojae historia*. This prose account of the Trojan War was to be widely used by medieval writers. The mythical claim was made for it that Dares of Phrygia had composed it as a pre-Homeric poem about the conflict. (Dares is named in the *Iliad* 5. 9 as a priest of Hephaestus at Troy). The Latin work may date from the fifth century AD; it has an alleged dedication by Sallust to Cornelius Nepos.[18] Presumably the Middle Eastern setting of the narrative was a factor in Geoffrey of Waterford's interest in the work.
>
> Eutropius, *Historia romana*. Eutropius took part in the Emperor Julian's Persian campaign (AD 363) and wrote a Latin history of Rome down to AD 364. As a historian he is said to show good judgement and impartiality. His writing was translated into Greek by Paenius about AD 380, and it received in addition a Greek adaptation by Capito of Lycia. It is not known when exactly Geoffrey translated it into French.[19]

16 Scott, 'Latin learning', p. 967.   17 The most recent study of Geoffrey is by Albert Henry, 'Un texte oenologique de Jofroi de Waterford et Servais Copale', *Romania* 107 (1986), 1–37. The author explores only the chapter on wine. Hayes Somers refers to Geoffrey as '*Godfrey* of Waterford' (p. 187).   18 Art. 'Dares of Phrygia' in Hammond & Scullard (eds), *The Oxford Classical dictionary*, 2nd ed. (Oxford, 1970), p. 313.   19 Art. 'Eutropius' in *The Oxford Classical*

Ps.-Aristotle, *Secretum secretorum*. Geoffrey made a French version of the *Secretum secretorum* attributed falsely to Aristotle: *Segre de segrez*.[20] The version is known in only one manuscript, Paris, BN fr. 1822. The *Secretum secretorum* proved an immensely popular work, surviving in 350 Latin manuscript witnesses. The original writing went back to the tenth century and to Syria, but it incorporated older material and first appeared with the title (in Arabic) *Book of the Policy for Ruling*; in other words it was a variant of the 'Mirror of Princes' genre. It is a compilation of widely-differing material, including passages from Aristotle's *Nicomachean Ethics*. Its final section contained medical material, herbal lore with magical overtones, and other material on poisons and the supposed healing powers of precious stones, amulets and talismans. Adaptations of the *Secretum* appeared in due course in Turkish, Persian and Hindi. Its Latin reception began with John Hispanus *c*.1135–42. In the thirteenth century an anonymous version was made which attributed the writing to 'Philip of Tripoli', thus making it pseudonymous. Commentaries were written on the *Secretum*, and Roger Bacon OFM took a considerable but critical interest in it. Vernacular versions of the same period included those in German, English and Scandanavian languages, as well as Castilian. The translation by Geoffrey was the third of the French versions (following after those of Pierre d'Abernon and Pierre de Peckham). But this new translation was a work enlarged by the translator himself, who brought in material of wider medical and natural interest. Continuing interest in his work is attested by its appearance in an incunabulum of 1497.

One of the most prolific translators of Arabic philosophical texts into Latin, the priest Michael Scotus, is sometimes claimed for Ireland.[21] Michael studied at Toledo and worked later at the imperial court of Frederick II, but nothing is known of his early life. His only definite connection with Ireland was his appointment as archbishop of Cashel by Pope Honorius III (1223). Michael refused the honour on the very honest grounds that he did not understand the language of the people there. This, and the fact that he held benefices in Scotland and England, suggests that he was of Scottish origin rather than Irish. He must have been born in the last quarter of the twelfth century and he died *c*.1235; by that time the Irish were no longer known as 'Scoti' but as 'Hibernici.'[22]

---

dictionary, pp 424–5. **20** Useful references are to be found in the art. 'Secretum secretorum' in *Lexikon des Mittelalters* 7. 1662–3 (D. Briesemeister). **21** As Michael Richter does: *Medieval Ireland: the enduring tradition*, New Gill History of Ireland I (Dublin, 1988), p. 179. **22** 'Michael Scotus' in *Lexikon des Mittelalters* 6. 606 (S. Ackermann).

A single work is attributed to '**Malachias**', but it is a writing that attained considerable popularity in the course of the later Middle Ages and which was widely diffused, namely *De septem venenis* ('On seven poisons', that is, the Seven Deadly Sins).[23] The poison-metaphor for sin was traditional and the title of the treatise may not have been original with Malachy, but numerous writings with similar titles were to appear well into the age of printing. Malachy could be the same person who, as a member of the Franciscan order at Limerick in 1279, was recommended by Archbishop Nicholas Mac Maol Iosa to Edward I as being 'young, provident and discreet', and on these grounds a suitable candidate for the see of Tuam. The election however was disputed.[24] Luke Wadding asserted that Malachy had earned a degree in theology at Oxford University about 1310, while living with the friars, but if the Franciscan historian had evidence for this claim it has not come down to us. The most one can say is that Malachy had learning and that he sought to put it to pastoral use; the fact that his treatise knew a wide circulation in England and was frequently associated with the name of Robert Grosseteste, the Oxford chancellor who became bishop of Lincoln (1235–53), could possibly indicate a connection between the friar and the university.

It is somewhat unsatisfactory for the historian to have to acknowledge that Malachy's authorship of the treatise on moral poisons is not certain and is supported by only a fraction of the manuscript evidence bearing on its authorship. A longer title for the *Tractatus de venenis* is attested, namely *Libellus septem peccatorum venenorum eorumque remedia describens, qui dicitur venenum Malachiae*,[25] which may be loosely paraphrased as: 'On the seven deadly sins and on the pastoral theology of Penance.' The book was a success: sixty-six manuscripts witness the text and more may still be identified. In nineteen of the manuscripts the writing is left anonymous, whereas twenty-five ascribe it to Grosseteste. The majority of the latter copies circulated in England, as might be expected.[26]

The authorship of Malachy is supported by only three attributions. Can he be considered the true author of *De venenis* when the numbers are so stacked up against him? Before the age of printing, the authorship of writings was frequently uncertain or contested, or simply unknown. The natural tendency existed to associate compositions of doubtful origin with well-known names,

23 The most perceptive account of Malachy is that given by Scott, 'Latin learning', pp 969–71. 24 This Malachy went to the papal court but his case for a papal provision to Tuam failed. Mario Esposito was the first to suggest a connection between the author of *De venenis* and the candidate for Tuam: 'Friar Malachy of Ireland', *English Historical Review* 33 (1918), 359–64. Katherine Walsh lists the complete bibliography on Malachy in her article on him in the *Oxford DNB*, 36. 269–70. 25 'A little book on the Seven Sins or Poisons also outlining their remedies which is called The Poison of Malachy.' 26 Two manuscripts are held in the library of Trinity College, Dublin: MS 115 (formerly A.5.3) and MS 281 (formerly C.2.18).

perhaps on the rather weak grounds that a given writing 'sounded like' St Augustine, say, or indeed *Lincolniensis* (Robert Grosseteste). In fact each great name of the patristic era and of medieval times functioned like a comet that drags a lengthy tail behind it or a planet that attracts foreign material into its orbit. The association of the treatise *De venenis* with Grosseteste was examined critically in 1940 by the latter's bibliographer, Samuel Harrison Thomson.[27] His studies had led him through the well-populated territory of Grosseteste-claimants and he was perfectly used to weighing the evidence for the authenticity of writings attributed to the famous bishop of Lincoln and making an adjudi-cation on the evidence before him. In the case in point he upheld the value of the three ascriptions to Malachias, arguing that 'any ascription at all to a relatively obscure person, provided it has intrinsic probability, has great weight'; besides, *De venenis* is not infrequently found in manuscripts alongside other works wrongly ascribed to Grosseteste. In Thomson's eyes the fact that Malachy is otherwise unknown as an author seemed to point in the right direction, whereas the authorship claimed so repeatedly for Robert Grosseteste could not be upheld. He noted furthermore the presence of Irish and Scottish references in the treatise, something which strengthens the claims to authorship on behalf of Malachy. Thomson's other service to the study of *De venenis* was more direct, for in addition to the total of thirty-three manuscripts known to Mario Esposito he identified a further eleven.[28] These identifications did nothing to advance the cause of Malachy, however, for seven of the new manuscripts ascribe the writing to Grosseteste whereas the remainder carry no ascription. The discussion of the authorship question by Thomson has not been superseded, and so his conclusion continues to stand: an otherwise unknown Irishman called Malachy was the author of the treatise *De venenis*.[29]

Malachy allegorizes each of the deadly sins in turn under the guise of a snake, reptile or insect. The chameleon for instance is compared to the hypocrite, the salamander to the false religious, the asp to envy in its different forms. Each poison however has a medical antidote, which is given, and a moral remedy, which the author develops in terms of the virtues, owing much in this regard to the *Moralia in Job* of St Gregory the Great. Regarding the animals, Malachy

---

27 S.H. Thomson, *The writings of Robert Grosseteste bishop of Lincoln 1235–1253* (Cambridge, 1940), pp 268–70.   28 Bloomfield was to add an additional 21 manuscripts and one has been added to the list by Sharpe to make a total of 66; see M.W. Bloomfield and others, *Incipits of Latin works on the virtues and vices, 1100–1500 AD* (Cambridge, MA, 1979), n. 5102; R. Sharpe, *A handlist*, n. 1028. Esposito's writings on Hiberno-Latin are still valued and have been collected by Michael Lapidge: Mario Esposito, *Latin learning in medieval Ireland*, and *Irish books and learning in medieval Europe* (2 vols, London, 1988, 1990).   29 Curiously, Thomson did not advert to the likelihood that the oft-repeated attribution of the *De venenis* to such a prominent author as Robert Grosseteste gave rise to an increase in the number of copies made, and also to the attention accorded to the treatise during the later Middle Ages.

draws his material from Pliny, Isidore and the Bestiary, making reference also to Aristotle's *De animalibus*, and to Avicenna for medical learning, supplemented by Constantine the African.

References to Ireland ('Scotia maior') and its people are quite frequent and strikingly candid. The Irish are descended from the Greeks and, like the Cretans of whom St Paul spoke unflatteringly (Tit 1: 12), are given to lying. The snakes were expelled from the land but its inhabitants still have some of their poison (Malachy moralizes) that comes out in the form of gross flattery (does he mean the class of *filí* or poets?), and in venom directed by 'bailiffs and administrators' against the poor and innocent. This looks like the even-handed criticism of a Franciscan regarding the two Irelands of his own time. With reference to sexual vice the author draws attention to the papal denunciation of the last high king of Ireland, Rory O'Connor, who had six wives and who surely incurred divine disfavour for his licentious ways. It is impossible to be certain whether Malachy was of Gaelic or of Anglo-Norman stock, though his name would suggest the former. If he was a Gael, he was censorious of his own people; on the other hand he did not spare the royal colony either.

The circulation of the treatise on the seven deadly sins was enhanced by its publication at Paris in 1518 by the famous printer Stephanus (Henri Etienne). In the now rare edition the writing is attributed to Malachias, who is given the title 'doctor theologiae'. Whether or not Malachy was a doctor, it is clear that he had made a study of theology following the usual formation in liberal arts and philosophy. It may be that he acquired his learning within the order to which he belonged – he refers to St Francis – rather than at the university, and it is possible that he also taught at a friary. The Stephanus edition kept the name of Malachy alive and placed it before bibliographers of early modern times, such as Bale and Tanner. His considerable learning is revealed through the numerous sources on which he drew, and which indicate his familiarity with a well-stocked library. Malachy's writing surely deserves a new edition bringing to bear on it all the contemporary resources of scriptural and patristic source-identification. This Franciscan of Irish origin wrote with an explicitly pastoral intention for, as he puts it, 'the instruction of simple men who have to teach the people.' This motivation makes plausible the idea that Malachy was a priest teaching his fellow friars in a provincial study-convent.

Mauritius Hibernicus a Portu/O'Fihely, *alias* **'Fildaeus', 'Flos Mundi'.** In his 1620 edition of the *Ordinatio* of Duns Scotus, Friar Hugh McCawell (1571–1626) paid the following warm tribute to an earlier Irish Franciscan editor of the same work:

> Our Maurice, a most learned and faithful disciple of Scotus, devoted great pains to the correction of the works of Scotus; he was attached to him by

the double bond of profession and nation, for of course each of them was Irish and of the Seraphic order [of St Francis].[30]

The 'Maurice' referred to with such respect by McCawell, and also by Luke Wadding, was the self-styled Mauritius a Portu ('Maurice from the Port') or 'Mauritius Hibernicus'.[31] He was a prominent Irish Conventual Franciscan, who was born Maurice O'Fihely, *c.*1460, either in Clonfert or in Baltimore (which was a small port). He died in Galway in 1513. It is sometimes stated that Maurice had pursued studies at Oxford, but J.I. Catto has pointed out that this claim, which goes back to Anthony Wood, is not supported by any contemporary evidence.[32] In 1488 he became regent at the Franciscan *studium generale* at Milan. He moved to the University of Padua in 1491, where he remained in the chair of Scotist Theology even after he was appointed archbishop of Tuam in 1506. He was a Father at the Fifth General Council of the Lateran (1512). He won recognition from his contemporaries as the best living connoisseur of the writings and thought of Duns Scotus. The honorific title 'Flos mundi' (Flower of the World) is thought to have been conferred on him in recognition of his gentle character and his exceptional learning. He edited many of the works attributed to John Duns Scotus, equipping them with commentaries, notes and scholia. For Maurice, Scotus was undoubtedly an Irishman, and one who had brought lustre to his native land through his unrivalled intellectual achievements. Through his editions of the writings of his hero and of works attributed to him Maurice became the first Irish figure to make a mark on the new printed literature, beginning in 1497. His editions appeared at Venice where he had a close connection with the eminent publisher of classical and contemporary Latin writings, Ottaviano Scotto, the printer being Bonetus Locatellus.[33] In his prefaces Maurice expresses his admiration for his fellow Franciscan and his own belonging to the 'Irish nation'. He composed an original work which he called the *Enchyridion fidei* (1509). In it were discussed, in Scholastic and Scotist manner, with many quotations, distinctions and questions, the favoured theological issues of the time such as predestination, divine foreknowledge of free contingent acts, fate and freewill. Not surprisingly, given the nature of several of these topics, Aristotle and Boethius figured large among the authorities he invoked. The writing, which was dedicated to Gearóid Mór Fitzgerald,

---

30 'Mauritius noster, doctissimus ac fidelissimus Scoti discipulus, duplici vinculo, professionis videlicet et nationis, (uterque quippe et Hibernus, et Religionis Seraphicae ad id adstrictus), in Scoti operibus castigandis multum elaboravit [...].' 31 Maurice's publications are discussed in greater detail by Martin Stone in the present volume. Few studies have been dedicated to him as yet. Scott has written valuable pages on his life and works ('Latin learning', pp 961–5). 32 J.I. Catto, 'Theology after Wycliffism', J.I. Catto & R. Evans (eds), *The history of the University of Oxford*, ii, *Late Medieval Oxford* (Oxford, 1992), p. 271. 33 On the Scotto publishing family see Claudio Sartori, 'La famiglia degli editori Scotto', *Acta Musicologica* (1964), 19–30.

eighth earl of Kildare, has not received a modern edition, though it probably deserves one.

Maurice was the first Franciscan to see in Friar John Duns Scotus an emblem for Irish intellectual achievement. The Franciscan school of Louvain and Rome in the seventeenth century regarded Scotus as their inspiration and Maurice as their fountainhead. In fairness, it was not simply misguided of them to regard Scotus as being of Irish origin, for the evidence linking him definitively to Scotland was not available during the medieval and early modern periods but was strengthened and placed beyond all possible doubt only in the nineteenth and twentieth centuries.[34] For the Irish Franciscans, such as McCawell and Wadding, in religious exile in post-Reformation Europe, to have Duns Scotus as the acknowledged fountainhead of their intellectual tradition (both national and Franciscan) was more than a source of pride, it was an important reference point for the new religious nationalism which they were promoting, amidst the disasters that were the everyday news reaching them from their country. They looked back to Mauritius Hibernicus as the originator of the school which they themselves were constructing. Brian Scott has paid Friar Maurice a handsome tribute: 'Like FitzRalph before him, [he remains] a shining example of an Irishman who integrated fully with the intellectual life of Europe at its highest and most rarefied level.'[35]

CONCLUSION

The surviving writings which can be classed as Irish contributions to the Scholastic movement are all related to academic settings outside the island itself. There are reasons for this. In the first place the cathedrals of Ireland do not appear to have developed a reliable system of higher education in the way they were meant to do. The religious and mendicant orders were more active and systematic in this regard, being bound to implement the constitutions laid down centrally for all their provinces to follow. Lectors were appointed to teach theology in each Dominican and Franciscan convent, and the brightest students were sent on to a *studium generale* of their order, often linked to a university and its degree awards. A higher *studium* was to be maintained by each province of the mendicant orders; the Franciscans for instance maintained such institutions at Galway and Drogheda; the Augustinian hermits made similar arrangements, as did the Dominicans. The Cistercians were actually required to have a *studium* in each monastery and to provide university education for chosen students. The

---

34 All the evidence was authoritatively reviewed by Charles Balić OFM, *John Duns Scotus: some reflections on the occasion of the seventh centenary of his birth* (Rome, 1966).   35 Scott, 'Latin learning', p. 964.

extent to which the different orders implemented their constitutional requirements is in some cases open to doubt. But in any case attendance at a university
meant Irish-born students leaving their country for England, France or Italy, the
efforts several times repeated to found a university in Ireland having resulted in
failure.[36]

In 1312 Pope Clement V gave permission to John Lech, the archbishop of
Dublin, to found 'a university, a corporation of scholars and a *studium generale* in
all permitted branches of learning and faculties.'[37] The institution was actually
set up by the next archbishop, Alexander de Bicknor, in 1320 and produced a few
graduates in theology and canon law. It seems to have faded way, and an attempt
made in 1358 to revive it proved unsuccessful.[38] A petition to the pope from
priests in Ireland complained in 1363 of the absence of any university institution
in the country, and Richard FitzRalph deplored the disadvantage under which
Irish students laboured, of having to seek further education across the sea. Later
attempts to found a university in Drogheda (1465) and Dublin (1475) produced
no result.[39] The negative consequences of the absence of any *studium generale*
included the lack of a suitable academic forum for intellectual discussion of a
kind that might crystallise in legal, philosophical or theological writings. The
same failure also entailed a relative disadvantage for the Gaelic Irish regarding
access to higher education, and the near monopoly in institutional terms of the
religious orders. France and southern Italy were regions where someone of
Norman descent leaving Ireland to study could adapt himself with some ease;
Peter of Ireland would seem likely to have been in this category. As we have seen,
Irish-born English speakers made it to Oxford University from *c*.1250 onwards.
But it would be another century or so before Gaelic-speakers would take the
same path in some numbers. Once they found their way to Oxford they established a well-trodden career path for clerics intending to qualify themselves in
order to return to their country with a view to preferment in the Church. Many
of the latter became bishops in the fifteenth century.

Ireland contributed to Europe a small number of scholars each of whom was
distinguished for some published achievement, as we have indicated. In this

36 Aubrey Gwynn SJ broke new ground with his article on 'The medieval university of St
Patrick's, Dublin', *Studies* 27 (1938), 199–212; 437–54. See also Fergal McGrath, *Education in
ancient and medieval Ireland* (Dublin, 1978), and A.B. Scott, 'Latin learning', pp 937–9.
37 Scott, 'Latin learning', p. 937. 38 'Money, leadership and scholarship all seemed to be
lacking…all that is known of Dublin in this period suggests that it would have been primarily an
Anglo-Irish institution and this very likely was another factor in its failure to take root': John
Watt, *The Church in medieval Ireland*, The Gill History of Ireland (Dublin, 1972), p. 129. 39
On the politically-inspired restrictions placed on Irishmen going to 'the scooles of Oxford
Cambridge or els where' (1410), 'of whom some were lieges of the king, but others were enemies
to him and his kingdom called wylde Irishmen' (1422), see Art Cosgrove, in id. (ed.), 'England
and Ireland, 1399–1447' in *A new history of Ireland*, ii, *Medieval Ireland 1189–1534*, 525–32 (in
particular, pp 528–9).

regard it was comparable to other marginal countries and regions of Western Europe such as Denmark (*Dacia*) and Portugal. The academic links and pathways forged by its scholars helped Ireland to overcome in some measure its geographical marginality and isolation, but the island proved unable to make itself self-sufficient regarding the provision of higher education for Church teachers and administrators.

APPENDIX

The names of writers connected with Ireland before AD 1540, as identified by Professor Richard Sharpe (in alphabetical order)

Adam Payne
Adomnan
Aethicus Ister
Aileran Sapiens
Albinus O'Molloy
'Animosus'
Cathulf
Celestine the Irishman
Cellanus of Péronne
Chilienus
Clemens Scottus
Cogitosus
Colmán (two)
Columba
Columbanus (two)
Conchubranus
Cruidmáel
Cú Chuimne
Cummianus (three)
David O'Bugey
David Scottus
Diarmait
Dícuil
Dionysius of Ireland
Donatus (two)
Dub Dúin
Dub Innse
Dubthach
Duncan the Irishman
Dunchad
Dungal of Pavia
Electus Scottigena
Eugenius of Ardmore
Eugenius of Armagh
Frigulus (?Fergil)

Gallus
Gille/Gilbert of Limerick
Gilbert of Oriel
Henry Crumpe
Henry of London (writing on Laurence O'Toole)
Henry of Marlborough
Henry of Sawtry (St Patrick's Purgatory)
Hugh of Ireland
Hugo de Scotia
James Yonge
John Allen
John Colton
John Cumin
John of Darlington
John of Fintona
John Foxholes
John Ireland (not Irish, probably)
Iohannes Scottus Eriugena
Iosephus Scottus
Laidcenn
Mael Ísu
Malachias (two, one of whom wrote the *De venenis*)
Malcalanus
Malsachanus
Marcus of Regensburg
Marianus Scottus (two)
Martin of Laon
Maurice O'Fihely
Michael Scot (not Irish, almost certainly)

Michael Tregury
Mo-sinu Moccu
Muiredach
Murchad O'Briain
St Patrick
Patrick Cullen
Patrick of Ireland
Peter of Ireland
Philip Flattisbury
Philip Norreys
Philip of Slane
Probus
Ralph of Bristol
Ralph Kelly
Richard FitzRalph
Richard Kenmore
Richard Ledrede
Robert Worksop
Ruben of Dairinis
Secundinus
Sedulius (two)
Simon of Ireland
    ?=Simon Simeonis OFM
Stephen Dexter
Stephen of Lexington
Thomas Colby
Thomas Cranley
Thomas Fich
Thomas of Ireland (two)
Thomas Kelly (?)
Thomas Radcliff
Thomas Scottus
Thomas Scrope of Bradley
Tírechán

Ultan
Vinnian
Virgil of Salzburg
Walter Jorz

William of Drogheda
William of Hotham (a
Yorkshireman)
William of Montoriel

William of Paull (bishop)
William of Pembridge

Scholars, schools and Scholasticism: aspects of the Irish language and medieval learning

RUAIRÍ Ó HUIGINN

From its beginning and throughout much of its early history, written literature in Irish has been associated with Christianity and with Latin. When Christianity arrived is a moot point. Tradition holds that a Briton named Patricius who was active in the second third of the fifth century was the first missionary. This perception, however, is probably due to later development of the Patrick legend and its propagation at the hands of Armagh clerics.[1] The truth, not that we can ever hope to recover it in its entirety, is somewhat more complex. It is true that the evangelisation of Ireland was brought about by British clerics, one or more of whom was called Patricius. According to a celebrated entry in Prosper's Chronicle for the year 431, Pope Celestine sent the bishop Palladius to minister to the *Scotti in Christum credentes*, giving to understand that there were already Christians in Ireland prior to this date. Elements of Irish tradition would support such an understanding.

Be it in the fourth or the fifth century, the introduction of Christianity to Ireland represented a major cultural revolution. This is true not only when we consider the establishment of a new religion to the apparent exclusion of others, but also when we look at the effect it had on many aspects of society as can be seen from the archaeological and literary records.[2] With regard to the former, the Christian imprint on the physical landscape of Ireland is appreciably greater than that of the invading or colonizing Celtic peoples who had arrived sometime in the first millennium BC. In a short space of time the new religion had taken root in the country. In its wake it brought a new language, Latin, and a new form of technology, writing. It exposed the Irish people to the heritage that was part and parcel of Christianity and to a new world of learning in which the Bible was central. Learning and its cultivation was carried out in monasteries or larger monastic cities, which now began to proliferate and dot the landscape quite densely. The extent of this proliferation has been demonstrated by NUI Maynooth's *Monasticon Hibernicum* project which now has identified some 5,500

---

1 On the question of St Patrick and Patrician legends, see D.A. Binchy, 'St Patrick and his biographers: ancient and modern', *Studia Hibernica* 2 (1962), 7–173. 2 See J. Carney, 'The impact of Christianity' in Myles Dillon (ed.), *Early Irish society* (Dublin, 1954), pp 66–78.

sites in the literary or archaeological record in the period down to AD 1200.[3] Many of these sites were in their time outstanding centres of learning, centres that housed monastic *scriptoria* or workshops for the production of religious artefacts wrought from precious metals.

The Irish took to the introduction of Christianity and its culture quite readily. In a brief period of time, the Latin alphabet had been adapted for use in Irish, and from a relatively early period texts in the vernacular begin to appear. What is accepted by many to be the earliest continuous work in Irish, *Amra Cholaim Chille*, is believed to have been written shortly after the death in AD 597 of St Colum Cille, whom it eulogizes.[4] This and other early texts such as the *Aibgitir Chrábuid* 'The Alphabet of Piety'[5] – written in quite a different style - show a developed and highly wrought literary language and one that evidently was being worked at for some time.

Down to the ecclesiastical reform of the twelfth century, learning in the form of the written word was conducted in the *scriptoria* of monastic settlements; for corresponding lay centres in the earlier period we have no clear evidence. The content of these monastic writings was multifarious. Apart from material of a devotional or overtly religious nature, we have annals, works on computistics, laws, histories, sagas and a host of other works, transmitted to us monolingually in Latin, later in Irish, or sometimes bilingually in a mixture of both. From the twelfth century down to the fall of the Irish nobility and the conquest of Ireland in the early seventeenth century, much native learning was carried out in non-ecclesiastical centres by learned families who enjoyed the patronage of local chieftains.

Looking at the extent of this literature, some would draw a divide between religious and secular material, and it has been argued that much of the secular material reflects native non-Christian learning taken from oral tradition. While there may be some truth in this, the division between types of learning may be more apparent than real. History, and in particular biblical history, was central to much of what was carried out in the monasteries. The world outlined in the Old Testament was a world in which Ireland did not exist, and between the sixth and the eleventh centuries much intellectual effort and imagination was expended in attempting to graft an Irish branch onto the tree of world history through the creation of legends and genealogies which formed an Irish prehistory that was connected to the world of the Bible.[6] The writing of sagas, and of origin legends, while they may contain elements of oral tradition, can also be seen as part of this process insofar as they are frequently fixed to or synchronized with important

---

3 On the *Monasticon* see A. Mac Shamhráin, 'The "Monasticon Hibernicum Project": a research tool for early and medieval ecclesiastical settlement in Ireland', *Monastic Research Bulletin* 14 (forthcoming).   4 Ed. W. Stokes, *Revue celtique* 20 (1899); 21 (1900).   5 Ed. V. Hull, *Celtica* 8 (1968), 44–89.   6 On the question of Irish 'synthetic' history, see J. Kelleher, 'Early Irish history and pseudo-history', *Studia Hibernica* 3 (1963), 113–27.

events in the annals of Christendom. Some of these traditions may well reflect elements of pre-Christian Irish tradition preserved orally, but it certainly came into being as literature written in monasteries under the influence of Christian learning.

Works, then, in Irish and in Latin were being produced in such centres of learning. Interestingly, however, the fate of material transmitted to us in each language was markedly different. While we have a considerable body of early material in Latin that was written by Irishmen, no all-Irish manuscript can be dated to earlier than the twelfth century. One important reason for this was that material in Irish was strictly for domestic consumption; manuscript written in that language were used and re-used and, when worn out, were copied and discarded. Material found in the earliest surviving all-Irish manuscripts, therefore, frequently represent the latest stage in a process of copying that had been in progress for many centuries beforehand and continued for many centuries afterwards. The earliest copy we have of the famous *Amra Cholaim Chille*, for instance, is found in the twelfth-century *Lebor na hUidre* (LU), a manuscript some five centuries removed from the probable time of this text's composition. Many other texts dateable on linguistic or contextual grounds to the seventh or eighth centuries are found in manuscripts of even later date than LU.

Of Latin manuscripts on the other hand we have many survivals from the earliest period, and indeed, were it not for the depredations of the seventeenth century, we would certainly have preserved many more.[7] Survival may in many instances be due to no more than chance; witness the discovery in 2006 of an eighth-century psalter in the Faddenmore Bog in Co. Tipperary. There were two other factors, however, that contributed to the preservation of Latin manuscripts. One concerns the nature of what they contained. Copies of the gospels, psalms and other material was not the type of work that would be changed linguistically or updated, so to speak, as frequently was the case with texts in Irish. A more important reason is the simple fact that many manuscripts were not kept in Ireland, but were brought at an early stage to continental Europe where they entered the libraries of the various Irish houses that were to become a feature of Europe in the Dark Ages, and there remained.

Among experts such as yourselves it is not my place to attempt to list or evaluate the contributions made by the many Irish *magistri* to philosophical thought and Scholasticism at this time.[8] What I have tried to do is to outline some elements of the cultural and learned background from which these

7 On this point see Donnchadh Ó Corráin, 'Cad d'imigh ar lámhscríbhinní na hÉireann?', *Oidhreacht na Lámhscríbhinní. Léachtaí Cholm Cille* 34 (2004), 7–27.   8 On this question see John J. Contreni, 'The Irish contribution to the European classroom', in D. Ellis Evans, John J. Griffith and E.M. Jope (eds), *Proceedings of the Seventh International Congress of Celtic Studies* (Oxford, 1986), pp 79–90.

peregrini came, and it is important to remember that for all their accomplishment in Latin, Irish was their mother tongue and was the language spoken among them. As a medium for textual expression, however, it took second place to Latin, the *lingua franca* in the intellectual world in which they now moved. The original works of masters such as Iohannes Scottus Eriugena or Sedulius Scottus were naturally geared towards an audience wider than the confines of their respective communities, and therefore were effected in Latin.

The degree to which these scholars immersed themselves in continental culture and learning may be hinted at by the form their nomenclature took. While many bore well-attested native Irish names such as Dungal, Dicuil and Murethach, others seem to have adopted common names of Christianity such as Iohannes, Martinus and Petrus, a nomenclature that is almost totally absent from the Irish pre-Norman genealogies. Despite such immersion in Latinity and its learning, Irish was not entirely absent from their work. In many cases, commentary and gloss appear in bilingual form; the text of the Pauline Epistles now found in the Stadtbibliothek of Würzburg contains a considerable amount of glosses and commentary in Irish that can be dated to the mid-eighth century.[9] An even greater body of such material appears in the Milan text of the psalms from roughly AD 800,[10] and a ninth-century text of Priscian's grammar found in the St Gall Stiftsbibliothek contains many Irish glosses and marginalia, including some Old Irish poetry.[11] Smaller collections of glosses on Priscian and on other texts are found in a number of other continental libraries. The presence of a small but significant number of such Old Irish glosses in the hand of Eriugena himself[12] serves again to remind us of his own linguistic background and formation.

Yet for all the evidence of Irish being the language of communication and quite possibly that of instruction among such émigré Irish communities, it is clear that its place in the intellectual world outside their immediate milieu was negligible. This is not to say, however, that the worlds of Scholastic and of Irish learning remained separate. There are a number of points where they intersect, two of which will concern us here.

We have mentioned the presence of Irish glosses in the St Gall copy of Priscian's grammar. This is in fact but one of a number of copies of this text that bears such glosses; similarly but far less extensively glossed copies are found, for instance, in libraries in Milan, Karslruhe and Leyden[13] and are testament to the

---

9 Ed. Stokes and Strachan, *Thesaurus Palaeohibernicus* (1901), i, 499–712.   10 Ed. Stokes and Strachan, *Thesaurus Palaeohibernicus* (1901), i, 7–483.   11 The Old Irish glosses are edited in Stokes and Strachan, *Thesaurus Palaeohibernicus* (1903), ii, 49–224; the poetry has been edited ibid. p. 290. See also R. Hoffman, *The Sankt Gall Priscian commentary* (Münster, 1996).   12 On this see *John Scottus Eriugena. Glossae Divinae Historiae. The biblical glosses of John Scottus Eriugena*, edited with an Introduction by John J. Contreni and Pádraig P. Ó Néill (Florence, 1997), pp 40ff.   13 Cf. Stokes and Strachan, *Thesaurus Palaeohibernicus* (1901), ii, pp xxiv, 225–32.

interest the Irish showed in a central area of Scholastic learning, namely, the study of language itself.

It has been pointed out that this interest in language may have developed through the manner in which the Irish had to confront and learn Latin. Unlike Britain, there was no sizeable community of Latin speakers in Ireland from which Irishmen might learn the language. In the absence of such a community, they were obliged to make use of written works, from which grew an interest in the nature of language itself. Some evidence of this can be seen in the manner in which Latin loanwords and terms were adopted into Irish. As can be expected, there was extensive borrowing of terms that had to do with concepts or objects unknown in Ireland prior to the introduction of Christianity. It is true that there was a native inherited pre-Christian religious vocabulary comprising words such as *Dia* 'a god', *anam* 'soul', *coimdiu* 'lord', *dúlem* 'creator', *creidim* 'I believe' etc. that could be 'recycled' for use in the new context of Christianity.[14] Terms specific to Christianity, however, had to be borrowed and this was done in accordance with the sound-laws of Irish at that time. Thus, while the different phonological systems of Irish and Latin resulted in early borrowings such as *Patricius* being rendered in Irish as *Cothraige*,[15] increasing familiarity with the sound-system of the new language and assimilation of once unfamiliar sounds into Irish gives us a later and more recognizable *Pátraic* (modern *Pádraig*).[16] Borrowing, which took place over the course of a number of centuries, was not solely restricted to Christianity and its vocabulary but also is used with terms connected with other spheres of life, where the Latin term in all probability denoted a new concept or object or one that was different or superior to the native: e.g. *Cásc* 'Easter' (< *Pascha*), *cruimther* 'priest' (< *presbyter*), *sacart* 'priest' (< *sacerdos*), *oifrend* 'Mass' (< *offerenda*), *bendacht* 'blessing' (<*benedictio*), *ponc* 'point' (< *punctum*), *scríbaid* 'writes' (< *scribere*), *fín* 'wine' (< *vinum*), as did a host of other words.

Beside borrowing, however, we also witness another and a more learned manner of adopting Latin words into Irish. This is through the process of calquing whereby an Irish word that approximates in meaning to the concept embodied by a Latin word is used. As might be expected, such calques are frequently to be found in grammatical terminology, but also occur elsewhere. For example, Ir. *tuisel* 'a falling' > 'a grammatical case' renders the Latin *casus* (<

14 The fact that *dia* and *creidim* were cognates of Latin *Deus* and *credo*, to which they bore a strong resemblance, was obviously an important factor in their being used in the new context. 15 Among other features the form *Cothraige* reflects the fact that Irish did not have a phoneme corresponding to the p-sound of Latin. Accordingly, though a process of phoneme substitution, it used the native sound felt to be closest to it, in this case /k/. 16 It should be remembered that as Latin was introduced to Ireland by British missionaries, it had already been influenced by the sound system of British Celtic. On the question of Latin borrowings into Irish see D. McManus, 'A chronology of the Latin loan-words in early Irish', *Ériu* 34 (1983), 21–71.

cadere 'to fall'). A more complex and sophisticated form of calque involves segmenting a Latin word and translating its constituent parts into Irish. These constituents are then 'reassembled', giving us an Irish term. Thus, *remsuidigiud* 'preposition' represents the Irish prefix *rem* 'before' and the verbal noun *suidigiud* 'placing', rendering the constituents of Latin *praepositio*; *comaccomal* 'conjunction', consisting of *com* 'together, with' and *accomal* 'joining', calques Latin *conjunctio*; *ranngabál*, consisting of *rann* 'part' and *gabál* 'taking' renders *participio*. *Imdibe* 'circumcision' is made up of *imm* 'around' and *dibe*, the verbal noun of *do-ben* 'cuts away'. Irish *briathar* 'word' translates *verbum*, but then comes to be used in other senses of the Latin word; it acquires the meaning '(grammatical) verb', and in the form *dobriathar*, with the prefix *do* 'to', serves to calque the Latin *adverbium*.

Calquing was not confined to glosses on Latin material. It has been shown that it is a strategy widely used in other contexts, not least certain sections of the Old Irish laws. Formerly held to be the product of a pre-Christian oral tradition, it has been demonstrated that some law-texts translate material taken from Irish canon law and rendered in a high and somewhat arcane register. As part of that process, certain Latin terms are calqued in Irish.[17]

Be it for the purposes of glossing or for the composition of texts, such a process evidently demanded a degree of linguistic awareness and sophistication. This most probably had been cultivated through the act of learning Latin from works such as those of Priscian or Donatus with which the Irish were acquainted at an early stage.[18] The Irish in turn produced Latin grammars of their own, such as the *Ars aspori* for use in their schools. Of similar tracts in Irish, however, we know only of one, the *Auraicept na nÉces* 'The Scholar's Primer', a brief tract on Irish grammar, which was compiled not later than the eighth century but which subsequently was to grow significantly through a process of accretion.[19] The *Auraicept* comprises a learned discussion and classification of some features of Irish grammar based on a Latin model. It is not a practical textbook; such a work would most probably have been superfluous. Its intellectual context more likely lies in the interest the Irish had developed in language in general and, just as they had laboured to establish for their traditions and for themselves a place in the scheme of world history as reflected in the Bible, they sought to extend to their own language the scholarly attention lavished on Latin and Greek.

While the works of Priscian and Donatus clearly were prominent in Irish libraries, another writing that made its way to the country proved to be highly significant. This was the first book of Isidore of Seville's *Etymologiae*, which was

17 See L. Breatnach, 'Canon law and secular law in early Ireland: the significance of *Bretha Nemed*', *Peritia* 3 (1984), 439–59. 18 On this see V. Law, *The insular Latin grammarians* (Woodbridge, 1982), p. 21. 19 Text and commentaries have been edited by G. Calder in *Auraicept na nÉces: The Scholars' Primer* (Edinburgh, 1917); the canonical text has been edited by A. Ahlqvist in *The early Irish linguist* (Helsinki, 1982)

known in Irish as the *Cuilmen* (< Lat. *culmen* 'summit'), and seems to have reached Ireland not long after its appearance in 636.[20] The extent of the influence this work was to have on certain aspects of Irish learning is hard to quantify, but the methodology Isidore employed therein, in looking at the various possibilities for segmenting words and providing etymologies for their constituents, is credited to a large extent with having introduced a similar approach to Irish, an approach that is evident not only in glosses on Latin or Irish texts, but also in glossaries such as Cormac mac Cuilleanáin's (d. AD 908) *Sanas Cormaic*[21] or the somewhat later *Cóir Anmann*,[22] a tract that which deals with the origins of certain Irish names.[23]

Isidorean etymologies were not confined to compilations of this kind, but are found throughout early Irish literature. The Irish law texts, for instance, were subject to extensive glossing whereby archaic or obscure words were furnished with etymologies which purported to explain their meaning or origin. More often than not, this etymologizing was quite speculative and the information contained in the gloss bears little relationship to the true meaning or etymology of the word in the text. Yet this practice was to give expression to a creative force which had a considerable impact on literature during the Middle (AD *c*.900–1200) and Early Modern Irish (*c*.1200–1650) periods. An aspect of etymology that held a fascination for the Irish was its application in the field of onomastics. *Cóir Anmann* 'The fitness of names', to which we have previously alluded, subjects the names of various figures of Irish mythology to etymological analysis on Isidorean lines, and several possible etymologies are suggested for each. To take an example: Fer Diad, foster-brother of Cú Chulainn, the great hero of the Ulster Cycle of tales, has his name thus etymologized: *Fear Diad .i. fer-niad .i. fer tren nó clama. Nam nia tren. Nó Fear Diad .i. fer da iath .i. comracc da ferund rod n-uccad. Is airi tuccad Fer Diad fair* ('Fer Diad, i.e. a warrior, i.e. a strong or brave man. For *nia* means warrior. Or Fer Diad, i.e. a man of two lands, i.e. he was born at the border of two territories').[24] Somewhat more pervasive was the application of this science to place-names. *Dindsenchas* 'the lore of places', while always prominent in Irish literature, was to prove a very productive feature during this later period. Thus, the Irish name of the royal centre of Tara, *Temair* (Modern *Teamhair*), is segmented as a compound of a (supposed) personal name *Tea* and the noun *múr* 'a rampart' (< Lat. *murus*). According to this legend, Téa is held to be a legendary queen, the daughter of a certain Lugaid

20 On the identification of the *Cuilmen* with Isidore's *Etymologiae*, see T. Ó Máille, 'The authorship of the Culmen', *Ériu* 9 (1921–3) 71–6. 21 *Sanas Cormaic: an Old Irish glossary*, ed. W. Stokes, in *Anecdota from Irish manuscripts* 4 (Halle, 1912). 22 'Cóir Anmann', ed. W. Stokes *Irische Texte* 3 pt. 2 (Leipzig, 1897), pp 285–444; *Cóir Anmann: a late Middle Irish treatise on personal names* (Part 1), ed. S. Arbuthnot, Irish Texts Society 59 (London, 2005). 23 For a brief discussion of Isidore's approach to etymology see R. Baumgarten, 'A Hiberno-Isidorian etymology', *Peritia* 2 (1983), 225–8. 24 *Cóir Anmann*, ed. Arbuthnot, pp 128, 144.

son of Íth. This etymology underlies alternative designations of Temair, such as *Múr Téa* or *Ráith* ('dwelling') *Téa*, found elsewhere in the literature.

Apart from the long tracts of poetry and prose that comprise the compilatory *Dindsenchas Érenn*,[25] the literary possibilities presented by the etymological analysis of place-names are exploited throughout a host of texts, including *Táin Bó Cúailnge* and *Acallam na Senórach*, the centrepieces of the Ulster and Fenian Cycles respectively. To attribute all such onomastic etymologizing to the influence of Isidore would probably be overstating the case. It is possible that in Ireland, as in other countries, a native tradition of folk etymology existed, and this may have contributed to the acceptance, development, and profound influence this aspect of continental learning had on Irish literature.

At the time works such as *Dindsenchas Érenn* were first being compiled, a fundamental change was taking place in the organisation of Irish learning. Church reform in the twelfth century led to the ecclesiastical centres, which hitherto had served as centres of literary production, now being used solely for religious purposes. As a result, the preservation and production of literature fell to certain families for whom the cultivation of different branches of learning became a hereditary profession. Enjoying the patronage of local potentates, such learned families provided professional services for their patrons and maintained schools for training their members in the branch of learning which was their calling.

A prominent branch of learning was medicine. Our information on Irish medical practice before the twelfth century is not extensive and is taken mainly from two lawtracts, *Bretha Crólige* 'Judgments on sick-maintenance'[26] and *Bretha Déin Cécht* 'The judgements of Dian Cécht'[27] which are concerned primarily with questions of liability for causing injury to another and the proper course to be followed in restoring the injured party to health. No medical textbooks as such have survived from this earlier period, and we are unclear as to how the practice of medicine would then have been organised. Following the changes of the twelfth century, however, we find this branch of learning being pursued by a number of learned families serving local chieftains in different parts of the country. Prominent among them were surnames such as Ó Caiside, (the Cassidys, hereditary medics to the Maguires of Fermanagh), Ó Duinnshléibhe (the Dunlevys/Livingstones who served the O'Donnells of Donegal), Ó hÍceadha (the Hickeys, medics to the O'Briens of Thomond), Ó Siadhail (the (O') Shiels who served the MacMahons of south Ulster), Ó Laidhigh (the Lees,

---

25 E.J. Gwynn (ed.), *The Metrical Dindshenchas: text, translation, and commentary*, 5 Parts (Dublin, 1903–35. Todd Lecture Series, 8–12); W. Stokes, 'The prose tales in the Rennes *Dindshenchas*', *Revue celtique* 15 (1894), 272–336, 418–84; 16 (1895), 31–83, 135–67, 269–312. **26** '*Bretha Crólige*', ed. and trans. D.A. Binchy, *Ériu* 12 (1934), 1–77; id. 'Sick maintenance in Irish law', *Ériu* 12 (1934), 78–134. **27** '*Bretha Déin Chécht*', ed. and trans. D.A. Binchy, *Ériu* 20 (1966), 1–66.

hereditary physicians to the O'Flahertys of West Connacht), and others such as Ó Nialláin (Neylon), Ó Ceanndubháin (Canavan), Ó Bolguidhe and Ó Callanáin (Callanan). Nor were such medical families unknown in Gaelic Scotland: Mac an Leagha (McKinlay), and Mac an Bheatha (Macbeth, Beaton etc.) were prominent practitioners in the eastern part of the Gaelic world. Some of these surnames reflect the hereditary profession of the bearer, e.g. Ó Íceadha (< Ícaidh 'healer'), Mac an Leagha (< Liaigh 'leech'), Mac an Bheatha (< Beatha 'life').[28]

From the schools such families maintained have been transmitted to us a sizeable number of medical manuscripts dating from the fifteenth to the seventeenth centuries. The texts these manuscripts contain do not belong to a native tradition of medical teaching, but are works that were translated or adapted from Latin. As such they reflect the medico-philosophical teaching of European schools such as those of Montpellier, Salerno or Bologna, some of which had attracted members of Irish medical families to their doors. Classical medical teaching mediated through Arab channels was the staple on the curricula in these schools and represented a form of medicine with a strong philosophical orientation.

Works emanating from this background that were rendered into Irish include *Rosa Anglica*, the medical textbook of the Englishman John of Gadesden,[29] Lanfranc's *Chrirurgia Magna*,[30] and the *Regimen Sanitatis* by Magninus of Milan.[31] The quality and nature of these Irish translations vary. Beside accurate rendition of the Latin into Irish we find cases where passages of the original text seem to have been misunderstood and are rendered incorrectly.[32] In other cases the Latin text has been adapted rather than translated verbatim, while some other works represent compilations garnered from different sources. The language used in these works is Early Modern Irish. Irish equivalents for the many technical terms found the original texts are used where possible, but in numerous cases the absence of any native term, especially for what in Ireland or Britain would be considered the exotic ingredients of medical remedies, results

---

28 For a discussion of medical scholars, schools and texts in the later medieval period see A. Ní Dhonnchadha, 'Medical writing in Irish 1400–1700', in J.B. Lyons (ed.), *Two thousand years of Irish medicine* (Dublin, 1999), pp 21–6; F.J. Shaw, 'Medieval medico-philosophical treatises in the Irish language' in J. Ryan (ed.), *Féil-Sgríbhinn Eóin Mhic Néill* (Dublin, 1940), pp 144–57; 'Irish medical men and philosophers' in B. Ó Cuív (ed.), *Seven centuries of Irish learning 1000–1700* (2nd edn, Cork, 1971), pp 75–87. 29 *Rosa Anglica*, ed. W. Wulff, Irish Texts Society, 25 (London, 1929). Wulff describes the original text as 'a hotch-potch of medical teaching, genuine or fabulous results of the application of remedies, oriental leechcraft and superstition, native English cures and charms, prayers and religious practices, interwoven with native beliefs of the people at different periods and the different parts of the country' (p.xvii). 30 Ed. W. Wulff, 'On the qualitees, maners and kunynge of a surgeon etc.', *Zeitschrift für celtische Philologie* 18 (1930) 249–86. 31 *Regimen na sláinte* ed. S. Ó Ceithearnaigh 3 vols. (Dublin, 1942–4). 32 See, for instance, *Regimen na sláinte* xvii–xviii.

in wholesale borrowing; or sometimes the Latin term is used without any accommodation to the Irish sound system.

The popularity some of these translations enjoyed is attested to by their
appearance in more than one manuscript witness. However, the practical
relevance that the teaching contained in such texts had in late medieval Ireland
is a matter of some debate. Besides advice on the treatment of ailments and
philosophical reflection on the nature of illness and health, quite a number of
dietary and herbal remedies require ingredients not native to Ireland and this
reflects the fact that the texts were composed in the warmer climes of southern
Europe.[33] This raises the question of the practical application of remedies which
would have required such material. It has been suggested that native plants or
herbs having similar medicinal properties might have been substituted for the
more exotic requirements ordained by medical texts. [34] This may certainly have
been possible in many cases, but one might expect that such practical information of no small significance to native medics would be incorporated in some
manner, be it in the translated text or by means of marginal glosses. The extent,
if any, to which such substitution may be indicated within medical texts cannot
be established until all these translations have been edited and published, a task
that is still in progress.[35]

In contrast to the so-called 'Golden Age' of Irish , when Irish scholars, played
a leading role and made a substantial contribution to European philosophical
debate through the medium of Latin, the late medieval period has been characterized as one of intellectual marginalization, as inward-looking men of learning
turned more to their own language.[36] It is true that the Irish contribution to the
European academy during this period declined significantly, but the evidence of
the medical texts shows no small degree of engagement with continental
learning, even if the Irish were accepting wholesale a philosophy and teaching
that was developed and refined elsewhere. Exempla and other religious material,
of which we have many translations into Irish, likewise testify to this
engagement. In time this was to result in a new flowering of Irish learning in the
writings of Counter-Reformation scholars such as Aodh Mac Aingil (Hugo
Cavellus) and Flaithrí Ó Maoil Chonaire (Florence Conry), who, like their illustrious forebears, wrote from seats of learning on the Continent. Ironically, this
late flowering took place just as the Tudor and Stewart conquest and
colonization was to bring the curtain down on late medieval learning in Ireland.

---

33 One course of medicine for pregnant women, for instance, has as a requirement roast oranges
and aloes; cf. *Regimen na sláinte* ll. 2367–9.   34 Wulff, *Rosa Anglica*, xxxviii.   35 The status and
respect accorded the medical families and their texts survived into modern folkore. An interesting
tradition which purports to tell how the Ó Laidhigh (Lee) family of Galway came into possession
of the celebrated 'Book of the Lees' is discussed by T. Ó Con Cheanainn 'Seanchas ar Mhuintir
Laidhe', *Éigse* 33 (2002) 179–226.   36 D. Ó Cróinín, *Early medieval Ireland, 400–1200* (New
York, 1995), p. 232.

Punch's riposte: the Irish contribution to early modern Scotism from Maurice O'Fihely OFMConv. to Anthony Rourke OFMObs.

M.W.F. STONE

Pro Scoto viriliter pugnandum, acrius decertandum, nervosius scribendum duco, in cuius nomine tota periclitatur Religio.

Luke Wadding[1]

In 1660 a diminutive and seemingly unassuming tome was published in Paris bearing the title *Scotus Hiberniae restitutus*.[2] The fact that so many other slender and more ample volumes were published in Paris that same year, did not lessen the impact of this potent little work, especially since the author was a celebrated Franciscan friar from Cork, John Punch (1599 or 1603–72/3),[3] who was known throughout Europe by his Latin name Poncius.[4] By the time that Punch's

1 Luke Wadding, *Annales Minorum*, ad. an. 1308, n. 71, VI (1931), p. 157: 'For Scotus, one should, in my opinion, struggle robustly, fight with force and write with vigor, since in his name [our] entire order is in the balance (lit. 'danger' = *periclitatur*).' 2 Joannes Hyacinthi Sbaralea, *Supplementum et Castigatio ad Scriptores trium ordinum S. Francisci*, 3 vols (Rome, 1921), ii, 118, quoting Joannes a San Antonio, *Bibliotheca Universa Franciscana*, 3 vols (Madrid, 1732), ii, 206, gives no indication of the book's size although he states that its was an octavo volume. In fact, it was a substantial little volume of more than 153 pages and an index in unpaginated form. The book contained the approbation of Edouard Tirel (fl. 1635),who was then superior of the Irish college (then a somewhat notional institution) in Paris. 3 There seems to be a good deal of confusion about the year of Punch's death. Most scholars give 1672–73, following the view of Geoffrey Cleary, *Father Luke Wadding and St Isidore's College* (Rome, 1925), p. 86; see Maurice Grajewski OFM, 'John Ponce, Franciscan Scotist of the Seventeenth Century', *Franciscan Studies* 6 (1946), 54–92, and most recently, Terry Clavin, 'Punch, John', *ODNB* (2004), pp 561–2. However, there is a good evidence to suggest that Punch might have died as early as 26 May 1661 in the Observant convent in Paris, and that he was buried there in the cloister. This can be established in the necrology, based on the *Archives Nationales* (series LL 1598-LL 1527A), published by J. Poulenc, 'Deux registres de religieux décédés au grand couvent de Paris au XVIIe siècle', *Archivum Franciscanum Historicum* 59 (1966), 323–84, see p. 344 for Punch. I am grateful to Jacob Schmutz for this information. 4 For the most recent attempt to set down the bare details of Punch's life and career see Terry Clavin, 'Punch, John'. See also Luke Wadding, *Scriptores Ordinis Minorum* (Nardecchia, ed.) (Rome, 1906), pp 149–50; San Antonio, *Bibliotheca*, ii, 205–6; Sbaralea, *Supplementum*, ii, 118; Geoffrey Cleary, *Father Luke Wadding and St Isidore's College Rome* (Rome, 1925), pp 83–6; and A. Teetaert, 'Ponce, Jean', *Dictionnaire de théologie catholique*, xii.2 (1935), cols. 2546–8. Among other achievements, Punch is also credited with the modern

opusculum was paraded before the cognoscenti, he was judged to be a theologian of international standing having made notable contributions to Scholastic thought in his *Philosophiae cursus integer* of 1643,[5] and *Cursus theologicus ad mentem Scoti* of 1652.[6] Punch had also secured for himself a reputation in Irish circles as a political controversialist, and his spirited writings in support of the cause of the Catholic Confederation against the wily machinations of the lawyer Richard Bellings (*c.*1605–77),[7] and the pitiable intrigues of the Jansenist John Callaghan (1605–50),[8] won him acclaim and opprobrium in equal measure.[9]

The slight appearance of the *Scotus Hiberniae restitutus* only served to disguise its author's more pointed aims, objectives that became obvious once the tract was prefixed to his 1661 definitive work of Scotist theology, the *Commentarii theologici in IV libros Sententiarum*.[10] Such as it was, Punch's little treatise was a work of principled polemic whose object was nothing less than the comprehensive refutation of its opponent's claims, and the exoneration and vindication of its own robustly stated position. The case that the Irish friar was moved to prosecute was twofold. First and foremost he sought to refute decisively the audacious assertion of an English Franciscan, Angelus a San Francisco (Angelus Mason), (1599–1678),[11] that the renowned medieval theologian John Duns Scotus or the *Doctor Subtilis* (1265/6–1308) had been English rather than Irish,[12] a view which ran contrary to the efforts of several Irish Franciscans, who in the

---

formulation of 'Ockham's Razor' in the Latin phrase: *entia non sunt multiplicanda praeter necessi-tatem*; see W.M. Thorburn, 'The myth of Occam's Razor', *Mind* 27 (1918), 345–53; and A.C. Crombie, *Medieval and early modern Science*, 2 vols (New York, 1959), ii, 30.   5 Poncius, *Philosophiae cursus integer*, 3 vols (Rome, 1643). This work was reproduced in an improved edition at Rome in 1645, and was republished at Paris in 1656, and again at Lyons in 1672, on this occasion with the inclusion of an additional treatise, '*Ethica*'. Punch's philosophy textbook provoked a dispute with the Conventual Franciscan Bartolomeo Mastrius (1602–73). As a result of the critical discussion of his treatise, Punch published at Paris in 1645 a reply to his critics, *Appendix apologetica ad praedictum Cursum*.   6 Poncius, *Cursus theologicus ad mentem Scoti* (Paris, 1652).   7 See Tadhg Ó hAnnracháin, 'Bellings, Richard', *ODNB* 5 (2004), pp 22–4.   8 P.J. Corish, 'John Callaghan and the controversies among the Irish in Paris 1648–1654', *Irish Theological Quarterly* 21 (1954), 32–50; and Thomas O'Connor, *An Irish Jansenist in seventeenth-century France: John Callaghan 1605–1650*, National University of Ireland – The O'Donnell Lecture 2004 (Dublin, 2005).   9 An active agent for the Catholic confederation since his time in Rome in 1640, Punch brought these concerns with him to Paris. His main works of controversy are *Deplorabilis populi Hibernici pro religione, rege et patria status* (Paris, 1651); and *Richardi Bellingi vindiciae eversae* (Paris, 1653). Cleary, *Father Luke Wadding and St Isidore's College Rome*, p. 85, also lists several letters that exist in manuscript. These writings and the context that produced them are discussed by Thomas O'Connor, *Irish Jansenists 1600–1670: religion and politics in Flanders, France, Ireland and Rome* (Dublin, 2008), pp 278–305.   10 Poncius, *Commentarii theologici quibus Ioannis Duns Scoti quaestiones in libros Sententiarum elucidantur et illustrantur*, 4 vols (Paris, 1661), the *Restitutus* can be found at the beginning, see i, cols. 1–39. All references are to this edition.   11 On Mason see San Antonio, *Bibliotheca*, i, 77–8; and Sbaralea, *Supplementum*, i, 44.   12 Angelus a S. Francisco, *Certamen seraphicum provinciae Angliae* (n.p., 1649).

years immediately before Punch's intervention had attempted to prove the long standing contention that Scotus was Irish.[13] Indeed, one of the Cork friar's former associates, the acclaimed hagiographer John Colgan (Séan Mac Colgán), (*c*.1592–1658),[14] had published at Antwerp in 1655 a detailed refutation of Mason's proposals,[15] a work that drew a terse response from the Englishman with the treatise *Apologia pro Scoto Anglo*, published at Douai in 1656.[16] Enervated by poor health, Colgan was unable to continue his dispute with Mason, and with his subsequent death in 1658, it was left to Punch to pick up the gauntlet and continue the valiant fight for Scotus' Irish *patria*.

Further to his cherished aim of claiming the *Doctor Subtilis* for Ireland, Punch's work set itself the task of explaining not only the specific bequest made by Irish Franciscans such as Aodh Mac Aingil or Hugh MacCaughwell (Latinized to Hugo Cavellus) (1571–1626),[17] Luke Wadding (1588–1657),[18] and

13 The evidence for Scotus' *patria* is presented and reviewed by Charles Balić, 'The life and work of John Duns Scotus', in J. Ryan and B. Bonansea (eds), *John Duns Scotus, 1265–1965* (Washington, DC, 1965), pp 1–28, esp. pp 2–14; and *John Duns Scotus: some reflections on the occasion of the seventh centenary of his birth* (Rome, 1966), see esp. pp 5–13, and 14–28. See also Colmán Ó hUallacháin, 'An Chunspóid faoi Dhúchas Duns Scotus', *Galvia* (1956), 30–46, who agrees with the claims of Balić. The Scottish origins of Scotus were well known and reasonably well attested throughout the Middle Ages, the crucial piece of evidence being that he was related to the Duns family of Grueldykes, who were landed gentry of the parish. For a recent attempt to shed some further light on Scotus' origins see Michael Robson, 'The birth-place of Blessed John Duns Scotus: Thomas Gascoigne, a hitherto unnoticed witness', *Miscellanea Francescana* 103 (2003), 703–18. 14 On Colgan's efforts in the field of hagiography see Brendan Jennings, *Mícheál Ó Cléirigh, chief of the Four Masters, and his associates* (Dublin, 1936), pp 175–84; Canice Mooney, 'Fr. John Colgan and the Louvain School', *Donegal Annual*, iv/1 (1958), 1–5; both of which are reprinted in Nollaig Ó Muraíle (ed.), *Mícheál Ó Cléirigh, his associates and St Anthony's College Louvain* (Dublin, 2008). See also Terence O'Donnell (ed.), *Father John Colgan OFM 1592–1658: essays in commemoration of the third century of his death* (Dublin, 1959); and Benignus Millet, *The Irish Franciscans 1651–1665*, Analecta Gregoriana, 129 (Rome, 1964), pp 487–92. 15 John Colgan, *Tractatus de Ioannis Scoti, Doctoris Subtilis theologorumque principis, vita, patria, elogiis encomiasticis, scriptis* (Antwerp, 1655). 16 Richard Angelus a S. Francisco Mason, *Apologia pro Scoto Anglo* (Douai, 1656). 17 The most recent synopsis of Cavellus' life and work can be found in Terry Clavin, 'MacCaughwell, Hugh', *ODNB* 12 (2004), pp 82–3. See also Wadding, *Scriptores*, col. 120; Nicholas Vernulaeus, *Rhetoricum Collegii Porcensis inclitae academiae Lovaniensis Orationum* (Louvain, 1657); and Tomás Ó Clérigh, *Aodh Mac Aingil agus an Scoil Nua-Ghaeilge I Lobháin* (Dublin, 1935; revised edition 1985). Other useful commentary can be found in: A. Goyena Pérez, 'Teólogos extranjeros formados en España: D. Fr. Hugo Cavello (MacCaughwell) Francisco, Arzobispo de Armagh (1571–1626)', *Estudios eclesiásticos* 6 (1927), 38–53, 281–336, esp. pp 281–8; Máirtín Mac Conmara, 'Mac Aingil agus an Scotachas Éireannach', *An Léann Eaglasta in Eireann 1200–1900* (Dublin 1988), pp 61–101; and Michael Dunne, 'Nicholaus Vernulaeus, Aodh MacAingil and the anonymous author from the *Collegium Pastorale*', *Léachtaí Cholmcille* 38 (2008), 151–71. 18 See Ignatius Fennessy, 'Wadding, Luke', in *ODNB* 56 (2004), pp 643–9, which includes an extensive bibliography. See also Cleary, *Father Luke Wadding and St Isidore's College Rome*; and The Franciscan Fathers (eds), *Father Luke Wadding commemorative volume* (Dublin & London, 1957); and Harold Francis, *Vita Fratris Lucae*

Colgan, to the modern school of Scotus,[19] but also of documenting the quite remarkable contribution made by exiled Irish clergy, regular and secular, to the Scholastic philosophy and theology of the period. Considering the recent exodus of priests, religious, and clerical students from the island of Ireland in the years following the Nine Years War, the defeat at Kinsale in 1601, and the so-called 'flight of the Earls' in 1607,[20] Punch's testimony is all the more extraordinary since it confirms that Irish Scholastics had assumed positions of genuine authority and institutional eminence in little more than fifty years since fleeing their homeland. In a significant passage in the *Restitutus*,[21] an excerpt which has largely escaped the attention of scholars,[22] Punch listed no fewer than 79 Irishmen, of whom 73 were Franciscans Observants, who had taught, or who were then teaching at some of the leading Catholic universities of Post-Tridentine Europe, or else gainfully employed in numerous *studia generalia*, seminaries, and other places of theological instruction. For Punch this was unequivocal evidence of a distinctive yet profound contribution made by the Irish to early modern Scholasticism, a gift which he thought ought to be celebrated, and which he believed followed as a consequence of their commitment to the intellectual heritage of Roman Catholicism, and the achievements of past Irish luminaries, among whom could be counted John Duns Scotus.[23] This was why he considered it propitious to preface his own *magnum opus* with such a rousing defense of Scotus' Irish origin.

Punch's dual riposte to his critics, that Scotus was a son of Ireland and that Hibernian thinkers, both Old Irish and Anglo-Irish,[24] were making a

Waddingi (first published as a prefix to *Epitome Annalium Waddingi*, Rome, 1662), third edition (Rome, 1931). **19** Poncius, *Scotus Hiberniae Restitutus*, p. 1. **20** On these events see John J. Silke, *Kinsale: the Spanish intervention in Ireland at the end of the Elizabethan wars* (Liverpool, 1970: reprint Dublin, 2000); Hiram Morgan, *Tyrone's rebellion: the outbreak of the Nine Years War in Tudor Ireland* (Dublin, 1993); Hiram Morgan (ed.), *The battle of Kinsale* (Bray, 2004); Colm Lennon, *Sixteenth century Ireland*, New Gill History of Ireland, 2 (Dublin, 1994), pp 266–304; and Thomas O'Connor and Mary Ann Lyons (eds), *Irish migrants to Europe after Kinsale, 1602–1820* (Dublin, 2003). **21** Poncius, *Scotus Hiberniae Restitus*, pp 23–4. For a translation of this notable passage, accompanied by critical notes, see Appendix 1. **22** One of the few recent scholars to take cognisance of this passage is Declan Downey Jnr., 'Augustinians and Scotists: the Irish contribution to Counter-Reformation theology in Continental Europe', in B. Bradshaw and D. Keogh (eds), *Christianity in Ireland: revisiting the story* (Dublin, 2002), pp 96–108, at p. 108. However, Downey provides no real analysis of its content or significance. **23** Poncius, *Scotus Hiberniae Restitutus*, pp 36–9. **24** It is pertinent to recall that Punch himself was Anglo-Irish, and was from south east Munster in the region of Cork. This did not, however, prevent him from adopting a cause, the Catholic Confederation, supported by friars and others of an Old Irish background. The differences between the exiled Irish friars in terms of race (Irish and Anglo-Norman) and language (Irish and English) could often be such as to foment conflicts and rivalries especially between individuals from Ulster and Munster and those of Leinster. For further discussion of this issue see the classic article by Canice Mooney OFM on the case of Luke Wadding, 'Was Wadding a patriotic Irishman?', in *Father Luke Wadding*, pp 15–92; and Declan Downey, 'Purity of blood and purity of faith in early modern Ireland', in Alan Ford and

palpable contribution to seventeenth-century theological and philosophical learning, provides a point of repose at which to examine the bequest made by the Irish Franciscans to early modern Scholasticism, and more specifically to the school of Scotism.[25] While it is certainly true that other exiled groups of Irish theologians and philosophers of different religious orders such as those Jesuits, Augustinian Hermits, Dominicans, Carmelites, Cistercians, Benedictines, and Capuchins named by Punch in the *Restitutus*, or else known through other sources,[26] and members of the secular clergy working in the universities and colleges of the Iberian peninsula,[27] Paris,[28] Louvain,[29]

John McCafferty (eds), *The origins of sectarianism in early modern Ireland* (Cambridge, 2005), pp 216–28. **25** The Scotism of the Irish friars is generally omitted from those few books that purport to explain the history of modern Irish thought. The best available studies, to which all students of the friars are indebted, are by Cathaldus Giblin, 'Hugh MacCaughwell OFM and Scotism at St Antony's College, Louvain', in *De doctrina Ioannis Duns Scoti. Acta Congressus Soctistici Internationalis Oxonii et Edinburgi 11–17 sept. 1966 celebrati*, 4 vols (Studia Scholastico Scotistica, 4), iv, 375–97; and Benignus Millet, 'Irish Scotists at St Isidore's College, Rome, in the seventeenth century', ibid., iv, 399–419. For more general overviews see Millet, *The Irish Franciscans*, pp 464–504, and Cathaldus Giblin, 'The contribution of the Irish Franciscans on the continent in the seventeenth century', in M. Maher (ed.), *Irish spirituality* (Dublin, 1981), pp 88–104. **26** See Appendix 1. On the contribution made by Irish secular clergy to Scholastic thought in Paris during the seventeenth and eighteenth centuries see Liam Chambers, 'Irish Catholics and Aristotelian Scholastic Philosophy in early modern Europe, *c*.1600–*c*.1750', in this volume. For a general discussion of the regular clergy see my 'Towards a cartography of Irish Scholasticism in early modern Europe (1): The Regular Clergy and their contribution to philosophical and theological thought from the aftermath Kinsale to the outset of the French Revolution', in Thomas O'Connor and Mary Ann Lyons (eds), *Awakening Irish identities: the Ulster earls in Baroque Europe* (Dublin, forthcoming). **27** See José Couselo Bouzas, *El colegio de irlandeses de Santiago de Compostela* (Santiago, 1935); María-José Arnáiz and José Luís Sánchez, *El colegio de los irlandeses* (Alcalá-Madrid, 1985); and the books by Patricia O Connell, *The Irish College at Alcalá de Henares, 1649–1785* (Dublin, 1997); *The Irish College at Lisbon, 1590–1834* (Dublin, 2001); and *The Irish College at Santiago de Compostela, 1605–1769* (Dublin, 2007). **28** A comprehensive history of the Irish college in Paris has yet to be written. However, some useful commentary can be found in Liam Swords, 'Collège des Lombards', in Liam Swords (ed.), *The Irish-French connection* (Paris, 1978), pp 44–62; Prionsias MacCana, *Collège des Irlandais Paris and Irish Studies* (Dublin, 2001); and Liam Chambers; 'Irish Catholics and Aristotelian Scholastic Philosophy', in this volume. Of further interest to the Irish presence in Paris is L.W.B. Brockliss and P. Ferté, 'A prosopography of Irish clerics in the Universities of Paris and Toulouse', *Archivium Hibernicum* 58 (2004), 7–166. **29** Until its closure in 1793 the University of Louvain was at different times home to four different Irish Colleges: the Franciscan College of St Anthony of Padua founded in 1607; the College of the Irish Dominicans founded in 1624/6; the Irish Pastoral College for secular clergy founded in 1624; and the Discalced Carmelites who maintained a college (Placet) of which little is known. On St Anthony's see Ignatius Fennessy, 'Guardians and staff of Saint Anthony's College Louvain, 1607–1999', *Collectanea Hibernica*, xlii (2000), 215–41; and N. Ó Muraíle, *Mícheál Ó Cléirigh, his associates and St Anthony's College Louvain*; and on the Dominican college see Hugh Fenning, 'Irish Dominicans at Louvain before 1700: a biographical register', *Collectanea Hibernica*, xliii (2001), 112–60. The other colleges await study. The most complete record of the Irish presence in Louvain is provided by Jeroen Nilis,

Rome,[30] and in the network of Irish colleges that graced the European mainland,[31] achieved distinction in many spheres of philosophy and theology, such persons cannot be said to match the accomplishments of the Irish Franciscans. For in their residences at Salamanca and Paris, and in their own colleges in Louvain, Rome, Prague, Boulay, and elsewhere,[32] the friars helped to transform Scholastic thought by means of a constant commitment to the intellectual heritage of the Subtle Doctor, their greatest monument being the publication at Lyons in 1639 of the *Opera omnia* of Scotus edited by Luke Wadding.[33] It is to these efforts that we shall now turn, in order that the collective industry and individual creativity of the friars can be recorded and analysed. Before examining their work, however, it is prudent to add a few details about the academic context in which the Irish friars wrote and taught. This will involve a comment or two about the Scholastic schools of seventeenth-century Catholic Europe, a description of the development of the *schola Scoti* to which they pledged their allegiance, and some further analysis of their determined if ultimately forlorn attempt to prove Scotus' Irish patrimony.

SCHOLASTICISM, THE SCHOOL OF SCOTISM, AND *SCOTUS HIBERNICUS*

Contrary to the once prevalent historical platitude that Scholasticism was a recalcitrant relic of the Middle Ages and thus a necessary casualty of modernity and putative 'enlightenment',[34] intellectual historians as well as historians of

'Irish students at Louvain university, 1548–1797', *Archivum Hibernicum*, lx (2006/7), 1–304, a work that improves upon and thereby completes the earlier article by Brendan Jennings, 'The Irish students at the University of Louvain, 1584–1794', in Sylvester O'Brien (ed.), *Measgra Mhichíl Uí Chléirigh* (Dublin, 1944), pp 74–97. 30 See Dáire Keogh and Albert McDonnell (eds), *The Irish College, Rome and its World* (Dublin, 2008). 31 For quite different introductions to the colleges in general see J. O'Boyle, *The Irish Colleges on the Continent: their origin and history* (Belfast, 1935); T.J. Walsh, *The Irish continental college movement* (Cork,1973); and D. Murphy, *A History of Irish emigrant and missionary education* (Dublin, 2000). 32 On these important institutions see Millet, *The Irish Franciscans*, pp 105–223. On Boulay and Prague, which have not been studied in great detail, see Brendan Jennings, 'The Irish Franciscans at Boulay', *Archivum Hibernicum*, xi (1944), 118–53; Canice Mooney, *Irish Franciscan relations with France, 1224–1850* (Killiney, 1951), pp 55–69; and Jan Pařez, 'The Irish Franciscans in seventeenth- and eighteenth-century Prague', in O'Connor and Lyons (eds), *Irish migrants in Europe after Kinsale, 1602–1820*, pp 104–17. 33 Luke Wadding (ed.), *Joannis Duns Scoti Opera Omnia*, 12 vols (Lyons, 1639). On this edition see C. Balić, 'Wadding the Scotist', in *Father Luke Wadding*, pp 486–504. 34 A stated bias against Scholasticism, and a refusal to acknowledge its place in modernity can still be said to persist, albeit in a less vociferous form, in several present day histories of modern philosophy. One prominent example is the recent attempt by Jonathan Israel in *Radical Enlightenment: philosophy and the making of modernity, 1650–1750* (Oxford, 2001), and *Enlightenment contested: philosophy, modernity, and the emancipation of man, 1650–1752* (Oxford, 2006) to map the philosophical origins of our present-day beliefs and practices without any

philosophy, theology, and science, are now much more attuned to the fact that the Catholic and Protestant Scholastic schools (*sectae*) of seventeenth- and eighteenth-century Europe and Latin America, made a genuine contribution to modern intellectual life.[35] Created by the fragmentation of late medieval philosophy and theology into competing 'ways' (*viae*) or movements,[36] and heavily conditioned by different ecclesial allegiances and responsibilities, the early modern schools exhibited considerable flexibility in their respective outlooks and were composed of disparate elements. More importantly, the *sectae* can be seen as responding to the needs of their own time rather than as movements concerned with the revival or uncritical preservation of medieval thought.[37] Two of the greatest in terms of number and influence were the Thomist and Scotist schools. Promoted by the Dominicans and Franciscans, although by no means their exclusive preserve, both *sectae* proved themselves reasonably adept at withstanding the intellectual pressures of the early modern

---

mention of the contribution or otherwise of Scholasticism. For an excellent account of the development of 'Scholasticism' throughout the ages, and of the different attempts made by modern historians to understand its ever changing scope see Riccardo Quinto, *Scholastica. Storia di un concetto*, Subsidia Medievalia Patavina, 2 (Padua, 2002). **35** A good illustration of this can be seen in the fact that the study of many of the canonical figures of modern philosophy and science, most notably Descartes, has been enriched by an analysis of the Scholastic context in which their ideas were formed and promulgated; see, for instance, Dennis Des Chene, *Physiologia: natural philosophy in Late Aristotelian and Cartesian thought* (Ithaca, NY, 1996); and Roger Ariew, *Descartes and the last Scholastics* (Ithaca, NY, 1999). On Protestant Scholasticism see Carl R. Trueman and R.S. Clark (eds), *Protestant Scholasticism: essays in reassessment* (Carlisle, 1999). Much more work needs to be done in charting the role and significance of Protestant Scholasticism, especially in its Anglican and Reformed manifestations, in early modern Irish thought. Such a study would help to illuminate the important contributions made by divines such as John Bramhall (1594–1663); Jeremy Taylor (1613–67); and James Ussher (1581–1656). Furthermore, it should be acknowledged that the subjects taught at Trinity College Dublin (e.g. logic, natural philosophy, mental and moral sciences) under the rubric of what we would now refer to as 'philosophy', followed a Aristotelian-Scholastic curriculum, especially in logic and natural philosophy, until the end of the eighteenth century. On this see R. B. MacDowell, David A. Webb, and F.S.L. Lyons, *Trinity College Dublin 1592–1952: an academic history* (Cambridge, 1982), pp 19, 29–32, and 169–171. The point of great interest here, is that even in a very different Christian confession to that inhabited by the Irish Franciscans, Scholasticism can be said to have made a distinctive contribution to modern intellectual life in the island of Ireland. **36** See Zenon Kaluza, *Les querelles doctrinales à Paris: nominalistes et réalistes aux confins du XIVe et du XVe siècles*, Quodlibet: ricerche e strumenti di filosofia medievale, 2 (Bergamo, 1988); and Russell L. Friedman, and Lauge Olaf Nielsen (eds), *The medieval heritage in early modern Metaphysics and modal theory, 1400–1700*, The New Synthese Historical Library: Texts and Studies in the History of Philosophy, 53 (Dordrecht, 2003). **37** This is especially evident in the innovative studies on the Jesuits and others by Richard Paul Blum, *Philosophenphilosophie und Schulphilosophie: Typen des Philosophierens in der Neuzeit* (Stuttgart, 1999); Sven Knebel, *Wille, Würfel und Wahrscheinlichkeit: Das System der moralischen Notwendigkeit in der Jesuitenscholastik 1500–1700* (Hamburg, 2000); and Marcus Hellyer, *Catholic Physics: Jesuit natural philosophy in early modern Germany* (Notre Dame, IN, 2005).

period.[38] Other major schools were sponsored by friars such as the Carmelites and the Augustinian Hermits, as well as new religious orders like the Theatines and Jesuits. Secular priests and laymen also contributed to Scholastic philosophy, as did thinkers in traditional monastic orders like the Benedictines and Cistercians.[39]

The 'school of Scotus' became an identifiable presence in European thought at the beginning of the sixteenth century when the works of the Subtle Doctor were collected, published in several editions, and systematically analysed. Though indebted to previous traditions of commentary in the fourteenth and fifteenth centuries,[40] early modern Scotism, both intellectually and geographically, was much more expansive than its medieval incarnations, providing a wider dissemination of the Subtle Doctor's ideas and methods. Its progress in Catholic Europe (for Protestants proved mostly resistant to the charms of Scotus),[41] and in the new colonies was assisted from 1501 onwards, when regulations of general chapters of the Franciscans recommended or directly prescribed the *doctrina Scotista* as the

38 As such, there is no complete history of early modern Thomism. Some illumination of several of its salient features can be found in B. Jansen, 'Zur Phänomenologie der Philosophie der Thomisten des 17./18 Jahrhunderts', *Scholastik* 13 (1938), 49–71; Sylvio Hermann de Franceschi, 'Thomisme et thomistes dans le débat théologique à l'âge classique. Jalons historiques pour une caractérisation doctrinale', in Y. Krumenacker and L. Thirouin (eds), *Les écoles de pensée religlieuse à l'époque moderne* (Actes de la Journée d'Études de Lyon, 14 janvier 2006), *Chrétiens et Sociétés. Documents et Mémoires* 5 (2006), 65–109; Jacob Schmutz, '*Bellum Scholasticum*: Thomisme et antithomisme dans les débats doctrinaux modernes', *Revue thomiste* 108 (2008), 131–182; and my 'Scholastic schools and early modern Philosophy', in Donald Rutherford (ed.), *The Cambridge companion to early modern philosophy* (Cambridge, 2006), pp 299–328, esp. pp 304–10. 39 See B. Jansen, 'Die scholastische Philosophie des 17. Jahrhunderts', *Philosophisches Jahrbuch*, 50 (1937), 401–44; Jacob Schmutz, 'Bulletin de scolastique moderne (I)', *Revue thomiste* 100 (2000), 270–341; and my 'Scholastic schools and early modern Philosophy', pp 302–10, and 313–20. 40 On the early school see C. Bérubé, 'La première école scotiste', in Z. Kaluza and P. Vignaux (eds), *Preuve et raisons à l'université de Paris. Logique, ontologie et théologie au XIVe siècle* (Paris, 1984), pp 9–24; and L. Honnefelder, 'Scotus und der Scotismus: Ein Beitrag zur Bedeutung der Schulbildung in der mittelalterlichen Philosophie', in Maarten J.F.M. Hoenen et al. (eds), *Philosophy and learning: universities in the Middle Ages* (Leiden, 1995), pp 249–462. See also Bert Roest, *A history of Franciscan education (c.1210–1517)*, Education and Society in the Middle Ages, 11 (Leiden, 2000), pp 187–96, for a discussion as to how the tradition of Scotus was conjoined to a more general 'Franciscan school' of theology. 41 Scotist ideas, however, did influence aspects of Reformed thought, as opposed to Anglican or Lutheran theology. In recent years, some scholars have argued that Calvin's theology bears a general resemblence to that of Scotus in respect of its emphasis on the Divine Will, and in other areas of theological epistemology; see T.F. Torrance, 'Intuitive and abstractive knowledge from Duns Scotus to John Calvin', in *De doctrina Ioannes Duns Scoti*, iv, 291–306. A much more definite Scotist influence, however, can be discerned in the writings of later Reformed theologians such as the Utrecht professor Gisbertus Voetius; see Andreas J. Beck, 'Gisbertus Voetius (1589–1676): basic features of his doctrine of God', in Willem J. van Asselt and Eef Dekker (eds), *Reformation and Scholasticism: an ecumenical enterprise* (Grand Rapids, MI, 2001), pp 205–26.

teaching to be followed by the Observant, Conventual, and Capuchin confections of the Franciscan order.[42] Furthermore, in the late fifteenth and early sixteenth centuries specialist chairs of Scotist theology were established at the universities of Paris, Rome, Coimbra, Salamanca, Alcalá, Padua and Pavia, thereby providing the school with a strong institutional foundation.[43]

The *schola Scoti* itself can be said to have approached its zenith in the first half of the seventeenth century, when one observer, the great Cistercian polymath Juan Caramuel y Lobkowitz (1606–82) was moved to remark: 'the school of Scotus is more numerous than all the other schools taken together'.[44] In the late seventeenth and early eighteenth centuries the movement still had an important following, especially in southern Germany and Austria,[45] Italy,[46] Spain,[47] eastern Europe,[48] and Latin America,[49] but subsequently fell into a slow decline, a state of affairs explicable by the repeated suppressions endured by Franciscan

---

42 See Maarten J.F.M. Hoenen, 'Scotus and the Scotist School: the tradition of Scotist thought in the medieval and early modern Period', in E.P. Bos (ed.), *John Duns Scotus (1265/6–1308): renewal of philosophy* (Amsterdam, 1998), pp 197–210. For a useful survey of the Franciscan orders at the advent of the early modern period see F. Meyer and L. Viallet (eds), *Identités Franciscaines à l'âge des Réformes* (Clermont-Ferrand, 2005). 43 On early modern Scotism see Dominique de Caylus, 'Merveilleux épanouissement de l'école scotiste au XVIIe siècle', *Études franciscaines* 24 (1910), 5–12, 493–502; 25 (1911), 35–47, 306–17, 327–645; and 26 (1912), 276–8. The information gathered in this article needs to checked against P. Uriël Smeets, *Lineamenta bibliographaie Scotisticae* (Rome, 1942). For a general synthesis see B. Jansen, 'Zur Philosophie der Skotisten im 17. Jahrhundert', *Franziskanische Studien* 23 (1936), 28–58. Despite their merits, these earlier studies have been eclipsed and superceded by Jacob Schmutz, 'L'Héritage des Subtils. Cartographie du Scotisme de l'âge classique', *Études philosophiques* 57 (2002), 51–81. 44 Juan Caramuel y Lebokowitz O.Cist., *Theologia moralis fundamentalis* (Lyon, 1657), Lib. II, disp. 10: '*Scoti schola numerosior est omnibus aliis simul sumptis*'. On the quotation see Felix Bak, 'Scoti schola numerosior est omnibus aliis simul sumptis', *Franciscan Studies* 16 (1956), 143–64. See also the remarks made by Wadding, *Annales*, ad an 1308, nn. 52 and 54. 45 For an interesting account as to how the debates of the Enlightenment impacted upon one Franciscan community see Thomas Kogler, *Das philosophisch-theologische Studium der Bayrischen Franziskaner: Ein Beitrag zur Studien- und Schulgeschichte des 17. und 18 Jahrhunderts* (Münster, 1925). 46 See Gabriele Panteghini, 'L'insegnamento della teologia nella facoltà delle arti dell'Università di Padova dal 1517 al 1807', in Camille Bérubé (ed.), *Regnum Hominis et Regnum Dei: Acta quarti congressus Scotistici internationalis, Patavii, 24–29 septembris 1976*, 2 vols, Studia Scholastico-Scotistica, 6–7, ii, 135–44; and Pietro Scapin, 'La metafisica Scotista a Padova dal XV al XVII secolo', in A. Poppi (ed.), *Storia e cultura al Santo di Padova fra il XIII e il XX secolo* (Vicenza, 1976), pp 303–23. 47 Bernardino De Armellada, 'El problema de sopranatural en la escuela escotista del siglo XVII', in Scotist Commission (ed.), *De doctrina Ioannis Duns Scoti.* iv, 421–59; and Manuel de Castro, 'Bibliografía de franciscanos escotistas españoles', in Camille Berubé (ed.), *Homo et mundus: Acta quinti congressus Scotistici internationalis Salamanticae, 21–26 septembris 1981*, Studia Scholastico-Scotistica, 8 (Rome, 1984), pp 437–58. 48 Viktoras Gidziunas OFM, 'Scotism and Scotism in Lituania', in *De doctrina Ioannis Duns Scoti*, iv, 239–48. 49 On the Franciscans and Scotism in the New World see Celina Ann Lértora Mendoza, 'El escotismo en el Río de la Plata (1600–1800)', in Camille Berubé (ed.), *Homo et mundus*, pp 501–17; and Mauricio Beuchot, *Historia de la filosofía en el Mexico colonial* (Barcelona, 1996), pp 15–43.

communities in many countries,[50] and by the increasing tendency of several popes in the years before the French Revolution to recommend the thought of Thomas Aquinas as normative for Catholic theologians and philosophers.[51] While the Scotist tradition in Catholic thought continued to demand the allegiances of Franciscans and others in the nineteenth and twentieth centuries up to the time of the Second Vatican Council (1962–5),[52] it never recaptured the vitality and purpose it possessed in the early modern period, an era which can now be looked upon as the 'golden age' of the movement.

As we have had cause to note with respect to Punch's *Scotus Hiberniae restitutus*, the Irish friars did not merely gravitate toward the teachings of the Subtle Doctor on account of their shared Franciscan heritage. There were much stronger connections that bound them to his thought, the most compelling of which was the long standing belief that Scotus himself was Irish, and that he had been born at Downpatrick in Ulster.[53] The very idea that the Subtle Doctor himself was one of their own provided the friars with sufficient motive to defend his honour against any attack on his reputation. A good example of such dedication to the cause is to be found in 1617, when a Polish Dominican

50 On the fortunes of the three orders of Franciscans, the Observants, Conventuals and Capuchins, see Owen Chadwick, *The Popes and European Revolution* (Oxford, 1981), pp 13–14, 26, 35, 43–6, 60–5, 162–9, 214–18, 526–7, and 593–5. On the many obstacles encountered by the Irish Franciscans during the first half of the eighteenth century, particularly with regard to sustaining their foreign colleges, see Hugh Fenning, *The undoing of the friars of Ireland: a study of the novitiate question in the eighteenth century*, Recueil de travaux d'histoire et de philologie, 6ème ser., 1 (Louvain, 1972). 51 See Schmutz 'L'Héritage des Subtils', pp 60–80; and my 'Scholastic schools and early modern Philosophy', pp 310–13. 52 In the last decades of the nineteenth century, especially after Leo XIII's encyclical *Aeterni patris* (1879), one finds fewer theological textbooks published in Europe under the rubric of *ad mentem Scoti*. In countries such as France, Italy and Germany, Scotism gave way to Neo-Thomism and other theological schools in the universities and seminaries. Still, there is some evidence that interest in the ideas of the Sutbtle Doctor remained constant. For one thing, the *Scotus academicus* by the French Scotist Claude Frassen (1620–1711), originally published in Paris 1672, continued to be reprinted until 1901 and remained a constant medium of instruction in Franciscan *studia generalia* and seminaries. In the late nineteenth century authors such as Déodat-Marie de Basly OFM (1862–1937), founded the *Revue Duns Scot*, and edited individual works of Scotus, while German theologians such as Parthenius Minges (1861–1926), wrote widely used textbooks that were strongly influenced by Scotist principles; see the latter's *Compendium theologicum dogmatica specialis et generalis* (Munich, 1901–2), and *Joannis Duns Scoti doctrina philosophica et theologica quoad res praecipuas proposita et exposita*, 2 vols (Ad claras Aquas, 1930), On the work of these indiviuduals see Siegfried Grän, 'P. Parthenius Minges ein Förderer des modernen Scotismus', in *De doctrina Ioannis Duns Scoti*, iv, 707–15; Crisóstomo de Pamplona OFM Cap., 'El Yo de Cristo y de las divinas personas segun Duns Escoto y Deodat Marie de Basly', ibid., iv, 717–37; and G. Baselli-Sani, 'Nel cinquantesmo anniversario della morte del. P.D.M. de Basly OFM', *Studia Francescana* 85 (1988), 105–8. 53 Cavellus, *Vita Scoti*, cap. 1. For an illuminating study of this text see James McEvoy, 'Hugh McCawell OFM, Scotist theologian of the Immaculate Conception of Mary', in M.W.F. Stone (ed.) *From Ireland to Louvain: the achievements of the Irish Franciscans and their contribution to early modern philosophy and theology* (Leuven, 2009).

Abraham Bzowski ('Bzovius') (1567–1637) penned a trenchant onslaught on the reputation of Scotus [54] that so appalled a whole generation of Irish friars and other Franciscans that they were moved to answer Bzowski's charges in ever greater detail.[55] Leading the first counter-attack against these perceived calumnies was Hugo Cavellus, who penned a *Vita Scoti* and an *Apologia* in order to counter Bzowski's animadversions.[56] Tellingly, Cavellus's students Bonaventure Magennis (fl. 1623),[57] followed in his footsteps with the publication of the *Apologia apologiae pro Ioanne Duns Scoto*, which was published at Paris in 1623, as did Anthony Hickey (Latinized to 'Hiquaeus') OFM (1586–1641),[58] with his *Nitela Franciscanae Religionis et absterio sordium quibus eam conspurcare frustra tentavit Abrahamus Bzovius*, which appeared in Lyons in 1627. After these others played their part, with William Casey (fl. 1638),[59] and the aforementioned Colgan and Punch all writing tomes of polemic to defend Scotus.

Added to this list of indignant tomes was the *Vita R.P. Joannis Duns Scoti* of Luke Wadding,[60] a work more circumspect about Scotus' *patria*,[61] but one just

---

54 A. Bzovius, *Annales ecclesiastici, XIII* (Antwerp, 1617), see 831–2. The gist of Bzowski's complaint was that the writings of Scotus were obscure and unintelligible, and lost in utter darkness. He even joked that the name 'Scotus' was derived from the Greek *skoteinos* meaning 'dark'. See ibid., p. 831: 'Hoc anno volens nolens ex humanis abiit Ioannes Dunsius [...] ob profundissimam dicendi scribendique obscuritatem *Skotinos*, id est, Tenebricosus, quod olim obscurissimi Anaxagorae cognomen fuit, cognominatus, et ob novam Scholasticae theologiae sectam de nomine suo dictam omnibus longe notissimus.' **55** See Matthaeus Ferchius (Mate Frkic) (1583–1669), *Apologia pro Ioanne Duns Scoto Doctore Subtili libri tres* (Bologna, 1620). Ferchius was a well known Conventual who taught at Padua; see N. Roscic, 'Mateo Frce (Ferkic, Ferchius): un grande scotista croato', in *Studia mediaevalia et mariologica see P. Carolo Balić OFM septuagesimum explenti annum dicata* (Rome, 1971), pp 377–402. **56** Both these works were included in Cavellus' edition of Scotus' *Commentary on the Sentences*, see *In quatuor libros Sententiarum*, 2 vols (Antwerp, 1620). Cavellus would eventually have to answer for his criticism of Bzowski when the Dominicans of Antwerp complained to their local bishop. In an effort to satisfy the Dominicans, the bishop appointed a censor who found in favour of Cavellus. The Dominicans then appealed to the papal nuncio at Brussels, who interviewed Cavellus and found no fault with his *Apologia*. Having tried and failed to induce another nuncio, this time on the Rhineland, to take their side, the Dominicans eventually brought their case to Rome, where Cardinal Robert Bellarmine, prefect of the Congregation, insisted that neutral judges should examine the charges. Finding for Cavellus, they imposed silence on Bzowski until he eliminated from his writings all falsehoods and slanders pertaining to Scotus. The story is relayed in Bonaventure Magennis, *Apologia apologiae pro Ioanne Scoti* (Paris, 1623), pp 2–8; see also Giblin, 'Hugh MacCaughwell OFM and Scotism at St Anthony's College Louvain', *De doctrina Ioannis Duns Scoti*, iv, 390–1, n. 74. **57** Very little is known about Magennis; see Giblin, ibid., at pp 390–1. **58** For the basic details of Hickey's life and writings see P. Édouard d'Alençon, 'Hickey, Anthony', *Dictionnaire de théologie catholique*, vi.2 (1914), cols. 2358–9; and Cleary, *Father Luke Wadding and St Isidore's College Rome*, pp 73–8. **59** William Casey, *Vindicationes apologeticae Doctoris Subtilis* (1638); this work is listed by San Antonio, *Bibliotheca*, i, col. 45. **60** This is added to the first volume of *Ioannis Duns Scoti, Opera omnia* (Lyons, 1639), i, cols. 1–34. The text was later published as self-standing tome, *Vita R.P.F. Ioannis Duns Scoti* (Mons, 1644). For further discussion see Balić, 'Wadding the Scotist', pp 463–74. **61** Wadding, *Vita R.P.F.*

as resolute in its defence of his thought and piety. Wadding, however, was not beyond making more definite pronouncements about Scotus' provenance. In the *Annales* he followed Cavellus, who had claimed that *Dun da Leathghlas* or Downpatrick, an ancient city in the north of Ireland, was the birthplace of the great theologian, and that the prefix '*Duns*' in Scotus' name was a contracted form of the adjective '*Dunensis*' or '*Dunius*'.[62] Wadding was prepared to acknowledge that: 'the Irish, the English, and the Scots dispute about [Scotus'] fatherland; for the glory of so great a man makes each of these provinces eager to claim him as their own, just as the Greek cities of old fought bitterly about the birthplace of Homer'.[63]

And yet despite his gallant efforts to mount a *prima facie* case that Scotus was indeed Irish, Wadding was a good enough historian to realise that the truth was far from certain. He ended his exposition with a plea that Scotus ought to belong to Ireland, because neither the English nor the Scots had exerted themselves or made such sacrifices for his glory as Irish scholars had done. Somewhat wearily, the great annalist concluded that 'if reward is due to merit, and recompense to labour, then Scotus can be awarded to nobody but to the Irish' (*etenim si pro meritis praemium, et pro labore merces adscribenda sit, nullis nisi Hibernis adiudicandus est Scotus*).[64]

Ioannis Duns Scoti, c. 1, p. 3: 'patria, aetas, mors, haec plus ceteris incerta'. **62** Wadding, *Annales*, ad annum 1304, nn. XVIII, XIX, pp 47–8. Such reasoning held no sway with Thomas Dempster (1579–1625), an indefatigable Scottish Catholic exile who devoted a good deal of his creative energies to claiming many Irish saints for Scotland. Dempster was especially irritated by Irish scholars like Wadding who asserted, the Scot claimed, that '*Duns* is a contracted form of *Dunesis*, but do not produce any codex where that contraction can be found' (*Quod Duns contracte pro Dunensi vocaretur, nec tamen ullum codicem producunt in quo contractio illa referiretur*); see his *Historia Ecclesiastica Gentis Scotorum* (Bologna, 1627), lib. xix, p. 228. On Dempster see Alexander Du Toit, 'Dempster, Thomas', *ODNB*, 15 (2004), pp 759–62. **63** Wadding, *Annales*, ad annum 1304, n. XVII, XIX, p. 46: 'De patria certant Hiberni, Angli, Scoti; tanti enim viri gloria desiderium excitat, ut unaquaeque ex his provinciis civem asserat suum; non aliter quam Graeciae urbes olim pro Homeri natalitiis acriter pugnarunt.' **64** Ibid., XXII, XIX, p. 50. 'Tantem vero ita haec pro Scoto Hibernis vindicando sincere congessi, ut minime me causam contra alios omnino evicisse putem; non enim tantum mihi tribuo, ut qui aliorum argumenta dixerim solubilia, mea judicaverim reponsionem omnem respuere. Novi enim non defuturos, qui his meis rationibus alias opponant, et ulteriori conatu Scotum repetant, civemque asserant suum. Id per me liceat, dum urbane et christiane absque livore et felle amaritudinis causam egerint: ut enim Scoti gloriae est, tot vindices habere, ita illis ignominiae vertetur, si modestiae fines transiliant. Hoc interim adiciam: quod si in causa dubia ferenda sit sententia, potiorem habendam esse Hibernorum rationem. Etenim si pro meritis praemium, et pro labore merces adscribenda sit, nullis nisi Hibernis adiudicandus est Scotus. Quis enim aliquando ex Scotis, aut Anglis in Scoto illustrando, aut operibus suis castigandis operam publicam insumpsit, aut laborem impendit? Quis eorum a calumnis defendit? Ultra omnes laboraverunt in hoc genere Hiberni [...].' See also ibid., p. 51: 'Itaque si Hibernorum calami et doctae elucubrationes Scotum illustrant, quos potius quam Hibernos illustrare debet Scoti nativitas? Scoto honorem diligenter impertiunt, ab eius ortu honorem sibi debitum vicissim reposcunt. Quare, si ipsa causae evidentia non evincunt, saltem meritorum titulo sibi Scotum adiudicandum non desperant. Suus est ex

By the seventeenth century Scotism constituted the very marrow of the theological bones of the Irish friars, but it was not always thus. At the end of the Middle Ages there is hardly any evidence to suggest that Franciscans in Ireland, who were predominantly Observants rather than Conventuals, were reading the works of Scotus with the same frequency, expertise, and enthusiasm as their early modern successors. Recent research on the late medieval friars paints a vivid picture of their religious, liturgical, and disciplinary concerns, revealing them to be much more exercised by the vicissitudes of preaching and other pastoral responsibilities than with the requirements of speculative theology and philosophy.[65] Support for this last claim can be found in a library catalogue that survived the destruction of the Youghal (Eochaill) friary in Munster,[66] and which provides a rare glimpse into the reading habits of the late medieval Irish friars. Revealingly, the codex does not mention Scotus at all, but lists many of the important works of Bonaventure, and other leading lights from the medieval Franciscan tradition, as well as books by Thomas Aquinas.[67] Though the Subtle Doctor is strikingly absent, the *Commentary on the Sentences of Peter Lombard* by the Scotist theologian Nicholas des Orbeaux ('Orbellus'), (d. 1472–2) is included.[68] It would be quite premature, however, to infer from the list of authors and works recorded in the Youghal catalogue that this group of Irish

meritis Scotus, suus etiam erit ex proborum iudicio.' **65** See the excellent study by Colmán N. Ó Clabaigh OSB, *The Franciscans in Ireland, 1400–1534: from reform to reformation* (Dublin, 2002), pp 42–80, and 106–57. More general analysis of the intellectual apostolates of the friars at this time is provided by Roest, *A history of Franciscan education (c.1210–1517)*, pp 272–324. **66** Youghal, Theo. Lat. Fol. 703, Staatsbibliothek Preussicher Kulturbesitz, Berlin. An edition of this interesting text can be found in Ó Clabaigh, *The Franciscans in Ireland*, pp 158–80, to which I am indebted. On the friary itself, which was probably the oldest in Ireland, being founded in 1224, becoming Observant in 1460, see ibid., pp 118, 142–3, 148–50; and D. Sullivan, 'Youghal, the first house of the Friars Minor in Ireland', J. O'Callaghan (ed.), *Franciscan Cork* (Dublin, 1953), pp 28–33 and 95; see also note 52 on p. 191. **67** For lists of works by Bonaventure see Ó Clabaigh, *The Franciscans in Ireland*, pp 162 n. 12, 164 n. 26, 165 n. 33, 172 n. 84, 174 n. 98, 175 n. 102, and 179 n. 147. Other important Franciscan *auctoritates* listed are the pentitential writers Astesanus of Asti (fl. 1317), p. 163 n. 21, and Angelo Carletti (Angelus) (1411–95), p. 173 n. 86; the enclyopediast Bartholemeus Anglicus (late 12th–mid thirteenth century), p. 166 n. 38; and the preacher Robert of Lecce, p. 169 n. 65, p. 173, 88, p. 177, n. 119, p. 178 n. 138. For Thomas Aquinas see pp 167 nn. 45 and 46, 174 n. 93, and 179 n. 142. Other important Dominicans to appear on the list are the canonist Raymund of Peñaforte (1175/80–1275), p. 167, n. 50, p. 170 n. 68, p. 172 n. 80; the theologian Peter of Tarantaise (*c.*1224–76), p. 166 n. 39; James of Voragine (*c.*1230–98) author of the *Legenda aurea*, p. 162, n. 13; and the moralists Johannes Nider (*c.*1380–1436), p. 173 n. 90, and Antoninus of Florence (1389–1459), p. 174, n.92. **68** Ibid., p. 174 n. 98, which lists *Item Dorpeli super sententias*, this being Orbellus' commentary. Completed around 1465 and printed in Paris in 1488, Orbellus' work was very popular, being printed no less than fourteen times in twenty six years. See F. Stegmüller, *Repertorium commentariorum in sententias Petri Lombardi* (Würzburg, 1947), pp 284–8, nn. 591, and 592; and E. Wegerich, 'Bio-Bibliographische Notizen über Franziskanerlehrer des 15. Jahrhunderts', *Franziskanische Studien* 29 (1942), 174–8.

friars was indifferent or else hostile to Scotist theology. Rather, their library was designed to meet their apostolic needs, pastoral responsibilities, and formation in the rules and objectives of the order; hence the strong representation in the catalogue of tomes concerning the Franciscan Rule, moral theology, preaching, and works concerned with spiritual discipline.[69]

The first ostensible connection between the Irish Franciscans and Scotism, however, seems to appear in the guise of an English Conventual, and former Observant, John Foxholes (*c*.1415–75).[70] A well-known exponent of Scotist theology, Foxholes enjoyed a considerable reputation in late fifteenth-century Rome and Bologna due to his prowess in the debate *De arcanis Dei* on divine foreknowedge.[71] For this and other reasons, he was raised to the position of archbishop of Armagh on December 16th 1471 by his old friend and fellow friar Franciscus della Rovere OFM (1441–84), Pope Sixtus IV.[72] Appearances in this case, however, are utterly deceptive; since due to unpaid debts owed to the Roman Curia by his predecessor on the archepiscopal *cathedra*, Foxholes was never able to enter his diocese, and finished his days languishing in the London convent of the Conventuals. So much, it seems, for the close relations between the Irish and Scotism at the end of the Middle Ages.

The exploits of another Conventual friar, this time a green-blooded Irishman, Maurice O'Fihely (Ó Ficheallaigh), (*c*.1460–1513), also known as Mauritius Hibernicus a Portu,[73] provide a more tangible link between the emerging Scotist school and the Irish friars. O'Fihely taught with great distinction at the

---

69 See Ó Clabaigh, *The Franciscans in Ireland*, pp 133–6. The Youghal library bears testimony to the fact that late medieval Irish friars continued to pursue the same sense of a Franciscan vocation as that of their predecessors, see Francis J. Cotter OFM, *The Friars Minor in Ireland: from their arrival to 1400* (St Bonaventure, NY, 2004), pp 75–122; and Colman Ó Clabaigh, 'Patronage, prestige and politics: the Observant Franciscans at Adare', in J. Burton and K. Stöber (eds), *Monasteries and society in the British Isles in the Later Middle Ages* (Woodbridge, 2008), pp 71–82. See also Canice Mooney, 'Irish Franciscan libraries of the past', *Irish Ecclesiastical Record* 5/60 (1942), 214–28.   **70** G.J. Etzkorn, 'John Foxal, OFM: his life and writings' *Franciscan Studies* 49 (1989), 17–24; and Lorenzo Di Fonzo, 'Il minorita inglese Giovanni Foxholes: Maestro scotista e arcivescovo (*c*.1415–1475)', *Miscellanea Francescana* 99 (1999), 320–46.   **71** On this debate and Foxholes' part in it see Chris Schabel, *Theology at Paris, 1316–1345: Peter Auriol and the problem of divine foreknowledge and future contingents* (Aldershot, 2000), pp 151, 163, 314, 325–6, and 328. See also G.J. Etzkorn's critical edition of the texts relating to the dispute in *De arcanis Dei*, I maestri francescani, 8 (Rome, 1997).   **72** On Sixtus see Egmont Lee, *Sixtus IV and men of letters* (Rome, 1978); and Lorenzo Di Fonzo, 'Sisto IV: Carriera scolastica e integrazioni biografiche (1414–1484)', *Miscellanea Francescana* 86 (1986), 1–491.   **73** Wadding interpreted the toponym *de Portu* as referring to the port town of Baltimore in Co. Cork, see *Annales*, XV ad claras Aquas 1933, 360, 502, and *Scriptores*, p. 173. Other writers see it as deriving from the Augustinian monastery *St Maria de portu puro* in the diocese of Clonfert; see E.B. Fitzmaurice, 'The birthplace of Maurice de Portu', *The Franciscan Tertiary* 7 (1896), 4–11; 'The Birthplace of Maurice de Portu', *Irish Ecclesiastical Record* 17 (1896), 325–32, 545–50; and J. Fahey, 'The birthplace of Maurice de Portu', ibid. 17 (1896), 444–9. See also I. Linchaeus, *De praesulibus Hiberniae* (Dublin, 1944), ii, 228–30.

University of Padua. The facts of his early career, however, are shrouded in mystery, and while it has been supposed that he studied at Oxford,[74] there is no available evidence to substantiate this claim since the details of his intellectual formation and apostolic activities before 1487 are a matter of speculation. Much more is known about the later stages of his life, and we possess a reliable record of his presence in Milan in 1488, followed by a protracted residence in Padua from 1491 onwards. O'Fihely was appointed archbishop of Tuam in 1506, but remained in Italy for six more years. He died in 1513, probably in Galway, en route to take up his bishopric. Before he vacated the Italian peninsula, it is known that in 1512 he attended the first two sessions of the Fifth Lateran Council, being a signatory to its *acta*.[75]

The murkiness that shrouds O'Fihely's early life and intellectual development makes his subsequent achievements all the more intriguing, especially since he won for himself a considerable reputation at a major university like Padua,[76] where he was known as *Flos mundi* ('Flower of the World') within a few years of his arrival.[77] Since his fame rested on what his peers deemed to be formidable expertise both as an exponent and editor of Scotist thought,[78] it is difficult to prevent onself from believing that O'Fihely might have been exposed to Scotus' ideas before he left for Italy, a thought which licenses the further supposition that his initial exposure to the Subtle Doctor could have occurred in a Franciscan

---

74 Anthony à Wood, *Athenae Oxiionienses*, 4 vols, second edition (London, 1721), i, 9. **75** The best available survey of the scanty evidence that attend his life and work is by Colman Ó Clabaigh, 'O'Fihily, Maurice', in *Dictionary of Irish philosophers*, pp 263–4. See also A.G. Little, 'O'Fihely, Maurice', *DNB*, xiv (1909), pp 902–3; and Benignus Millet, 'The Irish Franciscans and education in late medieval times and the early Counter-Reformation', *Seachas Ard Mhacha* 18 (2001), 1–30. **76** Padua had been a recognized place of Scotist learning since the first half of the fourteenth century; see Paolo Marangon, 'Le origini e le fonti dello scotismo padovano', in Bérubé (ed.), *Regnum Hominis et Regnum Dei*, ii, 11–52. **77** J. Neary, 'Maurice O'Fihily, *Flos Mundi* and his times', *Irish Ecclesiastical Record* 25 (1925), 176–81; and P. Scapin, 'Maurizio O'Fihely editore e commentatore di Duns Scoto', in *Problemi e figure della scuola scotista del Santo*, Pubblicazioni della Provincia patavina dei frati minori conventuali, 5 (Padua, 1966), pp 303–8; and A. Poppi, 'Il contributo dei formalisti padovani al problema delle distinzioni', ibid., pp 601–790, esp. pp 624–6. See also Patrick Conlan, *St Isidore's College Rome* (Rome, 1982), pp 61–2. **78** On his writings see G. Franchini, *Bibliosofia e memorie letterarie di scrittori francescani Conventuali* (Modena, 1693), p. 454; Wadding, *Scriptores*, cols. 172–3; H. Hurter, *Nomenclator litterarius theologiae catholicae*, 4 vols (Innsbruck, 1906), ii, 1104–5; Scapin, 'Maurizio O'Fihely', p. 305; M. Walsh, 'Irish books printed abroad', *The Irish Book* 2 (1963), 23–4; and R.A. Sharpe, *A handlist of the Latin writers of Great Britain and Ireland before 1540: additions and corrections (1997–2001)*, publications of the Journal of Medieval Latin, 1 (Turnhout, 2002), pp 375–376. O'Fihely's main philosophical work is *Epitomata castigationum, conformitatum atque elucidationum in questiones metaphysice, de primo principio tractatum, atque theoremata doctoris subtilis fratris Ioannis Duns Scoti*. This work was published for the first time as an appendix to his edition of Scotus' *Commentary on the Metaphysics, Ioannes Duns Scotus Questiones subtilissime in Metaphysicam* (Venice, 1497). The most recent reprint of Mauritius' work is Wadding's edition of the *Joannis Duns Scoti Opera Omnia*, vi.

studium in Ireland. Such an assertion, while neither outlandish nor unreasonable and one which is lent some credence by O'Fihely's own personal testimony,[79] is still compromised by the lack of firm corroborating evidence. Until such times as adequate proof is forthcoming, the contribution which O'Fihely's Irish Franciscan formation did or did not play in his development as one of the foremost Scotist theologians of late fifteenth-century Europe must remain a matter of conjecture.

As with Foxholes, O'Fihely's immediate influence on the intellectual direction of the Irish friars is difficult to quantify, not least for the reason that the last twenty-three years of his life were spent teaching in Padua, a university which by the end of the fifteenth century had an established chair of Scotist theology.[80] An obvious consequence of his foreign residency was that O'Fihely had little or no contact with his native brethren (except those who may have studied at Padua),[81] and this makes it perilous to gauge the extent of his authority among his Irish peers. In any case, the protracted squabbles and unseemly rivalry between the Conventuals and Observants in late medieval Ireland may well have mitigated the extent of his influence had he returned to the land of his birth in the years before his episcopal election.[82] That said, O'Fihely did exert a captivating influence on a later generation of Irish friars by means of his textual labours, especially the acclaimed edition of Scotus' *Commentary on the Metaphysics* which was consulted by countless Scotists at Padua,[83] and praised by seventeenth-century editors such as Cavellus and Wadding. Even modern scholars such as the editors of Scotus' *Opera philosophica* have incorporated his suggestions in their own versions of the relevant texts.[84] His place in the

---

79 In a letter to his fellow Paduan Scotist, Antonio Trombetta, O'Fihely remarks that he has been nourished on Scotus' throught from the cradle; see O'Fihely (ed.), *Ioannes Duns Scotus Questiones subtilissime in Metaphysicam*, f. 99, 1–2: '*movit enim nos, et Doctoris Scoti conterranei mei singularis benevolentia, et eius doctrina, cujus lacte ab incunabulis sum nutritus, amor non mediocris*'. As far as I am aware, this is the best piece of evidence we possess concerning O'Fihely's prior exposure to Scotist thought before he went to Italy. A part of this letter is quoted in Wadding's reprint of Cavellus' 'Iudicium' in *Joannis Duns Scoti Opera Omnia*, iv, fifth page unpaginated. 80 On Scotism at fifteenth-century Padua see Edward P. Mahoney, 'Duns Scotus and the School of Padua around 1500', in Bérubé (ed.), *Regnum Hominis et Regnum Dei*, ii, 215–28; A. Poppi, *Ricerche sulla teologia e la scienza nella Scuola padovana del Cinque e Seicento* (Venice, 2001); and Marco Forlivesi, '*Quæ in hac quæstione tradit Doctor videntur humanum ingenium superare*': Scotus, Andrés, Bonet, Zerbi, and Trombetta Facing the Nature of 'Metaphysics', *Quaestio* 8 (2008), 53–111. 81 There is little evidence, however, that there were many Irish Franciscan students, be they Conventuals or Oberservants (which is highly unlikely), at Padua during the time of O'Fihely. The origin of most of the resident friars was Italian, with sizeable minorities from Slavic countries, especially Croatia and Bohemia. For a list of the masters and students see B. Bordin, 'Profilo storico-spirituale della communità del santo', in *Problemi e figure della Scuola scotista del Santo*, pp 15–115. 82 On the tensions between the Observants and Conventuals in late medieval Ireland see Ó Clabaigh, *The Franciscans in Ireland*, pp 19–42, and 58–79. 83 Edward P. Mahoney, 'Duns Scotus and the School of Padua around 1500', pp 217–18. 84 See

pantheon of Irish Franciscan scholars was confirmed when in 1672 his image was immortalized by Fra Emanuele di Como in a fresco painted in the Theological Hall of St Isidore's College, Rome.[85]

Some insight into O'Fihely's mind and working practices can be found in a letter to Pietro Barozzi, bishop of Padua (1487–1507), which is included at the very beginning of his joint edition of the *Theoremata*, the questions on the *Metaphysics*, and the *De primo principio*.[86] There, he praises Scotus' eminence in metaphysics and exclaims that he was moved to edit the works of his fellow countryman (once again we meet a steadfast belief in Scotus' Irish origins), lest they remain hidden and continue to be neglected. Since the texts were corrupt, O'Fihely states that he has examined them great care. In a further letter to be found in the same volume, addressed on this occasion to one of the leading figures in the Paduan Scotist school, Antonio Trombetta (1436–1517),[87] the Irish friar yet again exclaims that he has had to expend much effort on old, rare and faulty manuscripts, but adds that since he has been nourished on Scotus' doctrine from his earliest days, and seeks in this work to provide something of usefulness to the followers of the Subtle Doctor, his efforts will not to be in vain.[88]

O'Fihely proved himself a consummate Paduan Scotist, displaying many of the traits that help to distinguish the Subtle's Doctor's supporters in the Veneto from those of their contemporary opponents. For one thing, there exists in his corpus a pugnacious attitude toward Thomas Aquinas and members of the Thomist school which is typical of Trombetta and other Paduan Scotists,[89] several of whom were engaged in protracted and bitter disputes with their Dominican rivals.[90] Then there is the Irish friar's implacable aversion to

for instance the remarks of the modern editors of the *Quaestiones super libros Metaphysicorum Aristotelis*, libri I-V, in *B. Ioannis Duns Scoti, Opera philosophica*, 5 vols (St Bonaventure, NY, 1997), iii, xxxi–xxxii.   85 Cleary, *Father Luke Wadding and St Isidore's College Rome*, p. 40.   86 O'Fihely (ed.), *Ioannes Duns Scotus Questiones subtilissime in Metaphysicam*, f. 1v. For further discussion of this epistle see Scapin, 'Maurizio O'Fihely', p. 304.   87 O'Fihely (ed.), *Ioannes Duns Scotus Questiones subtilissime in Metaphysicam*, f. 99, 1–2. O'Fihely also discusses his activities as an editor in a letter to Cardinal Domenico Grimani to be found in *Commentaria Doctoris Subtilis Joannes Scoti in 12. li. Metaphysicae Aristotelis, Scripta recollecta et ordinata ab ipsius discipulo Antonio Andreae* (Venice, 1503), f. 1v.   88 On Trombetta, who proved himself an implacable foe of the famous Thomist Cardinal Cajetan, see Wadding, *Annales*, XV, pp 513–14; Sbaralea, *Supplementum*, i, 98; and Hurter, *Nomenclator*, ii, 1105–6. For a discussion of his writings see Antonino Poppi, 'Lo scotista patavino Antonio Trombetta', *Il Santo* 2 (1962), 349–67, *Causalità e infinità nella scuola padovana dal 1480 al 1513* (Padua, 1966), pp 373–434, and 'Il contributo dei formalisti padovani al problema delle distinzioni', in *Problemi e figure della Scuola scotista del Santo*, pp 273–348. See also Pietro Scapin, 'La metafisica scotista a Padova dal XV al XVII secolo', ibid., pp 501–9.   89 *Commentaria Doctoris Subtilis Joannis Scoti in 12. li. Metaphysicae Aristotelis, Scripta recollecta et ordinata ab ipsius discipulo Antonio Andreae*, f. 103v, 1; f. 116, 1; f. 117, 2; and f. 124v, 2.   90 On these disputes see Edward P. Mahoney, 'Duns Scotus and School of Padua', pp 225–7; and Paul Oskar Kristeller, *Medieval aspects of Renaissance*

Averroism.[91] At one point he speaks of 'the sword of Scotist ingenuity and the shield of Aristotelian truth' (*gladium solertiae scoticae et scutum sincerae veritatis aristotelicae*) to be used against the Averroists.[92] O'Fihely's total commitment to the cause of Scotism is also apparent in his later undertaking of editing the works of Franciscus de Mayronnes (*c.*1288–d. 1328),[93] to whom in a letter to Cristoforo Marcello, written at Padua in 1504, he refers to as 'a stalwart defender of the school of Scotus' (*acerrimus sectae scoticae propugnator*).[94]

Maurice O'Fihely was a learned editor and sagacious commentator of the Subtle Doctor, one whose work has yet to be studied in the detail it deserves. Writing at the end of the fifteenth century, and in the context of the revival of Scotism at the University of Padua, he stands out as the first Irish friar to make a notable contribution to early modern Scholasticism and to the school of the Subtle Doctor. The fact that his works were used and consulted throughout the seventeenth century and beyond, as can be illustrated in the near effusive testimony of Cavellus and Wadding,[95] is proof enough of his editorial skill and theological acumen. For this reason alone he is most undeserving of the ungracious comment by a celebrated historian of the Franciscan order that 'he added

---

learning, new edition (New York, 1992), pp 29–94. **91** On the Scotist aversion to Averroës at Padua and its more general relationship to the discussion of Averroes's ideas in the Renaissance see Dag Nickolaus Hasse, 'Aufsteig und Niedergang des Averroismus in der Renaissance: Niccolò Tignosi, Agostino Nifo, Francesco Vimercato', in Jan A. Aersten and Martin Pickavé (eds); *"Herbst des Mittelalters"? Fragen zur Bewertung des 14. und 15. Jahrhunderts*, Miscellanea Medievalia, 33 (Berlin, 2006), pp 68–86. See also his 'The attraction of Averroism in the Renaissance: Vernia, Achillini, Prassicio' in Peter Adamson, Hans Baltussen, and M.W.F. Stone (eds), *Philosophy, science and exegesis in Greek, Arabic and Latin commentaries*, 2 vols (London, 2004), i, 131–47. **92** *Commentaria Doctoris Subtilis Joannes Scoti in 12. li. Metaphysicae Aristotelis, Scripta recollecta et ordinata ab ipsius discipulo Antonio Andreae*, f. 102, 2. For further discussion of the war waged on Averroism by the Paduan Scotists see Antonino Poppi, 'L'antiaverroismo nella scolastica padovana alla fine del secolo XV', *Studia patavina* 11 (1964), 102–24; and Edward P. Mahoney, 'Duns Scotus and School of Padua', pp 219–27. **93** An important Franciscan theologian of the first part of the fourteenth century. An independent follower of Scotus, Francis made significant contributions to philosophical theology, metaphysics, and practical philosophy; see P. Lapperent, 'L'oeuvre politique de François de Meyronnes, ses rapports avec celle de Dante', *Archives d'Histoire Doctrinale et Littéraire du Moyen Âge* 15–17 (1940–2), 5–151; and Chris Schabel, *Theology at Paris, 1316–1345*, pp 149–55. **94** The letter to Marcello can be found in *Illuminati doctoris Francisci de Mayronis In primum sententiarum foecundissimum scriptum conflatum nominatum* (Venice, 1504), sig. AA2–AA2v. **95** Cavellus in *J. Duns Scoti Questiones subtilissimae et Expositio in Metaphysicam Aristotelis* (Venice, 1625), p. 4: 'Mauritius noster Hybernicus de universa scotistarum Schola optime meritus, magno labore et diligentia hos tractatus primum in lucem dedit; sed, ut ipse fatetur, tot et tantae difficultates et obscuritates occurrebant, ut multa futuris condiscipulis in operis expurgatione et exornatione praestanda reliquerit'; and Wadding, *Scriptores*, pp 172–173: 'Cum a iuventute annos quadraginta in Italia inter patres conventuales versaretur, et diu in universitate patavina theologiam profiteretur... totus in explicanda sui conterranei Scoti doctrina occupatus, multa in huius finem opera composuit.'

nothing new to human thought'.[96] The work of Mauritius Hibernicus would act as a template for all subsequent Irish contributions to the school of Scotus.

SALAMANCA

From the temperate climes of the Veneto our story moves on to the arid plains of Castille. For despite the industry of O'Fihely, the seeds of the long attachment of the Irish friars to Scotism were sown neither in Ireland nor in Padua but in Salamanca. Due to the exigencies of political conflict in late sixteenth- and early seventeenth-century Ireland, many students and clerics made their way to Spain in order to begin or else resume an education denied to them at home due to the bleak realities of civil strife and displacement.[97] Those inclining to a career with religious orders like the Observant Franciscans gravitated to their houses of studies in universities like Salamanca,[98] and these students were quickly inculcated into a sophisticated theological culture that had long been enchanted by the writings of Scotus,[99] and which on the eve of the seventeenth century was one of the leading centres of early modern Scholasticism.[1]

96 John R.H. Moorman (1905–89), former Anglican bishop of Ripon and ecumenist, see his *History of the Franciscan Order* (Oxford, 1968), p. 539. Moorman here is echoing the earlier view of A. Renaudet, 'Préréforme et Humanisme à Paris pendant les premières guerres d'Italie (1494–1517)', *Bibliothèque de l'Institut français de Florence*, première série, 6 (Paris, 1916), pp 98, 468, 656.   97 For a fascinating set of insights into how an assortment of Irish exiles, clerics and lay, negotiated the new challenges of Spanish society, and of the many rivalries they brought with them, see Igor Pérez Tostado, *Irish influence at the court of Spain in the seventeenth century* (Dublin, 2008); Karin Schüller, 'Irish migrant networks and rivalries, 1575–1659', in O'Connor and Lyons (eds), *Irish migrants in Europe after Kinsale*, pp 88–103; Thomas O'Connor, 'Irish migration to Spain and the formation of an Irish College network, 1589–1800', in Luc François and Ann Katherine Issacs (eds), *The sea and European history* (Pisa, 2001), pp 109–25; and Óscar Recio Morales, 'Irish émigré group strategies of survival, adaptation and integration in seventeenth- and eighteenth-century Spain', in Thomas O'Connor and Mary Ann Lyons (eds), *Irish communities in early modern Europe* (Dublin, 2006), pp 240–66.   98 For an invaluable assessment of the relationship between the Irish friars and Salamanca, albeit one specified to consider the activities of Luke Wadding, see Manuel de Castro OFM, 'Wadding and the Iberian Peninsula, in *Father Luke Wadding*, pp 119–70. Of more general interest is Manuel Rodríguez Pazas, 'De Nuestro Archivo Compostelano: Religiosos Irelandeses de la Provincio de Santiago', *El Eco Franciscano* 62 (1945), 168–211. See also Thomas Morrissey, 'The Irish student diaspora in the sixteenth century and the early years of the Irish college at Salamanca', *Recusant History* 14 (1978), 242–60; and Monica Henchy, 'The Irish college at Salamanca', *Studies* 70 (1981), 220–7.   99 See Issac Vázquez, 'La enseñanza del escotismo en España', in *De doctrina Ioannis Scoti*, iv, 191–220, esp. pp 191–207, and 211–17. The Salamanca enthusiasm for Scotus went back many years and as early as 1350 it is reported that a likeness of Scotus with his head surrounded by a halo was publicly venerated in the city; see E.M. Giusto, *Vita del B. Giovanni Duns Scoto* (S. Maria degli Angeli, 1921), pp 322–3.   1 Not only was Salamanca home to an important Scotist

In the Convento de San Francisco, the Franciscan priory and *studium* in the university,[2] Scotus was venerated as *Beatus*, and it is recorded by the Gallician theologian Mateus de Sousa (fl. 1629),[3] that an sizeable image of him was kept in a prominent place in the choir. Significantly, the effigy eventually found its way into the chamber of Francisco de Herrera (1551–1609) one of the teachers of Cavellus, and one can suppose that the Irish friar would have been familiar with its stature and presumed qualities of spiritual edification.[4] Of the six theological chairs in the university at the close of the sixteenth century one was specifically devoted to the study of Scotism.[5]

Before the Irish friars arrived, the Franciscans at Salamanca had already made a significant contribution to recent Catholic theology. Andréas de Vega (*c.*1498–1549), and Alfonso de Castro (1495–1588), to name but two, had helped to inform several important theological debates on justification at the Council of Trent.[6] Their legacy was upheld and enhanced in the crucial years of the early seventeenth century when the Irish friars were in residence. Among the leading Scotist theologians at this time were Francisco de Ovando (fl. 1577),[7] Juan de Rada (*c.*1545–1608),[8] the aforementioned Francisco de Herrera,[9] and Juan

school of theology, but it was also one of the leading centres of Thomist learning as exemplified by the famous Dominican convent of *San Esteban*; see Juan Belda Plans, *La Escuela de Salamanca y la renovación de la teología en el siglo XVI* (Madrid, 2000). Further to this, it was also graced by important Jesuit and Augustinian houses; on these see A. Astrain, *Historia de la Compañia de Jesús en al asistencia de España*, 6 vols (Madrid, 1920), iv, 20–250; and G. Díaz, 'La Escuela Augustiniana desde 1520 hasta 1650', *La Ciudad Dios* 176 (1973), 63–84, 189–234.   2 On this institution see Enrique Esperabé Arteaga, *Historia de la Universidad de Salamanca*, 2 vols (Salamanca, 1914–17), see i and ii; and Juan Antonio Domínquez, *Chrónica Seráfica y proseción de al Arbol chronológico* (Santiago, 1750).   3 Sousa's main work was *Optata diu articulatio et illustratio libri primi Sententiarum Doctoris Subtilissimi I.D. Scoti, cum fidelissima integritate et puritate Thomae modum redactae* [...] *nec non et controversiis, quae circa textum Scoti cum excitantur*, 2 vols (Salamanca, 1629).   4 An enthused description of the picture provided by De Sousa is cited by A. López, 'Notas de bibliografia franciscana', *Archivo Ibero-Americano* 14 (1927), 57; see also Giblin, 'Hugh MacCaughwell and Scotism', p. 381, n. 35.   5 Cavellus himself writes on this chair, see *Ioannes Duns Scotus, In quatuor libros Sententiarum*, i, p. xxvii: 'Florentissima Academia Salmanticensis, hisce temporibus in theologia Scholastica nulli in universo scholae secunda, sicut habet peculiarem cathedram pro Sacra Scriptura explicanda, et aliam pro Magistro Sententiarum, et aliam pro D. Thomae doctrina edocenda et defendenda; ita instituit specialem cathedram in qua legitur Scoti doctrina, non pro conclusione tantum et summatim, sed clare exponendo et tuendo eius literam.'   6 On this see B. Oromi OFM, *Los Franciscanos españoles en el Concilio de Trento* (Madrid, 1947); and R. Varesco OFM, 'I Frati Minori al Concilio di Trento', *Archivum franciscanum historicum* 41 (1948), 94–8, 99–104, and 132–3. On Vega see also Henricus Recla, *Andreae Vega OFM doctrina de iustificatione et Concilium Tridentinum* (Madrid, 1966), and Heiko A. Oberman, *The dawn of the Reformation* (Edinburgh, 1992), pp 204–233. For Castro see D. Müller, 'Ketzerei und Ketzerbestrafung im Werk des Alfonso de Castro', in F. Gunert and K. Seelmann (eds), *Die Ordnung der Praxis: Neue Studien zur spanischen Spätscholastik* (Tübingen, 2001), pp 333–48.   7 Ovando's principal work was the *Breviloquium Scholasticae theologiae in quatuor libros Magistri Sententiarum* (Salamanca,1584; Madrid, 1587).   8 Rada was the author of the influential *Controversiae theologicae inter S. Thomam et Scotam super quatuor libros*

Ovando de Paredes (d. 1610),[10] all of whom wrote works of speculative theology that added to the depth and sophistication of the Scotist school. The reflections of these individuals were guided and sustained by a near zealous concern to explain and analyse the works of Scotus, in order that his doctrines could then be applied to the issues and problems deemed important by the schools. Interestingly, these same Franciscan doctors of Salamanca came to understand the meaning and relevance of Scotus' doctrines in a multiplicity of ways, and the pluralism of their divergent approaches to the Subtle Doctor's ideas and texts was to have a lasting influence on the theoretical predilections of the Irish friars.

Francisco de Ovando, the first of this quartet, was a Spaniard who spent many years in Peru before becoming bishop of Trujillo.[11] His published corpus displays a thorough grasp of Scotus' thought as that had been handed down to him by earlier Salamancan professors, and by the leading figures of the fifteenth-century Scotist school. Eschewing any great novelty and exuding a lucid if tame orthodoxy in his approach to Scotus' ideas, Ovando's writings were designed to afford students clear and simple instruction in the opinions of Scotus and his medieval interpreters. For the Spaniard, the timeless teaching of the Subtle Doctor could be transposed to any period, and he remained steadfast in his conviction that all known problems of theology could be resolved by effective recourse to the wisdom of Scotus.

The methods of Ovando were not those of Juan de Rada. An eirenic thinker with an overt penchant for synthesis, he sought to contrive a conciliation between Scotism and the rival schools of early modern Scholasticism, especially Thomism and Durandianism, as these were practised in Iberia and elsewhere.[12] Rada was possibly less of a doctrinal Scotist than many of his Salamanca

Sententiarum, published at Salamanca in 1586, with later printings at Venice, 1601, 1604, and 1617, and at Cologne, 1620. **9** Herrera's important works are *Disputationes thelogicae et commentaria in primum librum Sententiarum doct. Subtilis a 28 usque ad 48* (Salamanca, 1589); *In Secundum* (Salamanca, 1600); and *Manuale theologicum et resolutissima dilucidatio principalium quaestionum quae communiter in quatuor libris Sententiarum disputantur* (Rome, 1607), with later editions at Paris, 1616, and Venice, 1644. For further discussion see D. Savall, 'La interpretación escotista en la provincia de Santiago: Fr. Francesco de Herrera ye el pecado de los angeles', *El Eco franciscano* 56 (1939), 438–59; and Issac Vázquez Janeiro, 'Fr. Francisco de Herrera, OFM, y sus votos controversia de auxiliis', *Verdad y vida* 23 (1965), 271–318. **10** Another influential Observant theologian in Spain, whose reputation was based on his work *Commentarii in tertium librum Sententiarum Ioannis* (Valencia, 1597); see Issac Vázquez Janeiro, 'Los Juan de Ovando: dos teologos homonimos del Siglo XVI', *Revista Española de Teologia* 38 (1978), 273–310. **11** See 'Ovando, Francisco', *Dictionnaire de théologie catholique*, xi (1932), col. 1674. **12** 'Durandianism' was a late medieval and early modern Scholastic school which took its impetus from the teaching of the Dominican Durandus of St Pourçain (*c*.1275–1332/1334). It had some influence on Iberian Scholasticism with chairs based in universities such as Coimbra. The school remains to be studied. Some information about its place in Portuguese Scholasticism can be gleaned from Friedrich Stegmüller, *Filosofia e Teologia nas Universidades de Coimbra e Évora no século XVI* (Coimbra, 1959), pp 32–4.

contemporaries, but his rehearsal of some of the more taxing issues of his time reveals an earnest yet inquiring mind that was suitably equipped to hound the minutiae of theological controversy. Rada's four-volume *Controversiae theologicae inter S. Thomam et Scotum* is a veritable emporium of Scholastic argument, not least for the fact that it evinces a profound understanding of the principal differences that attended the schools of Scotus and Thomas on issues pertaining to metaphysics and theology.[13] His knowledge of the detail of these disputes served him well in his contribution to the debate on pure nature,[14] and also when he was summoned to Rome to serve on the *De auxiliis* congregation.[15] The *Controversiae theologicae* also displayed an appreciation of the ideas of modern Scholastic thinkers (known as *recentiores* or *neoterici*) such as Cajetan and Suárez, and was moved to bring the teaching of Scotus into dialogue with the current views of the schools. In the later writings of Irish friars such as Cavellus, and more importantly, Punch, one can discern a similar commitment to engage with the latest arguments of prominent Scholastic theologians on the topical issues of their time.

De Herrera and Juan Ovando de Paredes were teachers of Cavellus,[16] and they helped to instill in the Irishman's mind an esteem for all things Scotist which he would impart to a fledgling generation of Irish friars at St. Anthony's College, Louvain.[17] De Herrera, who was ever present in the Covento de San Francisco, was a major figure in Salamancan Scotism, and who wrote a detailed study of the first and second parts of Scotus' *Commentary on the Sentences*.[18] His gifts as an exegete aside, he also pioneered a distinctive theological approach to Scotus, which was minded to work within the spirit rather than the letter of the Subtle Doctor's teaching. De Herrera's acclaimed and interesting *Manuale theologicum* of 1607, bears witness to his independent outlook and willingness to revise and improve upon established Scotist arguments, in order to propose solutions to then current problems in the schools concerning divine grace and human freedom.[19] Less original than de Herrera, Ovando de Paredes was a thorough if remorseless exponent of Scotist doctrine. His narration and analysis of the

13 For a synopsis of this work see George Marcil, 'Joannes de Rada and the argument for the primacy of Christ in his *Controversiae theologicae*', in Bérubé (ed.), *Homo et Mundus*, pp 138–44.
14 See Bernardino de Armellada, 'Dos teólogos franciscanos del siglo XVI ante el problema del sobrenatural: Francisco Liqueto y Juan de Rada', *Revista española de teología* 19 (1959), 373–422. See also Marcil 'Joannes de Rada', pp 139–43 for further comment on his theological method.
15 Issac Vázquez Janeiro, 'El arzobispo Juan de Rada y el molinismo', *Verdad y vida* 20 (1962), 351–96. 16 Cavellus informs us of this at *Ioannes Duns Scoti* [...] *in primum et secundum Sententiarum questiones subtilissimae* (Antwerp, 1620), i, p. xxxix. 17 See Giblin, 'Hugh MacCaghwell OFM and Scotism at St Anthony's College Louvain', in *De doctrina Ioannis Duns Scoti*, iv, 386–9. 18 Francisco de Herrera, *Disputationes theologicae et commentaria in primum librum Sententiarum doct. Subtilis a 28 usque ad 48* (Salamanca, 1589); and *In secundum* (Salamanca, 1600). 19 Vázquez Janeiro, 'Fr. Francisco de Herrera, OFM, y sus votos contro-versia de auxiliis', pp 300–16.

Subtle Doctor's third book of *Commentary on the Sentences* advanced a systematic treatment of a multitude of theological antinomies, especially those pertaining to the Trinity and Christology. Ovando's handling of each issue is characterised by an impeccable attention to explicating the *sensus et intentio* of the mind of Scotus.[20]

The theological outlook of the Irish friars would be yet further formed by their inheritance of another feature of Salamanca Scotist theology, mariology; and its specific commitment to a reasoned defense of the teaching of the Immaculate Conception.[21] At the outset of the seventeenth century, an extraordinary wave of devotion to the Immaculate Conception of Mary consumed Spain. An ancient piety which stretched back to the time of the Fathers, and which had been nurtured in the Middle Ages by Franciscan theologians such as Scotus, who had argued that Mary's Immaculate Conception was anticipatory of Christ's redemptive work,[22] the teaching now found mature expression in the Scotist school of Iberia as well as enthusiastic support among the laity.[23] Due to the furore created in the Spanish universities by the cause of the Virgin Mary, many of the traditional objections to the doctrine were recycled, especially those of Thomas Aquinas and the Dominican order, who had denied the theological position because they thought it undermined the universality of redemption through Christ.[24] The reintroduction of this position only served to exacerbate latent tensions and further estrange the disputing Franciscan and Dominican parties. In an effort to remedy the growing discord among his theologians and their lay supporters, Philip III decided to send a series of special delegations to Rome,[25] the most famous being led in 1618 by the influential Franciscan bishop

---

20 Vázquez Janeiro, 'Los Juan de Ovando: dos teologos homonimos del Siglo XVI', pp 280–90, and 300–10.   21 On the devotion and its complicated history see X. Le Bachelet, 'L'Immaculée Conception', *Dictionnaire de théologie catholique*, vii (1922), cols. 845–1218, esp. cols. 1150–76; and C. Balić, 'The medieval controversy over the Immaculate Conception up to the death of Scotus', in E. O'Connor (ed.), *The dogma of the Immaculate Conception: history and significance* (Notre Dame, IN, 1958), pp 161–222.   22 See Scotus, *Opus Oxoniense*, III d. 3, q. 1, and III d. 18, q. 1, n. 14; and *Rep.* III. d. 3, q. 1. On Scotus' arguments and their influence see C. Balić, *Ioannes Duns Scotus et historia Immaculatae Conceptionis* (Rome, 1955); L. Amorós, 'La significación de Juan Escoto en la historia del dogma de la Immaculada Concepción', *Verdad y Vida* 14 (1956), 265–378; R. Zavalloni and E. Mariani (eds), *La dottrina mariologic di Giovanni Duns Scoto*, Spicilegium Pontificii Anthenaei Antoniani, 28 (Rome, 1987); and Alfonso Pompei, 'Mariología', in José Antonio Merino and Francisco Martínez Fresneda (eds), *Manuel de Teología Franciscana* (Madrid, 2004), pp 251–322, esp. pp 294–311.   23 A. Uribe, 'La Immaculada en la literatura franciscana española', *Archivo Ibero-Americo* 15 (1955), 201–495.   24 See Thomas Aquinas, *Summa theologiae*, III, q. 27, aa. 1–3; and Ulrich Horst, *Die Diskussion um die Immaculata Conceptio im Dominikanerorden: ein Beitrag zur Geschichte der theologischen Methode*, Veröffentlichungen des Grabmann-Institutes zur Erforschung der mittelalterlichen Theologie und Philosophie. Neue Folge, 34 (Paderborn, 1987).   25 Lemes Frias, 'Felipe III y la Immaculada Concepción: instancias a la Sta. Sede por la definición del misterio', *Razón y Fé* 10 (1904), 21–33, 145–56, 293–308; 11 (1905), 180–98; 12 (1905), 322–36; 13 (1905), 62–75.

of Cartagena, Antonio de Trejo (d. 1639),[26] to ask the Holy See to define the dogma.

The young Luke Wadding, fresh from his recent experience of teaching Scotist theology at Salamanca, was appointed theologian to this delegation and asked to prepare its theological petition and *vota*, which would be presented in Rome by the Spanish ambassador. Some years later in a work known as the *Legatio*, Wadding published a revised version of the views he had originally set down in the petition.[27] Drawing on his formative education in the Marian theology of the Jesuit Francisco Suárez (1548–1617) and the Augustinian friar Gil da Presentaço (1593–1629) at the University of Coimbra,[28] he produced a learned case which reflected the current thinking of his Franciscan colleagues at Salamanca.[29] Attempting to defuse the growing tension and acrimony in the schools, Wadding aimed to explain that the general authority of Thomas Aquinas was not impugned if his views on the issue of the Immaculate Conception of Mary gave way to those of Scotus.[30] Moreover, if the doctrine were accepted, Wadding argued, Thomas's opinions would not have to be condemned,[31] but only one of his theses would need to be rejected.[32] In this manner Wadding strove to uphold the authority of Scotus' position while not riding roughshod over the Thomist sensibilities of his Dominican critics.

The Mariological writings of Scotus and the defence of the doctrine of the Immaculate Conception would remain pervasive themes in the theological writings of the Irish friars. Further to Wadding, Flaithrí Ó Maolchonaire or Florence Conry (Latinized to 'Conrius') OFM (*c*.1560–1629),[33] Cavellus,[34] and

26 On the good bishop and the mission to Rome see Jose Maria Pou y Marti, 'Embajadas de Felipe III a Roma pidiendo de la definición de la I. Concepión de Maria', *Archivo Ibero-Americano* 34 (1931), 371–417, 508–34; 35 (1932), 72–88, 424–34, 481–525. For De Trejo see ibid. 35 (1932), 72–88. 27 Luke Wadding, *Legatio Philippi III et IV catholicorum regum Hispaniarum ad SS.DD.NN. Paulum PP. V et Gregorium XV de definienda controversia Immanculatae Conceptionis B. Virginis Mariae per Ill. mum ed. Rev mum Dom. D. F. Antonium a Trejo* (Louvain, 1624). 28 See M. De Castro, 'Wadding and the Iberian peninsular', pp 120–62. On Suarez's Mariology see Robert Fastiggi, 'Mary's Coredemption according to Francisco Suarez, S.J. (1548–1617)', in *Mary at the foot of the cross – IV: Mater Viventium. Acts of the Fourth International Symposium on Marian Coredemption* (New Bedford, MA, 2004), pp 338–51; and for Fray Gil see Eloy Domínguez Carretero, 'Tradición Immaculista agustiniana a través de Egidio de la Presentación', *La Ciudad de Dios* 66 (1954), 343–86. 29 See M. De Castro, 'Wadding and the Iberian peninsula', in *Father Luke Wadding*, pp 159–62. 30 Wadding, *Legatio*, pp 278–81. See also *De redemptione B. Mariae Virginis* (Rome, 1656), pp 24–5, for Wadding's most candid endorsement of Scotist teaching. 31 Wadding, *Legatio*, p. 284: 'cum in rebus dubiis illa semper fuerit D. Thomae opinio vel doctrina quam Ecclesia postea definierit, ut et ipse dixit in morte; et omnes pii et catholici doctores parati sunt id potius sequi, quod Ecclesia statuerit, quam quod aliquando ipsi docuerint.' See also ibid., pp 281, and 283. 32 As Wadding pointed out, see ibid., p. 281, when the Church praises Thomas (and indeed other saints and doctors), it does not intend to lay down that '*ipsa [opera] in omni sua parte sint vera et in nullo a vero tramite aberrent*'. 33 Florence Conry, *De Augustini sensu circa B. Mariae Virginis Conceptionem* (Antwerp, 1619). 34 Cavellus'

1 Revd (later Canon) Denis O'Keeffe 1882–1952

2 Dr (later Monsignor) Arthur Ryan 1897–1982

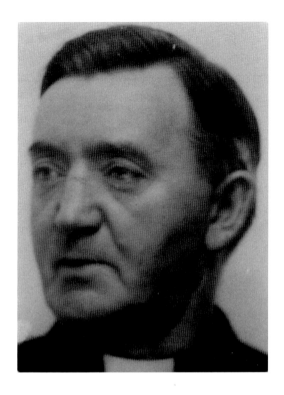

3 Revd Professor Theodore Crowley OFM 1910–1990

4 Dr (now Cardinal) Cahal Brendan Daly 1917–

5 Revd Professor James McEvoy 1943–

6 Group shot from the June 2008 Conference

Front Row from left: Padre Apollonio, Rev. Professor James McEvoy, Cardinal
Cahal Daly, Monsignor Ray Murray, Bishop John Fleming
Middle Row from Left: Fr Gavan Jennings, Angelo Bottone, Dr Declan Lawell,
Denise Ryan, Sarah Otten, Sandra Gilpin, Professor William Desmond, Dr
James Daly, Dr Mette Lebech, Mr Éamonn Gaines, Dr Catherine Kavanagh,
Dr Ian Leask, Dr Frank Gourley, Francis Creagh, Professor John Rooney
Back Row from Left: Fr Joseph Gunn, Dr Michael Haren, Dr Kevin O'Reilly,
Gaven Kerr, Jonathan Watson, Dr William Desmond Jr, Dr Cyril O'Donnell,
Dr Hugh Bredin, Martin McDonnell, Professor Philipp Rosemann, Professor
Martin Stone, Sean De Bhulbh, Dr Liam Chambers

Thirteenth Meeting.

At Belfast, 16th April, 1909.

The Commissioners met at ten o'clock.

PRESENT:- His Honour Judge Shaw, Chairman, in the Chair, the Vice-Chancellor, Professor Dill, Sir Donald MacAlister, Mr. R. T. Martin, Sir Arthur Rücker and Professor Symington.

The Minutes of the twelfth meeting were approved.

The Commissioners further considered Draft Statutes (Third Proof) and fixed the salaries of certain of the officers and teaching staff of the University according to the Schedule annexed.

The Commissioners decided to make appointments to the following additional Professorships :- Modern History, Economics, French and Romance Philology, and Botany. They also decided to make appointments to the following additional Lectureships or Readerships :- Archaeology and Ancient History, English Language, Celtic Languages and Literature, Logic and Scholastic Philosophy, Physics, Geology, Organic Chemistry, and Bio-Chemistry.

The Commissioners rose at half-past five o'clock and visited the Municipal Technical Institute, where they were received by Sir James Henderson, D.L., Chairman, and other members of the Library and Technical Instruction Committee, and members of the Staff of the Institute.

JAMES J. SHAW.

7 From the minutes of the meeting
of QUB commissioners
dated 16 April 1909

8 The Revd Denis O'Keeffe replies accepting

others,[35] would all make significant contributions to a cause they inherited from the Salamancans. While the intellectual labours of the Observant Irish friars would come to maturity in the subsequent decades of the seventeenth century, it was at the Convento de San Francesco that they were first tutored in the ideas of Duns Scotus and his Mariological heritage. The greatest debt of the friars in the first decades of their exile was then to Salamanca and other universities of Iberia. For it was there that they were given respite from the troubles of their homeland, and the leisure to pursue a programme of study sufficient to furnish them with the skills needed to make a genuine contribution to early modern Scholasticism. Wherever Conry, Cavellus, and Wadding roamed, and whenever they lectured and published, they remained steadfast in their allegiance to a Scotist and Mariological outlook that had been fashioned in Salamanca.

'DRAMATIS PERSONAE'

When one comes to examine individual works of philosophy and theology by the Irish friars one is immediately struck by the vivid personality of several authors, who despite their editorial or expository responsiblities to a particular text or theological problem, leave the reader with a fetching imprint of their own temperament, struggles, and even peculiar foibles. Nowhere is this more common than in the introductions to apparently dry works of Scotist scholarship, such as the revelatory prefaces and epistles that grace the epistles of O'Fihely,[36] or the autobiographical reminisces of Cavellus in his charming description of the environs of Downpatrick when relating the life of Scotus.[37] These features can also be combined with other indications of a colourful personality, such as exasperated ruminations on the limitations of current pastoral practices, as can be found in the writings of Conry,[38] the nervous anxiety of Wadding that the cause of Scotus must be prosecuted at all costs lest the faith

---

Rosarium Beatae Maria is included as an appendix at the end of his edition of the Third Book of Scotus' *Sentences Commentary*, see ii, 267ff. Punch also inserted this work as an appendix to the third volume of his 1661 *Commentarii theologici*, appearing after page 696 running for eighteen pages. On the *Rosarium* itself see McEvoy, 'Hugh McCawell OFM, Scotist theologian of the Immaculate Conception of Mary', in Stone (ed.), *From Ireland to Louvain*.   **35** See also Hickey, *De Conceptione Immaculata B. Mariae Virginis*, listed by San Antonio, *Bibliotheca*, i, 82 (no copy of this work has been found despite reliable attestations of its existence since 1648); and Bonaventure Baron, *Elegia de Immaculata Conceptione B.V.M.* (Rome, 1642), see Sbaralea, *Supplementum*, i, 185. Others worthy of mention are: Bonaventure O'Connor Kerry (alias A.S. Patritio), *Quintuplex Pentekaedechryris Mariana* (Trent, 1658), Cleary, *Father Luke Wadding and St Isidore's College*, Rome, pp 135–6; and James Miles (Milesius), (d. 1639), *Typus Conceptionis Immaculatae Virginis Mariae* (Naples, 1631); this work was originally written in Italian, see ibid., p. 83.   **36** O'Fihely, see above, p. 153, nn. 86–8.   **37** Cavellus, *Vita Scoti*, cap. 1.   **38** Florence Conry, *De statu parvulorum*, pp 5–11; and *Desiderius* or *Sgáthán an chrábhaidh*, p. 5.

be lost,[39] or else the elegant and leisured Latinity of Bonaventure Baron (1610–1696), who manages to impose a literary precision upon the compact and multifarious thoughts of Scotus.[40] Even restrained and seemingly more 'academic' writers such as Hickey, Punch, Anthony Broudin (d. 1675),[41] and Bonaventure O'Connor Kerry (fl. 1660),[42] could all wear their hearts on their sleeves whenever a suitable cause forced itself on their time and attention.

The relevant point here is that those friars whose writings came to prominence in the schools of seventeenth and eighteenth century Europe were varied characters of broad range and great depth. Their complex personalities and elaborate intellectual interests were often heightened rather than dissipated by their emotional attachment to the causes of Ireland, the Immaculate Conception, and Scotus. And when these divergent allegiances were combined with the literary skills and personae of Conry and Cavellus, both highly trained bards (*ollamhain*) in the Old Irish tradition,[43] or Baron with his humanist elegance, or Punch with his analytical acuity and dry wit, the resulting works of theological and philosophy that issued from the friars' pens were expressive of a humanity so often lacking in other quarters of early modern Scholasticism. With this in mind, let us now review the speculative achievements of the Irish Franciscans from Conry to Rourke and beyond, in order that we may learn how they put their Scotist allegiances and Salamancan inheritance to good use.

Florence Conry

In years that led up to the establishment of the college of St Anthony of Padua at Louvain in 1607 the first theologian of repute among the Irish friars was Florence Conry,[44] an individual whose intellectual interests, political passions,

---

39 Wadding, *Annales*, vi, 157.   40 Baron, *Ioannes Duns Scotus* [...] *de Deo trino, contra adversantes quosque defensus* (Lyons, 1668), pp 1–6.   41 On Broudin see Cleary, *Father Luke Wadding and St Isidore's College Rome*; pp 134–138; Thomas Wall, 'Bards and Bruodins', in *Father Luke Wadding*, pp 438–62; and Micheál MacCraith and David Worthington, 'Aspects of the literary activity of the Irish Franciscans in Prague, 1620–1786', in O'Connor and Lyons (eds), *Irish migrants in Europe after Kinsale*, pp 118–34, esp. pp 130–4.   42 Cathaldus Giblin, 'Bonaventure O'Connor Kerry: a seventeenth-century Franciscan abroad', *Journal of the Kerry Archaeological & Historical Society* 17 (1984), 37–60. One of the O'Connors of Kerry, he was educated in Rome and taught in Bolzano and Prague. His work of controversial theology, *Lumen Orthodoxum spargens duodecim radios* (Bolzano, 1661), was composed for priests on the mission to England and Ireland. A very personal work, it presents a series of summaries of the main dogmatic differences between Catholics and Protestants, as well as a discussion of other problems associated with the vagaries of recusancy.   43 On the literary training and repute of Conry and Cavellus see O'Rahilly, 'Introduction', in *Desiderius*, pp viii–xvi; and Tomás O Cléirigh, *Aodh MacAingil agus an scoil nua-Ghaeilge i Lobháin*, pp 10ff.   44 The most recent biographical sketches of Conry are by Terry Clavin, 'Conry, Florence', *ODNB*, 12 (2004), pp 996–998; Declan Downey, 'Archbishop Florence Conry of Tuam', in Duddy (ed.), *Dictionary of Irish philosophers*, pp 86–90; and Anthony McKenna et al., 'Florent Conry', in J. Lesaulnier and A. McKenna (ed.), *Dictionnaire de Port Royal* (Paris, 2004), p. 293. See also Pazas, 'Religiosos irelandeses de la Provincio de

quizzical personality, and general approach to theology place him at an orthogonal position to his colleagues.[45] Although he maintained a resolute interest in traditional Scotist doctrines such as the Immaculate Conception, thereby affirming an impeccable Salamancan pedigree,[46] there is a sense in which Conry was not a 'Scholastic' not at least in the sense in which that term might be used to characterize the methods and arguments employed by Cavellus, Hickey, Punch, and Baron. For unlike this distinguished quartet, he drew his inspiration not from the medieval schoolmen but from the Fathers, specifically from the writings of Augustine.[47] Though his highly personal theological outlook never caused him to quarrel with Scotism as such,[48] it did prompt him to query the validity of the pronouncements of many contemporary Scholastic theologians, especially members of the Jesuit order whom he particularly disliked, on topics such as grace, nature, limbo, and infant baptism.[49] Conry could not withhold himself from pointing out that elements of their teaching were contradicted by the dicta of the ancient Church as upheld by Augustine.

The first Guardian of the College of St Anthony of Padua at Louvain,[50] Conry's posthumous reputation has undoubtedly suffered as a result of his less than cordial association with Cornelius Jansenius (1585–1638),[51] and the fact that

Santiago', pp 200–11. **45** Something of the man is captured in the following studies: F. O'Byrne, 'Florence Conry, archbishop of Tuam', *Irish Rosary* 31 (1927), 845–7, 896–904; and ibid. 32 (1928), 346–51, 454–60; O'Connor, *Irish Jansenists, 1660–70*, pp 64–72, 171–80; and Declan M. Downey, 'A Salamancan who evaded the Inquisition: Florence Conry, pro-Habsburg archbishop, diplomat and controversial theologian (*c.*1660–1629)', in Declan M. Downey and Julio Crespo MacLennan (eds), *Spanish-Irish relations through the ages* (Dublin, 2008), pp 87–103. The most complete study of Conry's public persona is Benjamin Hazard, 'The political career of Florence Conry: *c.*1590–1629', PhD NUI, Maynooth, 2008. **46** Conry's debt to Salamanca is on full display in his work of Marian theology, *De Augustini sensu circa B. Mariae Virginis Conceptionem*, as well as in his writings on grace See also, C. Heaney, *The theology of Florence Conroy OFM* (Drogheda, 1935), pp 67–72; and Downey, 'A Salamancan who evaded the Inquisition', pp 89–93. **47** The best available studies of Conry's theology, which still awaits a comprehensive reassessment are C. Heaney, *The theology of Florence Conroy OFM*; Lucien Ceyssens, 'Florence Conroy, Hugh de Burgo, Luke Wadding, and Jansenism' in *Father Luke Wadding*, pp 295–404, esp. 303–31; and O'Connor, *Irish Jansenists*, pp 64–72. According to Wadding, *Scriptores*, p. 109, Conry immersed himself in the works of Augustine at Madrid before he left the Spanish court in 1618. **48** This is probably due to the fact that Scotus' own theology is heavily reliant upon many facets of Augustine's thought. The Augustinian residue in Scotism is famously chronicled in the useful, if contested, work by Étienne Gilson, *Jean Duns Scot: introduction à ses positions fondamentales* (Paris, 1952), esp. pp 11–115. **49** Beside his disdain for certain aspects of their theology, Conry's antipathy to the Jesuits was also sharpened as a result of running conflict with the Society, personified in the figure of James Archer (1550–1620), to gain control of the Irish colleges in Spain and the Irish mission. For further discussion see Karin Schüller, 'Irish migrant networks and rivalries in Spain, 1575–1659'; and Benjamin Hazard, 'Confessor, adviser and favourite': the early career of Florence Conry OFM', in Stone (ed.), *From Ireland to Louvain*. **50** Fennessy, 'Guardians and staff of Saint Anthony's College', p. 215. **51** Jansenius often refers to Conry in his letters, see Jean Orcibal (ed.) *Correspondance de*

many of his writings were circulated after his death by Antoine Arnauld (1612–94) and other supporters of the cause of Port-Royal.[52] While it is true that he shared several points in common with these individuals, especially with respect to theological anthropology, it would be unfair to view him as an influential figure in the development of the movement that bore Jansenius' name.[53] For when his work is liberated from the false perspective that he was a 'proto-Jansenist', Conry can be appreciated as a historically engaged theologian whose position on the questions of his day is constructed on the basis of a detailed reflection upon the texts of the bishop of Hippo. Moved to read Augustine's treatises with an eye to discerning the details of their author's development, and thus to locating their salience and truth,[54] Conry's entire corpus is devoted to the advancement and defence of an Augustinian theology.

The initial fruits of his rich interactions with the *Doctor Universalis* can be seen in his translation into Irish of a Catalan work, known in Castilian as *Tratado llamado el Desseoso, y por otro nombre, espejo de religiosos*,[55] which Conry called *Sgáthán an chrábhaidh* (Mirror of piety) or *Desiderius*.[56] The *Sgáthán*'s content is indicative not only of his general catechetical concerns but also of a more specific aspiration to form the Irish in an orthodox 'Augustinian' faith, that eschewed the sort of compromising attitude towards the Protestant state Conry had so roundly condemned in his 1615 letter to Irish Catholic Members of Parliament.[57]

Jansenius, Les origines du Jansénisme, 1 (Paris & Louvain, 1947), and these documents reveal an uneasiness in their relationship despite their shared enthusiasm for Augustine. For commentary on these letters see Ceyssens, 'Florence Conry, Hugh de Burgo and Luke Wadding, and Jansenism', in *Father Luke Wadding*, pp 311–30; and O'Connor, *Irish Jansenists*, pp 68–70. See also Jean Orcibal, *Jansénius d'Ypres (1585–1638)* (Paris, 1989), pp 110–16. 52 Ceyssens, 'Florence Conry, Hugh de Burgo, Luke Wadding, and Jansenism', pp 303–31; and O'Connor, *Irish Jansenists*, pp 171–80. 53 Ruth Clark, *Sojourners and strangers at Port-Royal* (Cambridge, 1930), pp 3–7. 54 On this see Jean-Louis Quantin, *Le Catholicisme Classique et les Pères de L'Église. Un retour aux sources (1669–1713)* (Paris, 1999), pp 128–30, and 137; and my 'Florence Conry on the *limbus infantium*: tradition and innovation in early modern Augustinianism', in Stone (ed.) *From Ireland to Louvain*. 55 The Catalan original had probably circulated in manuscript before being published, anonymously, in 1515. On the dispute concerning the authorship of the work see Seán Ua Súilleabháin, 'Údar sgáthán an chrábhaidh', *Maynooth Review* 14 (1989), 42–50. 56 See Thomas F. O'Rahilly (ed.), Flaithrí Ó Maolchonaire, *Desiderius* otherwise called *Sgáthán an chrábhaidh*, Medieval and Modern Irish Series, XII (Dublin, 1955); see also Brian Ó Cuív, 'Flaithrí Ó Maolchonaire's Catechism of Christian Doctrine', *Celtica* 1 (1946–50), 161–206. 57 Conry, 'Remonstrance by Florence Conry to the Catholic members of the Parliament held in Dublin, 1613' [Valladolid, 1614] cited in C.P. Meehan, *The fate and fortunes of Hugh O'Neill, earl of Tyrone and Rory O'Donnell, earl of Tyrconnell* (Dublin, 1868), pp 395–7. On Conry's extensive political activities see Brendan Jennings (ed.), *Wild Geese in Spanish Flanders 1582–1700* (Dublin, 1964), pp 155, 209, 212–15, and 217–19; M. Walsh, 'The last years of Hugh O'Neill', *Irish Sword*, 7 (1965–6), 5–14, 136–46, and 327–33; J.J. Silke, *Kinsale: the Spanish intervention in Ireland at the end of the Elizabethan Wars* (New York, 1970), pp 148, 161, 166–7; G. Henry, *The Irish military community in Spanish*

Further testimony of his commitment to a rigidly Augustinian anthropology can be found in *De statu parvulorum*, perhaps his best known theological work, where he treats the thorny issue of unbaptized infants. The immediate stimulus for the tract, Conry revealed in the preface, was his own pedagogical experience, and former attempts to make sense of the sufferings of the just.[58] Some theologians, he claimed, had been tempted, perhaps in the interests of pastoral sensitivity, to adopt a benevolent line on the issue, by offering the hope of some version of eternal felicity to infants who died unbaptized. Conry would allow nothing of the sort, since Augustine and Sacred Scripture, he avowed, denied any middle place between the eternal life of the kingdom and the perpetual punishment of hell.[59] As there was no limbo, the infants would suffer the pains of hell, albeit in a manner less horrific than that endured by the damned. Here was an issue, Conry asserted, that revealed Scripture and Augustine to have greater authority than the conjectures of contemporary Scholastics.[60]

Following *De statu parvulorum*, Conry pursued another project which dealt more explicitly with the question of grace. This manuscript was entitled *Peregrinus*, and though completed by 1625, it remained unpublished for sixteen years. The work provides the most complete account of Conry's engagement with the anti-Pelagian writings of Augustine, and his attempt to translate them into a tractable pastoral programme. As such, the book amounts to nothing more than a strong defence of an Augustinian theory of grace and predestination. Significantly, the dominant conclusion of the work proved exceptionally popular with some of the students at St Anthony's College. John Barnewall OFM (fl. 1627),[61] for instance, in his lectures reiterated Conry's grim doctrine,[62] and in

Flanders (Dublin, 1992), pp 136, 142–3; Thomas O'Connor, 'Perfidious machiavellian friar: Florence Conry's campaign for catholic restoration in Ireland, 1592–1616', *Seanchas Ard Mhacha* 16 (2002), 91–105; Mícheál MacCraith, 'The political thought of Florence Conry and Hugh MacCaughwell' in Ford and McCafferty (eds), *The origins of sectarianism in early modern Ireland*, pp 183–202; and Benjamin Hazard, 'Confessor, adviser and favourite'.   **58** This was probably a reference to his tract *De flagellis justorum juxta mentem Sancti Augustini*, which dealt with the sensible punishment of original sin; see Heaney, *The theology of Florence Conry*, pp 41–2. No copy of this tract is known to exist. It appears to have been a substantial piece as Conry writes, in *De Statu parvulorum*, '*late alibi tractavimus*', p. 5, and '*alibi operose poenas originalis in hac vita deduximus*', see p. 33.   **59** Conry, *Tractatus de statu parvulorum sine baptismo decedentium ex hac vita juxta sensum B. Augustini* (Louvain, 1623), pp 2–18. For a full discussion of Conry's complicated views on this subject see my 'Florence Conry on the *limbus infantium*', in Stone (ed.) *From Ireland to Louvain.*   **60** Conry, *Tractatus de statu parvulorum sine baptismo decedentium ex hac vita juxta sensum B. Augustini*, pp 50–75. For further brief discussion of this aspect of Conry's thought see Downey, 'Augustinians and Scotists', pp 96–108; see also Heaney, *The theology of Florence Conry*, pp 28–77.   **61** Barnewall, who later became provincial of the Irish Observants, also defended a thesis (set out in hexameters!) on Scotus, *Universa theologia iuxta mentem Doctoris Subtilis* (Louvain, 1620). The little information on him that exists is recorded by Ceyssens, 'Florence Conry, Hugh de Burgo, Luke Wadding and Jansenism', pp 308, 310, 312, 324–5, 326, 344–5; and O'Connor, *Irish Jansenists*, pp 71 and 286.   **62** Peter Walsh, *History and Vindication of the Loyal*

1627 he presided over a thesis entitled *Sententia S. Augustini* [...] *de gratia, libero arbitrio, praedestinatione et reprobatione ac simul proponitur disputatio de justifica-tione ac merito bonorum operum,* defended by one Francis O'Farrell OFM (fl. 1627).[63] The presentation of Barnewell's lectures and O'Farrell's thesis indicates that Conry's views on grace and predestination had set down roots among the early Franciscans at Louvain. Indeed, some years later, when following the publication of Jansenius' *Augustinus* in 1640 an ensuing controversy had polarised theological opinion both in Louvain and elsewhere, the Franciscan propositions were reprinted.[64] In this different and slightly hysterical context, Hugh Bourke (*c.*1592–1654), Patrick Brenan (fl. 1627), and other Irish Franciscans came under pressure from anti-Jansenist quarters to disown the 1627 propositions. They refused to do so, and with some justice denied that their position emanated from the mind of Jansenius, adding that it was nothing more than the teaching of Augustine as interpreted by the scrupulously orthodox Florence Conry.[65]

In retrospect one might view Conry as being semi-detached from the theological views that are more readily associated with the Irish Franciscans of the seventeenth century, not least for the reason that he promoted a neo-Augustinian theology that rejected a good deal of the apparel of early modern Scholasticism. His stalwart enthusiasm for the doctrine of the Immaculate Conception, however, helped to keep him within the theological mainstream of his Order rather than that of his adopted home of Louvain, where the theolo-gians viewed the doctrine with suspicion.[66] For all that, however, Conry still cuts

Formulary or Irish Remonstrance (London, 1674), Fourth treatise, p. 75. Peter Walsh (Petrus Valesius) (1610/8–1688) was an Irish Franciscan who had been educated at Louvain and was initially well disposed to Jansenism; see Clark, *Strangers and sojouners at Port-Royal*, pp 206–7; and Millet, *The Irish Franciscans*, pp 418–63. On Farrell see Ceyssens, 'Florence Conry, Hugh de Burgo, Luke Wadding and Jansenism', p. 325; and O'Connor, *Irish Jansenists*, pp 287–88, 330–2, and 334–42. 63 *Sententia D. Augustini eximii ecclesiae doctoris de gratia, lib. Arbit, praedestina-tione et Reprobatione publice defense, Lovanii in Collegio S. Antonii de Padua FF. Minorum Hibernorum strictioris observantiae, praeside V.F.P. Ioanne Barnewallo Sacrae Theologiae Lectore. Respondente F. Patricio Brinan, die 9. Septembris 1627, hora 9. Ante et 3 post meridiem. Facta omnibus oppugnandi Copia. Secunda editio. Lovanie, apud Iacobum Zegers anno 1641.* See Dom Gabriel Gerberon, *Histoire générale du jansénisme,* 3 vols (Amsterdam, 1700), i, 21–3. On the theses published by the Irish friars see Ignatius Fennessy, 'Canon E. Reussen's list of Irish Franciscan theses in Louvain, 1620–1738', *Collectanea Hibernica* 48 (2006), 21–66. 64 Ceyssens, 'Florence Conry, Hugh de Burgo, Luke Wadding and Jansenism', p. 324. The propo-sitions were originally published by Jacob Zegers in Louvain and were later republished in Paris, in 1641. 65 Lucien Ceyssens, 'Florence Conry, Hugh de Burgo, Luke Wadding and Jansenism', p. 324. 66 The doctrine of the Immaculate Conception did not find favour among the *Lovanienses,* even from the foundation of their Theology Faculty in 1432. Their reluctance to embrace the idea was further strengthened by their allegiance in the early modern period to several neo-Augustinian doctrines rightly or wrongly associated with 'Jansenism'. For Jansenist opposition to the Immaculate Conception see Wenceslaus Sebastian OFM, 'The controversy after Scotus to 1900', pp 267–70.

quite a dash in the intellectual landscape of his age, not least for his articulate advocacy of the view that Catholic theology should always be firmly grounded in the authority of Scripture and the Fathers, so that it might avoid heresy and uphold the ancient verities of the Church.

Hugo Cavellus
The learned Hugo Cavellus arrived in Louvain sometime in the summer of 1607 having received a thorough education in Scotist thought at Salamanca. Nothwithstanding the earlier efforts of O'Fihely, the modern tradition of Irish exegesis and reflection on the Subtle Doctor might be said to have begun with him, not least by dint of his influence on a whole generation of friars, and by virtue of his creativity as a commentator and editor of Scotus' works.[67] In 1620, while still at Louvain, Cavellus published at Antwerp his two volumes of commentaries on the four books of *Sentences* according to Scotus. This indefatigable work of nearly one thousand pages of large folio contains an edition of the *Opus Oxoniense* (this being the *Sentences* commentary which Scotus composed at Oxford), a life of Scotus which includes a picturesque description of the environs around Downpatrick which Cavellus took to be the birthplace of Scotus,[68] the aforementioned defence of Scotus against Bzowski, and a small Marian *opusculum* entitled *Rosarium Beatae Mariae Virginis*.

Sometime in the summer of 1623 Cavellus left Louvain and went to Rome, where he was appointed professor of theology at the Franciscan convent of Aracoeli. In synergy with his teaching responsibilities, he continued to work with great energy on further editions of Scotus he had begun while in Louvain, and

---

67 On Cavellus' life and work see Cathaldus Giblin, 'Hugh McCaghwell, OFM, Archbishop of Armagh (†1626): aspects of his life', originally published in *Seanchas Ard Mhaca* xi (1983–5), 259–90; reprinted in B. Millet and A. Lynch (eds), *Dún Mhuire Killiney 1945–95: Léann agus Seanchas* (Dublin, 1995), pp 63–94; and 'Hugh MacCaghwell OFM and Scotism at St Anthony's College Louvain', in *De doctrina Ioannis Duns Scoti*, iv, 375–97; and James McEvoy, 'Hugh McCawell OFM, Scotist Theologian of the Immaculate Conception of Mary', in Stone (ed.), *From Ireland to Louvain*. A list of Cavellus' Latin works is provided by Cathaldus Giblin, 'Hugh MacCaughwell OFM and Scotism at St Anthony's College Louvain', pp 391–3, and An tAth. Anraí Mac Giolla Comhaill, in *Bráithrín Bocht ó Dhún* (Dublin, 1985). Cavellus' learning was quite remarkable, as can be displayed by an examination of his writings in the Irish language, on this see Tomás Ó Cléirigh, *Aodh MacAingil agus an scoil nua-Ghailge I Lobháin*. Of further interest are his pastoral writings such as the *Sgáthán Shacramuinte na hAithridhe* of 1618; on this see Salvador Ryan, 'Steadfast saints or malleable models? Seventeenth-century Irish hagiography revisited', *Catholic Historical Review* 91 (2005), 251–77; and MacCraith 'The political and religious thought of Florence Conry and Hugh MacCaughwell', in Ford and McCafferty, *The origins of sectarianism in modern Ireland*, pp 192–200. 68 Of course Cavellus' description of these places is given extra spice by virtue of his personal acquaintance with Downpatrick and its historical sites. On this see Cathaldus Giblin, 'Hugh McCaghwell, OFM, archbishop of Armagh', pp 89–94; and, importantly, James McEvoy, 'Hugh McCawell OFM, 'Scotist theologian of the Immaculate Conception of Mary', in Stone (ed.) *From Ireland to Louvain*.

by 1625 no less than six further tomes had appeared in Venice and Cologne.[69] Two further volumes, editions of the *Reportata Parisiensia* and *Quaestiones quodlibetales*, were published some nine years after his death in 1635. Even a cursory examination of Wadding's later edition will reveal that he drew lavishly upon these earlier attempts to make Scotus' writings available to the modern age, and for this reason it is important that Cavellus be apportioned sufficient credit for his part in the Irish celebration of the theological heritage of Scotus.[70]

Given the size of Cavellus' theological corpus, it is perhaps unsurprising that few scholars have attempted to present a synoptic analysis of its content and quality. This is to be regretted, since much is to be learned about early modern Catholic thought in the early seventeenth century from a study of its teaching on grace, divine providence and the sacraments. Like his fellow Irish commentators, Cavellus is rarely content to restate the views of Scotus (here we find shades the influence of his teacher De Herrera), but rather uses the text of the Subtle Doctor as a canvas on which he paints his own views on a diversity of topical subjects. Though committed to depicting Scotus' thought in the best possible light, Cavellus is not above going beyond the letter of the Scotist position, and proves himself most able in teasing out the ambiguities and obscurities that attend the text.[71]

If we lack a solid treatment of his theological ideas, then the very same thing could be said of Cavellus' philosophy. His account of the epistemology of decision-making in a disputation on evidence and certitude, this being a part of his edition of the *Quaestiones Scoti De anima*, which features a fresh analysis of concepts such as doubt (*dubia*) and probable certainty (*certitudo probabilis*), as well as his more general account of human psychology, are two topics which could be usefully studied by historians of early modern philosophy.[72] Likewise a

---

69 See Giblin, 'Hugh MacCaughwell OFM and Scotism at St Anthony's College Louvain', pp 391–3. **70** To be fair to Wadding he was generous in his acknowledgement of Cavellus's achievements see *Annales*, vi, cols. 50–1. There, Cavellus is praised as an industrious and successful editor who was able to shed light on the most inaccessible aspects of Scotus' teaching: 'Hugo Cavellus, Hibernicus, archiepiscopus Armachanus et Hiberniae Primas, eadem denuo expolivit, ad autographorum veritatem reduxit, spuria a genuinis distinxit, adiectis notis marginalibus, citatisque Doctoribus, pulchriora fecit, et insertis ad omnes dubias, obscuras aut ab aliis impugnatas sententias doctissimis scholiis, pro omnium votis, cum omnium laude, ultra quam dici possit, egregie clarificavit, ita ut summo desiderio et pretio conquirantur, quae prius negligebantur, et dum aliae priores editiones ubique prostabant absque emptore, huius postremo non sit invenire volumen.' **71** This is certainly true of his views on probabilism, which Cavellus holds independently of its basis in any text of Scotus and of the teaching of Franciscan moral theologians. See Disputatio III, vi–x, in *Quaestiones Scoti De anima* (*Opera Omnia*, 1639, ii, 635–41), which contains a lengthy discussion of evidence and certitude. **72** An excellent start, in this regard, has been made by Michael Dunne, 'Hugo Cavellus (Aodh Mac Aingil, 1571–1626) on Certitude' in Stone (ed.), *From Ireland to Louvain*. See also P. Alessandro M. Apollonio, *L'intellezione dei singolari materiali nelle "Annotationes" di Hugo Cavellus alle* Quaestiones super libros Aristoteles de Anima *attribuite al Beato G. Duns Scotus*, PhD Pontificia Universitas Sanctae

full and impartial treatment of his work as a textual scholar of Scotus is warranted.[73] On any general assessment, Cavellus was an interventionist editor prepared to gloss, embellish, omit, and restore anything he believed to be either superfluous or else necessary to the understanding Scotus' texts.[74] While his particular editorial traits have been admonished by modern scholars of the Subtle Doctor,[75] it would still be of great interest to learn just how his methods of preparing a critical edition helped to fashion Scotism in the early modern period, and the degree to which this school was or was not faithful to the persona of the 'historical Scotus', the one that is studied by scholars of medieval philosophy today.[76] Cavellus left an impressive corpus in the fields of theology, philosophy, and textual editions, and an equally notable legacy in terms of students. Several among these, made estimable contributions to Scotist thought:

Crucis, Rome 2003. Giblin, 'Hugh McCaghwell, OFM archbishop of Armagh', cites evidence that Cavellus influenced Descartes, see pp 91–2. In my view such a link is tenuous since on the basis of the available evidence it appears that Descartes was never really cognisant of the central debates of seventeenth-century Scholasticism, let alone Irish Scotism, and that his interest in the schools was highly selective, and always driven by his own scientific research. Still, other scholars have attempted to place some of Descartes' views in the context of Parisian Scholasticism (which was heavily influenced by Scotism), and have argued that such links are by no means spurious. See Roger Ariew, *Descartes and the last Scholastics*, pp 39–57.   **73** See Dunne, 'Hugo Cavellus (Aodh Mac Aingil, 1571–1626) on certitude', for some helpful guidance on this question. See also, Máirtín Mac Conmara, 'Mac Aingil agus an Scotachas Éireannach', pp 61–101.   **74** At one instance, Cavellus tells us that in the first book of the *Sentences* he alone made four hundred changes; see *In quatuor libros Sententiarum*, see I, ad lectorem: 'Restituuntur loca quamplurima in editionibus ultimis depravata, quae translatione, appositione vel ademptione unius aut plurimum verborum, nullum vel contrarium auctori sensum reddebant. Nonnumquam integrae clausulae, antea omissae, sunt restitutae, et aliae superfluae a quibusdam additae, nunc omnio delentur, ita ut in primo libro 400 ad minus loca sint restituta.'   **75** See, for instance, C. Balić, *Les Commentaires de Jean Duns Scot sur les quatre livres des Sentences: Étude historique et critique*, Bibliothèque de la Revue d'Histoire ecclésiastique, 1 (Louvain, 1927); and the comments made by the various modern editors of the *B. Ioannis Duns Scoti Opera Philosophica*, iii, pp i–l; and v. 1*–144*, regarding texts edited by Cavellus. For a reasoned defence of Cavellus's editorial practices see Máirtín Mac Conmara, 'Mac Aingil agus an Scotachas Éireannach', p. 80; and Dunne, 'Hugo Cavellus [...] on Certitude'. That said, it is not without interest that the modern editors of Scotus' *Opera philosophica* state that Cavellus was a sagacious reader of Scotus. At vol. iii, *Quaestiones de Anima* p. 127*, the editors note that one of the reasons why scholars doubted the authenticity of the work is that in it Scotus seems to take a position regarding the hylomorphic composition of the spiritual substances which is diametrically opposed to what he defends in all of his other known writings. Cavellus, however, had noted (in *Annotationes* ad q. 15: conclusion 1): *Doctor non ponit hanc conclusionem ut suam, sed tantum ait probabiliter deduci ex fundamentis Philosophi, et Divi Thomae* [...]. Thus, it happens that present day historical research on the text and the sources upholds the original judgment of the Irish friar.   **76** For useful illustrations of the ways in which Scotus is currently studied by leading practitioners of medieval philosophy in the English-speaking and Francophone traditions, see Thomas Williams (ed.), *The Cambridge companion to Duns Scotus* (Cambridge, 2003); and Olivier Boulnois et al. (eds), *Duns Scot à Paris 1302–2002* (Turnhout, 2002).

Thomas Fleming (*c*.1590–1651) taught philosophy in Aachen and Cologne, later becoming archbishop of Dublin;[77] his namesake, Patrick Fleming (1599–1631),[78] who taught in Rome, and Louvain, and then in Prague where he was martyred;[79] Didacus Gray (fl. 1630) who was a professor in Cologne,[80] and Anthony Hickey who taught theology at St Isidore's College, Rome. In terms of his formation of a new generation of Irish Scotists, and through his editorial work and published research, Cavellus was one of the most important Scotists of the seventeenth century; his work is surely deserving of greater attention.

Anthony Hickey

In most histories of the seventeenth-century Irish friars Anthony Hickey plays something of a Cinderella part in the story, not least due to the fact that his figure is so often obscured by the long shadows cast by his teacher Cavellus and his pupil Punch.[81] Still, he can be considered an important conduit through which Scotist thought was filtered onto the stage of European letters, and his writings (though for the most part unstudied) are of some consequence. Hickey received the habit at Louvain on 1 November 1607, and then joined Cavellus on his journey to Rome to attend the general chapter of the Order in 1612. There he distinguished himself in the midst of his brethren by defending theological theses, and by 1619 his reputation was such that he was teaching theology back in Louvain and then in Cologne. His Rhineland sojourn was cut short when he was summoned to Rome to assist Wadding in his multiple scholarly endeavours. There Hickey remained until his death in 1641, becoming the first professor of theology at the College of St Isidore in June 1625.[82]

Ever faithful to the intellectual legacy of Cavellus, Hickey, through his research and teaching, helped to make St Isidore's one of the most renowned centres of Scotistic studies in the seventeenth century.[83] Originally intending to write commentaries on all the four books of *Sentences* '*iuxta mentem Scoti*', a project which remained incomplete at the time of his demise, Hickey did

---

77 See P.F. Moran, *History of the Catholic archbishops of Dublin* (Dublin, 1864), pp 295–309; Donal F. Cregan, 'Counter Reformation bishops', in A. Cosgrove and D. McCartney (eds), *Studies in Irish history* (Dublin, 1979), pp 85–117; and O'Connor, *Irish Jansenists*, pp 126–7, and 150–69.   78 On Patrick Fleming see Cleary, *Father Luke Wadding and St Isidore's College in Rome*, pp 141–2; and Millet, *The Irish Franciscans*, pp 492–5.   79 Fleming was murdered, with another friar, Matthew Hore, by a group of Czech Lutheran peasants while en route to Vienna, see Anthony Broudin, *Propugnaculum Catholicae Veritatis* (Prague, 1669), who provides a suitably lurid description of the sad event. Broudin's work is especially important since it was one of the first tomes written for a Central European public that sought to explain the history, past and present, of Catholic Ireland.   80 Details on Gray are few and far between; for what little there is see Alphons Bellesheim, *Geschichte der katholischen Kirche in Irland*, 3 vols (Mainz, 1890–1), ii, 327, and 730.   81 On Hickey's writings see Wadding, *Scriptores*, 26–7; and Harold Wadding, *Vita fratris Lucae Waddingi*, pp 24 and 32.   82 See Cleary, *Father Luke Wadding and St Isidore's College*, pp 74–8.   83 Millet, *The Irish Franciscans*, pp 465–87.

succeed in compiling the commentaries of the fourth book and these were later published by Wadding in 1639 as volumes eight, ten, and eleven of the *Opera omnia* of Scotus. Hickey used the text of the fourth book which had been corrected and emended by Cavellus in 1620, and followed verbatim the *scholia* adopted by his former teacher. Apart from his polemical *Nitela Franciscanae Religionis*, which he published under the pseudonym Dermitius Thaddaeus, Hickey also published a work on the Immaculate Conception.[84] Though his fame at the time of his death was such that his pupil, John Punch, intended to publish his work,[85] the volumes never saw the light of day. Hence Hickey remains an enigmatic figure known to few and read by fewer.

An insight into Hickey's prowess as a theologian can be found in his discussion of the issue of the natural or supernatural desire for beatification in post-lapsarian human beings. This proved to be one of the most contested problems in Catholic theological anthropology during the early modern period, and exercised the attention of many of the best minds of the schools.[86] Following on from a notable succession of Franciscan treatments of this theologico-moral puzzle by Italian and Iberian Scotists such as Philip Fabri (d. 1630),[87] Jerónimo Tamariz (fl. 1622),[88] Mateo de Sousa,[89] and Angel Volpi (d. 1647),[90] Hickey's extensive coverage of the problem in his Commentary on Scotus' *Ordinatio* IV. d. 49, qq. 7–11[91] reflects a singular determination to vindicate the teaching of Scotus. The Subtle Doctor had claimed 'that God is the natural end of man, although He is attained not naturally but supernaturally',[92] the point being that

---

84 Originally cited in H. Maracci, *Bibliotheca Mariana* (Rome, 1648), p. 125, and by San Antonino, *Bibliotheca*, i, 82. **85** John Punch, *Commentarii theologici*, iii, 109: '[…] id quod etiam ultimus omnium doctissime et eruditissime fecerat magister meus P. Antonius Hiquaeus, cuius de hac materia lucubrationes brevi imprimendas spero.' **86** On this complicated problem see J. Alfaro, *Lo natural y lo sobrenatural: estudio histórico desde Santo Tomás a Cayetano* (Madrid, 1952); Henri De Lubac, *Le mystère du surnaturel* (Paris, 1965), and *Augustinisme et théologie moderne* (Paris, 1965); and my 'Michael Baius (1513–89) and the debate on 'pure nature', grace, and moral agency in sixteenth-century scholasticism', in Jill Kraye and Risto Saarinen (eds), *Moral philosophy on the threshold of modernity*, The New Synthese Historical Library, 57 (Dordrecht, 2005), pp 51–90. **87** Fabri, *Disputationes theologicae, secundum seriem distinctionum Magistri Sententiarum et quaestionum Scoti ordinatae* (Venice, 1613), see proleg. q. 3, disp. 8, cc. 1–2. On Fabri's work and influence see G. Panteghini, 'La teologia speculativa al Santo dal Concilio Trento al secolo XX', in Poppi (ed.), *Storia e cultura al Santo di Padova*, pp 415–83, esp. 418–25. **88** Tamarit, *Flores theologicae in primum librum Magistri Sententiarum* (Valencia, 1622), see II, c. 2, n. 8; see B. De Armellada, 'El problema del Sobrenatural en la Escuela Escotista del siglo XVII', pp 425–6. **89** Sousa, *Optata diu articulatio et illustratio Oxoniensis libri primi Sententiarum Doctoris Subtilis I. Duns Scoti* (Salamanca, 1629), n. 22, pp 89b–92b; B. De Armellada, 'El problema del Sobrenatural en la Escuela escotista del siglo XVII', pp 426–8. **90** Volpi (Vulpes), *Sacrae theologiae summa Ioannis Duns Scoti*, 12 vols (Naples, 1622–46), see I, disp. 23, a. 3, pp 224a–227b; see Schmutz, '*Bellum Scholasticum*', pp 138ff. **91** Duns Scotus, *In IV Sent.*, d. 49, qq. 7–11 (*Opera Omnia*, 1639, x, 479–94, 498–502, 503–4, 505, 506–12, 514–38, 541–4, 553–60, and 562–72). **92** Duns Scotus, *In I Sent.*, prol. q. 1, a. 12 (*Opera Omnia*, 1639, viii, 22): 'Concedo Deus esse finem naturalem hominis, licet non naturaliter adspicendum sed

the desire for union with God, though particular to a human person, was ultimately caused by the action of divine grace rather than grace acting so as to perfect some aboriginal or 'natural' appetite within that same individual. For Hickey, the pithy statement of Scotus was the very nub of the entire issue. Thus, with his fellow Scotists he was not prepared to countenance the view of Jesuit thinkers like Gabriel Vázquez (1549–1604)[93] and Suárez,[94] who had argued, following the earlier thesis of Cajetan,[95] that there was a natural appetite for God in human beings even in their fallen state. For Hickey, such a position was simply false, being condemned by the teaching of the Fathers and by the schools.[96] What is revealing about his treatment of the issue is its clear deference to an Augustinian theory of predestination which makes fallen human beings utterly dependent on the grace of God, disavows any idea of a natural desire or state of 'pure nature', and stresses that despite the existence of freedom of choice (*liberum arbitrium*), human beings do not contribute to their own salvation by their own merits, but are reliant upon the grace of God.[97] Though a committed Scotist, Hickey was just as convinced as Florence Conry had been, that far too many contemporary Scholastics painted an excessively optimistic picture of human beings in their fallen condition. For this Irish theologian, one advantage of the school of Scotism was its contiguity with the teaching of the Fathers and Augustine on post-lapsarian human nature, a tradition which Hickey believed avoided the snares and seductions of the semi-Pelagianism of the *recentiores*.[98]

supernaturaliter'. For a useful discussion of Scotus' thought on this issue, one which is at partial variance with the interpretation of Hickey, see Alan Wolter 'Duns Scotus on the Natural Desire for the Supernatural', *New Scholasticism* 23 (1949), 281–317. 93 Vàzquez, *Commentariorum in primam-secundae S. Thomae*, 2 vols (Alcalá, 1598–1605); see i, disp. 7, cap. 1. On his ideas see José A. de Aldama, 'Un parecer inédito del P. Gabriel Vàzquez sobre la doctrina agustiniana de la gracia eficaz', *Estudios Eclesiásticos* 23 (1949), 515–20. 94 Suàrez, *De gratia*, proleg. IV (Francisco Suàrez, *Opera omnia*, vii, 179–219). Suàrez's views are expertly discussed by Blaise Romeyer, 'La théorie suarézienne d'un état de nature pure', *Archives de philosophie* 18 (1949), 37–63. 95 Cajetan, *Commentarius In III*, q. 9, a. 2, ad. 3 (Thomas Aquinas, *Opera omnia iussu Leonis*, Rome, 1930, xiii, 141–2). 96 Hickey, *Commentarius in Ord.* IV, d. 49, q. 10 (Scotus, *Opera Omnia*, 1639, x, 507): 'respondetur sequelam absolute falsam esse in forma et materia, si loquamur in stylo Patrum et Scholae, et secundum rigorem sermonis'. For further discussion see B. De Armellada, 'El problema del Sobrenatural en la Escuela Escotista del siglo XVII', pp 437–8. 97 Hickey, *Commentarius in Ord.* IV, d. 49, q. 11 (Scotus, *Opera Omnia*, 1639, x, 547–53). See also my 'Michael Baius (1513–89) […]', pp 69–81. 98 Hickey, *Commentarius in Ord.* IV, d. 49, q. 10 (Scotus, *Opera Omnia*, 1639, x, 541–4). For further discussion of this point, albeit not with regard to Hickey, see P. Minges, 'Duns Scotus und die thomistisch-molinistischen Kontroversen', *Franziskanische Studien* 7 (1920), 14–29.

Luke Wadding

It should never be forgotten that the great historian of the Franciscan Order, Luke Wadding, was a skilled theologian.[99] Since his literary production was gargantuan,[1] it is important to discriminate among his published works in order to highlight works of greater theological moment. Beside the publication in 1639 of the Subtle Doctor's *Opera omnia*, which is surely his greatest gift to the cause of Scotism, Wadding's four learned tracts defending Scotist Mariology must surely rank among his more valuable theological accomplishments.

His first Mariological work, the aforementioned *Legatio*, was published at Louvain in 1624 and in a second edition at Antwerp in 1641. For a volume that contains many sober documents relating to the official Spanish mission to the Holy See to plead the cause of the Immaculate Conception,[2] its dogmatic content is surprisingly fresh and full of unique insights, revealing Wadding's own position on the Immaculate Conception as that doctrine had been debated by late medieval theologians and recently clarified by Franciscan masters at Salamanca. Three other *opuscula* on the death,[3] the redemption,[4] and the baptism of the Virgin Mary,[5] were published in Rome between 1655–1656, and yet again were the by-product of Wadding's membership of the Spanish mission.

The first and second of these tracts purport to be a commentary on Scotus' own teaching concerning the preservative redemption of the Virgin Mary, but as modern scholars such as Balić have remarked,[6] Wadding's extensive theological learning and use of clear Scholastic logic were such that they helped to ground and justify the dogmatic definition of the doctrine for a new generation of Catholic theologians. In this respect, the Waterford friar's Mariological writings rank among the more significant of the early modern period, and hold up in comparison with the achievements of his former teacher Suárez.[7] With his other theological *opuscula*, they serve to illustrate the manner in which Wadding's hard won erudition, gained from long hours of study of original documents and ancient texts, was applied to one of the contentious theological debates of the age.[8]

---

99 This fact is brought out in convincing detail by Balić in 'Wadding the Scotist', pp 463–507. **1** See Canice Mooney, 'The writings of Father Luke Wadding, OFM', *Franciscan Studies* 18 (1958), 225–39; and Benignus Millet, 'Guide to material for a biography of Father Luke Wadding', in *Father Luke Wadding*, pp 235–42, and *The Irish Franciscans*, pp 464–7. **2** On the work's content and the circumstances in which it was composed, see Balić, 'Wadding the Scotist', pp 474–80. **3** *Immaculatae Conceptioni B. Mariae Virginis non adversari eius mortem corporalem. Opusculum primum* (Rome, 1655). **4** *De redemptione B. Mariae Virginis. Opusculum secundum* (Rome, 1656). **5** *De baptismo B. Mariae Virginis. Opusculum tertium* (Rome, 1656). **6** Balić, 'Wadding the Scotist', pp 474–475. **7** A useful analysis of the achievements of Suárez and his relevance to Mariology can be found in Sarah Jane Boss, 'Francisco Suárez and modern Mariology' in Sarah Jane Boss (ed.), *Mary: a resource book for study* (London & New York, 2007), pp 256–78. **8** See Ceyssens, 'Florence Conry, Hugh de Burgo and Luke Wadding, and

The greatest Scholastic accomplishment of Wadding, however, was the critical edition of Scotus published in 1639.[9] Even though the Scotist school was firmly established in the European university system at the start of the early seventeenth century, a new and complete edition of the works of Scotus was still deemed to be a *desideratum* among his assorted admirers. These supporters hoped that the publication of such a work would act as a futher impetus to the school, in much the same way as late sixteenth-century editions of the writings of Thomas Aquinas and Bonaventure[10] were credited with furthering the development of the Thomist and the 'Seraphic' schools.[11] Assistance finally came in the form of a general chapter of the Observant Franciscans at Toledo, which issued a decree stating the need for a publication of the desired work. The newly appointed minister general of the Order, Giovanni da Campagna,[12] gave his full support to Wadding in this undertaking, and assigned him to St. Isidore's in Rome, where the work was to be completed. In 1634, the very same minister general granted Wadding leave to suspend all other scholarly activities, especially his on-going project of the *Annales*, and to devote himself to Scotus. The general also provided him with help in the form of two other Irish friars, the highly capable duo of Punch and Hickey, and with two further colleagues resident in Lyons, the eventual place of publication, to correct the proofs, the new editorial team set to work. Within the short space of four years Wadding and his collaborators succeeded in producing twelve folio volumes of the works of Scotus, entitled *Joannis Duns Scoti Opera Omnia*. The philosophical volumes occupy the first four volumes; the *Opus Oxonense* runs from five to ten; volume eleven contains the *Opus Parisense*, and volume twelve contains the *Quodlibeta*. The edition included the earlier efforts of O'Fihely, Franciscus Pitigianis (*c*.1533–1616),[13] and Cavellus, newly edited texts by Wadding, as well as commentary on individual works by the Italian Franciscus Lychetus (*c*.1465–1520),[14] Hickey, and Punch. The entire edifice was dedicated to the

Jansenism', in *Father Luke Wadding*, pp 355–404, for a helpful assessment of Wadding's views on the thorny issues of grace and nature.   9 See D. Scarmuzzi, 'La prima edizione dell'*Opera Omnia* di G. Duns Scoti', *Studi Francescani* 27 (1930), 381–412, to which I am indebted. Further details are provided by Balić, 'Wadding the Scotist', pp 486–507.   10 Influential editions of the complete works of Thomas Aquinas and Bonaventure were both published in 1588.   11 Though modest when compared with other Scholastic schools, the 'Seraphic' or Bonaventurian *secta* found expression in parts of Spain, France, and Italy. Its membership was usually confined to members of the Capuchin order such as Petrus Trigosus (1533–93), *Sancti Bonaventurae Summa thelogiae* (Rome, 1593). In the seventeenth century the school was represented by other Capuchins such as Hyacinthus Olpensis (1647–95), *Cursus philosophicus ad mentem Seraphici Doctoris*, 3 vols (Barcelona, 1691).   12 See Castro, 'Wadding and the Iberian peninsula', pp 157–8; and Balić, 'Wadding the Scotist', p. 487, 489, and 498.   13 Sbaralea, *Supplementum*, i, 294; and De Caylus, 'Merveilleux épanouissement de l'école scotiste au XVIIe siècle', p. 33; and Wegerich, 'Bio-Bibliographische Notizen über Franziskanerleher des 15. Jahrhunderts', pp 134–50.   14 See De Caylus, 'Merveilleux épanouissement de l'école scotiste au XVIIe siècle', pp 32–3; and Wegerich, 'Bio-Bibliographische Notizen über Franziskanerleher des 15. Jahrhunderts', pp 169–74.

reigning king of Spain, Philip IV, as a mark of gratitude to those who had sponsored the doctrines of Scotus in the Spanish universities. In this way, Wadding and his confrères acknowledged their profound debt to Salamanca and other Iberian universities for instructing them in the *via Scoti*.

While the shortcomings of Wadding's edition have been duly noted by a succession of contemporary scholars,[15] and it has been replaced by the work of the Scotist Commission in Rome[16] and the new *Opera Philosophica* produced at the Catholic University of America, Washington DC,[17] its influence on the future labours of the Scotist school, and the renewed momentum it afforded to important Scotist thinkers in the second half of the seventeenth century, should never be underestimated. As a result of Wadding's labour, authors such as Mastrius, Punch, Bonaventura Belluto (1600–76), Frassen, and Franciscus Henno (1662–1714),[18] put Scotus' ideas before a new readership, be they members of the Scholastic schools or else disinterested spectators in the European 'Republic of Letters'.[19] For over three hundred years Wadding's edition would be the first port of call in any scholar's attempt to grapple with the challenging thoughts of Scotus, and as such it helped to condition how Scotus was read and interpreted from the moment of its publication to the second half of the twentieth century.[20]

John Punch

The most remarkable philosophical talent among the Irish friars was John Punch of Cork, who proved to be one of the more creative yet controversial Scholastic metaphysicians of the mid-seventeenth century. As with Cavellus, Punch's

15 For a general set of criticisms of the Wadding edition see C. Balić, 'The nature and value of a critical edition of the complete works of Scotus', in Ryan and Bonansea (eds), *John Duns Scotus, 1265–1965*, pp 368–79. 16 The Scotist Commission, founded in 1930, is committed to publishing a complete edition of all Scotus' theological works. Since 1950, 16 volumes of parts of *Ordinatio* and *Lectura* have been published. See Balić, 'Wadding the Scotist', pp 500–2. 17 The Washington edition was founded to publish the *Opera Philosophica* of Scotus. This appeared in five volumes from 1997 to 2000. 18 Franciscus Henno, *Theologia domatica, moralis ac Scholastica, opus principiis thomisticis et scotisticis, quantum licuit, accomodatum, complectensque casus omnes obvios ex firmis Scripturae, conciliorum, canonum et sanctorum Patrum sententiis resolutos*, 8 vols (Douai, 1706–13; 1718; 1720; Cologne, 1718; Venice, 1719, 1768, 1785, 1788; Madrid, 1795). On Henno, who was a Franciscan Recollect who taught in French-speaking Belgium, see Servais Dirks, *Histoire littéraire et bibliographique des frères mineurs de l'observance en Belgique* (Antwerp, 1886), p. 362; and Edouard d'Alençon, 'François Henno', *Dictionnaire du Théologie Catholique*, VI. 2 (1914), cols. 2152–3. 19 On the wider circulation of Scotist ideas within early modern philosophy see Ludger Honnefelder, *Scientia transcendens: die formale Bestimmung der Seiendheit und Realität in der Metaphysik des Mittelalters und der Neuzeit (Duns Scotus, Suárez, Wolff, Kant, Peirce)* (Hamburg, 1990); and Schmutz, 'L'Héritage des Subtils', pp 78–80. 20 It should added that the Wadding edition was reprinted, with the addition of the treatise *De perfectione statuum*, by the great nineteenth-century publisher of early modern Scholastic texts, Ludovicus Vivès, at Paris between 1891 and 1895. The resulting work filled 26 volumes

corpus of published work is imposing, presenting itself as a mixture of original philosophical and theological reflection accompanied by exacting commentary on the texts of Scotus.[21] Though heartily committed to Scotism, an allegiance which expressed itself with such great spirit in the *Scotus Hiberniae restitutus*, Punch's mind was blessed with a cultivated critical acumen that is indispensable to the successful prosecution of abstract argument.[22] Tellingly, his achievements are spread over the central areas of Scholastic philosophy: logic and metaphysics, coupled with intelligent excursions into areas of natural philosophy, psychology, and ethics.[23] His theological corpus is also broad and ambitious, broaching all manner of subjects through a sustained engagement with Scotus' ideas.

Initially educated at Louvain, before being groomed by Hickey at St Isidore's, Punch assisted Wadding in the preparation of the Scotus edition, and in 1642–3 published the *Integer philosophiae cursus ad mentem Scoti*. This work, which enjoyed a further edition in 1649 and two reprints in 1659 and 1672, was the cause of his prolonged clash with the Conventual Scotist Bartolomeo Mastri da Meldola or 'Mastrius'.[24] In 1648 Punch left Rome bound for France, teaching in Lyon before moving to the Franciscan convent in Paris. There, in 1652 he published his *Integer theologiae cursus ad mentem Scoti*, which was reprinted in 1671. In 1661 his six-volume *Commentarii theologici* on Scotus' *Commentary on the Sentences* completed his cycle of published works.

What is quite striking about all these volumes, especially the latter, is Punch's sense of autonomy and originality which led him away from many positions associated with the heritage of Scotus, toward ideas more readily associated with other Scholastic schools, most notably those of the Jesuits.[25] For this and other

---

21 Maurice Grajewski OFM, 'John Ponce, Franciscan Scotist of the Seventeenth Century', *Franciscan Studies* 6 (1946), 54–92, esp. pp 71–92; and Marco Forlivesi, "*Ut ex etymologia nominis patet*": the nature and object of Metaphysics according to John Punch', in Stone (ed.), *From Ireland to Louvain*.   22 For recent studies which demonstrate this feature of his work see J. Coombs, 'The possibility of created entities in seventeenth-century Scotism', *Philosophical Quarterly* 43 (1993), 447–59; S. Sousedik, 'Der Streit um den wahren Sinn der scotischen Possibilienlehre', in L. Honnefelder et al., *John Duns Scotus. Metaphysics and Ethics*, pp 191–204; Tobias Hoffmann, '*Creatura intellecta*': *Die Ideen und Possibilien bei Duns Scotus mit Ausblick auf Franz von Mayronis, Poncius und Mastrius* (Münster, 2002), pp 263–76.   23 A synoptic portrayal of his philosophical achievements is furnished by M. Grajewski, 'John Ponce, Franciscan Scotist of the seventeenth century', although some points of his analysis have been surpassed by the more recent scholarship listed above, n. 22.   24 On Mastrius see B. Crowley, 'The life and works of Bartholomew Mastrius OFM Conv.', *Franciscan Studies* 8 (1948), 97–152; and the important study by Forlivesi, *Scotistarum princeps: Bartolomeo Mastri (1602–1673) e il suo tempo*, Fonti e studi francescani, 11 (Padua, 2002); and his more recent edited collection, *Rem in Seipsa Cernere. Saggi sul pensiero filosofico di Bartolomeo Mastri (1602–1673)* Subsidia mediaevalia Patavina, 8 (Padua, 2006).   25 For an excellent discussion of this issue, which takes place in the course of an analysis of Mastrius, see John P. Doyle, 'Mastri and some Jesuits on possible and impossible objects of God's knowledge and power', in Marco Forlivesi (ed.), *Rem in Seipsa Cernere: Saggi sul pensiero filosofico di Bartolomeo Mastri (1602–1673)*, pp 440–68, esp. pp 443,

reasons, Punch's philosophical labours began to attract the censure of some of his fellow Franciscans, and he met his match in the form of two highly capable Italian Conventuals, Mastrius and Belluto,[26] authors of one of the most influential Scotist textbooks of the late seventeenth century,[27] who individually and together sought to take the Irish friar to task.

For Belluto, and especially Mastrius, Punch was a renegade Scotist whose ideas had strayed too far from the original and authoritative texts of the school's founder. Should anyone be disposed to view strict fidelity as a hallmark of intellectual excellence, then the case of the Italian Conventuals could be conceded, especially since it is clear that in important areas of metaphysics Punch is very much his own man, being led by the force and direction of an argument rather than by an appeal to prior authority.[28] This is not to say, however, that Mastri and Belluto were servile Scotists concerned to cuff Punch's ears for doctrinal impurity,[29] but that, unlike them, the Irish Observant took the view that, in specific instances, Scotus was not always the best guide for resolving questions that had arisen as a result of profound changes in Scholastic philosophy that had occurred since his death.[30]

The disagreements between Punch and his Franciscan critics are instructive because they demonstrate the extent of principled dissension that existed within the Scotist school, especially on some of the more rarefied aspects of metaphysics and ontology. On this last topic, which concerns the study of being and other cognate concepts, Punch advanced a radically essentialist position, whose merits and drawbacks would be debated by successive generations of Observant theologians. Even as late as the eighteenth century, a Franciscan of

452–3.   **26** On Belluto see D. Scaramuzzi, *Il pensiero di Scoto nel Mezzogiorno d'Italia* (Rome, 1927), 215ff.; and V. Di Giovanni, *Storia della filosofia in Sicilia dai tempi antichi al secolo XIX* (Palermo, 1872), i, 144ff.   **27** Belluto and Mastrius, *Cursus integer philosophiae ad mentem Scoti* (Venice, 1678; with later editions in 1688, 1707 and 1727). Lest it be concluded that Observant and Conventual Franciscans were always at daggers drawn, and that such rivalry provides the context for the Punch-Mastrius dispute, it should be noted that Mastrius and Belluto had cause to consult with Wadding on matters of Scotist scholarship. See Forlivesi, *Scotistarum Princeps*, p. 175: 'Nello *In Organum* si legge che Luke Wadding, durante il periodo di tempo in cui inventariava le opere autentiche di Scoto, avrebbe detto a voce a Mastri e Belluto che un certo testo non era attribuibile a Scoto', Mastrius-Bellutus, *In Organum*, d. 1, q. 5, a. 2, 'Explicatur distinctio realis' (Venice, 1639), p. 235b; and second edition (Venice, 1646), n. 70, pp 217b–218a.   **28** See Poncius, *Inter philosophiae cursus ad mentem Scoti*, 'Metaphysica', disp. II, q. 3, c. 2, nn. 20–33, third edition (Lyon, 1659), pp 888b–891a.   **29** For a useful discussion of Mastrius's general approach to Scotus see Francesco Bottin, 'Bartolomeo Mastri: dalla 'subtilitas' scotiana all 'eremeneutica 'generalis', in Forlivesi (ed.), *Rem in Seipsa Cernere*, pp 189–204.   **30** For informative discussions of the Punch-Mastrius dispute see the very different interpretations advanced by Hoffmann, *Creatura intellecta*, pp 263–304; Lukás Novak, 'Scoti de conceptu entis doctrina a Mastrio retractata et contra Poncium propugnata', in Forlivesi (ed.), *Rem in Seipsa Cernere*, pp 237–58; and Marco Forlivesi, 'The nature of transcendental being and its contraction to its inferiors in the thought of Mastri and Belluto', ibid., pp 261–338.

Irish origin based at Valladolid in Spain, Anthony Rourke or Ruerk (fl. 1746), published a *Cursus theologiae Scholasticae*, which advanced several trenchant criticisms of Punch's theory of 'autonomous possibles'.[31] Other areas of Punch's philosophical system which elicited criticism were its dependence upon a weak nominalist epistemology,[32] and his account of the necessity of an abstract intelligible species.[33] This last metaphysical ingenuity was later employed by Juan Caramuel y Lobkowitz in his account of mental reservation.[34]

The thorough scrutiny and protracted discussion of Punch's work stands testimony to the fact that his writings were widely debated within Scholastic circles and that he enjoyed a reputation for innovation and rigour, even if his views were not always greeted with universal approval. A technically proficient philosopher who wrote at the highest level of abstraction, and whose use of dense argument and incremental analysis is reminiscent of the methods used in contemporary English-speaking philosophy, Punch's ideas are not readily accessible to those uninitiated in the Scholasticism of his time. And yet, his extant corpus reveals a metaphysican of the highest calibre who commanded the respect and attention of a whole generation of European schoolmen. Long before 'God-appointed Berkeley' was universally acclaimed (if not by W.B. Yeats) as Ireland's foremost modern philosopher, by proving 'the world a dream',[35] John Punch was hard at work thinking his way through the more prosaic if no less important issues of metaphysics.

Bonaventure Baron

Nephew of Luke Wadding, Bonaventure Baron of Clonmel not only acquired considerble expertise as a theologian but was also a respected Latin stylist, composing some of the most accomplished verses among his generation of Irish *érudits*.[36] Baron enjoyed the favour and friendship of Popes Urban IV and Alexander VII, as well as Cardinal Barberini. This learned friar also taught at St.

---

31 *Cursus theologiae Scholasticae in via venerab. P. Subt. que doct. Joannis Duns Scoti, decursus per quatuor eiusdem sententiarum libros*, 6 vols (Valladolid, 1746–64); see i, §§ 387–98. For further discussion of this debate in the seventeenth century see Coombs, 'The possibility of created entities in seventeenth-century Scotism', and S. Sousedík, 'Der Streit um den wahren Sinn der scotischen Possibilienlehre', in L. Honnefelder et al., *John Duns Scotus. Metaphysics and Ethics*, pp 193–7.   32 This is explained by Forlivesi, "*Ut ex etymologia nominis patet*". The nature and object of metaphysics according to John Punch', in Stone (ed.), *From Ireland to Louvain*. 33 See L. Spruit, "*Species Intelligibilis": from perception to knowledge*, 2 vols (Leiden, 1995), ii, 341–51.   34 Juan Caramuel y Lebokowitz, *Haplotes*, in *Trismegistus theologicus*, t. III (Viglevani, 1679), pp 171–4, t. IV, pp 8–12.   35 W.B. Yeats, 'Blood and the Moon II', *Collected Poems* (London, 1933), p. 268.   36 See Terry Clavin, 'Baron, Bartholomew', *ODNB* 4 (2004), pp 13–14; Cleary, *Father Luke Wadding and the College of St Isidore*, pp 85–100; Benignus Millet, 'Bonaventure Baron, OFM, *Hibernus Clonmeliensis*', in P. O'Connell and W.C. Darmody (eds), *Siege of Clonmel commemoration: tercenternary of the siege of Clonmel* (Clonmel, 1950), pp 41–6, reprinted in *The Irish Franciscans*, pp 469–73.

Isidore's College, and then spent some time in Hungary engaged in duties for his order. Later, he was appointed provincial commissary for the Franciscan Order, and in 1676 Cosimo de Medici, the grand duke of Tuscany, honoured him with the office of historiographer in recognition of his eminence as a scholar and Latinist.[37] After a period of residence in Florence, his last years were spent back at St. Isidore's in Rome. Apparently a humble man, who was moved nevertheless to quarrel with several of his colleagues and was burdened by a far from easy relationship with his uncle, Baron is said to have declined several bishoprics, and even the rectorship of the college.

The Clonmel friar's elegant and learned publications were extensive, ranging from occasional verse to philosophical and theological treatises of a definite Scotist disposition.[38] Of special interest are his tract *De Deo uno*,[39] which presents a nuanced discussion of some of the central conundrums of philosophical theology, especially in its treatment of the divine attributes, and a small *opusculum* on angels which aimed to situate Scotus' own views on the heavenly host in the on-going modern debate about the nature and role of these spiritual creatures.[40] These works were the fruit and development of Baron's lectures in the classrooms of St Isidore's, as indeed was his major philosophical textbook, the *Universam philosophiam* published in 1664.[41] Together they represent a solid addition to the school of Scotus.

While it would be unfair to compare Baron's philosophical and theological works with the acute and penetrating analysis of Punch, or the magisterial understanding of Scotus to be found in O'Fihely and Cavellus, the careful yet penetrating exegesis of Hickey, the impressive historical learning of Wadding, or even the sheer theological audacity of Conry, his reasoned and balanced approach reveals something of his own considerable talent. For Baron provides earnest instruction in the doctrines of the Subtle Doctor by means of crisp, lucid, and economical Latin prose, a style that more often than not helps to render the salient features of Scotus' thought less obtuse and more amenable to

---

37 On Baron the humanist see T. Wall, 'A distinguished Irish humanist: Bonaventure Baron O.F.M', *Irish Ecclesiastical Record* 67 (1946), 92–102, and 'Parnassus in Waterford', ibid. 69 (1947), 708–21; and John J. Silke, 'Irish scholarship and the Renaissance, 1580–1673'. 38 The principal philosophical and theological works of Baron are: *Panegyrici sacro-prophani* (Rome, 1643) and (Lyons, 1656); *Prolusiones philosophicae, logicis et physicis materiis bipartitae* (Rome, 1651); *Divus Anitius Manlius Boectius absolutus: sive De consolatione theologiae, libri quatuor* (Rome, 1653); and *Opuscula* (Lyons, 1669). A full list of his works can be found in Sbaralea, *Supplementum*, pp 185–6. 39 Baron, *Ioannes Duns Scotus* [...] *de Deo trino, contra adversantes quosque defensus* (Lyons, 1668). 40 Baron, *Ioannes Duns Scoti defensus et amplificatus de Angelis* (Florence, 1676). On Scotus' views on angels see Gilson, *Jean Duns Scot*, pp 391–431; and on the early modern debate see Peter Marshall and Alexander Walsham (eds), *Angels in the early modern world* (Cambridge, 2006). 41 Baron, *Fr. Ioannes Duns Scoti per universam philosophiam, logicam, physicam, metaphysicam, ethicam contra adversantes defensus, quaestionum novitate amplificatus*, 3 vols (Cologne, 1664)

philosophical reflection.[42] An acknowledged master of Latinity, Baron managed to communicate the sense and meaning of Scotus' often taxing concepts in simple terms, without contrivance and exaggeration. Though not as original in his interpretations of the texts as many of his peers, Baron ought to enjoy the plaudits of posterity for helping to make one of the difficult thinkers of the Middle Ages tractable to the sensibilities of his own time. His engaging rehearsals of Scotist thought in graceful Ciceronian Latin are a worthy addition to theological corpus of the Irish friars.

'MILLET'S LIST' AND THE END OF A GOLDEN AGE?

Forty years ago the admired historian of the early modern Irish Franciscans, Benignus Millet OFM (1922–2006), appended a useful catalogue to his indispensable study of the Scotism of the Irish friars based at St Isidore's College.[43] The list made mention of many unknown and unstudied friars who made an active contribution to the Scotist school through their teaching and publications. Having performed this very valuable service, Millet then supplied a little additional comment as to the quality or otherwise of those individuals included in his inventory, thereby confirming the common assumption among scholars of the time that the death of Bonaventure Baron witnessed the end of the 'golden age' of the Irish Franciscans. With other distinguished historians of his order, most notably Canice Mooney OFM (1911–63),[44] Millet laboured under the presumption that by the close of the seventeenth century, there were few, if any, among the friars that could match the achievements of those persons whose work has been appraised in this essay. On this understanding, the venerable theological tradition of the Irish friars came to an abrupt end, or else was on the wane, by the advent of the eighteenth century. Even with the continuation of the Franciscan colleges down to the very last years of the *ancien régime*, and the presence of well-known friars in prestigious universities like Louvain such as Patrick Duffy (1640–1705)[45] and Francis Porter (1632–1702),[46] scholars such as

---

42 Baron, *De Deo trino*, pp 45–60.   43 Millet, 'Irish Scotists at St Isidore's College, Rome, in the seventeenth century', pp 412–19.   44 Canice Mooney, 'The Golden Age of the Irish Franciscans, 1615–1650', in S. O'Brien (ed.), *Measgra i gCuimhne Mhichíl Uí Chlérigh*, pp 21–33. For Mooney, the so-called 'Golden Age' did not last as long as that proposed by Millet; see his companion piece to the above article, 'The Irish Franciscans 1650–99: "Rough and uncultured men"', *Catholic Survey* 1 (1953), 378–402.   45 Lucien Ceyssens, 'François Porter, franciscain irlandais à Rome (1632–1702)', in Isidoro de Villapadierna (ed.), *Miscellanea Melchor de Pobladura*, 2 vols (Rome, 1964), i, 387–41. For the context of his time see Toon Quaghebeur, 'A Jansenist intermezzo at the Irish Pastoral College at Leuven 1689–1708', in Stone (ed.), *From Ireland to Louvain*.   46 Lucien Ceyssens, 'P. Patrice Duffy OFM et sa mission antijanséniste', *Catholic Survey* 1 (1951–53), 76–112, and 228–66; see also Toon Quaghebeur, 'A Jansenist intermezzo at the Irish Pastoral College at Leuven 1689–1708', in Stone (ed.), *From Ireland to*

Millet and Mooney were adamant that the Irish friars had forsaken the status they once enjoyed in the Scholastic schools.[47]

There are good grounds to query at least one aspect of this assessment, while not impugning the veracity of the more general conclusion that the outset of the eighteenth century witnessed a profound change in the academic fortunes of the Irish friars.[48] We would do well *not* to endorse uncritically the judgement that the death of Baron ushered in a period of intellectual stagnation among the friars, for the simple reason that so many of their works remain unstudied. Until such times as eighteenth-century texts and manuscripts of those Irish friars resident in colleges and universities have been catalogued and analysed, we cannot rule out the possibility that there might be other Irish contributors of repute to the early modern Scotist school.[49] A detailed analysis of these materials is surely mandatory, since only then will we be in a position to judge the speculative quality of the extant works of philosophy and theology, and venture any sort of opinion as to whether or not the 'Scotist' tradition instituted by O'Fihely, Conry, Cavellus, Hickey, Punch, and Baron was continued in a robust, revised, or an etiolated form.

Part of the reason why even learned scholars such as Millet and Giblin have presumed that Baron's death witnessed the dying embers of a once great of Irish tradition of theology, can be attributed to their further acceptance of the view (tacitly accepted in their work), that the eighteenth century was a period in which the Scotist school was in headlong retreat. Try as we might, this position insists, we will never discover individuals of the calibre of Cavellus, Wadding, and Punch, or Frassen, Mastrius, and Belluto, in the Scotist school of the *ancien régime*.[50] While it is certainly true that there was a definite decline in the quality of Scotist works of this period,[51] it is still noteworthy that Irish friars (and

---

Louvain. **47** Millet, 'Irish Scotists at St Isidore's College, Rome, in the seventeenth century', p. 410. See also Patrick Conlan, 'Irish Franciscan studies in the 17th century', *Donegal Annual* 48 (1996), 110–22. **48** In the case of the Irish friars this infelicity was combined with other factors that threatened their existence; see Fenning, *The undoing of the friars of Ireland*, pp 354–73. **49** This research should also encompass a systematic treatment of those 'B' and 'C' manuscripts, relating to Scotist theology and philosophy in the period after the death of Baron, of the Franciscan Library Killiney, now housed in the archives of University College Dublin. See Ignatius Fennessy, 'The B Manuscripts in the Franciscan Library Killiney', in *Dún Mhuire Killiney, 1945–1995*, pp 150–208. The 'C' manuscripts still await formal study and an adequate catalogue. **50** This is certainly the case with regard to the Scotism championed by the Italian Conventuals in the eighteenth century. They appear to have taken the view that whatever could be said to further the Scotist cause had already been said by Mastrius, and thus urged that Mastrius should be reprinted rather than any new works of Scotist theology be commissioned; see Forlivesi, *Scotistarum Princeps*, pp 314–18. **51** See Schmutz, 'L'Héritage des Subtils', pp 79–81; and Stone, 'Scholastic schools and early modern philosophy', pp 312–313. It is somewhat ironic that the decline in the fortunes of Scotism throughout Europe at this time was accompanied by a process of expansion among the religious orders in terms of numbers and wealth, see Derek Beales, *Prosperity and plunder: European Catholic monasteries in the age of revolution,*

others) continued to write theological works *ad mentem Scoti*, and that these efforts were neither derisory nor wholly derivative.

Two works from the early eighteenth century deserving of comment are by Francis O'Devlin OFM (fl. 1710), and the aforementioned Anthony Rourke OFM of Valladolid. Of the elusive O'Devlin we know next to nothing, except that he or his superiors published in Nuremberg in 1710 a four-volume work that presented an articulate synthesis of Scotist and Aristotelian philosophy.[52] The book reveals a broad knowledge of the early modern Scotist heritage and of the writings of individual Irish friars, especially Cavellus, and some of the arguments used by Punch in his *Integer cursus philosophicus*, but rarely advances points of original commentary or introduces novel opinions.[53] Written as a textbook and heartily committed to its reader's formation in the principles of Scholasticism, it does not offer any real insight into the possible sources of innovation among Scotist thinkers at this time, but merely serves to confirm that the school still enjoyed an institutional profile in southern Germany and Bohemia, and that it saw the need to sustain itself by commissioning new manuals of instruction.[54]

Rourke was a Scotist theologian of Irish origin who taught in the Spanish Province of the Immaculate Conception.[55] Not much is known about his life, nor his stature within the University of Valladolid. He produced a lengthy course of Scotist theology, the *Cursus theologiae Scholasticae*, which is a work of genuine substance and not just a *vademecum* of Scotist doctrine in the fashion of O'Devlin. Rourke's book is firmly engaged with the topical debates of his time, and one feature of the *Cursus* is its protracted criticism of several theses advanced by prominent members of the early modern Thomist school. Figures such as Juan González de Albelda OP (d. 1622),[56] Jean-Baptiste Gonet OP (1615–1681),[57] and John of St. Thomas (João Poinsot) (1589–1644),[58] are all

1650–1815 (Cambridge, 2003). **52** Francis O'Devlin OFM, *Philosophia scoto-aristotelica universa, intentioni volentium cito et sufficienter philosophicum cursum consummare*, 4 vols (Nürenberg, 1710). O'Devlin was also the author of a theological work entitled *Gladius Spiritus* (Prague, 1698). See Pařek, 'The Irish Franciscans in seventeenth- and eighteenth century Prague', pp 110–11. **53** Ibid., iii, 27–51. **54** See Kogler, *Das philosophisch-theologische Studium der Bayrischen Franziskaner*, pp 75–100. **55** For the Scotist tradition at Valladolid see Germán Zamora, 'Jaque mate al escotismo en la universidad de Valladolid', in Bérubé (ed.), *Homo et Mundus*, pp 459–73. Further study must be undertaken to locate Rourke's book in that tradition of exposition and commentary. **56** Juan González de Albelda was a major figure in Complutensian Thomism. See his *Commentaria et disputationes in primam partem Angelici Doctoris Divi Thomae*, 2 vols (Alcalà, 1621); and Igor Agostini, *L'infinità di Dio. Il dibattito da Suárez a Caterus (1597–1641)* (Rome, 2008), pp 154–5, 199–202, 278, 281. **57** Gonet was a highly regarded French Thomist who taught in Bordeaux. Among his principal works are *Clypeus theologiae thomisticae*, 6 vols (Lyon, 1681); see B. Peyrous, 'Un grand centre de thomisme au XVIIe siècle. Le couvent des Frères Prêcheurs de Bordeaux et l'enseignement de J.-B. Gonet', *Divus Thomas* (Pl.), 77 (1974), 452–73. **58** Perhaps the greatest Thomist of the early modern period, Poinsot's writings have proved to be very influential, especially his *Cursus philosophicus* of

singled out for disparagement and correction whenever they are deemed to contradict the teaching of Scotus.[59] Not content with attacking his Dominican opponents, Rourke reserved his more virulent censure for several of his fellow Franciscans, with Francisco de Herrera and John Punch falling short of his own high standards of Scotist orthodoxy. Rourke was especially hostile to Punch's doctrine of the 'autonomy of possibles', a theory which he was convinced had dramatically departed from the accepted teaching of Scotus, and which he believed had no place in the schools.[60] The Valladolid theologian's animadversions against Punch are of great interest, not least for the fact that they show that the the Cork friar's metaphysics was still ruffling feathers in certain quarters of the Scotist school many years after his demise.

As we all know, two swallows, let alone one solitary incumbent, do not make a summer; and would be quite wrong to infer from the existence of these tomes that the Irish school of Scotus remained in fine fettle well into the eighteenth century. Much more needs to be discovered about the context, formation, and associates of both O'Devlin and Rourke, especially the latter's presumed Irish background, before we can make any reliable assessment of their volumes and the extent or otherwise of their influence. Still, the fact that the works were written at all, and were of suitable range and sophistication, show that in this instance at least, eighteenth-century Scotism was not a mere afterthought to the seminal achievements of the previous century, but a continuing intellectual tradition to which the Irish friars made a contribution.

It is perhaps fitting to conclude our extended journey through the annals of Hibernian Scotism by drawing attention to the last embodiment of that venerable tradition, the Dublin-born Franciscan Colmán Ó hUallacháin (1922–79).[61] Educated at Galway and at Louvain, writing a doctoral thesis on Scotus in the early 1950s,[62] Ó hUallacháin taught epistemology at Galway and ethics at Maynooth, before devoting the greater part of his academic career to the study of the Irish language and linguistics.[63] In 1958 he famously combined his first two interests of *Gaeilge* and philosophy in the publication of *Foclóir Fealsaimh* or *Philosopher's Dictionary*,[64] a work which despite its age remains a

1631, and the *Cursus theologicus* of 1637. See Marco Forlivesi, *Conoscenza e affettività. L'incontro con l'essere secondo Giovanni di san Tommaso* (Bologna, 1993). **59** Rourke, *Cursus theologiae Scholasticae*, ii, §§ 25–36, and iii, 50. **60** Ibid., i, §§ 387–99. **61** See the short entry on his work by Thomas Duddy, in Duddy (ed.), *Dictionary of Irish philosophers*, pp 264–5. I am most greatful to Father Joseph MacMahon OFM, and Rev. Prof. Mícheál MacCraith OFM for further information on Father Ó hUallacháin. **62** A copy of this dissertation is not known to exist, either in Louvain or else in the Franciscan provinical library, Dún Mhuire, Killiney. I am very grateful to Father Ignatius Fennessy OFM, librarian, for his generous (if sadly unsuccessful) efforts in trying to recover a copy of this work. **63** The essay by Tadhg Foley and Fiona Bateman, 'English, history, and philosophy', in Tadhg Foley (ed.), *From Queen's College to National University: essays on the academic history of QCG/UCG/NUI Galway* (Dublin, 1999), pp 83–90, provides a very useful sketch of the intellectual context in which Ó hUallacháin taught. **64** Colmán Ó hUallacháin, *Foclóir Fealsaimh* (Dublin, 1958).

landmark in the all too few attempts to furnish the modern Irish language with an adequate philosophical vocabulary.

But it is Ó hUallacháin's studies on Scotus, published over a nine-year period, which bind his work irrevocably to the Irish friars of early modern times. For like Cavellus, Hickey and Punch he sought to make a case for Scotus against the competing claims of Thomism, a school even more entrenched in the theological culture of Catholic Ireland of his own day than in the European universities of the seventeenth century.[65] In addition to this, Ó hUallacháin sought to clarify, as Cavellus and Wadding once did, the meaning of the opening of Scotus' *Ordinatio*,[66] and was moved to follow this with a study of that same work's teaching on certainty.[67] And in a famous article in the Irish language, he joined the historical chorus of friars from times past to debate the vexed subject of Scotus' Irish *patria*.[68] Bowing to the inevitable, and endorsing the incontrovertible findings of Balić and others, he graciously acknowledged that Scotus was indeed a Scot, thereby bringing to a definitive end the project begun by his illustrious predecessors when they sought to refute the claims of Bzowski and Angelus a San Francisco. With great learning lightly worn, Ó hUallacháin's writings might be said to bring the distinguished tradition of the Scotism of the Irish friars to a gentle conclusion.

The theologians and philosophers of the Irish Franciscan Observance made a genuine contribution to early modern Scholasticism. From O'Fihely to Rourke they contrived to say something sensible about an imposing range of subjects, and they made an active contribution to the depth and erudition of the Scotist school by means of comprehensive manuals of instruction, works of commentary, original treatments of topical problems, and major textual editions. They left an impressive intellectual inheritance in terms of books and ideas, which later generations of Scholastics were only too happy to adapt, appropriate and scrutinize. And yet, in the land of their birth their speculative achievements are for the most part unknown and generally unrecognized, and they very rarely grace histories of Irish thought. Let us hope that with the welcome development of a greater interest in the more cerebral, as opposed to the purely gossipy, political, economic, and social activities of Irish exiles in early modern Europe, and with the thawing of previously negative attitudes towards seventeenth-century Scholasticism, the texts and ideas of the Irish friars will become objects of rigorous yet agreeable study.[69]

---

65 Ó hUallacháin, 'A Scotist criticism of St Thomas on the necessity of Revelation', *Irish Theological Quarterly* (1949), 264–7. **66** Ó hUallacháin, 'On the recent studies of the opening question in Scotus' *Ordinatio*', *Franciscan Studies* 15 (1955), 3–31. **67** Ó hUallacháin, 'Scotus' *Ordinatio* on Certain Knowledge', *Philosophical Studies* 8 (1958), 105–14. **68** Ó hUallacháin, 'An Chunspóid faoi Dhúnchas Duns Scotus', a part of which was put into English in 'Duns Scotus and 13th century philosophy', *University Review* 1/10 (1956), 38–43. **69** I am very grateful to James McEvoy, Michael Dunne, Jacob Schmutz, Liam Chambers, Colmán Ó

APPENDIX I

Johannes Poncius, *Scotus Hiberniae Restitutus*,
in *Commentarii theologici in IV libros Sententiarum* (Paris, 1661), i, pp. 23–4.

The following appendix contains a transcription and annotated translation of the above passage from Punch's *Restitutus*. I have endeavoured to replicate in English Punch's somewhat prolix Latin prose style, in order to preserve his characteristic manner of exposition, and the spirit of his remarks. In my annotations I have attempted to provide further information about the individuals named by Punch, and have directed the reader to the best available primary and secondary sources.

TEXT

Quot Hiberni lectores recepti in alienis Provinciis aut in ipsis incorporati, ac saepissime etiam sine ulla incorporatione, pro caritate et humanitate eximia eorundem praeferuntur ad praelegendum ipsismet nativis illarum Provinciarum, quamvis non desint qui id muneris sufficientissime subire possent? R. admodum P. Iacobus Arthurus Ordinis sancti Dominici non ante multos annos factus est primus Cathedraticus Universitatis Conimbricensis, cui statim sucesserat P. Ricardus Vvaddingus Ordinis sancti Augustini. P. Petrus Vvaddingus Iesuita multis annis in Belgio Professor, tandem factus est Cancellarius Universitatis Pragensis. P. Lucas Vvaddingus aeternae memoriae Theologiam apud nostros docuerat Salamanticae, et post ipsum P. Franciscus a Sancta Maria, qui ante docuerat Tolosae et Romae in Conventu Aracelitano, in quo ante ipsum docuerat primus Professor P. Cavellus postea factus Achiepiscopus Ardamacanus et Primas Hiberniae. Compostellae diu legerat primam lectionem P. Dionysius Driscollus postea assumptus in Archiepiscopum Brundusinum. Vallisoleti apud Iesuitas diutissime Theologiam professus est cum summo honore P. Lucas Vvaddingus eiusdem Societatis vir celeberrimus, et eodem tempore apud nostros ibidem meus carissimus frater et discipulus P. Edmundus Poncius. Salamanticae Regii Collegii Iesuitarum Cathedrae Vespertinae moderator erat P. Ricardus Linceus eiusdem Societatis. In Hetruria Professor erat P. Petrus Coganus Ordinis Cistercensis postea factus Abbas celeberrimi Monasterii S. Crucis in Hibernia. Coloniae docuerunt Theologiam PP. Antonius Hiqueus et Didacus Graecus, ac Philosophiam P. Thomas Flammingus postea factus Archiepiscopus Dublinensis. Neapoli Theologiae professores erant P. Ieremia Herbertus qui ante in Gallia docuerat, et P. Ioannes Conorus. Philosophiae vero P. Bernardinus Barry qui etiam docuerat ante Romae in Conventu Aracelitano, et P. Philippus Rochaeus. Panormi Theologiam docuerunt PP. Thadaeus Daly, Daniel Bruaduir, Antonius Faluaeus, qui postea docuerat Placentiae in Hispania, et Ioannes Hestenan. Siracusae P. Didacus Barry, Messinae P. Thomas Lea, et P. Antonius Theig. Mediolani P. Franciscus Bremminganus. Bononiae P. Maurus Mathaeus, Mantuae P. Nicolaus Valesius. Viterbi P. Franciscus Brenanus. Taurini P. Ludovicus Durcan. Venetiis P. Franciscus Copperingus.

Clabaigh OSB, Joseph MacMahon OFM, Micheál MacCraith OFM, and Amos Edelheit, for conversations on the issues raised by this paper. *Do chum glóire Dé 7 onóra na hÉireann.*

Genue P. Michael Duffius, qui mortuus est ibidem cum magna sanctitatis opinione, et P. Bonaventura Conorus. In Austria et Styria PP. Iacobus Geraldinus, Bernardinus Clanchy, Franciscus Omoloy et Patricius Vitaeus. In Moravia apud Cistercienses PP. Franciscus Bern, et Petrus Higginus. In provincia Tirolensi PP. Bernardus Conorus, Eugenius Calananus, et Gulielmus Kenedy. In provincia Bavariae: PP. Thomas Kironan et Marcus Graius. In Hungaria PP. Antonius ô Brien, Antonius Haly, Bonaventura Rannel, et Richardus Blake. In Uuestphalia PP. Philippus Relly, Antonius Brenanus, Iacobus Keonius, Thomas Ferallus. Augustae Vindelicorum PP. Bonaventura de la Hoid, Eduardus Tyrellus, et Edmundus Braius. In provincia Bosnae P. Andreas Vitalis, Rhotomagi P. Malachias Fallonius, qui posteae docuit Pragae in Collegio Cardinalitio, et obtinuit ab Imperatore Collegium Hibernorum Pragense. Pontisarae P. Eugenius Cahanus, qui ante docuerat Barlectae in Apulia. Nancaei P. Patricius Conorus, in Aquitania P. Antonius Macarty, Andegavi P. Boneventura Condonus, Vastinii P. Ioannes Conrius, et postea Pragae in Bohemia. Viennae in Gallia P. Bonaventura Gradius, qui etiam Parisiis docuit apud Religiosos sancti Antonii. In Brittania Armorica, PP. Franciscus Verdonus multis annis diversis locis, et P. Thomas Haroldus, qui ante docuerat in provincia sanctae Mariae Magdalenae. In Collegio Cardinalitio Prage docuerunt PP. Bernardus Cauocus, Franciscus Ferallus, Eduardus Tyrellus, Patricius Vardaeus, Hugo Canauanus, Daniel Bruadair, Bernardus Higginus, qui etiam iam docet in Monasterio Plastensi apud Cistercienses, Antonius de Burgo, Bernardinus Clanchii, Bonaventura Bruadin, Franciscus Fenellus, Antonius Ferallus, Franciscus Vardaeus postquam ante docuisset Vvarsouiae in Polonia, Franciscus Haroldus, Antonius Donelly et alii quorum nomina non recordor; nec aliorum plurium, qui in variis aliis provinciis Philosophiam et Theologiam docuerunt ex nostra Religione Hiberni; sicut nec quamplu-

ABBREVIATIONS

ODNB   *Oxford Dictionary of National Biography*, 60 vols. (Oxford, 2004);

Wadding, *Scriptores*   Luke Wadding, *Scriptores Ordinis Minorum* (Nardecchia, ed.) (Rome, 1906);

San Antonio, *Bibliotheca*   Joannes a San Antonio, *Bibliotheca Universa Franciscana*, 3 vols (Madrid, 1732);

Sommervogel   Carlos Sommervogel SJ (ed.), *Bibliothèque de la Compagnie de Jésus*, 12 vols (Heverlee, 1960);

Cleary   Geoffrey Cleary, *Father Luke Wadding and St Isidore's College* (Rome, 1925);

Millet   Benignus Millet, *The Irish Franciscans 1651–1665* (Analecta Gregoriana, 129) (Rome, 1964);

Millet, Irish Scotists   'Irish Scotists at St Isidore's College, Rome, in the Seventeenth Century' in Scotist Commission (eds), *De doctrina Ioannis Duns Scoti: Acta congressus Scotistici Internationalis Oxonii et Edimburgi 11–17 sept. 1966 celebrati*, 4 vols (Rome, 1968), iv, 399–420;

Mooney   Canice Mooney, *Irish Franciscan Relations with France* (Dublin, 1962);

Parez   Jan Pařez, 'The Irish Franciscans in seventeenth- and eighteenth-century Prague', in Thomas O'Connor and Mary Ann Lyons (eds.), *Irish Migrants in Europe after Kinsale 1602–1820* (Dublin, 2003), pp 104–117.

rimorum aliorum ex aliis Ordinibus Benedictinorum, Cisterciensium, Dominicanorum, Augustinianorum, Carmelitarum. Quis iam audeat dicere provinciam aut Regnum Hiberniae sterilem esse ingeniorum? Nullus profecto nisi vel maleuolus, vel inuidus, cui nemo probus fidem habebit, quorum defectuum Adversarium nullo modo accusaverim, quem interpretor locutum de temporibus antiquioribus ab adventu Anglorum in Hibernia, et de ingeniis, quae tradiderunt posteritati aliqua litteraria monimenta, quorum tum pauca fuisse in Hibernia fateor, propter continua tot centenis annis bella, et defectum Universitatum, quarum beneficium non concesserant Angliae Reges propter rationes politicas, ut ingenue fatetur, *P. Franciscus à S. Clara.*

ANNOTATED TRANSLATION

How many Irish lecturers admitted to foreign provinces or incorporated in them (but mostly without any incorporation) have been chosen by virtue of their charity and their extraordinary humanity to teach the natives themselves of these provinces, although there are plenty of native inhabitants who could perform this duty more than sufficiently? After a short time Reverend, formerly Father, James Arthur of the Dominican Order[70] was appointed not many years ago as the first chairholder of the University of Coimbra, whom Father Richard Wadding of the Augustinian Order immediately succeeded.[71] For many years the Jesuit Father Peter Wadding was professor in Belgium;[72] eventually he was appointed as chancellor at the University of Prague. Father Luke Wadding, whom we will eternally remember, had taught theology to our brethren in Salamanca,[73] and after him Father Francis of Saint Mary who had taught earlier in Toulouse and Rome in the Aracoeli Convent,[74] where Professor Father (Hugo) Cavellus had taught before him, later appointed archbishop of Armagh and Primate of Ireland.[75]

70 James Arthur OP born in Limerick, educated in Salamanca (1610–16), and then taught in León, Naples, and Avila. From 1627 to 1628 he occupied one of the chairs of theology at Salamanca, before becoming regent of studies at the graduate College of San Gregorio, Valladolid. In 1640 he was nominated by Philip IV to the first chair in theology at Coimbra, and died in Lisbon on 1 February 1644. A devoted Thomist, he wrote a series of commentaries on the entire *Summa theologiae*, entitled *Commentaria in totam fere S. Thomae de Aquino Summam*, which survive in manuscript form in several Iberian libraries; see J. Quétif and J. Echard, *Scriptores Ordinis Praedicatorum Recensiti, Notisque Historicus et Criticis Illustrati*, 2 vols (Paris, 1719–21), ii, 536; and Thomas S. Flynn OP, *The Irish Dominicans, 1536–1641* (Dublin, 1993), pp 101, 106, 118, 148, 155, 285, and 310.   **71** Richard Wadding OSA. Cousin of Luke Wadding OFM (n. 73); Richard was an Augustinian Hermit who taught in Coimbra.   **72** Peter Wadding SJ. Another cousin of Luke Wadding OFM (n. 73). Born in Waterford 1583, died in Graz 1644, he taught at the Jesuit colleges of Louvain and Antwerp, before teaching in Prague. See Sommervogel, viii, cols. 928–31; and Paul O'Dea, SJ, 'Father Peter Wadding, SJ: Chancellor of the University of Prague, 1629–41', *Studies* 30 (1941), 337–48.   **73** Luke Wadding OFM. Born in Waterford 1588 died in Rome 1657. See The Franciscan Fathers Dún Mhuire Killiney (eds), *Father Luke Wadding. Commemorative Volume* (Dublin, 1957); Canice Mooney, 'The writings of Father Luke Wadding, OFM', *Franciscan Studies* 18 (1958), 225–39; and Ignatius Fennessy, 'Wadding, Luke', *ODNB*, 56 (2004), pp 643–9.   **74** Francis of Saint Mary (Franciscus a S. Maria) or Francis Tully OFM. See Cleary, pp 81–2; and Millet, 'Irish Scotists', p. 418.   **75** Aodh MacAingil (Hugo Cavellus) OFM. Born in Downpatrick, Co. Down, in 1571, died in Rome

Long since in Compostela Father Dennis O'Driscoll delivered the first lecture; later he was appointed to be archbishop of Brindisi.[76] In Valladolid with the Jesuits, Father Luke Wadding,[77] most honorable member of the Society of Jesus, professed theology for a very long time to his greatest honour, and at this very time at the Franciscan convent in the same place my most dear brother and disciple Father Edmund Punch.[78] In the Royal College of Jesuits at Salamanca, the moderator of the chair of the vespers was Father Richard Lynch of the Society of Jesus.[79] In Tuscany Father Peter Cogan of the Order of Cistercians was professor, later he was appointed as abbot of the most renowned monastery of the Holy Cross in Ireland.[80] In Cologne, Fathers Anthony Hickey[81] and Didacus Gray taught theology,[82] Father Thomas Flemming taught philosophy,[83] who was later appointed as archbishop of Dublin. In Naples, Father Jeremiah Herbert,[84] who formerly had taught in France, and Father John Conor were professors in theology;[85] in philosophy Father Bernardine Barry,[86] who also had formerly taught in Rome at the Aracoeli convent, and Father Philip Roche.[87] In Palermo, Fathers Thaddaeus Daly,[88]

1622. See Terry Clavin, 'MacCaughwell, Hugh', *ODNB* 12 (2004), pp 82–83. See also Wadding, *Scriptores*, col. 120; Nicholas Vernulaeus, *Rhetoricum Collegii Porcensis inclitae academiae Lovaniensis Orationum* (Louvain, 1657); San Antonio, *Bibliotheca*, ii, 85–6; and Tomás Ó Clérigh, *Aodh Mac Aingil agus an Scoil Nua-Ghaeilge I Lobháin* (Dublin, 1935; revised edition 1985).   **76** Denis O'Driscoll of Castlehaven, bishop of Brindisi, died 23 August 1651. He was bishop from 1640 to 1650.   **77** Luke Wadding SJ. Yet another cousin of Luke Wadding OFM (n. 73). Born in Waterford 1593, died in Madrid 1651. Luke taught with distinction at Salamanca and was actively involved in the defence and clarification of Molinism; see L. McRedmond, *To the greater glory: a History of the Irish Jesuits* (Dublin, 1992), pp 63 and 83; and Sven Knebel, 'The other Luke Wadding', in Stone (ed.), *From Ireland to Louvain* (Leuven, 2009).   **78** Edmund Punch OFM. See Cleary, pp 126–7. Brother of John Punch OFM, Edmund taught philosophy in Segovia and theology at Valladolid. Touchingly referred to by his brother as 'most dearest brother and disciple' (*meus carissimus frater et discipulus*).   **79** Richard Lynch (Linceus) SJ. Born Galway 1610, died Salamanca 1676). See Sommervogel, v, cols. 218–20; A. Morán, 'El primer catedrático Jesuita de "prima" de teología en la antigua Universidad de Salamanca', *Miscelanea Comillas* 14 (1950), 83–142, at 140–1; and Sven K. Knebel, *Wille, Würfel und Wahrscheinlichkeit: Das System der moralischen Notwendigkeit in der Jesuitenscholastik 1550–1700* (Hamburg, 2000), pp 272, 307, 340–2, 345, 503, and 514.   **80** Peter Cogan OSCO. For the context of his times see Colmcille Ó Conbhuidhe, *Studies in Irish Cistercian history* (Dublin, 1998).   **81** Anthony Hickey OFM. A native of Thomond, died in Rome 1641. See Wadding, *Scriptores*, 26–7; San Antonio, *Bibliotheca*, i, 108–9; Harold Wadding, *Vita fratris Lucae Waddingi*, third edition (Rome, 1930), pp 24 and 32; Cleary, pp 73–9; and Millet, 'Irish Scotists', pp 402–4.   **82** Didacus Gray OFM. See Alphons Bellesheim, *Geschichte der katholischen Kirche in Irland*, 3 vols (Mainz, 1890–1), ii, 327, and 730.   **83** Thomas Flemming OFM. Born around 1590, died in 1651. A pupil of Aodh MacAingil (Cavellus) (n. 6) at St Anthony's College Louvain, he taught philosophy in Aachen and Cologne, later becoming archbishop of Dublin. See P.F. Moran, *History of the Catholic archbishops of Dublin* (Dublin, 1864), pp 295–309; and Donal F. Cregan, 'Counter Reformation bishops', in A. Cosgrove and D. McCartney (eds), *Studies in Irish history* (Dublin, 1979), pp 85–117.   **84** Jeremiah Herbert OFM. See Millet, p. 136; and Millet, 'Irish Scotists', p. 416.   **85** John Conor OFM.   **86** Bernardine Barry OFM. See Cleary, pp 102–3; Millet, pp 39–41; and Millet, 'Irish Scotists', p. 412.   **87** Philip Roche (Rochaeus) OFM. See Cleary, p. 100; Millet, p. 434, n. 52; and Millet, 'Irish Scotists', p. 418.   **88** Thaddaeus Daly OFM. See Cleary, pp 86–7; and Millet, 'Irish Scotists', p. 415.

Daniel Brouder,[89] Anthony Falvey,[90] who later taught in Placencia in Spain, and John Hestenan taught theology.[91] In Syracuse, Father Didacus Barry,[92] in Messina Father Thomas Lea,[93] and Father Anthony Tighe.[94] In Milan, Father Francis Bermingham.[95] In Bologna, Father Maurus Matthews,[96] in Mantua, Father Nicholas Walsh.[97] In Viterbo, Father Francis Brenan.[98] In Turin, Father Louis Durcan,[99] in Venice Father Francis Coppinger,[1] at Genoa Father Michael Duffy,[2] who died there with a great reputation for sanctity, and Father Bonaventure O'Connor.[3] In Austria and Steiermark, Fathers James [sic] Geraldine,[4] Bernardine Clancy,[5] Francis O'Molloy[6] and Patrick White.[7] In Moravia, with the Cistercians Fathers, Francis Beirne,[8] and Peter Higgins.[9] In the province of Tirol, Fathers Bernard Conor,[10] Eugene Callaghan,[11] and William Kennedy.[12] In the province of Bavaria, Fathers Thomas Kironan[13] and Mark Gray.[14] In Hungary, Fathers Anthony O'Brien,[15] Anthony Halpin,[16] Bonaventure Rannel,[17] and Richard Blake.[18] In Westphalia, Fathers Philip Reilly,[19] Anthony Brennan,[20] James Keony,[21] Thomas

---

89 Daniel Brouder (Bruoder) OFM. See Cleary, pp 128–9; and Millet, 'Irish Scotists', p. 413. Also taught in Prague see n. 41, p. 190. **90** Anthony Falvey (Falvaeus) OFM. See Millet, pp 361–2; and Millet, 'Irish Scotists', p. 415. **91** John Hestenan OFM. See Cleary, p. 113; Millet, pp 121–4; and Millet, 'Irish Scotists', p. 416. **92** Didacus Barry OFM. See Cleary, pp 124–5; and Millet, 'Irish Scotists', p. 412. **93** Thomas Lea (Lee) OFM. See Cleary, p. 125; Millet, 'Irish Scotists', p. 416. **94** Anthony Tighe (Mac Taidgh) (Antonius Thadaei) OFM. See Millet, pp 124–8; and Millet, 'Irish Scotists', p. 418. **95** Francis Bermingham OFM. See Cleary, p. 131; Millet, pp 124–8; and Millet, 'Irish Scotists', p. 412. **96** Maurus Matthews (Mathaeus) OFM. See Cleary, pp 112–13; and Millet, 'Irish Scotists', p. 417. **97** Nicholas Walsh (Valesius) OFM. See Cleary, p. 140; and Millet, 'Irish Scotists', p. 419. **98** Francis Brenan OFM. See Cleary, pp 139; Millet, p. 365; and Millet, 'Irish Scotists', p. 413. **99** Louis Durcan OFM. See Millet, p. 364; and Millet, 'Irish Scotists', p. 415. **1** Francis Coppinger OFM. See Cleary, p. 138; Millet pp 318, 435, and 454; and Millet, 'Irish Scotists', p. 414. **2** Michael Duffy OFM. **3** Bonaventure O' Connor OFM. See Millet, pp 362, 363, 482, 483, and 486–7. Not to be confused with Bonaventure O' Connor Kerry OFM, see ibid., pp 165, 325, 362, 366, 482–5, 486, and 487, and the correction of Cleary, pp 134–6. **4** Probably a reference to Francis Geraldine OFM who taught in Bavaria; see Cleary, p. 140. **5** Bernardine Clancy OFM. See Millet, pp 40, 47, 136, 139, 149, 150, 152, 156, 157, 159–66, 210, 211, 217, 218, 222, 356, 367, and 494. **6** Francis O' Molloy OFM. See Cleary, pp 104–108; and Millet, 41, 58–9, 65, 69, 70, 97, 124, 125, 127, 243, 405, 414, 447, 480, 528, 529–30, 532, 536–41, and 479–80. **7** Patrick White (Vitaeus) OFM. See Millet, 'Irish Scotists', p. 419. **8** Francis Beirne (O'Beirne) OFM. See Millet, pp 135, 136, 527, and 528. **9** Peter Higgins OFM. See Millet, pp 136, and 137. **10** 'Bernard Conor' another reference to Bonaventure O'Connor Kerry OFM, see Millet, pp 165, 325, 362, 366, 482–5, 486, and 487. See also Cathaldus Giblin, 'Bonaventure O'Connor Kerry: a seventeenth-century Franciscan abroad', *Journal of the Kerry Archaeological & Historical Society* 17 (1984), 37–60. **11** Eugene Callanan (Calananus) OFM. See Millett, pp 26, 87, 116, 361, 376, and 490; and Millet, 'Irish Scotists', p. 414. **12** William Kennedy OFM. See Millet, p. 361; and Millet, 'Irish Scotists', p. 416. **13** Thomas Kironan OFM. **14** Marcus Grady OFM. **15** Anthony O'Brien OFM. See Cleary, p. 103–4; Millet, p. 125, n. 98; and Millet, 'Irish Scotists', p. 417. **16** Anthony Halpin OFM. See Millet, pp 367–8. **17** Bonaventure Rannel OFM. **18** Probably Anthony Blake OFM. See Millet, p. 367. **19** Philip O' Reilly OFM. Could be the same friar who was associated with the college at Prague, see Millet, pp 15–21, 45–8, 52–4, and 158–63. **20** Anthony Brennan OFM. **21** James Kernoy OFM.

Farrell.[22] In Augsburg, Fathers Bonaventure de la Hoid,[23] Edward Tyrell,[24] and Edmund Bray.[25] In the province of Bosnia, Father Andrew McVeigh,[26] in Rouen Father Malachy Fallon,[27] who later taught at Prague in the Cardinal College and obtained from the Emperor the Prague Irish College. In Pontoise, Father Eugene O'Cahan,[28] who had taught before in Barletta in Apulia. In Nancy, Father Patrick O'Connor,[29] in Aquitaine Father Anthony MacCarthy;[30] in Angers, Father Bonaventure Condon,[31] in Gâtinais Father John Conry and later in Prague in Bohemia.[32] In Vienne in France, Father Bonaventure Grady,[33] who also in taught in Paris with the followers of St. Anthony. In Brittany, Father Francis Verdon for many years and in different places,[34] and Father Thomas Harold,[35] who had taught before in the province of St. Mary Magdalen. In the Cardinal College of Prague taught Fathers Bernard Cavoc,[36] Francis Farrell,[37] Edward Tyrell,[38] Patrick Warde,[39] Hugh Canavan,[40] Daniel Brouder,[41] Bernard Higgins,[42] who now teaches in the monastery of the Cistercians at Plasy, Anthony Burke,[43] Bernardine Clancy,[44] Bonaventure Bruodin,[45] Francis Fennell,[46] Antony Farrell,[47] Francis Ward after he had taught before in Warsaw in Poland,[48] Francis Harold,[49] Anthony Donnelly and

22 Thomas Farrell OFM. See Millet, pp 125, and 179; and Millet, 'Irish Scotists', p. 415. 23 Bonaventure de la Hoid OFM. See Cleary, pp 123–124; and Millet, 'Irish Scotists', p. 415. 24 Edward Tyrell OFM. See Millet, p. 212. 25 Edmund Bray OFM. See Millet, pp 22, 24, 40, 80, 121, and 222; and and Millet, 'Irish Scotists', p. 413. 26 Andrew McVeigh (Andreas Vitalis) OFM. See Millet, pp 125, 366, 371, and 488; and Millet 'Irish Scotists', p. 417. 27 Malachy Fallon OFM. See Millet, 45–6, 151, 157, and 158–9; and Pařez, pp 105, 107, and 121. 28 Eugene O'Cahan OFM. See Cleary, pp 148–9; Millet, pp 256–7, and 539; and Millet, 'Irish Scotists', p. 417. 29 Patrick O' Connor OFM. See Millet, p. 484; and Millet, 'Irish Scotists', p. 417. 30 Anthony MacCarthy OFM. See Mooney, p. 27; and Millet, 'Irish Scotists', p. 416. 31 Bonaventure Condon OFM. See Millet, p. 365; and Millet, 'Irish Scotists', p. 414. 32 John Conry OFM. See Millet, p. 165, 278, 328–30; and Millet 'Irish Scotists', p. 414. 33 Bonaventure Grady OFM. 34 Francis Verdon OFM. See Cleary, pp 129–30; Mooney, pp 28, 43, 48, and 79; Millet, p. 364; and Millet, 'Irish Scotists', p. 418. 35 Thomas Harold OFM. See Millet, pp 77, 291–2, 307, 319, 31–2, 365, 379, 435, and 503. 36 Bernard Cavoc (Cavocus) OFM. See Pařez, p. 107. 37 Francis Farrell OFM. Born 1557, died probably in 1663. See Millet, pp 14–15, 42–5, 53, 62, 76, 101, 151, 280, 283, 294, 310, 335, 438, 443, 506, 524, 541; Millet, 'Irish Scotists', p. 415; and Pa_ez, p. 107–108. 38 Edward Tyrell OFM. See Millet, p. 212; and Pařez, p. 107. 39 Patrick Warde OFM. See Millet, pp 135, and 136; and Pařez, p. 107. 40 Hugh Canavan (Hugo Canavamus) OFM. See Millet, 'Irish Scotists', p. 414; and Millet, 'Irish Scotists', p. 414. 41 Daniel Brouder (Bruoder) OFM. Same person as n. 89, p. 189. See Millet, pp 121, 135, 136, 149, 156, 162–3, 217, and 218; and Millet, 'Irish Scotists', p. 413. 42 Bernardine Higgins OFM. See Mooney, p. 27; Millet pp 135, 159, 217, 218, 367, and 368; and Millet, 'Irish Scotists', p. 417. Higgins taught for thirteenth years in the Cistercian convent in Plasy, Western Bohemia; see Pařez, p. 117, n. 80. 43 Anthony Burke OFM. See Millet, pp 135, 136, 149, 150, 164, and 485. 44 Bernardine Clancy OFM. Born 1612, died 1638. See Millet, pp 40, 47, 136, 139, 149, 150, 156, 157, 159–66, 210, 211, 217, 218, 222, 356, 367, and 494; and Pařez, p. 108. 45 Bonaventure Bruodin OFM. See Cleary, pp 153–6; Millet, pp 136, 152, 161, 162, 164, 217, 367, 437, 494, 495, and 545; and Millet, 'Irish Scotists', p. 413. 46 Francis Fennell OFM. See Millet, pp 367, and 368; and Millet, 'Irish Scotists', p. 415. 47 Anthony Farrell OFM. See Millet, pp 48, 136, 137, 148, 149, 159, 164, 222, and 494. 48 Francis Ward OFM. 49 Francis Harold OFM. See Cleary, pp 108–12; Millet, pp 15, 29, 36, 40, 59, 61, 77, 81, 124, 125, 127, 128, 131, 149, 156, 162, 164, 165, 196, 198, 199, 200, 201, 244, 269, 272, 291, 307, 319,

others whose names I do not remember.[50] Neither do I remember the names of many other Irishmen of the Franciscan order, who taught philosophy and theology in several other provinces; nor as many others of the other Orders of Benedictines, Cistercians, Dominicans, Augustinians, Carmelites. Who still dares to state that the province or kingdom of Ireland is deprived of ingenious men? No one at all, unless he is malevolent, or jealous, whom no honest man ever will trust; of these failures I could never accuse an enemy in any way, whom I hear speaking about the most ancient times since the arrival of the English in Ireland, and about the talented, whom transmitted to posterity some literary monuments, of which I confess there were few at that time in Ireland because of so many wars for hundreds of years, and because of the lack of universities, the benefit of which was not allowed by the English kings because of political reasons, as Father Francis of Saint Claire openly confesses.[51]

379, 461, 467, 484, 489–90, 519, 527, 535, 536, and 546; and Millet 'Irish Scotists', p. 416. **50** Anthony Donnelly OFM. See Millet, pp 135, 137, 159, 160, 161, and 165. **51** Francis of St Clare or Christopher Davenport OFM whose religious name was *Franciscus a Sancta Clara*. Born in 1598, died in 1680, Davenport was an English diplomat, Franciscan historian and polemical theologian; see San Antonio, *Bibliotheca*, i, 375–6; and John Berchmans Dockery, *Christopher Davenport, friar and diplomat* (London, 1960). See also O'Callaghan, 'Some medieval religious houses in the barony of Imokily, Co. Cork', *Journal of the Cork Historical and Archaeological Society* 50 (1945), 89–111. O'Callaghan was unaware of the library catalogue referred to by Pádraig Ó Riain, 'Deascán Lamhscribhinní: a manuscript miscellany', ibid., 108 (2003), 62–8.

The contribution of Hugo Cavellus OFM (d. 1626) to the theory of the understanding of material individuals

ALESSANDRO M. APOLLONIO FI
Translated by Michael Dunne

Hugo Cavellus was born at Downpatrick, Co. Down (lat.: *Dunensis*) in Ireland, in 1571.[1] His name as transliterated into English became Hugh MacCaghwell (or 'Caughwell') but he was also known as Aodh Mac Aingil. He entered the Franciscan order in 1603 or at the beginning of 1604, at the age of 33 or there-abouts. At Salamanca he encountered important theologians such as Andrés de la Vega, Alfonso de Castro and Juan Lobera, who had taken part in the Council of Trent. As teachers for his philosophical and theological formation to become a priest, he had Francisco de Herrera and Juan de Ovando, who are counted among the best-known Spanish Scotists of the seventeenth century. They would not have had much difficulty in directing Cavellus towards the study of Scotism, since in those times, especially among the Irish friars, the birthplace of Bl. John Duns Scotus was held to be Downpatrick, the same as that of Cavellus.[2] In the

---

1 As regards his birthplace we follow the unequivocal evidence given by two of his students, Antonius Hiquaeus (Anthony Hickey) and Bonaventura Magennis (cf. Archivum Vaticanum, *Processus datariae*, v, 1626, ff. 145rv. 147v.; *Processus Consistoriales*, xxiii, 1626, ff. 762v. 763r), even if many authors state that Hugo Cavellus was born at Saul (cf. C. Giblin, 'Hugh MacCaghwell OFM and Scotism at St. Antony's College, Louvain', in *De doctrina Ioannis Duns Scoti. Scotismus decursu saeculorum*, Acta Congressus Scotistici internationalis Oxonii et Edimburgi 11–17 sept. 1966 celebrati, cura Commissionis Scotisticae, iv (Rome, 1968), pp 375–97 at p. 375, note 2. The biographical details given here have been taken from: L. Wadding (recensuit), *Scriptores Ordinis Minorum, quibus accessit syllabus illorum*, ex Typographia Francisci Alberti Tani (Rome 1650), pp 177–8; cf. ibid., editio novissima, ed. Nardecchia (Rome, 1906), p. 381; T. Ó Cléirigh, *Aodh Mac Aingil agus an Scoil Nua-Ghaeilge i Lobháin* (Dublin 1985, 1ª ed. 1935). 2 Nowadays it seems that the controversy regarding the birthplace of Bl. John Duns Scotus has been resolved in favour of Scotland. More precisely, he was born, it seems, at Duns, a village in the south of Scotland in the county of Berwick (cf. Carlo Balić OFM, *John Duns Scotus: some reflections on the occasion of the seventh centenary of his birth* (Roma, 1966), p. 22. Some scholars have also put forward less compelling arguments, but which cannot be ignored, for another birthplace: Maxton on Tweed, in the county of Roxburgh, where his father Ninian Duns owned some property and which is not far from Duns itself (cf Bettoni, *Vent'anni di studi scotisti (1920–1940)* (Milan, 1943), p. 2 ff.; *ibidem, Duns Scoto filosofo*, Milano 1966², p. 5 ff.; Francesco Saverio da Brusciano, 'Giovanni Duns Scoto nel suo ambiente storico,' in *Giovanni Duns Scoto nel VII centenario della nascita*

convent of Salamanca, as in the city itself, Duns Scotus was venerated as a saint since 1350 at least, the year in which his image with a halo appeared as the object of public devotion.[3] Since the end of the sixteenth century, one of the six chairs in theology of the University of Salamanca was held by the Franciscans and was reserved for the teaching of the doctrine of Duns Scotus, '*non pro conclusione tantum et summatim, sed clare exponendo et tuendo eius literam*'.[4]

In June 1607 Hugo Cavellus was among the founders of the College of Saint Anthony, the college of the Irish Franciscans at Louvain, where he was rector for many years. There he publicly taught theology for fourteen years, handing on to his many students an enthusiastic and lasting admiration for Duns Scotus and his doctrine; these then carried Scotism to many parts of Europe, and they defended the arguments of Scotus against attacks coming from the Thomist school. Among the best disciples of Cavellus engaged in the '*apologia pro Ioanne Duns Scoto*' one could mention: Anthony Hickey (Antonius Hiquaeus), Bonaventura Magennis (future bishop of Down and Connor), William Casey, John Colgan and John Punch (Ioannes Poncius, a student of Antony Hickey). All of the aforementioned, like the majority of the exponents of Scotism in the seventeenth century, quoted in their works from the *Vita Scoti* and the *Apologia* of Hugo Cavellus.[5] One can indeed state that with Hugo Cavellus the great Scotist tradition of the Irish friars begins. A century before him, the only Irish Franciscan who distinguished himself in the field of Scotist studies was the conventual friar Maurice O'Fihely (Mauritius a Portu), archbishop of Tuam, who died at Galway in 1513.

Other famous students of Cavellus were the following: John Barnewall, Didacus Gray (future professor at Cologne), and Thomas Fleming (future archbishop of Dublin).

In July 1623 Cavellus arrived in Rome where he taught theology in the friars' convent of Aracoeli. Having become professor emeritus, he was then *definitor generalis* and finally, by the decision of Pope Urban VIII, archbishop of Armagh and primate of All Ireland. The fact that he belonged to the Spanish Franciscan province and spent most of his life away from his homeland was of course due to the political situation at home and the religious persecution of Catholics in Ireland.

Cavellus' chief merit and concern in the field of theology is that of having carefully examined the commentaries of Duns Scotus on the four books of the *Sentences* and having cleared them of innumerable errors by using manuscripts and the earliest printed editions. He also enriched the text with the addition of

(Naples, 1967), p. 15). **3** See, E.M. Giusto, *Vita del B. Giovanni Duns Scoto* (S. Maria degli Angeli, 1921), pp 322–3. **4** This is what Hugo Cavellus himself wrote in the preface to: Ioannes Duns Scotus, *In primum et secundum Sententiarum quaestiones subtilissimae. (Nunc noviter recognitae, et habita collatione cum selectioribus antiquis editionibus, ac vetustissimo codice manuscripto* [...] *per P.F. Hugonem Cavellum*), apud J. Keerbergium (Antverpiae, 1620), p. xxvii. **5** See below.

marginal notes and with quotations from the most famous writers, and inserted *indices* and *scholia* into the text. His edition of the *Opus oxoniense* was published for the first time at Antwerp in 1620 in two volumes, and was printed again by Wadding in his *Opera omnia Scoti*[6] in 1639, together with the notes by Francesco Lichetus. At that time there was no notion of a 'critical edition' as we now understand it; editors, and Cavellus was among them, were more concerned with making the thought of an author clear and intelligible, rather than searching for more authentic readings. Faithfulness to the author was to be considered more with reference to the 'spirit' rather than the letter. In this, Hugo Cavellus was the product of his time, and it would be a mistake for someone to criticize him for using then a method which nowadays would be considered not to be objective and in any case inferior.

Among the works of Hugo Cavellus are the following:

- *Scoti vita.*
- *Appendix diffusa ad quaestionem primam distinctionis tertiae libri tertij positam in calce eiusdem libri, pro asserenda immaculata Conceptione Virginis Mariae.*
- He was also responsible for the *Reportata parisiensia* of the *Quaestiones quodlibetales*, and for the *Quaestiones in libros de Anima*, which appeared in the Wadding edition. These show the same expertise and competence as in the edition of the commentary on the four books of the *Sentences.*
- He also edited the *Quaestiones in Metaphysicam*, the *Tractatus de primo principio,* the *Theoremata*, with the addition of commentaries and *conclusiones*, published in Venice in 1625 by Marco Ginammum.
- *Apologia Apologiae*, namely a defence of the *Apologia* in favour of Duns Scotus.
- *The Mirror of the Sacrament of Penance* (*Scáthán Shacramuinte na hAithridhe*) in Irish, printed in Gaelic typeface.

Cavellus died six months after being consecrated bishop and before being able to return to Ireland. He is buried in the College of St Isidore's,[7] beside the minister general Benignus of Genova (1618–25), and near to Luke Wadding and Antony Hickey.

The study undertaken by Cavellus of the questions of the Subtle Doctor places him within the current of thought most typical of the Franciscan School, which is marked by the clear recognition of a 'particular' understanding of the individual. Faced with the problems arising from some rather ambiguous statements, Cavellus as commentator was clearly guided by what he acknowledged to

6 Ioannes Duns Scotus, *In primum et secundum Sententiarum quaestiones subtilissimae*, op. cit.; Ioannes Duns Scotus, *In tertium et quartum Sententiarum* [...], ibid.   7 'In hoc collegio': the reference is to the Irish College of S. Isidoro dei Frati Minori, at Rome (via degli Artisti, n. 41).

be the Franciscan tradition. Bérubé rightly affirms that 'indirect understanding through reflection on the phantasms or the gathering together of accidents was not acceptable to him'.[8] Indeed, we shall see that he aims at explaining the doctrine of the knowledge of the individual by means of a representative species or likeness of the individual or by means of an intuition of a 'vague' individual (*individuum vagum*). These are the two more interesting solutions which represent a coherent development of the general theory of knowledge of individuals in line with the position typical of the Franciscan School. Cavellus, without trying to harmonize or resolve the differences, and without entering into polemics, as a Franciscan studies the texts of Scotus which were considered by the Franciscans to be sources of primary importance for intellectual formation.[9]

Given the fundamental importance of Cavellus's contribution to the twelve volumes of the edition of the *Opera omnia Scoti*, which far exceeds that of other commentators and collaborators of Luke Wadding, together with his crucial influence on the beginnings of the flourishing Irish Scotist School, one hopes that in the future greater attention will be paid to this author by Scotist historiography.

THE PROBLEM OF THE KNOWLEDGE OF INDIVIDUALS

If we look at the philosophical debates which were to the fore during the hundred years after 1240 and which include authors between Jean de la Rochelle OFM (d. 1245) and William of Ockham OFM (d. 1349), it is easy to see that the problem of the knowledge of individuals began to become more and more important. The great philosophical battle around the theory of universals, which will have a rather sad end with the decadence of Scholastic metaphysics due to nominalism, had its origin in the reaction to the exaggerated abstractionism of Aristotle's epistemology, summed up in the well-known phrase:

> The perception of individuals happens through an act of sensation, intellectual knowledge deals with universals.[10]

The enthusiasm for the rediscovery of Aristotelianism thanks to the mediation of the Arabic commentators led Western philosophers initially to

---

8 C. Bérubé, *La connaissance de l'individu au Moyen Age*, cit., p. 138: '... l'intellection indirecte par réflection sur les phantasmes ou par la collation des accidents n'a pas l'air de lui plaire'.
9 Further bibliographical information regarding Cavellus can be found in: *Dictionnaire d'histoire et de géographie ecclésiastiques*, t. XXV, F. Vesoul (1994–5), col. 246 (listed as 'Hugues Mac Caghwell'); *Dictionnaire de Théologie catholique*, t. XII/2 (Paris, 1910), cols. 2045–6. Mistakenly, according to the D.Th.C., Mac Caughwell was buried in the church of Aracoeli: 'Il est enseveli dans l'église de l'Ara-Caeli.' See also A. Bertoni, *Le bienhereux Jean Duns Scot*, cit., p. 497.
10 Aristotle, *De Anima*, III v, 20b.

adopt a rigid position against the intelligibility of the individual. However, in Jean de la Rochelle inasmuch as he can be considered as a precursor of St Thomas (d. 1274),[11] and even more so in Roger Bacon OFM (d. 1294), we can already detect a desire to soften the rigidity of the Aristotelian principles in favour of some kind of possible intellectual knowledge of the individual. Notwithstanding the strong reaction of Aristotle's most convinced supporters, led by Siger of Brabant (d. 1265), the Franciscan masters with few exceptions will form a united front after 1275 in order to defend and demonstrate the understanding of the individual. Even if it sometimes happens that the debates become sidetracked into various complicated theories of knowledge, when terms and categories come into play which are not always clearly defined, such as 'intuition' or 'direct knowledge,' they all have as their basis the one fundamental and undeniable metaphysical 'given' of the knowability of being, as already formulated by Avicenna.

Perhaps because of the ever-growing number of more complicated and more overly critical secondary questions, sight had been lost of that which the problem took to be obvious, and with this, the very soul of Scholasticism was also lost:

> From an initial simplicity, the problem reached its greatest complexity and saturation with the Subtle Doctor, to be then radically pared down by the use of Ockham's razor.[12]

The undeniable merit of Hugo Cavellus is to have faithfully presented the complex thought of Bl. Duns Scotus, adapting it into an ordered, systematic and clear piece of writing, making coherent choices where Scotus had left space for various opinions, and brilliantly resolving the apparent *aporemata* internal to the discourse itself.

ST THOMAS AND THE ARISTOTELIAN TRADITION

Duns Scotus, and Hugo Cavellus with him, fall within the current of this tradition, and so it is useful to know something about it in general. The particular contribution of Franciscan thinkers is the Augustinian 'colouring' of Aristotelianism, begun by St. Thomas but left unfinished on a number of points, such as that of the intellectual knowledge of the individual. The solution of the Franciscan School, intuited by the genius of Duns Scotus and expertly propounded by Hugo Cavellus, can be considered as a case in point of the progressive completion of the integration of these two great philosophical traditions of Christian thought.

11 See below.   12 C. Bérubé, *La connaissance de l'individu au Moyen Age* (Montréal & Paris, 1964), p. 8.

What Camille Bérubé defined as 'the indirect knowledge of the individual which is characteristic of the position of St Thomas and his school and which corresponds to the theory of the *conversio ad phantasmata*,' even if it represents in part an attempt to overcome the impasse of extreme Aristotelian abstractionism, is still not, strictly speaking, an intellectual knowledge of the individual. In fact, if we keep to the precise meaning of the terms, the turning to the phantasms is nothing other than a falling back upon sensitive knowledge in accordance with Aristotle's saying *'sensus sit singularium, scientia vero universalium.'*[13] As long as one tries to find the solution within this principle one remains in a certain sense imprisoned by it, and cut off from the possibility of accepting a true intellectual (even if only inadequate) knowledge of the individual.

St Thomas turns to the problem of the knowledge of individuals many times both in his philosophical as well as in his theological work; a clear sign that he considered the matter to be of considerable importance. Initially his solution seems to be a daring innovation and one which seems to be completely incompatible with Aristotle's position; it represents the first stage on the road on which medieval thinkers set out towards the acceptance of the intellectual knowledge of the individual. However, if from the perspective of philosophical psychology the solution of St Thomas did justice to everyday experience, which clearly manifests a certain 'practical' knowledge of the individual, the exact relationship between the *conversio ad phantasmata* and the Aristotelian principle which attributed only universal knowledge to the intellect did not seem as straightforward. In fact, Thomas' efforts inexorably run counter to the Aristotelian dogma of universalism; if it is true that the intellect by its very nature knows only the universal, the turning to the phantasms can only mean that the higher faculty, as soon as it realizes its own inadequacy, falls back upon the lower. Notwithstanding the 'turning', and the complex interrelations which tend to unify the two faculties, the intellect still remains by its nature on a different level from that on which sensation operates. The unity of these two simultaneous and parallel forms of knowledge happens then despite the fact that they are clearly distinct, inasmuch as they are not autonomous and independent faculties but rather are related, and are dependent in their being and activities upon the same subject.

Despite these considerations, there has always been among the followers of St Thomas a desire to show that the turning to the phantasms, about which their teacher spoke so much, is not a mere game of words but that it includes a real intellectual knowledge of the individual. Without doubt this attempt is praiseworthy, but it has to be understood as a development and thus as going beyond the thought of St Thomas itself, rather than as an exegesis of it.

---

13 St Thomas, *De Anima*, n. 377.

St Theresa Benedicta of the Cross (Edith Stein) is an example of this 'going beyond' or overcoming of the thought of Aquinas, or, if one wishes, of this natural leaning of Thomism towards Scotism. The Carmelite philosopher dealt with the problem in her philosophical masterpiece, *Finite and Eternal Being*, where she clearly shows the limits of Thomas' theory regarding the principle of individuation, upon which the position of the non-knowability of the individual depends. By way of conclusion, the Carmelite saint, after a series of acute observations regarding the transcendental relation between matter and form which is proper to corporeal beings, affirms:

> Matter as such and in itself is indeterminate and common to all corporeal beings. Nor can it ever be the basis of individuation, of *numerical difference*. This basis is rather determinate and divided matter because it is subordinate to extension […]. What however is this determination and subordination if not the receiving of a first form?[14]

For this reason, she coherently concludes against the position of her venerated master, St. Thomas: 'We attribute individual being to the form of the thing.'[15]

In a footnote she adds:

> It should be understood that Duns Scotus does the same thing: he considers the *principium individuationis* to be a positive quality of the thing which separates the essential individual form from the universal form (cf. R. Messner [OFM], *Das individualprinzip in skotistischer Schau*, in *Wissenschaft und Weisheit*, I [1934] 8ff.).[16]

The movement of Edith Stein from St Thomas to Bl. Duns Scotus enables us to understand that on this problem, as in all others, the Subtle Doctor should be considered as someone who completed the work of the Common Doctor and not as his antagonist. It also shows the contemporary relevance of the 'popularizing' synthesis carried out by Hugo Cavellus, since his clarity of expression deserves to be appreciated through the direct reading of his texts. They have the merit of correctly interpreting, and presenting in a clear and orderly fashion, the thought of Duns Scotus, someone who is notoriously difficult and extraordinarily complex.

The value of the commentary of Hugo Cavellus on the *De anima* of Scotus has been recently enhanced by the publication of the critical edition of Scotus' text,[17] which is now acknowledged to be an authentic work of Scotus despite the

---

14 E. Stein, *Endliches und ewiges Sein* (Freiburg, 2006), pp 403–4.   15 Ibid., p. 404.   16 Ibid., pp 408–9.   17 B. Ioannis Duns Scoti, *Quaestiones super secundum et tertium de anima*, in *Opera philosophica*, v, ed. gen. Timothy Noone (New York, 2006), pp 295 (including 148* pp. of intro-

hesitation of some scholars.[18] A comparison between the critical edition and that commented upon by Hugo Cavellus (and printed in the Wadding-Vivès edition) shows that, despite some variations in the words used, they are substantially the same, at least as regards the doctrine of the knowledge of individuals contained above all in q. 22.[19]

THE ANNOTATIONS OF HUGO CAVELLUS TO THE Q. XXII OF
THE 'DE ANIMA', ED. WADDING, II, 576–80)

Conclusion I: It is false that the individual is not intelligible
[11] St. Thomas (in the *Summa theologiae* I, n. 86, a. 1) holds that the material individual is not intelligible. The Subtle Doctor refutes this position with five clear arguments [...]. He adds [...] that if matter inasmuch as it is part of the composite were not intelligible, it would follow that no natural thing would be intelligible; because everything which is natural is composed of matter and form. It would also follow that material universals would not be intelligible, since one of their essential parts is matter. If, on the other hand, one were to take the matter to stand for individuality, it would follow that an angel would not be an individual.[20] The refutation which Scotus puts forward in that text, which is taken from the definition of the university of Paris, is to be found among the articles condemned by the same university, and prefaced to the various editions of the Master of the Sentences.[21]

duction).   18 See, for example, C. Bérubé, *La connaissance de l'individu au Moyen Age*, p. 224.
19 'The result of the editors' [Wadding-Cavellus] procedure is probably the most contaminated redaction of the *Quaestiones De anima* in the whole textual tradition' (B. Ioannis Duns Scoti, *Quaestiones super secundum et tertium de anima*, in *Opera philosophica*, v, 84*).   20 Here Cavellus writes *intelligibile*, but that does not make much sense. Again, the reference to the text of Scotus and to the condemnation of 1277 says that if individuation is in matter and the angel is without matter, then the angel is without individuation.   21 The Paris condemnations of 7 March 1277 by Bishop Stephen Tempier, which struck at the excesses of Aristotelianism and at some Thomistic theses, were mirrored in condemnations at Oxford by the archbishop of Canterbury, the Dominican Robert Kilwardby, and by his successor, the Franciscan John Peckham. News of the condemnations at Paris and Oxford reached the general chapter of the Franciscans at Assisi in 1279, where Franciscans were officially banned from teaching the condemned theses without, however, indicating any particular reservations with regard to Thomism as such. It is not surprising, therefore, that when Duns Scotus arrived in Paris for the first time in the autumn of either 1292 or 1293 he began his personal philosophical and theological reflections by confronting Aristotelianism in general (including that of St Thomas), while making some of it his own and attacking at the same time the Augustinianism of Henry of Ghent. The Dominicans only managed to have these condemnations revoked in 1325, two years after the canonization of Aquinas. The following are the propositions referred to by Cavellus which were condemned: [42] God cannot multiply individuals of the same species without matter. [43] Since the intelligences [that is, angels] do not have matter, God cannot create more than one of the same species. [15]

Conclusion II: The individual can in itself be known intellectually by us in an absolute manner.

[12] Duns Scotus proves this conclusion: firstly, because the individual is a more perfect being with respect to the universal, thus it is a more perfect intelligible; secondly, because if the individual were not intelligible in itself it could not be known even by God. Thirdly, the individual adds nothing to the universal other than individuality, something which does not impede understanding; otherwise neither an angel nor a separated soul could know the individual in an intellectual manner. It seems to me that there is nothing controversial in this conclusion, if one means knowledge in a life different from the present state.

Conclusion III: The individual is known in the present life.

The Subtle Doctor proves this conclusion with five most beautiful and most clear arguments, to which this can be added, that our intellect distinguishes between the universal and the individual. The Philosopher in Book III n. 145 of the *De Anima* proves with this kind of argumentation that there is a *sensus communis*,[22] because sensation knows the limits of what can be sensed inasmuch as it perceives that there is a difference between things. Moreover, the will moderates the act of the cogitative faculty, thus the intellect knows it; but this is an individual [and so the intellect knows the individual]. Again, art and prudence fall under the competence of the intellect and refer to an individual, as the Philosopher states in Book III of the *Ethics*, ch. 3.

With regard to the fourth argument it should be noted that even if we cannot assign a term to something which we do not know, yet a term may signify the thing nominated in a more distinct manner, insofar as the person who assigns the term understands it; otherwise in this life we would be unable to impose on a substance, a term by means of which the substance itself would be distinctly signified. This however is false, because as soon as the word 'man' is heard an angel or a separated soul[23] knows in a distinct manner that which the one who assigns the term knows only in a confused manner inasmuch as it lies under those accidents. See Scotus *Ordinatio* I, 1, d. 22, q. 1[24], where he questions whether God can be known by a term which signifies His own individual essence.

[13] Secondly, note that, as Scotus teaches in the *Ordinatio* I, II d. 5, q. 9, n. 11[25] and in the most subtle *Questions on the Metaphysics* I, vii, q. 15, there are two kinds of knowledge, abstractive, which abstracts from the existence of the object,

God cannot know the individual (in: Denifle-Chatelain, *Chartularium Universitatis Parisiensis*, i (Paris, 1889), pp 543 ff.) **22** See, Duns Scotus, *De anima*, q. VI, § 13. **23** Obviously, there is no sense knowledge in an angel or in separate souls. The term 'sensible' here is to be understood in an analogical way, with its basis in the theory of angelic knowledge which for Duns Scotus happens also by means of the direct intuition of the proper species and not only by infusion on the part of God. **24** Ed. Vaticana: q. un., nn. 6–11. **25** Ed. Vaticana: d. 3, qq. 9.11.

and intuitive, which is concerned with existence as such. The former includes the individual and the universal (even if it commonly regards the universals), because the individual also abstracts from existence.

Thirdly, note also that according to Scotus, in book VII of the *Metaphysics* q. 15 (n. 1), the individual is considered in two ways: one way inasmuch as it abstracts from all accidents such as from the here and now, from quantity and quality, etc., and so it includes only the *haecceitas*, namely the individuality; in another way inasmuch as it is the subject of accidents in the here and now. We refer here to material individuals, because in the present life we cannot grasp any spiritual being except under the common concept of being, or of substance, or of accident, as has been shown many times. The third conclusion should be taken in the second sense, in which it is completely proved by the arguments of the Subtle Doctor, not in the first sense, as will appear evident from the arguments used in the following conclusion.

Apart from Scotus and his followers other authors have also held that the individual is intelligible for us, at least with regard to the present life: Gregory of Rimini, Richard of Middleton, Durandus of Saint Pourçain, John of Jandun, Fonseca, Paleatinus Manelianus, the Coimbricenses, Francisco Suárez, Toletus. Again Antonius Andrea and Antonio Trombetta deal fully with this problem.

Conclusion IV: None of our faculties in the present life knows an individual intrinsically, that is, the intrinsic individuality.
[14] The Subtle Doctor proves this conclusion with a single, most effective argument: neither our senses nor our intellect can distinguish between two individual things which are completely equal in appearance – for example two eggs of the same shape, colour and size, or two rays of light. Thus none of our faculties knows the intrinsic reasons for the individuality of these things which are only known by means of extrinsic appearances and common sensibles, namely by means of extrinsic accidents. Otherwise we would be able to distinguish between two rays of light which blend together; which is false, because we judge that there is only one ray. The implication is clear, because someone who knows something with a proper knowledge of the object distinguishes it from all others. Thus since we distinguish one individual from another only by means of extrinsic accidents, we know nothing about it except these accidents as referring to the proper concept. From this it is clear that Suárez was mistaken when he presented Scotus as someone favourable to the position according to which we have in this life a proper and distinct concept of the individual, both because here Scotus explicitly holds the contrary, and again because at the references given by Suárez, *Op oxon.* l. IV, d. 45, q. 3[26] and *Op. oxon.* l. II, d. 3, q. 1, n. 4,[27] Scotus holds the opposite.

---

26 Ed. Wadding: n. 17.   **27** Ed. Vaticana: n. 21.

The arguments against these conclusions are solved

[15] It will be immediately objected that according to book III of the *De anima* nos. 15–16, material realities are not intelligible in act but only in potency. Thus the material individual is not intelligible in act but only inasmuch as it is abstracted from matter, namely as considered universally. To which it is replied that the arguments prove the existence of that abstractive knowledge of which Aristotle speaks in that text, inasmuch as the individual is knowable in act by that abstractive knowledge, but only by means of the abstraction of the species. Nonetheless, the individual is intelligible in act also in an intuitive manner, confusedly in this life but distinctly in a future state. And when Aristotle says in the text that the intelligible is without matter he is talking about abstractive knowledge, and by matter he means the individual difference – otherwise according to him no natural thing would be capable of being known.

Since Aristotle in the same text divides those things which can be known into sensible and intelligible, he means that there are only non-sensible intelligibles but not vice versa. The passage from *De anima* II, ch. 5 should also be explained in the same way, where he says 'the senses are for the individuals, the intellect for the universals'. In this regard see the better explanation given by Scotus in *Op. oxon.* l. IV d. 45, q. 3, ad 2.[28] We reply to the argument, stating that Aristotle only means that in order to know material things it is necessary for them to be freed from matter so as to become similar to the intellect, something which happens by means of the species which are probably also required for intellectual knowledge of them. However, immaterial beings are in themselves similar to the intellect, and if the species were necessary in order to know them (something which is probable even in intuitive knowledge) it would not be in order to be made similar to the intellect. It is clear that this is the preferred solution, because as regards abstractive knowledge the material being is not more intelligible in potency than the spiritual being, and both become intelligible in act by means of the impressed species. Thus the first solution is not satisfactory when it is said that according to the Philosopher the material being becomes intelligible in act only insofar as it is abstracted from the material individual.

[16] Secondly, it is argued that if the individual is individual in itself, there is no need of the agent intellect because it is posited only inasmuch as it carries out the function of abstracting the species from the phantasms which represent the universals, which in turn represent the individuals. To which we reply that the agent intellect is affirmed inasmuch as it produces the spiritual species, by means of which the nature is known abstractly in a spiritual manner, and for this reason it is necessary that the individual is known in itself in an intuitive manner.

Thirdly, it is argued that if the intellect knows individuals, then the knowledge which the senses have of the same would be superfluous. This is denied, since it

28 Ed. Wadding, n. 17.

is necessary to know the same things by means of a material as well as a spiritual knowledge. If the argument were valid, the knowledge of the particular senses would also be superfluous, as would the *sensus communis*.

Fourthly, it is argued that the material individual is not disposed in such a way as to act on the intellect, which is spiritual. To which the reply is made that the material individual acts as a partial cause; which is not unsuitable. Even the opponents hold that the phantasms, even if they are material, act upon the intellect.

In order to investigate this problem further the following question is raised:

Must one accept the existence in our intellect of the proper species of individuals?
[17] It should be noted that here we are dealing with sensible individuals, because no immaterial being and no substance has a proper species in our intellect, from what has been said regarding question 17.[29]

Secondly, it should be noted that the individual, whether material or not, plays a role in producing its species; it produces it completely if it is spiritual, partially if it is corporeal with respect to the angelic intellect or the separated intellect; otherwise an angel could not have an abstractive knowledge of those things which it sees intuitively with the use of its natural forces; which is false, as Scotus well shows in *Op. oxon.*, l. II, d. 3, q. 11.[30] The problem does not, therefore, refer to the species of the individual in the separate intellect, because it perhaps never knows intuitively without the intervention of the intelligible species by means of which it can know the same object in an abstractive manner, since it remains in the intellect. On this one could look at Scotus, *Quodlibet 15*; *Op. oxon.*, l. I, d. 3, q. 6, n. 11;[31] l. II, d. 3, q. 8, n. 10.[32] In the first reference given, Scotus teaches that the intelligible species is completely produced by the spiritual object. The reason is clear since the spiritual object does not have a lesser effectiveness than that which the corporeal object has in respect of the sensible species. Thus without this an angel cannot know an immaterial object as a material agent producing a species in the intellect. In the second and third texts referred to, the Subtle Doctor seems to teach that an angel cannot 'see' a sensible being intuitively[33] without the species. It would seem however that there is a difference, because whereas the spiritual object is intuited, the species is

---

29 The concept is said to be proper in two senses. In the first, a concept is proper which is appropriate to one thing and not to another. In this sense we have also got a proper concept of God, infinite being [...]. In the second sense a concept is proper which derives immediately from the thing itself, or from its likeness, without analogy or similarity. And it is this sense which we mean (Cavellus, *De Anima*, XVII, n. 30). In the present life we cannot have any knowledge of a substance except by means of a sensible accident, as the Philosopher often says. 30 The critical edition (Vaticana) considers this question to be an interpolation and not authentic, and so has deleted it from the *Opera omnia*. 31 Ed. Vaticana, d. 3, pars 3, q. 1, nn. 367–8. 32 Ibid. 33 'See', in the sense of knowing intellectually.

produced as a prior effect and not as the cause of the intuition; and this is so because the intelligible object in act and the faculty are enough for knowledge. However, as regards the sensible objects, their species is produced as the cause of knowledge because the sensible object existing as such is not intelligible in act. I acknowledge that these things are not certain but are a matter of dispute among Scotists [...].

[18] Thirdly, it should be noted that insofar as Scotus says, in *Op. oxon.*, l. II, d. 3, q. 11,[34] that the species of the universal nature cannot represent individuals in their proper understanding,[35] because the universal does not include the existence of individuals, neither does it include their ability to be known.

Fourthly, note that probably the species of the individual represents the common nature. This can be deduced from what Scotus says in *Op. oxon.*, l. I, d. 3, q. 2, n. 18,[36] according to which, probably by means of a species which is less universal, the more universal species is known. The reason is that the more universal species is contained in that which is less common, and the common nature in the individual. This conclusion is held also by Suárez in Book IV of the *De anima* ch. 3, n.12. And if it is objected that Scotus in his commentary on Book IV of the *De anima* q.6, n.5 teaches that the same species cannot be both of the individual and of the universal, we can reply with Bargius, again on the *De anima* l. IV, *Reply to the fifth argument*, that this is true in a formal sense; and yet the species can be formally of the individual and virtually of the universal. Moreover, in the same text Scotus argued only against Henry of Ghent, who denied the species; and it is not necessary that each individual point made in an argument should be successful. Add as well that according to Scotus there are probably no species but that the phantasmata are enough, something of which he often speaks throughout q. 17 of the *De anima*.

[19] Having stated the above one can reply to the question by saying that in the present life we do not accept that there is a proper species of individuals by means of which the very intrinsic individuality is presented. This is what Scotus says in *Op. oxon.*, l. III, d. 14, q. 3[37] at the end, and it is evident because of the argument of the fourth conclusion, otherwise we would not have a proper knowledge of this individuality in this life; the opposite of which we have proved here. Nevertheless we do accept the species of individuals which represent them in a confused way. It has been fully stated in q. 16 of the *De anima* what it means to represent something confused or distinctly. This thesis is successfully proved by the arguments of Scotus in n. 6[38] in favour of the second conclusion, because

---

34 Nowadays this question is regarded as inauthentic and so has been excluded from the critical edition. See above.   35 As has been said above, a 'proper understanding' or 'proper concept' is that intentional entity produced in the intellect by its respective real referent.   36 Ed. Vaticana, n. 61.   37 Ed. Vaticana, n. 123.   38 Actually, the arguments in favour of the second conclusion that 'the individual can be understood by us in the present life' are to be found in nos. 4 and 5 of the Wadding edition.

otherwise we would not know individuals in this life. It is also probable that this species of the individual represents the universal, such that there is a single species of both, as has been said above; and which Scotus hints at here in replying to the fourth objection.[39] This thesis is proved first of all by the argument adopted in the fourth conclusion above,[40] and secondly, if the agent intellect were to abstract two species of 'man', one individual and the other universal, the same would happen for all of the higher grades. Thirdly, someone who sees only whiteness would not easily distinguish it from colour. This is a sign that whiteness does not have a different species with regard to colour, because by means of different species one can easily distinguish one from the other. In this way the individual would be known as follows: when the intellect abstracts many different species of the same essence from various phantasms, these individual species have something in common with each other, namely all of the essential predicates which they represent, and something else by which they differ from each other, namely individuality. The intellect can know what they have in common, and so it knows the universal; or those aspects in virtue of which they differ, and in this regard it tends towards the individual.

It is objected that 'whatever is received in the receiver is received according to the mode of the receiver', thus the sensible individual cannot be in the intellect, nor can there be anything which represents it. In reply it should be said that the sensible species of the individual is entitatively spiritual like the intellect in which it is received, but [inasmuch as it represents the material] it is material from the point of view of the capacity for being represented.

[20] Secondly, it is objected that the species represents the object according to that same essence by which the object itself has been produced; thus if it is not produced by individuality, neither does it represent it. We reply together with Scotus (cfr. *Op. oxon.* l. I, d. 3, q. 6, ad 1, n. 16):[41] 'Individuality is not the reason for acting but for the condition of the agent.' Moreover the reason for acting is the nature which is individual; thus the nature in itself is represented and its status is represented in a confused way. Secondly, the Subtle Doctor says that when the species is completely produced by the object, as happens in the pure spirits, then it represents everything which is in it, including individuality; for this reason the separated intellect cannot distinguish the individuality in itself by means of its proper species. This however is not valid for the sensible species, even if it is totally produced by the object; otherwise sight would distinguish between two whites which are completely identical, which is false according to Conclusion IV. The defect, on the other hand, does not lie with the species, as it might seem, but with the faculty, which can only know individuality in a confused way.

---

39 See Wadding, n. 10. 40 See above, n. 18. 41 The quotation in the Wadding edition is not in no. 16, but in no. 15; Ed. Vaticana, d. 3, pars 3, q. 1, n. 380.

Thirdly, it is objected that if the same species represents the individual and the universal, it will be useless to admit another species which represents the universal. To which we reply that the species of the individual has the individual as the first, adequate object and the universal as the secondary, inadequate object, so it is not useless to admit the species of the universal insofar as it is in itself, and of the adequate object. This happens when the agent intellect abstracts not only from material conditions but also from individuality itself. Add that perhaps we should admit only the species of the individual which also represents the universal, because nothing would oblige us to admit another if the species of the individual were sufficient. Nonetheless, it is probable that there is also a universal species, so that the intellect can immediately and without hindrance grasp the essence of the individuality, as experience bears out.

Another question: Is the individual known directly or only in a reflexive manner?
[21] Those who deny that the individual is intelligible in itself, and to whom I have referred above at n. 5, said that it is known only in a reflexive manner; but from what has been said it is clear that it is known directly. Everything which is known by means of a proper species is in fact known directly. This is clearly proved also by the fact that the separated soul preserves the memory of individuals which it had present during its earthly life, as is evident from the dialogue between the Rich Man and Abraham, of which Scotus speaks superbly in *Op. oxon.* l. IV, d. 45, q. 3.[42] Those who hold that the individual is known only in a reflexive way explain it differently. St Thomas in the work cited above and in *De veritate* q. 2 a. 6, states that they are known inasmuch as the intellect, after knowing the universal nature, turns to the phantasm and by means of this knows the individual.

Against. The intellect knows the individual in the phantasm either as in the object which is known or as in a species; not in the first way, because then the phantasm would be known first, which is not borne out by experience, since many people know the individuals and do not know the phantasms.

Moreover the phantasm itself is individual; thus if it were known the individual reality in it would also be known, and thus the individual would be directly known, something which the opponents themselves deny.

Thirdly, if one were to know in the phantasm, this would happen by means of the species in the universal which is indifferent with regard to each individual by means of which it is directly known, otherwise it would not be known at all.

Nor can one accept the second way,[43] namely that the individual is known by means of the phantasm as by means of an intelligible species, because the intellect does not make use of a corporeal or material species. Moreover every faculty makes use of only those species which inhere in it.

42 See above.   43 See above ('Against'): 'the intellect knows the individual [...] in the object known'.

[22] [...] Others teach that the individual is known by means of the whole known through its accidents. Against: I wonder whether these accidents are known as individuals. If so we have proved our thesis, namely the direct knowledge of individuals; if on the other hand they were only known universally, then individuals would not be known by means of them.

Again, against all these ways of acknowledging that there is only a reflexive knowledge of individuals: an uneducated person knows individuals and yet does not know that he is carrying out this reflection; in fact he does not even know the universal nature. Secondly, if by means of a universal species, for example that of 'man', one were to know every individual of 'man' once a species is produced, even if other men were encountered the intellect would not produce any further species, and so it would not know them, because it would not derive any species from their phantasms. Thirdly, neither creation nor experience necessitates the denial to our intellect of a direct knowledge of individuals, because that cannot arise either from its perfection, because then it would not happen with God or an angel, or from its imperfection, otherwise it would not happen to sensation.

Conclusion V: Firstly the vague individual is known, then the nature, and finally the determinate individual.

[23] [...] We prove the first part of this conclusion [that firstly the vague individual is known]. Firstly, art and the intellect imitate nature. However, nature in its acting does not tend towards the universal, otherwise once the body is produced it would not continue to act so as to animate it. Nor does it tend towards the determinate individual, otherwise it would cease its activity as soon as it produced it. Thus it should be said that it tends first of all towards the vague individual; and so the species will represent this individual in the first place, then the nature in itself, without considering the individual in the essence of the subject, so that it unites many individuals together in the way of knowing the universal, which has already been stated; which perhaps corresponds more to the mind of Scotus in *Op. oxon.* l. I, d. 3, q. 6, n. 5,[44] where he speaks of the physical universal.

Secondly, it is clear to experience that we sometimes know a vague individual without knowing any species. The minor premise is clear, as when we see something from afar.

Thirdly, it can be proven through what the Philosopher says in Book 1 of the *Physics* n. 12. It also fits in well with what he says in Book I of the *Posterior Analytics* n. 12, that whatever is closer to the senses is better known.

Proof of the second part of the conclusion [that the nature is known next].

The nature is known in itself in that way when it is represented without considering the determining circumstances, which means that the nature is abstracted from lower things.

---

44 Ed. Vaticana, d. 3, pars 3, q. 1, n. 379–381.

We now explain the third part of the conclusion [that the last thing to be known is the determinate individual].

Turning to the nature as grasped according to the circumstances of place, time, shape, size, etc., we understand that there is something under there which resists being divided into many parts. However, we do not know its proper essence, otherwise we would be able to distinguish it from any other individual; which is false, as is clear from experience. For this reason this is not a simple concept, but it is somehow produced by the various concepts of the circumstances, which is explained well by the Subtle Doctor with an example, because we cannot otherwise explain the concept of the determinate individual (*signatum*) except by means of these various circumstances. When he says that the signate individual is known by the intellect by means of the concepts of the various circumstances added to the concept of the universal, he means that the individual and the universal are represented by the same species.

[24] However there is a serious difficulty because Scotus (above in q. 16, n. 3 and in *Op. oxon.* l. I, d. 3, q. 2, n. 21),[45] teaches that what is first conceived is the most specific species (*species specialissima*); here on the other hand he teaches that it is the vague individual. We reply that in those works cited one is speaking about those things which are known in their proper essence and inasmuch as there is something essentially or virtually contained in them. The first of these things to be known in the proper essence is the most specific species; but the individual in the present life is not known in its proper essence, as is clear from Conclusion IV, otherwise we would be able to distinguish this ray of light if it were to merge together with another completely the same; and so the contradiction is removed.

Secondly, it can be said that in those texts Scotus compares the lowest species (*species infima*) with the universals, not with its individuals upon which the knowledge of the lowest species itself depends because it is abstracted from them.

The third argument of Scotus in that text seems to support this inasmuch as he affirms that the most specific species is known first of all because a natural cause produces first of all the most complete effect. However this is not valid for those things the knowledge of which is as it were by means of the knowledge of that species.

Moreover, the knowledge of the individual is perhaps more perfect if it happens by means of the same species through which the universal is known. And this is because, since there is more entity in the individual, there is also a greater intelligibility.

You might object that it is a confused knowledge and not according to the proper essence of the individual, and so it is more imperfect with regard to the

45 Actually it is to be found in no. 22 of Wadding; ed. Vaticana, d. 3, pars 1, q. 1–2, n. 73.

knowledge of the universal nature. To which it can be replied that, admitting that this is a confused knowledge and not in accordance with the proper essence of the individual, nonetheless it is a proper knowledge of the nature to which some modification is added, by means of which the nature is determined in conformity with the knowledge of the vague individual, as the Subtle Doctor implies here.

[25] In a subject which is so unclear and in which generally one proceeds by means of conjecture, it seems to me that one should not accept that there is a species which in this life represents the individual and is distinct from the universal species. However the same species of the universal – or rather the nature, which is neither individual nor universal except in an accidental manner, according to what Scotus says in *Op. oxon.* l. II, d. 3, q. 1[46] – represents the individual in a confused way by means of the addition of concepts, just as the species of the creatures in the present life represent God in a confused manner, as Scotus explains in *Op. oxon.* l. I, d. 3, q. 2, n. 18[47] when he teaches how we form the concept of God as the most actual, Highest Good, from the species of highest good and of act.

That this really corresponds to the mind of Duns Scotus can be proved from what he says in *Op. oxon.* l. I, d. 3, q. 6, n. 15,[48] namely that the species in itself, at least in this life, only represents the nature. However, from what he adds we can deduce that this nature is limited, even if we do not see the essence itself which limits it. And this happens in two ways: firstly when I understand that nature in something which is indivisible and in a plurality, which means understanding that nature in a subject, namely the vague individual. Secondly, when I understand that nature as modified by its circumstances of place, time, size, etc.; and this is the knowledge of the determinate individual, where many species are to be found together, as the Subtle Doctor says in the same text, no.10.

CONCLUSION

The fundamental question to which Cavellus seeks to give an answer in his theory of knowledge is the following: Is the individual intentional existence of corporeal beings, present to the human intellect, known in this life?

From the substantially affirmative reply to the question arises a significant strengthening of the position of realism which is proper to perennial Christian philosophy. The process of understanding begins from an immediate perception of the real which is a confused knowledge of the individual, beginning from the initial intuition of being; since the first act of the intellect which attributes a

---

46 Ed. Vaticana, d. 3, pars 1, q. 1, n. 31. 47 Ed. Vaticana, d. 3, pars 1, q. 1–2, nn. 61–2.
48 Ed. Vaticana, d. 3, pars 3, q. 1, nn. 379–81.

vague, objective but certainly individual being to the sense data must correspond to the sensory act which perceives the presence of something. Beginning from this primordial notion of being, which is proportionate to the sense data, and for this reason individual, the process of abstraction begins, which continues with the universal concept of the *species specialissima* and concludes with the reflection upon the phantasms, completing the original intuition of the individual being.

The intelligible species of the individual is not necessarily other with respect to that of the universal, even if it is its ultimate perfection. Just as the *haecceitas* is not a form added to that of being but is its ultimate perfection, so the same is true analogically on the intellectual plane.

Perhaps it is worthwhile to go over matters again and to take some examples so as to clarify what can at times seem a quite abstruse argument.

The only species with a double capacity for representation is ultimately a dynamic intellectual impression. The intellect, like a sort of spiritual camera lens, can move from a panoramic vision back to the individual and vice versa. Unlike a camera lens, however, the intellect sees all of the universal in the individual, because it 'reads into' the proper and formal content of the essence (genus and difference) even before turning to subjects in which the essence is multiplied in reality.

To conclude, the 'Franciscan' theory of the knowledge of individuals is not necessarily opposed to the spirit of Thomistic epistemology but only to some of its particular applications, mainly the 'rigid' intellectual universalism, and to a materialistic understanding of the principle of individuation.

As a very important exponent of the Franciscan school, Hugo Cavellus knew how to grasp the overall significance of the problem and to propose a harmonious and coherent synthesis of the philosophical doctrine which justifies the intellectual knowledge of material individuals.

In overall terms, here are the three main points which Cavellus makes with regard to the *vexata quaestio*:

a) the intellectual knowledge of individuals is direct, that is, by means of individual species abstracted directly from the phantasms, and not only indirectly by means of reflection upon the phantasms;

b) the intellectual knowledge of individuals as such is not, in this life, a knowledge of the intrinsic reason for their individuality, but is the point of contact between the sensible and the intelligible order;

c) the following are the stages of the intellectual process: firstly there is the knowledge of the vague individual, then the universal nature (*species specialissima*), and finally the nature with all of the details which accompany it (the *individuum signatum*).

There are other problems which are connected with that of the material individuals, especially in the moral order. For example, the exercise of prudence which evaluates the application of universal laws to individual cases, and the law of friendship which is directed towards individual concrete persons. These facts clearly postulate an intellectual knowledge of individuals, because *nihil volitum quin praecognitum*, 'nothing is desired unless it is already known.' These are the practical consequences of the problem of the theory of knowledge, which at all events is not a mere quibbling about words.

The examination of the problem from both a theoretical and a historical point of view clearly shows the existence of a flourishing Scotist school in the sixteenth to eighteenth centuries (one only has to think of Bartolomeo Mastrius, Sebastian Dupasquier and Jerome da Montefortino), in which there was a considerable uniformity of judgment with regard to the understanding of material individuals, founded upon the philosophical principles outlined by Hugo Cavellus.

Irish Catholics and Aristotelian Scholastic philosophy in early modern France, *c*.1600–*c*.1750

LIAM CHAMBERS

While historians and philosophers have been reticent about studying early modern Aristotelian Scholasticism,[1] research on higher education curricula in Europe during the seventeenth and eighteenth centuries has emphasized repeatedly the enduring significance of a philosophy rooted in Aristotle and mediated through the great schools created in the Middle Ages.[2] This has important implications for assessments of the intellectual formation of Irish Catholics in the early modern period. From the middle of the sixteenth century until the end of the eighteenth Irish Catholic students attended universities, colleges and seminaries across continental Europe, where they were introduced to the debates and controversies which marked early modern Aristotelian Scholasticism.[3] From the later seventeenth century they would have been acutely conscious of the challenges to the philosophy curriculum from versions of the 'new philosophy', though they would have noted too the resilience of the traditional curriculum which ensured that in many parts of Europe some form of Aristotelian Scholasticism remained important well into the eighteenth century. Moreover, the Irish were more than the passive receptors of existing curricula. Some Irish students found employment as university professors of philosophy and a smaller number published textbooks and treatises. Put simply, as students, readers, teachers and writers, Irish Catholics engaged with Aristotelian Scholasticism, often critically, throughout the early modern period. The present article draws attention to this phenomenon and offers a preliminary assessment. It focuses on Irish activity in France, the most significant centre for Irish Catholic student migrants, though it also ranges more widely as appropriate. The present state of research means that the article is more suggestive than

---

1 For a comment on the difficulties inherent in describing 'Aristotelian Scholastics' see M.W.F. Stone, 'Aristotelianism and Scholasticism in early modern philosophy' in Steven Nadler (ed.), *A companion to early modern philosophy* (Oxford, 2002), p. 7. 2 L.W.B. Brockliss, 'Curricula' in Hilde de Ridder-Symoens (ed.), *A history of the university in Europe, volume two: universities in early modern Europe (1500–1800)* (Cambridge, 1996), pp 578–89. 3 There is no satisfactory general account of Irish student migration to early modern Europe, though there is a growing body of literature on particular Irish Colleges and student communities. For an introduction see T.J. Walsh, *The Irish continental college movement* (Cork, 1973).

conclusive, but it is hoped that it will help to open up a subject that has been neglected for far too long.

While early modern Aristotelian Scholasticism has always generated scholarly interest, as the work of the French historian of philosophy Étienne Gilson illustrates,[4] in the past two decades it has begun to receive much closer attention.[5] Recent historians and philosophers have argued strongly that Aristotelian Scholasticism was not the tired bulwark depicted by its opponents in the seventeenth century, but a fertile, complex and plural phenomenon. There was no agreement about what constituted 'Aristotelian' philosophy among its proponents, while those writing within particular 'Scholastic' traditions could diverge sharply.[6] Moreover, Aristotelian Scholasticism has been scrutinized as the dominant intellectual influence against which the new philosophies of the period emerged.[7] In France, it was Descartes and the Cartesians who offered the most serious challenge to the Aristotetelian Scholastic mainstream. In recent years considerable attention has been devoted to the intricate debates which engaged Aristotelian Scholastics and Cartesians in the second half of the seventeenth century and into the early eighteenth century, especially as they battled for control of the philosophical curriculum in the universities. This scholarship has further emphasized the view that neither Aristotelian Scholasticism nor Cartesianism were monoliths. Just as there were Scholastic Aristotelianisms, so there were Cartesianisms, as well as attempts to integrate the two.[8]

---

4 Étienne Gilson, *Index Scolastico-Cartésien* (Paris, 1913); idem, *Études sur le rôle de la pensée médiévale dans la formation du système Cartésien* (Paris, 1930). For a mid-twentieth century approach see: Leonora Cohen Rosenfield, 'Peripatetic adversaries of Cartesianism in 17th century France', *Review of Religion* 22 (1957), 14–40. 5 For useful overviews see: Michael Edwards, 'Aristotelianism, Descartes and Hobbes', *Historical Journal* 50:2 (2007), 449–64; Jacob Schmutz, 'Bulletin de scolastique moderne (I)', *Revue Thomiste* 100 (2000), 270–341. 6 Stone, 'Aristotelianism and Scholasticism in early modern philosophy', pp 7–24; idem, 'Scholastic schools and early modern philosophy' in Donald Rutherford (ed.), *The Cambridge companion to early modern philosophy* (Cambridge, 2006), pp 299–327; Christian Mercer, 'The vitality and importance of early modern Aristotelianism' in Tom Sorrell (ed.), *The rise of modern philosophy: the tension between the new and traditional philosophies from Machiavelli to Leibnitz* (Oxford, 1993), pp 33–67; Charles B. Schmitt, *Aristotle and the Renaissance* (Boston, 1983). 7 For a good example in relation to Descartes see: Jorge Secada, *Cartesian metaphysics: the late scholastic origins of modern philosophy* (Cambridge, 2000). It should be noted that there is a tension between claims that early modern Aristotelian Scholasticism deserves scholarly attention *per se* and the fact that much recent work has been motivated by a desire to contextualize the *novatores* of the seventeenth century. For a comment see: Edwards, 'Aristotelianism, Descartes and Hobbes', 456–8. See also comments in Stone, 'Aristotelianism and Scholasticism in early modern philosophy', p. 8; idem, 'Scholastic schools and early modern philosophy', p. 301. 8 For overviews see: Edwards, 'Aristotelianism, Descartes and Hobbes'; Eric P. Lewis, 'Cartesianism revisted', *Perspectives in Science* 15:4 (2007), 493–522. Good examples include: Charles Alan Kors, *Atheism in France 1650–1729, volume 1: the orthodox sources of disbelief* (Princeton, 1990); Roger Ariew, *Descartes and the last scholastics* (Ithaca, 1999); Tad Schmaltz (ed.), *Receptions of Descartes: Cartesianism and anti-Cartesianism in early modern Europe* (Abingdon, 2005); Tad Schmaltz, *Radical Cartesianism:*

This brings us to a final preliminary point: the recognition that there were early modern Irish Aristotelian Scholasticisms. Scholars have long recognized the crucial role played by the Irish Franciscans in the revival, development and dissemination of Scotism in the seventeenth and eighteenth centuries.[9] The networks created around key individuals like Luke Wadding, as well as the colleges established by the Order in Louvain, Rome and Prague, ensured that the Irish Franciscan commitment and contribution to Scotism has received significant scholarly attention, and the four-hundredth anniversary of the establishment of St Anthony's College, Louvain, has encouraged a fresh wave of interest.[10] Research on other aspects of Irish Scholastic Aristotelianism remains underdeveloped. In part, this is because there was no equivalent to the Irish Franciscan Scotist network for the other great school of the period, Thomism, which drew inspiration from the philosophy of Thomas Aquinas. While the Irish Dominicans and Jesuits were more likely to be formed within a Thomist framework, they did not have the philosophical commitment to Thomas to mirror the Franciscan commitment to Scotus, which was derived in large part from the knowledge that the Subtle Doctor was a Franciscan but also the conviction that he was an Irishman. The philosophical positions of the Irish secular clergy and laity are less clear again. The present article focuses on non-Scotist Irish Aristotelian Scholasticisms, while Irish Scotism is the subject of an important article elsewhere in this volume.[11]

II

Irish students attending classes at a university or other higher education institution in early modern Europe would have followed a course of studies which began with humanities (essentially Latin), before progressing to philosophy and, for the most able and ambitious, culminating in one of the three higher faculties of law, medicine or theology. From the work of the historian Laurence Brockliss

the French reception of Descartes (Cambridge, 2002); François Azouvi, *Descartes et la France: histoire d'une passion nationale* (Paris, 2002). See also the works of Laurence Brockliss cited in note 12 below.   9 See, for example, D. de Caylus, 'Merveilleux éponouissement de l'école scotiste au XVIIe siècle', *Études Franciscaines* 24 (1910), 5–21, 493–502; 25 (1911), 35–47, 306–17, 627–45; 26 (1912), 276–88; Charles Balić, 'Wadding, the Scotist' in The Franciscan Fathers (ed.), *Father Luke Wadding commemorative volume* (Dublin, 1957), pp 463–507; Cathaldus Giblin, 'Hugh MacCaghwell OFM and Scotism at St Anthony's College, Louvain' in *De Doctrina Joannis Duns Scoti* iv (1968), 375–97; Benignus Millet, 'Irish Scotists at St Isidore's College, Rome, in the seventeenth century' in *De Doctrina Joannis Duns Scoti* iv (1968), 399–419.   10 See M.W.F. Stone (ed.), *From Ireland to Louvain: the achievements of the Irish Franciscans and their contribution to early modern philosophy and theology* (Leuven, forthcoming 2009).   11 See M.W.F. Stone, 'Punch's riposte: the Irish contribution to early modern Scotism from Maurice O'Fihely OFMConv. to Anthony Rourke OFMObs' in this volume.

on the French higher education system in the early modern period, we know that throughout the seventeenth and early eighteenth centuries Irish students experienced a philosophy curriculum which was broadly Aristotelian Scholastic, though with important qualifications.[12] He argues that of the four components of the curriculum – logic, metaphysics, ethics and natural philosophy (or physics) – only the natural philosophy section changed radically. This is not to suggest that the courses offered in logic, metaphysics and ethics did not change at all. For example, Brockliss points out that the section of the logic course on 'method' (*de methodo*) greatly expanded in the late seventeenth century, clearly influenced by the challenge of Cartesianism.[13] However, the impact of the work of Descartes and the Cartesians was most strongly felt in natural philosophy, culminating in the replacement of Aristotelianism, though this was a slow process. Brockliss offers two stages of development. First, between 1640 and 1690 'Aristotelianism went on the defensive.'[14] Increasingly this meant discussing (if only to refute) aspects of the 'new learning'. A small number of Parisian professors began to teach an eclectic mix of Aristotelian and Cartesian natural philosophy, reflected in the appearance of textbooks like Jean Baptiste du Hamel's *Philosophia vetus et nova ad usum scholae accomodata* (4 vols, Paris, 1678). The second stage delineated by Brockliss spans the period 1690 to 1740. During the 1690s Aristotelian natural philosophy was increasingly replaced by Cartesian mechanism. However, in some quarters this process was very slow. Aristotelian Scholastic concerns about the apparent inability of Cartesians to provide a natural philosophy compatible with the Catholic doctrine of the Eucharist, as well as worries that Cartesianism opened the door to the dangers of Spinozism, ensured that as late as the 1720s and 1730s it is still possible to find courses in Aristotelian natural philosophy.[15] It is also important to note that there was little agreement among Cartesian professors about what constituted a 'Cartesian' natural philosophy, and in any case they soon found themselves under attack from Newtonian professors.[16] The pattern of development and change varied

12 The following section draws on the work of L.W.B. Brockliss: 'Philosophy teaching in France 1600–1740', *History of Universities* 1 (1981), 131–68; idem, 'Aristotle, Descartes and the new sciences: natural philosophy at the University of Paris 1600–1740', *Annals of Science* 38 (1981), 33–69; idem, *French higher education in the seventeenth and eighteenth centuries: a cultural history* (Oxford, 1987), pp 185–227, 337–90; idem, 'Discoursing on method in the university world of Descartes's France', *British Journal for the History of Philosophy* 3 (1995), 3–28; idem, 'Descartes, Gassendi and the reception of the mechanical philosophy in the French *collèges de plein exercice*, 1640–1730', *Perspectives on Science* 3:4 (1995), 450–79; idem, 'The moment of no return: the University of Paris and the death of Aristotelianism', *Science and Education* 15 (2006), 259–78. 13 Brockliss, 'Philosophy teaching in France 1600–1740', 136–7. See also: idem, 'Discoursing on method in the university world of Descartes's France', 3–28. 14 Brockliss, 'Philosophy teaching in France 1600–1740', 147. 15 The significance of the Eucharist is discussed in J.-R. Armogathe, *Theologia Cartesiana: L'explication physique de l'eucharistie chez Descartes et Dom Desgabets* (The Hague, 1977) and Schmaltz, *Radical Cartesianism*. 16 Brockliss, 'Philosophy

depending on the institution, but the key point is that Irish students experienced an Aristotelian Scholastic curriculum until the 1690s and, with qualifications, beyond then.

Analysing the attitudes of Irish students towards the philosophy curriculum they experienced in France, or elsewhere on the continent, is a difficult task, and much of the research required to do this has yet to be undertaken. However, it is interesting that Éamon Ó Ciosáin has identified a satirical and critical image of Irish students and scholars, which recurred in a number of French sources, and depicted them as backward and slavish Scholastics.[17] A key text in the development of this stereotype was a satire published by Nicolas Boileau in 1671, in which the author poked fun at the attempts of the University of Paris, in the same year, to censor Cartesian ideas.[18] As Ó Ciosain has noted, Boileau particularly identified the Irish (*Hybernois*) with the Scholastic position.[19] When, in 1722, the philosophy of the Angers Oratorian and Cartesian, Jacques Guillou, was censored in the local university a satirical response appeared criticising the censorship with the unlikely title: *Lettre des Hibernois et des Arabes à l'Université d'Angers* (s.l., s.d.).[20] A number of Enlightenment writers propagated the motif, most famously Montesquieu in his *Lettres Persanes*.[21] A similar view found expression in Ireland. One visitor to Kerry in the late seventeenth century recorded that the local inhabitants were especially noted for 'their gaming, their speaking of Latin, and inclination to philosophy and disputes therein [...]. When they can get no one to game with them, you shall often find them with a book of Aristotles or some of the Commentators Logic which they read very diligently till they be able to pour out nonsensical words a whole day about *universale a parte rei, ens rationalis* [*sic*] and suchlike stuff.'[22] Right at the end of the century Louis-Sébastien Mercier offered an explanation for the bewildering attachment of the Irish to Scholasticism in his utopian description of Paris, *L'an deux mille quatre cent quarante*: 'Nous avons découvert que les bancs sur lesquels s'asseioient ces docteurs hibernois, étoient formés d'un certain bois, dont la funeste vertu dérangeoit la tête la mieux organisée, et la faisoit déraisonner avec méthode.'[23] There are a number of ways of explaining the recurring image of

teaching in France, 1600–1740', pp 150–1.   17 Éamon Ó Ciosáin, 'Attitudes towards Ireland and the Irish in Enlightenment France' in Graham Gargett and Geraldine Sheridan (eds), *Ireland and the Enlightenment 1700–1800* (London, 1999), pp 141–6.   18 [Nicolas Boileau], *Requeste des maistres es arts, professeurs, & regens de l'Université de Paris presentée à la cour souveraine de Parnasse: ensemble l'arrest intervene sur ladite requeste* (s.l., 1671).   19 Ó Ciosáin, 'Attitudes towards Ireland and the Irish in Enlightenment France', p. 142; [Boileau], *Requeste des maistres es arts*, p. 12.   20 Jacques Maillard, *L'Oratoire à Angers aux XVIIème et XVIIIème siècles* (Paris, s.d.), pp 193–4, 224–5. For the seventeenth-century context: Roger Ariew, 'Oratorians and the teaching of Cartesian philosophy in seventeenth century France', *History of Universities* 17 (2001–2), 47–80.   21 Charles-Louis de Secondat, baron de Montesquieu, *Persian Letters*, trans. C.J. Betts (1721; London, 1993), p. 90.   22 Cited in W.B. Stanford, *Ireland and the Classical tradition* (Dublin, 1984), p. 27.   23 Louis-Sébastien Mercier, *L'an deux mille quatre cent-*

Irish scholastics in France. Like any migrant group, the Irish were particularly susceptible to stereotyping, especially so in the light of ill-informed French knowledge of Ireland. As Ó Ciosáin has argued, Irish migrants frequently had to live on their wits and may have gained a reputation for disputatiousness as a result.[24] It is interesting that the prominent writer Charles Perrault recalled that when he was student at the Collège de Beauvais in Paris in the early seventeenth century, he boasted to his professor of philosophy that 'mes argumens étoient meilleurs que ceux des *Hibernois*'.[25] The highly visible Irish Franciscan commitment to the philosophy of John Duns Scotus may have underlined the Irish-Scholastic connection to would-be satirists, like Boileau. Some of the key works emanating from this network were printed in France, including Wadding's edition of the *Opera omnia* (Lyons, 1639) and John Punch's forceful re-statement of Scotus' Irish background, *Scotus Hiberniae restitutus* (Paris, 1660).[26] Boileau may also have been targeting the Irish Scholastic philosopher Michael Moore, who was probably involved in the attempt to censor Cartesianism in Paris in 1671.[27] Indeed, Boileau was educated, like Perrault, at the Collège de Beauvais, where he may well have encountered the Irish professor of philosophy, Roger O'Moloy.[28]

There are a number of ways of ascertaining the philosophical positions adopted by Irish students in the course of their studies and afterwards. Surviving student notebooks are an important, though almost entirely untapped, source. The philosophy notebook of Thomas Medus, compiled in 1622, begins with a two page poem in honour of Thomas Aquinas. It contains notes on the four sections of his philosophy course, beginning with logic (taking in Porphyry's *Isagoge* and Aristotle's works), followed by physics (encompassing Aristotle's *Physica, De anima, De generatione et corruptione,* and *De coelo*) and finishing with sections on metaphysics and ethics. The notebook is dominated by logic and physics, while ethics accounts for by far the shortest section.[29] Alexius Stafford's philosophy notebook, dated 1667, shows that he studied the work of the Coimbra commentators in detail while he was a student in Lisbon.[30]

quarante: rêve s'il en fût jamais (3 vols, [Paris], 1786), i, 65. **24** Ó Ciosáin, 'Attitudes towards Ireland and the Irish in Enlightenment France', p. 146. **25** Charles Perrault, *Mémoires de ma vie*, ed. Paul Bonnefon (Paris, 1909), p. 20. **26** For Irish Franciscan connections with France see Canice Mooney, *Irish Franciscans and France* (Dublin, 1964). **27** On this and related issues see Liam Chambers, 'Irish Catholics, French Cartesians: Irish reactions to Cartesianism in France, 1671–1726' in Eamon Maher & Grace Neville (eds), *Ireland and France: anatomy of a relationship* (Frankfurt am Main, 2004), pp 137–40. **28** L.W.B. Brockliss and P. Ferté, 'A prosopography of Irish clerics in the Universities of Paris and Toulouse', *Archivium Hibernicum* 58 (2004), 32. **29** Thomas Medus, 'Philosophiae universae compendium per Thomam Medum Ibernum' (1622) (Marsh's Library, Dublin, MS Z3.5.16). It is not clear where he studied, but Paris is a possibility. A student with the same name was registered at the University of Paris in the mid-seventeenth century. See Brockliss and Ferté, 'prosopography', 156–7. **30** Alexius Stafford, 'In universam Aristotelis logicam' (1667) (Marsh's Library, Dublin, MS Z4.5.3). On

Source material like this is not lacking. The Russell Library, Maynooth, holds a large collection of philosophy notebooks, many compiled in eighteenth-century France by students residing at one of the Irish Colleges.[31] The extensive early seventeenth-century philosophy notebooks of Cornelius Lery are available in Cambridge University Library and run to hundreds of pages. Lery's philosophy thesis is bound in with the same collection and points towards another significant, but again largely untapped, source.[32] Philosophy theses sustained by Irish students may be found scattered among a number of French libraries. For example, surviving theses from the late 1650s and 1660s indicate that Irish professors of philosophy at the University of Paris (in this case Michael Moore and Roger O'Moloy) presided over the theses of their compatriots.[33] Works of philosophy also circulated in manuscript. A good example is a mid-seventeenth century Irish manuscript, which contains a lengthy transcription from Charles François Abra de Raconis' popular textbook *Summa totius philosophiae*, first published in 1617.[34] Manuscript philosophy treatises written in the seventeenth century by Nicholas French, the future bishop of Ferns, and Peter Pippard, an Irish Jesuit, survive, as do works by Spanish philosophers, which circulated in manuscript in early seventeenth-century Dublin.[35]

Private libraries offer another indicator of philosophical attitudes. Michael Moore, the most prominent Irish Aristotelian Scholastic in Paris in the late seventeenth and early eighteenth centuries, unsurprisingly had a large collection

Stafford see: Richard Roche, 'Alexius Stafford: "the popish dean of Christ's Church"' in *History Ireland* 8:3 (2000), 32–4; Patricia O Connell, *The Irish College at Lisbon, 1590–1834* (Dublin, 2001), p. 95. **31** See the listings in Richard J. Hayes, *Manuscript sources for the history of Irish civilization* (11 vols, Boston, 1965), vi, 291 and *First supplement, 1965–75* (3 vols, Boston, 1979), ii, 289–90. **32** Commentaries of Cornelius Lery on various works of Aristotle, *c.*1630s (Cambridge University Library, MS 1804). **33** For example, Henri LeBrun, *Conclusiones philosophicae* (Paris, 1659); Peter Comminge, *Conclusiones philosophicae* (Paris, 1661); John Purcell, *Conclusiones philosophicae* (Paris, 1666). Further examples of philosophy theses are listed in Tony Sweeney, *Ireland and the printed word: a short descriptive catalogue of early books, pamphlets, newsletters and broadsides relating to Ireland printed 1475–1700* (Dublin, 1997). **34** Royal Irish Academy, MS 3.B.40. The transcription occupies fos. 1–119 and is followed by transcriptions relating to the history of the Fitzgerald and Butler families. **35** Nicholas French, Notebook containing sections on 'physica' and 'metaphysica', undated (Marsh's Library, Dublin, MS Z4.4.15). There is no title or date, which the library catalogue provides without explanation: 'Dictata physicalia et metaphysicalia' (1630). Walter Harris knew of the manuscript and noted that French 'wrote [...] a course of philosophy, which (I believe) was never thought worth printing': Sir James Ware, *The whole works of Sir James Ware concerning Ireland, revised and improved*, ed. Walter Harris (2 vols, Dublin, 1739–45), ii, 166. In fact, this may be a student notebook. On French's student career see: Jeroen Nilis, 'Irish students at Leuven University, 1548–1797' in *Archivium Hibernicum*, 60 (2006–7), 62. Peter Pippard's treatise is: 'Disputationes in libros Aristotelis De Anima', early seventeenth century (Trinity College, Dublin, MS 437). For the works of Spanish philosophers see Juan José Pérez-Camacho, 'Late renaissance humanism and the Dublin scientific tradition (1592–1641)', in Norman McMillan (ed.), *Prometheus's fire: a history of scientific and technological education in Ireland* (Carlow, 2000), pp 56–7.

of Scholastic philosophy and theology, largely Thomist, but also including the works of Scotus. He donated the library to the Irish Collège des Lombards in the French capital on his death in 1726.[36] Clerical libraries of this period belonging to bishops Piers Creagh, William Daton and Luke Wadding, as well as the Dominican John Donnelly (who taught philosophy at Louvain) and the Augustinian community in Galway all reveal late Aristotelian Scholastic content.[37] The library of the Galway Augustinians indicates a preference for the works of their colleagues, presumably a feature of other libraries belonging to the regular clergy.[38] Dennis Molony, who graduated from the University of Paris as a master of arts in 1683, owned a copy of Aquinas' *Summa theologiae*, but also possessed the integrationist philosophy of Jean Baptiste du Hamel (mentioned above), which he may well have picked up as a student.[39]

A small number of Irishmen were professors of philosophy at one of the colleges attached to the University of Paris in the seventeenth and eighteenth centuries.[40] Eight found employment in the seventeenth century, Michael Moore straddles the seventeenth and eighteenth centuries, while three Irishmen were professors in the eighteenth century. Most gained a position very early in their career, perhaps in order to facilitate their theological studies, though it should not be assumed that these posts were easily acquired.[41] This was especially

---

36 Liam Chambers, 'The library of an Irish Catholic émigré: Michael Moore's bibliothèque, 1726', *Archivium Hibernicum* 58 (2004), 210–42.   37 Canice Mooney (ed.), 'The library of Archbishop Piers Creagh' in *Reportorium Novum* 1:1 (1955), 126–7; Patrick J. Corish (ed.), 'Bishop Wadding's Notebook' in *Archivium Hibernicum* 29 (1970), 55–6, 58, 61, 64, 67, 79, 80, 84, 86; Hugh Fenning, 'The library of Bishop William Daton of Ossory, 1698', *Collectanea Hibernica* 20 (1978), 40, 46; idem, 'The library of a preacher of Drogheda: John Donnelly, O.P. (d. 1748)' *Collectanea Hibernica* 18–19 (1976–7), 73, 80, 84, 91–4, 97; Hugh Fenning (ed.), 'The library of the Augustinians of Galway in 1731', *Collectanea Hibernica* 31–2 (1989–90), 166, 170, 183, 184. Daton also had a copy of a work by Descartes (Fenning, 'The library of Bishop William Daton of Ossory, 1698', 37).   38 Fenning (ed.), 'The library of the Augustinians of Galway in 1731', 170, 183–4.   39 *A catalogue of the library of Denis Molony esq; late of Gray's-Inn, deceas'd* (London, 1728), p. 8. For an edition see John Bergin & Liam Chambers, 'The library of Denis Molony (1650–1726), an Irish Catholic lawyer in London' in *Analecta Hibernica* 41 (2008), forthcoming.   40 Malachy Queeley, Collège de Boncourt, 1617; Henry Stanihurst, 1622; Nicolas Pouerus (Power), 1622; John O'Molony, Collège des Grassins, 1623; Roger O'Moloy, Collège de Beauvais, 1629?–70; Edouard Tirel, Collège des Grassins, 1635; James Dulaeus (Daly), Collège du Plessis, 1642–3; Nicolas Poerus (Power), Collège de Lisieux, 1650; Michael Moore, Collège des Grassins, 1663–70s, Collège de France, 1703–20; James Wogan, Collège de Navarre, 1729; Luke Joseph Hooke, 1736; James MacDonagh, Collège du Plessis, 1772. This list (including dates) is drawn from Brockliss and Ferté, 'Prosopography', 32, 35, 81–2, 85, 87–90, 93, 105, 107–8, 113, 119. Some sources list other Irishmen as professors of philosophy in early modern Paris, but the evidence is not strong. For example, Richard Hayes asserts that Maurice Aherne was a professor of philosophy at the Collège de Navarre in the 1760s. See Richard Hayes, *Biographical dictionary of Irishmen in France* (Dublin, 1949), p. 2.   41 Boris Noguès, *Une archéologie du corps enseignant: les professeurs des collèges parisiens au XVIIe et XVIIIe siècles (1598–1793)* (Paris, 2006), pp 82–3. More generally: Brockliss, *French higher education*, pp 37–51.

pronounced in the seventeenth century when Irish students lacked strong connections within the university and were therefore unable to gain access to the institutionally and financially more elevated chairs of theology. By the next century, especially from the 1730s, Irishmen regularly progressed to chairs of theology. For example, James Wogan and Luke Joseph Hooke both began their careers teaching philosophy before progressing to theology. Moreover, the establishment of a permanent Irish College in Paris in the 1670s offered an alternative source of employment. Of the seventeenth-century philosophers, it is significant that many proceeded to successful careers. Queeley, O'Molony and Daly became bishops. Tirel, who provided an approbation for John Punch's *Scotus Hiberniae restitutus* (Paris, 1660), was superior of the Irish College (albeit a virtual institution) in the mid-seventeenth century.[42] Roger O'Moloy was therefore unusual, for he was a professor of philosophy for his entire career.[43] In 1641 the doctor and writer Gui Patin recommended to a friend that he send his son to the Collège de Beauvais, 'parce qu'il y a un Hibernois excellent philosophe.'[44] Unfortunately, we know very little about O'Moloy's teaching activities, though we do know that he supervised the philosophy theses of a number of Irish students and played a prominent role in the Irish student and academic community in Paris.[45] In fact, only one Irish professor of philosophy at the University of Paris published works of philosophy during his career: Michael Moore. The most that we can say about the others is that they do not seem to have been controversial, which, for the seventeenth century at least, suggests that they taught a fairly orthodox Scholastic Aristotelianism.[46]

III

This makes the career of Michael Moore all the more important, for he provides an indication of an Irish response to the philosophical curriculum at a moment of dramatic change.[47] Born in Dublin around 1639, Moore was educated in Nantes and Paris. He began teaching philosophy at the Collège des Grassins (one of the teaching colleges attached to the University of Paris) in 1663, before switching to rhetoric in the 1670s when he also became vice-principal. Moore returned to

---

42 John Punch, *Scotus Hiberniae restitutus* (Paris, 1660), unpaginated.   43 Brockliss, *French higher education*, pp 46–8.   44 Gui Patin à M. Belin, 22 Août 1641 in Gui Patin, *Lettres de Gui Patin*, ed. Joseph-Henri Reveillé-Parise (3 vols, Paris, 1846), i, 81.   45 Priscilla O'Connor, 'Irish clerics in the University of Paris, 1570–1770' (unpublished PhD thesis, NUI, Maynooth, 2006), pp 114–15; Brockliss and Ferté, 'Prosopography', p. 32. For supervision of philosophy theses see above.   46 However, it should be noted that Henry Stanihurst provided advice to Marin Mersenne concerning alchemy in 1625. See Antonio Clericuzio, *Elements, principles and corpuscles: a study of atomism and chemistry in the seventeenth century* (Dordrecht, 2001), p. 51.   47 The following section draws on Liam Chambers, *Michael Moore, c.1639–1726: provost of Trinity, rector of Paris* (Dublin, 2005).

Dublin in 1686 and played a prominent role during the reign of James II. He was briefly provost of Trinity College, before a public attack on the king's ecclesiastical policies resulted in his return to France. During the 1690s the conflict between Aristotelians and Cartesians within the University of Paris, essentially over the content of the natural philosophy component of the course, reached a crescendo. In 1691 eleven propositions allegedly taken from the work of Descartes were banned by the university authorities. This represented a concerted, if ultimately futile, effort on the part of the church, the state and the university to determine the philosophy curriculum and reveals the extent of official antipathy to Cartesianism.[48] It was at this point that Moore published his most important work: *De existentia Dei et humanae mentis immortalitate secundum Cartesii et Aristotelis doctrinam disputatio* (Paris, 1692). Moore spent the 1690s in Italy, but he returned to Paris in 1701 where he was elected rector of the university and was appointed principal of humanities students at the Collège de Navarre (1702) and professor of Greek and Latin Philosophy at the Collège de France (1703). Two works based on his lectures at the Collège de France were later published: *Vera sciendi methodus* (Paris, 1716) and *De principiis physicis, seu corporum naturalium disputatio* (Paris, 1726). Moore retired in 1720 and died in Paris six years later.

Michael Moore's *De existentia Dei* contributed to the debates involving Aristotelian Scholastics and Cartesians in later seventeenth-century France.[49] He was especially concerned with the content of the philosophy curriculum at the *collèges de plein exercice* at the University of Paris and, by extension, the rest of France.[50] More specifically, he was targeting those philosophers, like Jean Baptiste du Hamel and his former colleague at the Collège des Grassins, Edmond Pourchot, who were arguing in the 1680s and 1690s that one could integrate aspects of Cartesianism with the existing Aristotelian curriculum.[51] Moore's clear purpose was to show that no accommodation was possible. To do this he focused on Descartes' 'Arguments proving the existence of God and the distinction between the soul and the body arranged in geometric fashion,' penned in response to Marin Mersenne's (second) set of objections to the *Meditations on first philosophy*.[52] This permitted Moore to range quite widely,

48 See Charles Jourdain, *Histoire de l'Université de Paris au XVIIe et au XVIIIe siècles* (Paris, 1862), pp 269–70. For attempts to censor Cartesianism in France see Roger Ariew, 'Damned if you do: Cartesians and censorship, 1663–1706', *Perspectives on Science* 2 (1994), 255–74; Thomas McLoughlin, 'Censorship and defenders of the Cartesian faith in mid-seventeenth century France', *Journal of the History of Ideas* 40:4 (1979), 563–82. On the 1691 censorship, see also the recent work of Tad Schmaltz, *Radical Cartesianism*, pp 217–20; idem, 'French Cartesianism in context: the Paris formulary and Regis's *Usage*' in idem (ed.), *Receptions of Descartes*, pp 80–95. 49 A fuller treatment may be found in Chambers, *Michael Moore*, pp 61–83. 50 See, for example, his comments on the 1601 statutes of the university, which demanded an Aristotelian philosophy course: Moore, *De existentia Dei*, pp 458–9. 51 Kors, *Atheism in France, 1650–1729*, pp 276–7; Mercer, 'The vitality and importance of early modern Aristotelianism', pp 58–9. 52 Moore, *De existentia Dei*, preface; René Descartes, *The philosophical writings of Descartes*,

while addressing the two metaphysical issues raised in the full title of the *Meditations*: 'the existence of God and the distinction between the human soul and body'.[53] In his dedicatory letter to the Sorbonne, Descartes claimed that he was motivated by the Fifth Lateran Council's assertion in 1513 of the philosophical truth of the immortality of the soul.[54] Moore's essential point was that neither of Descartes' alleged demonstrations stood up to close scrutiny.

The result is a lengthy and complex critique of Cartesian metaphysics. In book one of *De existentia Dei* Moore subjected each step in Descartes' 'Arguments' to a forensic analysis, in each case carefully unpacking Descartes' position, before offering alternatives (drawn especially from Aristotle and Thomas Aquinas, but also from Plato and Augustine), and settling on a conclusion. In this way he analyzed the definitions, postulates, axioms and propositions (or demonstrations) which constituted the basic fabric of Cartesian metaphysics.[55] In book two he provided Aristotelian Scholastic demonstrations of the existence of God and the immortality of the human soul.[56] Moore's discussion of the soul is particularly interesting, for it underlines the need to think of plural Aristotelian Scholasticisms in the early modern period. Moore argued that Descartes' distinction between mind and body did not entail a demonstration of the immortality of the mind or soul. Challenged on just this point by Mersenne, Moore argued that Descartes had retreated into a kind of fideism.[57] Therefore Descartes was unable to provide a demonstration of an essential Christian truth 'despite his disciples' assertions'.[58] Moore's focus on the soul was a shrewd decision, given that, in the later seventeenth and early eighteenth centuries, Cartesians were struggling to defend Descartes' rational demonstration of Christian truths.[59] Moreover, Moore recognized the difficulties with Aristotle's theory of the soul. For this reason he confronted head on the 'secular' or 'radical' (or Averroist) position adopted by Pietro Pomponazzi in his *De immortalitate animae* (1516). He had argued that Aristotle had not provided an argument in favour of immortality, a truth which had to be accepted on the basis of faith, not reason.[60] This would have undermined the superiority of the Aristotelian position and Moore rejected it. He adopted the Thomist

trans. J. Cottingham, R. Stoothoff and D. Murdoch, 2 vols (Cambridge, 1985), ii, 113–20. 53 This was the wording in the second edition. The first edition carried the wording 'in which are demonstrated the existence of God and the immortality of the soul.' Descartes, *The philosophical writings*, ii, 1. For a recent discussion on the publication history of and context to the *Meditations* see Desmond Clarke, *Descartes: a biography* (Cambridge, 2006), pp 184–217. 54 Moore also addressed his work to the dean and doctors of the faculty of theology: *De existentia Dei*, epistola. 55 Ibid., pp 7–330. 56 Ibid., 331–451. 57 Ibid., 321–30. 58 Ibid., 322. 59 Jonathan Israel, *Radical Enlightenment: philosophy and the making of modernity, 1650–1750* (Oxford, 2001), pp 491–4. 60 Pietro Pomponazzi, 'On the immortality of the soul', introduced by J. Herman Randall Jr, in E. Cassirer, P.O. Kristeller & J.H. Randall (eds), *The Renaissance philosophy of man: selections in translation* (Chicago, 1967), pp 257–381. For Moore's discussion of Pomponazzi, see *De existentia Dei*, pp 411–51.

position that the intellective part of the soul (*mens*) in humans is separable from the body because it has operations proper to itself.[61] It is interesting that Moore drew Pomponazzi into the debate (he was still widely discussed in the late seventeenth century) and that he implicitly associated the dangerous ideas of the secular Aristotelian with the Cartesian.

While the natural philosophy courses at Paris largely succumbed to Cartesianism in the 1690s, the other parts of the philosophy curriculum were less dramatically affected and, in any case, some support for the Aristotelian position remained strong for the first two decades of the eighteenth century.[62] Moore's courses at the Collège de France were an important indicator that Aristotelian Scholasticism had not disappeared and his position as *professeur royal* accorded his work significant status. Two books emerged from his teaching in the early eighteenth century. *Vera sciendi methodus* reflected the expansion of the 'method' section of the logic course in the face of Cartesian challenges. In this work Moore attacked the appeal to mathematics as the basis for the study of nature and the geometric method of demonstration, instead outlining an Aristotelian logic rooted in the syllogism. In *De principiis physicis* one finds a stripped down late Aristotelian natural philosophy, a re-statement of the importance of matter and form, his theory of the soul and an attack on the influential Oratorian Nicholas Malebranche. Throughout his work Moore stressed the Christian utility of Aristotelian Scholasticism and the dangers presented by Cartesianism. In his early eighteenth-century teaching and writing he led the call for a renewal of philosophy based on Aristotle and the Scholastic approach.[63] Moore is therefore especially important because he confronted the Cartesian challenge in natural philosophy and attempted to fight a rearguard action well into the eighteenth century.[64]

IV

Moore was not the only Irish writer to publish works of (non-Scotist) Aristotelian Scholastic philosophy in the seventeenth and early eighteenth centuries. In the early seventeenth century Bernard Morisanus published a textbook, *In Aristotelis logicam physicam ethicam apotelesma* (Frankfurt, 1625), as well as a commentary on the medieval astronomy of John de Sacrobosco: *In spheram Joannis de S. Bosco commentarius* (Frankfurt, 1625).[65] Christopher

---

61 Moore, *De existentia Dei*, pp 350–1. 62 L.W.B. Brockliss, 'Aristotle, Descartes and the new sciences', p. 52. 63 For fuller analysis see Chambers, *Michael Moore*, pp 116–29. 64 For an interesting discussion of the historiographical issues thrown up by early modern Aristotelian natural philosophy see: Christoph Lüthy, 'What to do with seventeenth century natural philosophy: a taxonomic problem', *Perspectives on Science* 8:2 (2000), 164–95. 65 Charles H. Lohr, 'Renaissance Latin Aristotle Commentaries: Authors L–M', *Renaissance Quarterly* 31:4

Holywood had produced an Aristotelian-Ptolemaic work over a decade earlier: *De meteoribus* (Paris, 1613).[66] James Piers, an Irish professor of philosophy at the Collège de Guyenne in Bordeaux, published a work on Aristotelian logic: *Brevis atque dilucida in logicam introductio quam vulgo summulus appellant* (Bordeaux, 1635).[67] Perhaps the most significant Irish Aristotelian Scholastic textbook (written outside the Scotist tradition) was the Galway Jesuit Richard Lynch's *Summa Philosophica Scholastica* (Lyons, 1654).[68] Irish writers produced polemics as well as textbooks. Peter Talbot, the archbishop of Dublin, published two strong attacks on the English neo-Aristotelians Thomas White (alias Blacklow) and John Sergeant.[69] The Dominicans had a particular investment in the Thomist school and a number of Irish friars made important contributions. Dominic Lynch, a Dominican from Galway, who taught for most of his career in Seville, published a full Aristotelian Scholastic course in France, his *Summa philosophiae speculativae juxta mentem & doctrinam Divi Thomae & Aristotelis* (4 vols, Paris, 1666–86).[70] In a long medieval and early modern tradition of rhyming philosophy treatises, another Dominican, Michael Corcran, published his *Rythmus pan-sophicus* (Morlaix, 1690).[71] Outside France, James Arthur had prepared a projected twelve-volume commentary on the *Summa* by the time of his death. Only two volumes appeared, under the title: *Commentaria in totam fere S. Thomae de Aquino Summam* (2 vols, Lisbon?, 1665).[72] John Baptist Hacket, a well-connected Irish Dominican who resided in Rome, published a series of philosophical texts in the mid-seventeenth century: *Synopsis summulistica* (Rome, 1659), *Synopsis physica* (Rome, 1659) and *Synopsis meteorica* (Rome, 1659), as well as a *Synopsis philosophiae* (2 vols, Rome, 1662). The latter was an abridgement of the philosophy of John of St. Thomas (João Poinsot), one of the most important Thomists of the seventeenth century.[73] Of course, some of these

(1978), p. 599.   **66** For a short discussion see Pérez-Camacho, 'Late renaissance humanism and the Dublin scientific tradition (1592–1641)', pp 57–60.   **67** Sweeney, *Ireland and the printed word*, p. 568.   **68** Thompson Cooper, 'Lynch, Richard (1610–1676)', rev. G. Martin Murphy, *Oxford dictionary of national biography* (Oxford, 2004) [http://www.oxforddnb.com/view/article/17258, accessed 21 July 2008]. Lynch's philosophy is discussed in: Sven K. Knebel, *Wille, Würfel und Wahrscheinlichkeit: Das System der Moralischen Notwendigkeit in der Jesuitenscholastik 1550–1700* (Hamburg, 2000).   **69** *Blacklonae haereses olim in Pelagio et Manichaeis damnatae* (Ghent, 1675); *Scutum inexpugnabile fidei adversus haeresem Blacklonam et clypeum septemplicum Joannis Sargentii* (Lyons, 1678). For context and some comment see Dorothea Krook, *John Sergeant and his circle: a study of three seventeenth-century English Aristotelians*; ed. Beverley C. Southgate (Leiden, 1993), pp 163–8.   **70** Thomas Burke, *Hibernia Dominicana, sive historia Provinciae Hiberniae Ordinis Praedicatorum* (Cologne, 1762), p. 545; J. Hardiman, 'The pedigree of Doctor Domnick Lynch [...] 1674', *Miscellany of the Irish Archaeological Society* 1 (1846), 44–90.   **71** Sweeney, *Ireland and the printed word*, p. 184.   **72** Ware, *The whole works of Sir James Ware*, ed. Harris, ii, 160.   **73** Burke, *Hibernia Dominicana*, p. 542–4; Ware, *The whole works of Sir James Ware*, ed. Harris, ii, 201; Thomas S. R. O'Flynn, 'Hackett, John Baptist (c.1606–1676)', *Oxford dictionary of national biography* (Oxford, 2004) [http://www.oxforddnb.com/view/article/11838, accessed 21 July 2008]; Stone, 'Scholastic schools and early modern philosophy',

authors, such as John Baptist Hacket and Richard Lynch, published important works of Scholastic theology as well.[74] Dominic Lynch had prepared a full course of Scholastic theology for publication, before it was lost at sea en route from Spain to France.[75] Indeed, the writings of a series of Irish Scholastic theologians deserve much closer attention. One of the best examples is Augustine Gibbon de Burgo, who published major works of Scholastic theology at Erfurt in the 1660s and 1670s.[76] The works of at least some of these authors found their way into the libraries of their compatriots. For example, the Irish bishop, Piers Creagh, owned a copy of Hacket's *Synopsis philosophica*, while the Dominican John Donnelly, at his death in 1748, owned a copy of Dominic Lynch's *Summa*.[77]

There is some evidence that Irish Catholic attitudes to Aristotelian Scholasticism were changing towards the end of the seventeenth century and into the early eighteenth century, in line with developments across the continent. The work of William O'Kelly of Aghrim (Aughrim) provides a good example of a shift in attitude. Educated in Paris, at least according to Walter Harris with whom he corresponded in the early 1740s, O'Kelly arrived in Prague in 1698 and was later appointed professor of philosophy and heraldry in Vienna. He wrote a string of works on philosophy, heraldry and Irish history, as well as compositions in Latin verse, during the late 1690s and early eighteenth century.[78] His major philosophical work was *Philosophia aulica juxta veterum, ac recentiorum philosophorum placita* (New Prague, 1701). The title seems to place it in within attempts to accommodate the 'old' and 'new' philosophies, though the presentation was relatively traditional (described by the author as 'the Parisian manner'), covering in turn logic, ethics, physics and metaphysics. The text was sympathetic to the 'new' philosophies of Galileo, Gassendi and Descartes. O'Kelly even incorporated the text of Boileau's 1671 satire in his introduction, though he silently expunged the references to the Irish.[79] Around 1741 O'Kelly

p. 309.   **74** For example, in the case of Richard Lynch, *Universae theologicae scholasticae tomus primus* (2 vols, Salamanca, 1679).   **75** Burke, *Hibernia Dominicana*, p. 545.   **76** On Gibbon de Burgo see John Hennig, 'Augustine Gibbon de Burgo: a study in early Irish reaction to Luther', *Irish Ecclesiastical Record*, 5th ser. 69 (1947), 135–51; Erich Kleineidam, 'Augustinus Gibbon de Burgo, OESA, und die Wiedererrichtung des theologischen Studiums der Augustinereremiten an der Universität Erfurt', *Analecta Augustiniana* 41 (1978), 65–112. For other authors see Benignus Millet, 'Irish literature in Latin 1550–1700' in T.W. Moody, F.X. Martin & F.J. Byrne (eds), *A new history of Ireland: iii, Early modern Ireland 1534–1691* (Oxford, 1976), pp 575–9.   **77** Mooney (ed.), 'The library of Archbishop Piers Creagh', pp 125–6; Fenning, 'The library of a preacher of Drogheda', p. 97.   **78** Ware, *The whole works of Sir James Ware*, ed. Harris, ii, 287; Brockliss and Ferté, 'Prosopography', p. 124; David Coakley & Zdenek Kalvach, 'Doctors in exile: William MacNeven O'Kelly (1713–1787) and William James MacNeven (1741–1841)', in Helga Robinson-Hammerstein (ed.), *Migrating scholars: lines of contact between Ireland and Bohemia* (Dublin, [1998]), pp 82–3. Some of his works are listed in: Hedvika Kucharová & Jan Parez, 'Po stopách Irskych emigrant u ve fondech strahoské Knihovny v Praze' in ibid., pp 174–6.   **79** O'Kelly, *Philosophia aulica*, unpaginated.

informed Walter Harris that he was working on a new edition of the *Philosophia aulica*, though no work appeared before his death ten years later.[80] O'Kelly's approach clearly contrasted with the Scotist philosophy and theology emanating from the Irish Franciscan College in Prague, which was beset by internal conflicts in the late seventeenth century.[81] Some Irish Catholics educated on the continent went further than O'Kelly. Bernard Connor, an Irish Catholic doctor educated in France in the 1680s and early 1690s, explicitly rejected Aristotelianism (and Galenism) in work published in the later 1690s, in favour of a mechanical theory of the human body, a theory which drew on Cartesianism. It is interesting therefore that Connor had settled in England and conformed to the Established Church in 1695, before publishing his most controversial work: *Evangelium medici: seu Medicina mystica; de suspensis naturæ legibus, sive de miraculis* (London, 1697).[82] The work of Connor and O'Kelly marked a shift away from Scholastic Aristotelianism on the part of some Irish thinkers on the continent and prefigured the emergence of Irish philosophers and mathematicians like Joseph Ignatius O'Halloran in Bordeaux and Patrick D'Arcy in Paris who were able, in the mid-eighteenth century, to embrace Newtonian mathematics and physics.[83]

There is also some evidence that the debates about the relative merits of Aristotelian Scholasticism and Cartesianism found expression among Catholics in Ireland. In 1731, Dennis McCarty published a short pamphlet in Dublin defending Descartes.[84] The work was the first of five projected 'philosophical conferences', though the author was concerned 'that some envious, malicious, and dwarf understandings [...] will endeavour rather by calumniating me (according to their actual manner) and nibbling at, and censuring what they understand not, to ruin and render abortive my design, than to confute it in

---

80 Ware, *The whole works of Sir James Ware*, ed. Harris, ii, 287. However, O'Kelly had earlier published another work of philosophy, presumably another edition or re-print of the *Philosophia aulica*, with the title: *Examen philosophicum: iuxta saniora veterum, ac recentiorum philosophorum placita* (2 vols, Frankfurt and Leipzig, 1703). 81 Jan Parez, 'The Irish Franciscans in seventeenth and eighteenth century Prague', in Thomas O'Connor & Mary Ann Lyons (eds), *Irish migrants in Europe after Kinsale, 1602–1820* (Dublin, 2003), p. 109. 82 See Liam Chambers, 'Medicine and miracles in the late seventeenth century: Bernard Connor's *Evangelium medici* (1697)' in Fiona Clark (ed.), *Ireland and medicine in the seventeenth and eighteenth centuries* (forthcoming). 83 John Ferrar, *The history of Limerick: ecclesiastical, civil and military* (Limerick, 1787), pp 370–1; 'Eloge de M. le Comte D'Arci', *Histoire de l'Académie Royale des Sciences, 1779* (1782), pp 54–70. 84 Dennis MacCarty, *A vindication of Monsieur Descartes: in five philosophical conferences* (Dublin, 1731). The identity of the author is not known, but it seems likely that he was a Catholic. In the dialogue, one of the two characters suggests repairing to a tavern called the 'London' (MacCarty, *Vindication*, p. 6). The 'London Tavern' was run by Tim O'Sullivan, originally from Kerry, in early eighteenth-century Dublin and was a meeting place for Kerry natives, perhaps suggesting the author's origins. See: Andrew Carpenter, *Verse in English from eighteenth century Ireland* (Cork, 1998), p. 87; J.T. Gilbert states that the tavern was destroyed by fire in 1729. See J.T. Gilbert, *A history of the city of Dublin* (3 vols, Dublin, 1854–9), i, 67.

publick writings by good and solid natural reasonings; but I hope that they will not succeed, and that *the impartial publick* will rather disappoint them, than listen to their calumnies.'[85] The work involved a dialogue between Claude (a Cartesian) and Gusman (his friend). At the start of the text Gusman welcomes Claude back to 'this country', presumably Ireland, but soon recoils in horror: 'I am very glad to see you – welcome to this country – let me embrace you – but good God pardon me for this crime I have just now committed, for I have caress'd a person who is, as I am inform'd, not only a Jansenist, an Heretick, but also an Atheist.'[86] Gusman explains that he believes Claude to be an atheist because he is a Cartesian and that he has heard reports that Descartes' denial of substantial forms is essentially heretical. Claude responds that, in fact, substantial forms are the road to atheism, while Cartesianism offers proof of God's existence. There follows a discussion on the proposition 'God alone is the true and efficient cause of all motion, being a preparatory proposition, in order to confute substantial material forms', in which Claude outlines the Cartesian position and offers solutions to various objections.[87] He draws not only from Descartes, but also from the Jesuit Ignace Gaston Paradies' *Discours de la connaissance des bestes* (Paris, 1672) and the Oratorian Nicholas Malebranche's *De la recherche de la vérité* (2 vols, Paris, 1674–5).[88] In the end, the larger work containing the remaining conferences did not appear, but this short pamphlet nonetheless points to the development of a *public* debate among Irish Catholics in the early eighteenth century about fundamental philosophical issues and a challenge to Aristotelian Scholasticism.[89]

V

Irish writers were involved in all aspects of early modern Aristotelian Scholasticism. However, research on the subject remains underdeveloped. At a basic level, there is no prosopography of Irish Catholic professors of philosophy in the early modern period.[90] Despite recent advances we still do not know enough about Irish interactions with philosophy curricula on the continent. For example, how important were the Irish Colleges in fostering philosophical attitudes? It is not surprising that there is evidence for a strong Aristotelian Scholastic influence among at least some Irish student communities. Balthasar

---

85 MacCarty, *Vindication*, p. 3. My italics. 86 Ibid., pp 5–6 87 Ibid., pp 7–27. 88 Ibid., pp 19–20, 22–3. 89 Despite the author's comments that 'This pious and godly doctrine, God alone, &c. is peculiar to the Cartesians, unless it be common to them with St Thomas and his Disciples, as I believe it is', the pamphlet is clearly an attack on what he calls 'Peripatetics [...] and all other anti-Cartesians' (ibid., p. 3). 90 For a list of ninety-four Irish Scotist philosophers who were students and/or professors at St Isidore's College, Rome, see Millet, 'Irish Scotists at St. Isidore's College, Rome, in the seventeenth century', pp 412–19; also this book, pp 185–91.

Tellez published a major textbook, *Summa universae philosophiae* (Lisbon, 1642), while he was superior of the Irish College in Lisbon.[91] The Irish Aristotelian James Piers was the superior of the Irish College in Bordeaux during the 1620s.[92] Malachi Kelly, who edited the philosophy textbook of his professor François Le Rées, was one of the founders of the Irish Collège des Lombards in Paris.[93] Also in the French capital, the professors of philosophy Roger O'Moloy and Michael Moore played a leading role in the Irish student community.[94] It is interesting that the first foundation (*fondation*) for Irish students in Paris was established by the royal professor of philosophy Jean Perreau in 1645 and stipulated *inter alia* that students would attend lectures in philosophy at the Collège de France. Four students were admitted to the *bourses* at a time, including two Irish, who were nominated by the superior of the Irish College, at the time of the establishment of the foundation Eduoard Tirel, himself a former professor of philosophy.[95] Where courses were taught internally, philosophical formation was clearly more amenable to supervision and control. This was the case at the colleges of Irish regular clergy, where philosophy courses must have mirrored the prevailing tendencies of their order. Therefore, it is hardly surprising that the course of philosophy followed by the Irish Dominicans at San Clemente in the eighteenth century was firmly Thomist.[96] However, many Irish Colleges did not provide courses of study, and students attended class and sat examinations at the local university. At some Irish Colleges a practice evolved whereby *conférences* (essentially revision lectures or classes) were provided, which permitted the monitoring of opinions picked up outside. For example, in 1773 a theology student resident at the Irish Collège des Lombards in Paris explained to a correspondent in Ireland how the daily timetable worked:

> Up at five and a half in the morning we meet at prayer at six, which finishes at six and a half, we then retire to our rooms untill eight and a quarter when the philosophers are called away to class where they continue till ten and a half. I have done with this disagreeable part of our duty as I am now in Theology. The divines study in their chambers until they are called away to

91 Charles H. Lohr, 'Renaissance Latin Aristotle commentaries: So–Z', *Renaissance Quarterly* 35:2 (1982), 191; O Connell, *The Irish College at Lisbon*, p. 39. 92 T.J. Walsh, 'Some records of the Irish College at Bordeaux', *Archivium Hibernicum* 15 (1950), 106; idem, *The Irish continental college movement*, p. 98. 93 Thomas O'Connor, *Irish Jansenists, 1600–70: religion and politics in Flanders, France, Ireland and Rome* (Dublin, 2008), p. 205. 94 Brockliss and Ferté, 'Prosopography', p. 32; Chambers, *Michael Moore*. On Moore see also the comments of the playwright Michael Clancy who met him in Paris in 1716: *Memoirs of Michael Clancy, M.D.*, 2 vols (Dublin, 1750), i, 27. 95 Collège de Reims, Fondation Perreau, 1645–70 (Archives Nationales, Paris, M 187, pièces 10–11); Henri Dacaille, *Étude sur le Collège de Reims à Paris, 1412–1763* (Reims, 1899), pp 51–4. 96 Hugh Fenning, 'SS. Sisto e Clemente, 1677–1797' in Leonard Boyle, *San Clemente Miscellany I: The community of SS. Sisto e Clemente in Rome, 1677–1977* (Rome, 1977), p. 49.

the several churches in which they officiate, and as they return breakfast at different hours. Dinner is served at twelve, at one the conference in philosophy, with which I have the misfortune to be charged for the ensuing year; at two the philosophers go to class 'till four.[97]

In general terms, it would appear that the location of the student and the nature of the institution he attended was crucial in forming (though not determining) intellectual attitudes. For example, the strong Jesuit influence on the Irish Colleges in the Iberian peninsula would suggest a significant Thomistic Aristotelian influence until well into the eighteenth century. However, much more research is required before stronger conclusions can be drawn.

We also need to know more about the relationship between philosophical attitudes and related social, cultural and political concerns. In *ancien régime* France the state and church required an intellectually satisfying philosophy curriculum, but also one which reflected their interests: the formation of rounded Christian subjects capable of taking their place within society, and especially the apparatus of the church and state.[98] For these reasons Cartesianism was viewed in some quarters with suspicion and even hostility until the early eighteenth century. In this context Irish philosophical orthodoxy, as represented by Michael Moore for example, was pragmatic and arguably reflected the Irish Catholic experience in the seventeenth century. Further afield, while William O'Kelly of Aghrim introduced readers to 'new' opinions, he was careful in his presentation.[99] The positions adopted by those who grappled with Aristotelian Scholasticism and the challenges it faced in the late seventeenth and early eighteenth centuries were important beyond the classroom. In recent work Laurence Brockliss has suggested that the overthrow of centuries of Aristotelian natural philosophy in favour of the Cartesian alternative in 1690s France *did* undermine *ancien régime* intellectual, political and social structures. 'In an important sense', he writes, 'the Cartesian revolution at the University of Paris was one of the initial stages on the road to 1789.'[1]

---

97 John [Baptist] Walsh to Vere Hunt [jun.], 30 August 1773 (Limerick City and County Archive, De Vere Papers P22/1/8). My thanks to Ursula Callaghan for bringing this letter to my attention. The practice of revision lectures was not new. The community of 'Escholiers Hybernois' observed a similar system in the late seventeenth century: 'Ceux qui étudieront en Philosophie ou en Theologie seront tous les mois une Conference sur leurs Estudes, ou l'un d'eux soûtiendra quelques Theses prises des cahiers qu'ils auront écrits ce mois là sous leurs Professeurs, & les autres disputeront contre luy, le Prestre qui sera chargé de leur conduite assistera à ces Conferences, ceux qui estudient aux Humanitez seront aussi tous les Samedis en sa presence des repetitions de ce qu'ils auront appris pendant la semaine' ('Reglemens que doivent observer les pauvres Escholiers Hybernois, qui composent la Communauté establie à Paris', Bibliothèque Nationale de France, MS Français 23494, f. 227). 98 Noguès, *Une archéologie du corps enseignant*, pp 190–3. 99 O'Kelly, *Philosophia aulica*, pp 111–17 (physics section). Each of the four sections of the work is paginated separately. 1 Brockliss, 'The

Engagement with Aristotelian Scholasticism was an important feature of the history of Irish migration to early modern Europe and Irish writers were very conscious of their intellectual and educational antecedents. For example, in the early seventeenth century David Rothe drew attention to the contributions of the medieval Irish scholars, John Scottus Eriugena and Clemens Scottus (Clement of Ireland), on the Continent.[2] This is not to suggest that there was no room for alternatives. For example, some Irish clergy on the Continent implicitly challenged the credentials of the Scholastic approach to philosophy and theology, especially during the early- and mid-seventeenth century, and placed more emphasis on scriptural and patristic sources of authority instead.[3] Others, like William O'Kelly or Bernard Connor, engaged positively with Cartesianism and other new philosophies. A fuller assessment of the significance of Irish Aristotelian Scholasticism in the seventeenth and early eighteenth centuries will await a closer study of textbooks, treatises, theses and student notebooks. This will enable us to place Irish *Aristotelian Scholasticisms* within the emerging field of 'Irish philosophy', as well as the history of philosophy in early modern Europe.

moment of no return: the University of Paris and the death of Aristotelianism', p. 274. 2 David Rothe, *Brigidia thaumaturga* (Paris, 1620), pp 77–81. Around the same time Bernard Morisanus claimed the astronomer and mathematician John de Sacrobosco (d. *c*.1236) for Ireland in his *In spheram Joannis de S. Bosco commentarius* (Frankfurt, 1625). On the grammarian Clemens Scotus see V.A. Law, 'Clemens Scottus (*fl. c*.814–826)' in *Oxford Dictionary of National Biography* (Oxford, 2004) [http://www.oxforddnb.com/view/article/5599, accessed 15 Sept 2008]. 3 On this subject see: O'Connor, *Irish Jansenists*. I would like to thank the Revd Professor James McEvoy, Professor Martin Stone and Dr Thomas O'Connor, who generously read and commented on earlier drafts of this essay.

Peter Coffey (1876–1943): from neo-Scholastic scholar to social theorist

GAVAN JENNINGS

'Ireland', wrote Yeats at the beginning of the twentieth century, 'is now plastic and will be for a few years to come.' Peter Coffey, priest and philosopher, dedicated his greatest energies in the attempt to mould this 'plastic Ireland' in the direction of what he saw as social justice. At the same time, through his three published philosophical textbooks, two translations into English of important works by De Wulf, and many scholarly articles, he played a significant part in the neo-Scholastic revival in the English speaking world. And yet he is relatively unknown today and, beyond short encyclopaedia entries and passing references, little has been written about him.[1]

His relatively short life – he died at the age of 66 – spans a period of intense socio-political upheaval in Irish life. He was born into an Ireland undergoing political land agitation as well as cultural renewal. At the end of the nineteenth century there was still great deprivation in urban and rural regions of Ireland. Countrywide the average life expectancy at the turn of the century was only fifty and in Dublin one third of people were estimated to be living in one-room tenements while one in four children born would not reach their first birthday. Emigration was the only option for huge numbers, so that by 1911 one third of people who had been born in Ireland were living abroad. And yet socially the situation was gradually improving: there had been a gradual change in land ownership in the country through the Land Acts of the turn of the century, so that while only three per cent of rural dwellers were land owners in 1870, 64 per cent were land owners in 1916. At the bottom of the scale, however, there had also been a huge increase in landless agricultural labourers. Michael Davitt's National Land League had been founded in 1879 to agitate for these underprivileged agricultural workers. In the 1890s the co-operative movement began in earnest in Ireland under the leadership of, amongst others, Horace Plunkett and Fr Thomas Finlay SJ (not to be confused with Fr Peter Finlay SJ who was a close supporter of Coffey). Their intention was to relieve small farmers and agricul-

---

1 See Felix Ó Murchadha, 'Peter Coffey' in *The dictionary of Irish philosophers* (London, 2004), pp 79–80; Thomas Kelly, 'Peter Coffey' in B. Lalor (ed.), *Encyclopedia of Ireland* (Dublin, 2003), p. 216 and P. Corish, *Maynooth College, 1795–1995* (Dublin, 1995), pp 313–15.

tural labourers of the burden of exploitation. The motivation driving the betterment of the poorer class was as cultural as it was economic and was very much linked to the movement of national regeneration of the end of the nineteenth century. For Plunkett the co-operative movement was ultimately an effort to rebuild the 'character' of the Irish people. James Connolly, much admired by Coffey, wrote that 'Every victory for labour helps to straighten the cramped soul of the Irish labourer.' The 1880s and 1890s saw the founding of cultural and religious associations which were to dominate Irish life for decades to come: the Gaelic Athletic Association (1884), the Gaelic League (1893) and the Pioneer Total Abstinence Association (1898). The latter quickly went on to become the country's largest lay movement.

As a boy in the Meath of the 1880s Coffey lived through the Land War, and perhaps these early experiences contributed to his irrepressible sympathy for the lot of the underprivileged. During his seminary days in Maynooth of the 1890s he was keenly aware of the cultural currents of the times, and even corresponded with the novelist Patrick Canon Sheehan (1852–1913), author of popular novels such as *My New Curate* (1899) and *Luke Delmege* (1901). Sheehan's appeal to Coffey was no doubt due in large part to the novelist's social concern, expressed not only in his novels but also through his work to better the lot of his parishioners. In *My New Curate*, the fictional parish priest, Fr Dan Laverty, ruminates on those same social projects that Sheehan himself was carrying out in Doneraile, Co. Cork: the buying out of holdings and the replacing of farm labourer cabins with modern housing, in line with the Land Purchase Acts and the Irish Labourers Act (1883) respectively; the promotion of modern agricultural methods, especially in tillage and dairy farming; and the installation of a modern water supply system and the building of an advanced electrification plant.

Coffey was a member of the Maynooth Columban League, re-founded in 1898 after a false start in 1894 as a Gaelic literary association, and was himself prominent in Maynooth student debating societies. He writes in his private notebook in 1900, the year of his ordination: 'For the last year or more my heart has been in the Gaelic movement, because I see in it a powerful means of preserving the simple faith and saintly piety of our ancestors among the Irish people. I fear I am a dreamer.'[2]

SCHOLASTIC TRAINING AT LOUVAIN

It was to Louvain that the 27-year-old Peter Coffey went in September 1903 to continue his studies after one year holding the chair of logic and metaphysics in Maynooth. Désiré Mercier (1851–1926), one of the pillars of the neo-Scholastic

2 Corish, *Maynooth College, 1795–1995*, p. 313.

movement, had visited Maynooth for its 1895 centenary celebrations and requested that the college might send some bright students to his newly-founded Higher Institute of Philosophy in Louvain. It appears that Maynooth decided to send members of staff rather than students, and so the first to travel was a Dr Forker, who was given a year's freedom from the duty of teaching in order to study there. Coffey had only recently joined the academic staff when he left to spend the two years studying for a doctorate in Louvain under Mercier. Ever thereafter Coffey held Mercier in great esteem, later dedicating two of his books to the 'enlightened exponent of the philosophy of the Schools', as well as writing a glowing tribute to his former professor in an obituary in *Studies*.[3] It was through Mercier and the Higher Institute of Philosophy that Coffey came into contact with the full force of the neo-Scholastic movement.

Like German romanticism and French traditionalism, the seeds of the neo-Scholastic revival can be seen as a response to the exaggerations of the Enlightenment and the system building of German idealism. It gathered momentum throughout the nineteenth century, particularly with Cajetano Sanseverino (1811–65) in Naples, Matteo Liberatore in Rome and the Jesuit periodical *Civiltà Cattolica*. The ascent of neo-Scholasticism was assured by the election to the papacy in 1878 of Joachim Pecci (Leo XIII) – a keen sympathizer with the Thomistic revival. The following year the new pope, Leo XIII, with the help of the German Thomist Josef Kleutgen, produced what was to be the charter of the neo-Scholastic movement, the encyclical *Aeterni patris* – 'On the restoration of Christian philosophy' – which sought 'to restore the golden wisdom of St Thomas, and to spread it far and wide for the defence and beauty of the Catholic faith, for the good of society, and for the advantage of all society'.[4] While the centre of the movement was the Accademia Romana di San Tommaso, nevertheless Leo XIII was very keen that the Catholic University of Louvain would also have a centre of neo-Scholastic studies, and so a chair of Thomistic philosophy was established there in 1880. Eleven years later, in 1891, through a brief of Leo XIII (and accompanied by a donation of 150,000 Belgian francs) the Higher Institute of Philosophy was founded. Mercier, himself a Louvain graduate, had already been chosen in the 1880s to lead the project. Mercier was the powerhouse of the Institute until his appointment as archbishop in 1906. He had a broad vision of neo-Scholasticism: encouraging the engagement of philosophy with science. He famously encouraged the young Belgian seminarian Georges Lemaître, the future theoretician of the Big Bang, to study Albert Einstein's theory of relativity. He also encouraged the close study of original texts rather than over-reliance on sometimes problematic commen-

3 'Cardinal Mercier and philosophical studies', *Studies* 15:57 (1926), 95–104.   4 *Aeterni patris*, 31. For discussions of the neo-Scholastic movement and its critics, see Fergus Kerr, *After Aquinas, versions of Thomism* (Oxford, 2002), ch. 2 and Tracey Rowland, *Ratzinger's faith: the theology of Pope Benedict XVI* (Oxford, 2008), pp 18–19.

tators such as Suarez, as well as the study of modern philosophers, in particular
Descartes and Kant – presumably on the basis of the need to know one's enemy.
In 1894 Mercier founded *La Revue Néo-Scolastique de Philosophie.*

THE RETURN TO MAYNOOTH

After being awarded a PhD in 1905 from the Higher Institute of Philosophy,
Coffey returned to his teaching post in Maynooth where he was to lecture till his
death in January 1943. For the next twelve years he dedicated himself to the
preparation of his classes – something he did meticulously – and his own
writing. This period saw an impressive production of book reviews and articles
on various aspects of Scholastic Philosophy in the *Irish Theological Quarterly* and
the *Irish Ecclesiastical Record.* Coffey also wrote several entries for *The Catholic
Encyclopedia* and produced translations from French of two works by the
Louvain, and later Harvard, neo-Scholastic philosopher Maurice De Wulf:
History of Medieval Philosophy (1909) and *Scholasticism Old and New* (1910).[5]
Soon to follow were his own substantial manuals of Scholastic Philosophy: in
1912 *The Science of Logic*; in 1914 his *Ontology*, and in finally in 1917 his
Epistemology.[6] These textbooks – 'the volumes' as Maynooth seminarians
jokingly referred to them – were studied by generations of seminarians, some of
whom, such as Bernard Lonergan, were in time to become philosophers of note.

How were these works received and what was their importance? They were
certainly influential books insofar as they were read by generations of English-
speaking seminarians. While this period sees much neo-Scholastic work in Italy,
France and Belgium, the work being done in the English-speaking world was
centered principally on the Jesuit College of Stonyhurst, and in particular the
Stonyhurst Philosophical Series.[7] The series was described 'as the most valuable
exposition of Scholastic Philosophy written in the English language'.[8] The
Stonyhurst authors dealing with the material of Coffey's three textbooks were
Richard F. Clarke SJ (logic) and John Rickaby SJ (ontology and epistemology),
but presumably Coffey judged that other manuals on these topics were needed.
His own works appear to have received a wide diffusion within the English-

---

5 The original works in French are: *Histoire de la philosophie médiévale* (Louvain, 1900) and
Introduction à la philosophie néo-scolastique (Paris, 1904).   6 *The science of logic, an inquiry into the
principle of accurate thought and scientific method*, 2 vols (London, 1912); *Ontology or the theory of
being, an introduction to general metaphysics* (London, 1914); *Epistemology or the theory of
knowledge*, 2 vols (London, 1917).   7 The series comprised the following works: by Richard F.
Clarke SJ, *Logic*; John Rickaby SJ, *First principles of knowledge*; Joseph Rickaby SJ, *Moral
philosophy*; Bernard Boedder SJ, *Natural theology*; Michael Maher SJ, *Psychology*; John Rickaby
SJ, *General metaphysics* and Charles S. Devas SJ, *Political economy*.   8 Joseph Louis Perrier,
Revival of Scholastic Philosophy in the nineteenth century (New York, 1909).

speaking seminaries, *Logic* and *Ontology* going into a second printing in 1918. *Studies* gave all three books very positive reviews: of *Logic* it says that 'the student of philosophy will find it difficult to meet anything better than Coffey's work'; *Ontology* is described as a 'singularly clear and closely reasoned treatise' (with, however, 'a certain lack of warmth and enthusiasm'), while *Epistemology* is judged superior to Mercier's manual on the same material.⁹ The author of the *Irish Theological Quarterly* review of *Epistemology* calls the book 'the longest and most detailed treatise on epistemology which has yet come from the schools of contemporary Scholasticism', and refers to the general acclaim of the work: 'Almost twenty reviews of these volumes lie open on my desk [...]. All twenty are loud in their praises.'¹⁰ All three textbooks were republished in later decades by Peter Smith, and facsimile versions of *Ontology* and *Epistemology* have recently been produced by Kessinger. Furthermore Coffey's works – because of their systematic treatment of their material – are widely referred to in later English-language introductions to philosophy, such as those of Celestine Bittle and R.P. Phillips in the 1930s, and Fernand Van Steenberghen and Henry Koren in the 1950s. These authors generally recommend the study of Coffey to their readers.

Beyond the seminary world, however, it is difficult to see the effect of the treatises. According to Rudolf Metz, Coffey's work was little noticed outside the confines of seminary studies: 'We owe to him a system of philosophy based on a Thomistic foundation, broadly planned and fully worked out, which is much used for instruction in Roman Catholic theological seminaries, but has hardly aroused any notice outside their walls.'¹¹ Professor Macquarrie remarked that Coffey's achievement 'was to bring back the ideas of the Scholastic Philosophy onto the philosophical map, and to win respect for them, while the more original developments and applications of these ideas were left to a younger generation of neo-Thomistic thinkers.'¹²

Perhaps unfortunately for Coffey, Ludwig Wittgenstein, then a young Cambridge logician, reviewed *The Science of Logic* for the *Cambridge Review* in March 1913. The review – Wittgenstein's first published work and his only book review – is scathing: 'The author has not taken the slightest notice of the great work of the modern mathematical logicians – work which has brought about an advance in logic comparable only to that which made astronomy out of astrology, and chemistry out of alchemy.'¹³ This contrasts with the *Studies* review which

---

9 These reviews from *Studies* are: *Logic:* 28 (1939), 701; *Ontology:* 3 (1914), 539; *Epistemology:* 7 (1918), 163. 10 *Irish Theological Quarterly* 13 (1918), 159–61. Review by John O'Neill. 11 Rudolf Metz, *A hundred years of British philosophy* (London, 1939), p. 819. 12 John Macquarrie, *Twentieth-century religious thought: the frontiers of philosophy and theology* (London, 1963), 282–3. 13 For a further discussion of the tendency to criticize the Scholastic manuals see the interview with Fergus Kerr OP: 'A Thomist, but not a medievalist', *Leuven Philosophy Newsletter* 16 (2007–8), 15–19.

praises the author of *Logic* in that he 'makes an honest effort to sympathize with what is best in philosophies other than his own and does not seem to think that the evolution of thought ceased with the thirteenth century.'[14] The animosity towards the Scholastic manual tradition apparent in Wittgenstein's review was later to find an echo within the Catholic academic world itself after the Second Vatican Council, an animosity which has no doubt accelerated the decline of interest in Coffey's achievements.

DISILLUSIONMENT

Coffey himself says that he was too busy during his early years as professor at Maynooth 'up to about 1917' with the preparation and publishing of text-books to devote his attention to the social question.[15] Till then he had dealt with the social question only in passing, for example in his 1906 pamphlet *The Church and the Working Classes* for the Catholic Truth Society of Ireland (CTSI). This contained the substance of two lectures given in Dublin as a 'protest against the charge that the church was always on the side of the rich.' During the period from 1912 to 1919 he kept himself informed about the social unrest in the country, marked by such events as the August 1911 lockout from Wexford foundries and the 1913 Dublin tramway men's strike which led in turn to the general lockout. At the same time he would have been aware of the thinking of other high profile intellectuals on the Catholic position with regard to the social question, in particular the distributism of G.K. Chesterton's *What's Wrong with the World* (1912) and Hillaire Belloc's *The Servile State* (1912). Besides, the social question was in the air in Maynooth itself: Walter McDonald publicly addressed social issues during this period in the seminary.[16] Outside the college, in June 1915, a Fr Michael O'Flanagan from Castlerea, Co. Roscommon (ordained in Maynooth the same year as Coffey) was involved in an incident in Sligo which was to become known as the 'Cloonerco Bog Fight'. O'Flanagan, then parish priest of Ahamlish, Co. Sligo, agitated on behalf of his parishioners for turbary (turf-cutting) rights on the Ashley demesne, as well as the redistribution of the extensive landlord-owned grasslands. The conflict came to a head when he led a contingent of parishioners to cut and remove turf from the landlord's property – for which action his bishop promptly transferred him from the parish.[17]

---

14 'The science of Logic', *ITQ* 7 (1912), 480–6. The reviewer is Denis O'Keeffe.   15 'Personal narrative', p. 1. Peter Coffey archive, Maynooth College Archives (undated).   16 See 'The sympathetic strike' – an article published in the *Dublin Leader* in 1913; and 'How I have studied the social question' – the text of a lecture given in Maynooth in 1915. Both appear as appendices to Walter McDonald, *Reminiscences of a Maynooth professor* (Cork, 1967), pp 280–6 and 287–99 respectively.   17 See Dermot Keogh, 'John Hagan and radical Irish nationalism, 1916–1930: a study in political Catholicism' in Dáire Keogh & Albert McDonnell (eds), *The Irish College,*

The period between 1917 and 1923 saw a new phase in the ongoing land war – exacerbated in part by the Great War. The government land purchases had been brought to a halt by the war, and at the same time the depressed agricultural economy benefitted large land owners most. In 1917 the introduction of a compulsory tillage scheme was made necessary by food shortages, and the idea appealed to small-holders and landless labourers. Popular agrarian revolt – with the support of Sinn Féin – pressed more vigorously for land break-up. Agrarian agitation, allied to the burning of 'big houses', reached such a pitch that in 1920 Dáil Éireann had to take measures to calm the situation.

Yet surprisingly it is to the issue of temperance that Coffey devoted most of his spare time during this period. What appears to be the only pamphlet he wrote between 1906 and 1920 contains lectures delivered by him on the temperance platform.[18] The problem of drunkenness was a national issue as evidenced by the fact that the Jesuit-run Pioneer Total Abstinence Association was Ireland's largest Catholic association at this time. (During the period the problem was a declining one: in the period 1891–2 there were an astonishing 100,500 arrests for drunkenness as compared with 15,000 convictions in 1914 and 7,000 in 1925). Coffey at one point was president of the Catholic Total Abstinence Federation of Ireland and led a deputation of the Total Abstinence Association to address Dáil Éireann in February 1922.

The publication in 1919 of the CTSI pamphlet *Between Capitalism and Socialism* inaugurated a remarkable change in focus for the Maynooth philosophy professor. Over the next decade Coffey went into print almost exclusively on the social question, in dozens of articles, pamphlets, and letters. And yet there was not a single philosophical paper from the same period. Coffey's 1917 two-volume textbook *Epistemology* appeared to be a valedictory to his career in philosophical writing. This forces us to ask how 'the most prolific neo-Scholastic writer'[19] of his day could turn his attention so completely away from writing philosophy. His transfer of allegiance from the cause of neo-Scholasticism to extra-academic matters, principally the social question, appears to have been total. What might account for this fact?

In his 'Personal narrative' – undated but written about 1930 – Coffey explained that by 1917 or thereabouts, after he had finished writing his textbooks, he had grown quite disillusioned with philosophy in Maynooth for various reasons. He had hoped to start an Irish periodical along the lines of Mercier's *Revue Néo-Scolastique*, but this came to nothing. Secondly he complained of how little importance was given to philosophy by the college authorities, saying that they could not be induced to oblige some of the best students to take an honours course in philosophy for the BA degree (this

Rome, and its world (Dublin, 2008), pp 242–57.   **18** *The newspaper: its influence for good and for evil* (CTSI, Dublin, 1912).   **19** Metz, *A hundred years of British philosophy*, p. 819.

suggestion having been made in 1916). They preferred, he says, the élite of the student body to specialize in 'classics, modern languages, science, mathematics, etc. so as to be able to staff the diocesan seminaries with competent teachers'.[20] Neither could the college trustees be induced to introduce a course in the Dunboyne Establishment (the postgraduate scholarship scheme of the college) for a college doctorate in philosophy. As a result, their capacity to confer the papal degree of doctorate was, in Coffey's words, 'a dead letter'. It is true that philosophy was the poor cousin of theology in Maynooth: the teaching staff was below the number required by Rome.[21] When even as late as 1933 the Congregation for Seminaries and Universities reported on their examination of the draft statutes of Maynooth, the philosophy course was singled out for criticism for its insufficient number of professors, too few specialized courses, and too few lectures in the history of philosophy (one per week).[22]

Following his return from Louvain, Coffey had remarked on how much better staffed the Belgian centre was than Maynooth – the former having ten professors for about seventy students in philosophy, physics, chemistry and physiology; the latter only three permanent and four extern lecturers for over two hundred students for the same subject.[23] Twenty-five years or so later, Coffey was unambiguous in his criticism of Maynooth's low academic standards: 'I may say in passing that as a consequence no priest educated in Maynooth is eligible as a candidate for a vacant chair in philosophy in the College.'[24] Similar criticisms of the seminary came from several other sources, including Coffey's colleague Walter McDonald: 'What is wrong with Maynooth, and has been wrong with it while I know it, is that we aim at producing good average men. The worst of it is that we succeed; for while our average man is very good, our best men are poor […].'[25] In his novel Luke Delmege (1901) even Canon Sheehan criticizes, albeit implicitly, the narrowness of the education imparted in his alma mater, while another novelist and Maynooth graduate, Gerald O'Donovan, did likewise but much more bitterly, in his Father Ralph (1913), the early portion of which is set in the college.[26]

Another source of disappointment to him was the failure to establish a chair of sociology in the college.[27] All of this culminated in a situation where the great student of Mercier felt precluded from 'finding a natural and congenial field for further work in my own strictly professional domain'.[28]

20 'Personal narrative', p. 2. 21 Corish, Maynooth College, 1795–1995, p. 241. 22 See Corish, Maynooth College, 1795–1995, pp 317–8. 23 'Philosophy and the sciences at Louvain – II', IER 4:17 (1905), 485–516 at p. 492, n. 2. 24 'Personal narrative', p. 2. 25 Walter McDonald, Reminiscences, p. 177. 26 Another interesting source of recollections from Maynooth from this period can be found in Neil Kevin, I remember Maynooth (Maynooth, 1995); originally published in London in 1938 under the pseudonym Don Boyne – a reference to Maynooth's Dunboyne House. 27 In 1914 Peter Coffey and Patrick Boylan, professor of Scripture, drew up a report on the question but without success. Similar efforts in 1919 and 1924 failed, and it was only in 1930 that the chair was established. 28 'Personal narrative', p. 2.

TAKING UP THE CAUSE OF THE POOR

Coffey's increasing disillusionment with Maynooth philosophy coincided with the completion of his textbooks and his mastering the courses he was teaching; he now found he had time on his hands to dedicate to an intensive study of the rise of modern industrial capitalism and church teaching on economic issues, devoting to this study much of his leisure time.[29] Coffey entered on an in-depth study of social issues, using in particular Devas' *Political economy*,[30] and, after 1920, Major Clifford Hugh Douglas' theory of social credit as outlined in *Economic democracy*.[31] The disillusioned philosopher appears to have been completely absorbed by these studies.

Over the next decade Coffey's approach to the social neglect was understandably not the hands-on approach of Sheehan and O'Flanagan, as he spent his life in academia and he never held a parochial position. His role was one of a pamphleteer and lobbyist. From 1919 onwards he began to submit articles to various reviews, primarily the *Irish Theological Quarterly*, the *Irish Ecclesiastical Record*, the *Dublin Leader* and the *Catholic Bulletin*. The latter, which was published from 1911 to 1939, tended towards an extreme nationalism which resulted eventually in its being shunned by all of its Maynooth subscribers, Coffey being the last to abandon the publication, around 1922 (returning to it one last time in 1931 for the publication of a previously banned publication). His pamphlets were generally published by the CTSI though later, to obviate problems with censors, he went to the *Irish Messenger*.

Seeing the formation of the new state as an opportunity to 'leaven the political intelligentsia' with his ideas, Coffey also engaged in some lobbying of the politicians forming the first Free State government. In October 1922 he proposed to the president of the Provisional Government, Liam Cosgrave, a scheme for the issue of currency and the building of 500 houses. Both were rejected by Cosgrave as the ideas of an 'amateur'. Coffey's efforts were not made any easier by the fact that the first government of the state was tending in a different direction socially, perhaps evidenced by the way it dealt with its first trade disputes, voting against the postal workers' right to strike and using police and military in strong-arm tactics against the strikers.

Coffey's thought on the social question takes its inspiration from Leo XIII's ground-breaking encyclical *Rerum novarum* (1891), in which the Catholic Church, perhaps belatedly, addressed the question of the plight of the workers

---

29 He writes in 1923: 'I devoted much of my leisure time, especially in the past four or five years, to the study of the whole question.' Letter to the Visitors of Maynooth, April 1923. Peter Coffey archive (The Visitors were a body of bishops appointed by the trustees of Maynooth to oversee the proper functioning of Maynooth College, including the Pontifical University.) **30** Charles Devas SJ, *Political economy*, Stonyhurst Philosophical Series (London, 1892). **31** C.H. Douglas, *Economic democracy* (London, 1920).

in the industrialized world. Against the socialist position on private property, the encyclical asserts the right to private property contained in natural law; while at the same time the church, state, employers and employees are obliged to build up a just social system.

Coffey tries to steer a course between the extremes of capitalism – which does too little to regulate the production and distribution of wealth, and socialism – which does too much. However, at least as far as Irish society was concerned, it was capitalism not socialism which was the dominant ideology, and certainly he had no sympathy for a system based on what he called the 'pagan, Protestant, ultra-individualist, post-Reformation idea of ownership as an absolute "right" devoid of all duties and limitations, and entitling the "owner" to "do what he likes with his own"'.[32] He deliberately opposed the excessively individualist and absolutist views of private ownership – 'the mentality of Capitalist hostility to the labouring classes as fostered by the *Irish Independent* and the *Irish Times*, and the inclination to brand the whole Labour Movement in Ireland as Socialistic'.[33]

He sees vagueness of language in socio-political questions as commonly causing some Catholics to brand as socialist, ideas which are in fact a sound Catholic rejection of capitalism. By way of clarification, he gives the attitude towards small-holdings and ownership as the touch-stone: if negative it is socialism; if positive not. Interestingly, judging by this criterion, Coffey stands to the right of the Land League founder Michael Davitt who, in his *Leaves from a Prison Journal*, argues for land nationalization and strongly opposes peasant ownership of the land, calling it 'simply landlordism in another form'.

While Coffey had earlier, perhaps imprudently, used the term 'Christian socialism',[34] he does not consider socialism, understood as the abolition of private property, to be the answer to social injustice. What is needed is 'a wider diffusion of private ownership of land and capital'.[35] Rather than simple profit-sharing or co-partnership (where in practice the proprietors hold on to the real power), he advocates co-operative industrial ownership of the agencies of production (the factories) and distribution (stores etc. – in order to protect the workers, as consumers, from exorbitant prices). On the question of agriculture in Ireland, he opposes what he sees as the sacrifice of Ireland's economic good to Britain's need for beef and mutton – a situation which had created a socially-unjust form of land use in the form of cattle grazing on vast ranches. He believed that what was needed was more labour-intensive tillage (or even mixed grazing and tillage) on smaller farms. He supported the efforts of the 'back to the land movement' to bring about a gradual reversion to smaller holdings

---

32 Letter to the Visitors of Maynooth, April 1923. Peter Coffey archive. 33 'The social question with its relation to official ecclesiastical censorship and authority in Ireland: report submitted to the Holy See', Peter Coffey archive, Nov. 1930, p. 4. 34 In his *The Church and the working classes* (CTSI, Dublin, 1906). 35 *The social question in Ireland: some principles and projects of reconstruction* (Irish Messenger, 1930), p. 4.

practising tillage farming through land redistribution. (The Land Act of 1923 established the Land Commission for the compulsory acquisition and redistribution of lands, though its effectiveness was lessened by a large number of loop-holes.[36] Fairer land distribution was among the welfare measures proposed by the fledgling Fianna Fáil Party in 1926; it entered legislation in their 1933 Land Act and finally was enshrined in the 1937 Constitution as the aspiration to establish on the land 'as many families as in the circumstances shall be practicable.')[37]

Regarding industry, the interests of both employer and employee are identical and are served by 'mutual understanding, agreement and co-operation; and [...] they are injured by paralysis of industry, by the discontent that leads to inefficient labour, by avoidable deadlocks and strikes'.[38] Provided industry is able to yield it, each adult male labourer is entitled to the family wage, and this is prior to the employer's rights to profits over and above his earnings. This could be seen as a precursor of the highly successful schemes for Public Partnership for Prosperity between trade unions and employer bodies in recent years.

These ideas were for the most part not novel; *Rerum novarum* had already rejected the socialist proposal of the abolition of private property as a solution for inequality. It encouraged property ownership, and state intervention to protect the poor when their rights were trammelled, and accepted as part of the natural law the right of workers to form trade unions, and criticized employers who defrauded their employees of wages. What is novel is Coffey's support for the more complex economic notion of 'social credit' or reform of the financial and banking system. Up to 1920 Coffey had concentrated on the question of private capital ownership and the admissibility of state intervention, but at this point he became acquainted with the theory of social credit through his reading of Douglas' *Economic Democracy*. The social credit movement had been spearheaded by Douglas, Alfred R. Orage (one time editor of *New Age*), Professor T. Loddy and M.A. Kitson against what they saw as an inherently unjust monetary system which necessarily led to the dominance of financial magnates. They proposed the abandonment of the gold-based monetary system in favour of a system of government credits released annually in proportion to the actual volume of production. Such reform of the monetary system would, they held, obviate the artificial creation of scarcity by large financiers and maintain a correlation between workers' wages and their purchasing power. Coffey became convinced that it was only through the reform of the financial system itself – in the manner proposed by Douglas – that the evils of capitalism could be defeated. The proposed system received little support from economists, and much criticism from opponents of socialism.

---

36 For a detailed treatment of land redistribution in the period, see Terence Dooley, *The big houses and landed estates of Ireland: a research guide* (Dublin, 2007), pp 55–62. 37 Article 45.2 38 *The social question in Ireland*, p. 14.

CLASHES WITH THE CENSORS

The War of Independence and subsequent Civil War caused an understandable nervousness among the hierarchy at the prospect of anarchy and revolution in the country. The Bolshevik 1917 coup in Russia stood as a grim warning of the threat posed by left-wing revolutionaries. All of this made it less likely that the left-leaning writings of Coffey would find sympathetic readers among the censors, and in 1922, as was perhaps to be expected, Coffey fell foul of the censor.39 The CTSI had approached Coffey with a request to re-publish his 1920 CTSI pamphlets (*Between Capitalism and Socialism* and *The Social Question in Ireland*) and also to write a pamphlet which was to be entitled *A Catechism of the Labour Question*. The original stock of the 1920 pamphlets had been destroyed in the wreck of the CTSI offices in O'Connell Street in 1922. This time however the articles were studied and rejected by the diocesan censor as excessively socialist. These writings appeared to condone the confiscation of all but a fraction of private property as a practical measure to meet present distress, and gave the impression that a person's right to private property extended only as far as property required for sustenance. Coffey admitted that his articles contained ambiguities that he would have preferred to have clarified. The manuscript of *A Catechism of the Labour Question* had already received a *nihil obstat* from Fr Peter Finlay SJ when it was rejected by two ecclesiastical censors. Finlay, when granting the *nihil obstat*, suggested to Coffey that 'the odd phrase appears to unduly favour extreme socialism, but nothing an honest Catholic thinker couldn't say'.40 Neither of the ecclesiastical censors concurred with Finlay's view. The first censor objected that Coffey's proposal was too statist: 'the state is all in all, and state providence is everywhere and the limits of state interference are apparently reached only when the state starves a man.'41 Furthermore, the church was not presented as an essential part of the solution to the labour question, and the censor remarks slightly petulantly that 'Dr Coffey would have us go to school rather to Major Douglas than to the Pope.' The second censor objects to the qualification of the right to own private property, and concludes with the dramatic warning that 'The book is thoroughly unsound and most dangerous as coming from a priest. If published it will do incalculable harm and cause surprise and scandal amongst our Catholic people.'42

39 Chapter 23 of the 1917 Code of Canon Law contains the canons governing censorship at this time. The relevant canon is 1385, §2 which establishes that the permission to print must be given by the ordinary either of the author, or of the place in which the book is to be published, or the place in which the book is to be printed; and that should one of these three deny the author permission to publish the latter should not seek the permission of another of the ordinaries without informing them of the prior refusal. 40 1940 addition to 'The social question' (manuscript) in Peter Coffey archive. 41 'Report of the censors', Peter Coffey archive. 42 Ibid.

   In his interlinear comments Coffey could not hide his annoyance at the objections of the censors: '*Quis custodiet ipsos custodes?*' he asks. One cannot but feel sympathy for him as at times the objections of both censors are simplistic and excessively conservative, such as when they reject the doctrine of social credit on the grounds that the theory is not to be found in *Rerum novarum*. They appear to view the right to private property as absolute, and so, beneath the second censor's assertion that an owner has 'perfect ownership' and that this gives him the 'right of complete disposal of the source and the products', the frustrated Coffey asks: 'With no qualifications and limitations whatsoever?'[43] Against the advice of the college president, James MacCaffrey, Coffey appealed the judgment to the Visitors – only to be turned down once again.[44] Initially Coffey vacillated with regard to the judgment of the ecclesiastical censors, wondering whether he was only being *advised* by the bishops not to publish – even anonymously – or whether he was being positively *prohibited* from publishing. Eventually he decided that the latter was the case. Throughout the rest of the decade there was a voluminous correspondence with the Maynooth authorities, with bishops and cardinals. In general the tenor of this correspondence was good-natured: Coffey for his part declaring his fidelity to the Church, and the bishops and cardinals for their part acknowledging his good will in the whole matter. There was the occasional flash of candor, as when his 'candid friend' Bishop Thomas O'Doherty of Galway wrote: 'your opinion [...] "that the Church in Ireland is avoiding discussion of the social question" is sheer nonsense', and 'nobody, lay or clerical, will regard you as an authority on the financial question'.[45] At the same time as publishing, or trying to publish, pamphlets, Coffey worked privately to influence 'statesmen, politicians and leaders of thought at home and abroad', attending for example the International Catholic Conference at Oxford in August 1925 (where he distributed copies of a circular to the hundred or so delegates) and the French *Semaine sociale* in Le Havre a year later.

   But Coffey's reputation had become tarnished – even as early as February 1923 Cardinal Michael Logue felt the need to warn him that he was creating for himself 'the reputation of having a strong leaning to communism'.[46] When in October 1929 he applied for the vacant Maynooth professorship of ethics, this tarnished reputation ensured that he would not get the job, although he certainly felt himself to be the obvious candidate for the post.

   Despite the failure to garner support from virtually any ecclesiastical source, Coffey doggedly continued to lobby and to try to publish articles, convinced that in conscience he simply had to do so. His campaigning years drew to a close in

---

43 Ibid.   **44** In this letter, April 1923, he complains that few priests in Ireland are making a study of the social, economic and labour question, despite the fact that Leo XIII had requested this.   **45** Letter, 27 Dec. 1929. Peter Coffey archive.   **46** Cardinal Michael Logue, letter, 14 Feb. 1923.

the 1930s with an appeal to the Holy See through the offices of the papal nuncio, Archbishop Pascal Robinson.[47] The response of the Holy See was to leave the matter in the hands of the local ordinaries.

CONCLUSION

Were Coffey's social ideas – as the censors thought – too socialist to be orthodox? Or was it simply that, as he thought himself, Catholics were over-reacting to the growing communist threat and retreating too far into the arms of *laissez-faire* economics? Aspects of Coffey's defence of what would in time become known in Catholic social teaching as 'the universal destination of goods' do appear to be ahead of their time.[48] Regarding his ideas on social credit theory, he felt that he had been somewhat vindicated by the 'unmistakable strictures on the prevailing world-policy of finance' contained in Pius XI's 1931 encyclical *Quadragesimo anno.*[49] Coffey never conceded defeat to his censors, considering rather that the story told by his memoirs 'may some day prove instructive and helpful for would-be pioneers in Catholic social teaching'.[50]

It has been suggested that priests in early twentieth-century Ireland could have done more 'to develop a social ideology that would have more belligerently attacked social neglect and decay'.[51] It is true that the bishops were divided in their attitude to the co-operative movement and there was no unequivocal support for the rural movements. Sheehan's *Luke Delmege* was heavily criticized in clerical circles for its advocacy of reforms. While this criticism cannot be levelled against Coffey, did his efforts to 'leaven the political intelligentsia' succeed? The Fianna Fáil government which took office in 1932 was certainly closer to Coffey on social matters than was Cumann na nGaedheal, though whether Coffey's writings and lobbying influenced Fianna Fáil social thinking is matter for another study. Nevertheless, it is hard to imagine that an amateur economist-priest (his only formal training in economics was a course in political economy he had followed in Mercier's Higher Institute of Philosophy under a certain Professor Defourney) trying to involve himself so actively in the

---

47 'The social question', Peter Coffey archive. 48 *'Christian tradition has never recognized the right to private property as absolute and untouchable* [...]. The principle of the universal destination of goods is an affirmation both of God's full and perennial lordship over every reality and of the requirement that the goods of creation remain ever destined to the development of the whole person and of all humanity': *Compendium of the social doctrine of the Church* (Rome, 2004), § 177. 49 1940 addition to 'The social question', Peter Coffey archive. Furthermore here he mentions the Canadian investigation carried out by a team of nine theologians into the social credit system theories of Père Levesque OP, which came to the conclusion that they contained nothing contrary to the Catholic faith. 50 'The social question', Peter Coffey archive. 51 Diarmaid Ferriter, *The transformation of Ireland, 1900–2000* (London, 2004) p. 85.

economics of the new state would achieve much, even in the clericalist atmosphere of the 1920s.

At times Coffey appears to have gone beyond the field of Catholic social theory, as embodied in *Rerum novarum*, into the realm of strictly economic theory. The problem here is that he – a neo-Scholastic scholar – discusses fairly complex economic matters in the light of church teaching in specifically Catholic journals and pamphlets. He could be accused of having gone too far from the field of Catholic theology into specialized economics.[52] Furthermore, and of more practical significance, his theories would not be given credence as he was essentially self-trained in economic matters.

But this brings us to two intriguing if hypothetical questions. Firstly, was Coffey's 'defection' to the cause of social action a loss for neo-Scholastic philosophy in Ireland? And secondly, could he have achieved more for the cause of social justice had he 'stuck to his last' – philosophy? It is unfortunate that in 1917 he felt he could no longer find a 'natural and congenial field for further work' within philosophy in Maynooth because as an institution it was not committed to serious philosophical research. Had he persevered, might he have eventually succeeded in founding a neo-Scholastic journal, or improved the standard of philosophical training of the seminarians? In part the problem was one of straightforward poverty: Ireland of the beginning of the twentieth century was simply too poor, even apart from its political turmoil, to be conducive to philosophizing. Its poverty put pressure on its priests to be practical men of action. The social ferment perhaps also made them too politically precocious, and too inclined towards political intervention.[53]

The second question is a much more important one: was there not room within his 'own strictly professional domain' to work on the fundamental issues underlying and causing social injustice? It would seem that Coffey considers the social question to be fundamentally an economic rather than philosophical or theological problem; or at least that the solution is to come through a change in economic policy rather than in a deepened appreciation of the human person and society. Contrast this for example with the work done during this period by such personalist philosophers as Max Scheler (1874–1928) and – a little later – Emmanuel Mounier (1905–50). The personalist philosophy attacks the radical individualism of capitalism so disliked by Coffey, but in a speculative way, rather

52 See the *Compendium of the social doctrine of the church* (2004), § 72: 'A decisive clarification [...] was made in the encyclical *Sollicitudo rei socialis:* the church's social doctrine "belongs to the field, not of *ideology*, but of *theology* and particularly of moral theology". It cannot be defined according to socio-economic parameters. It is not an ideological or pragmatic system intended to define and generate economic, political and social relationships, but is a *category unto itself.*'
53 By way of example, thirty-three priests were involved in the campaign in the Galway constituency in the 1927 elections (all incidentally supporters of the Cumann na nGaedheal government).

than through advocating specific economic measures, and was to influence in time the course of thinking on the person and society.[54] In this light, the lack of connection between social action and philosophical thought in Coffey does appear slightly strange. Is this partly a failing of the ahistorical temper of his neo-Scholastic training? In a sense the years dedicated almost wholly to lecturing, writing and translating philosophical works appear an interlude in a life otherwise devoted to the campaign for a Gaelic Ireland, marked by the Irish language and temperance, but above all social justice.

APPENDIX I

Peter Coffey's published works

This is the first bibliography of Peter Coffey's works; some references are incomplete and some works may be missing altogether.
Abbreviations used:

IER	*Irish Ecclesiastical Record*
ITQ	*Irish Theological Quarterly*
CTSI	Catholic Truth Society of Ireland
Cath. Bulletin	*Catholic Bulletin*

1901
1. 'Agnosticism; a general sketch', *IER* 4:10 (1901), 289–310. The causes of modern agnosticism, with special attention to British empiricists.
2. 'Agnosticism; a special sketch', *IER* 4:10 (1901), 513–39. Examination of the role of Herbert Spencer in the development of modern agnosticism.

1903
3. 'Students and temperance reform', *IER* 4:14 (1903), 109–25. Text of address to Total Abstinence and Pioneer Association in Maynooth College, April 1903.

1905
4. 'Philosophy and the sciences at Louvain – I', *IER* 4:17 (1905), 385–408.
5. 'Philosophy and the sciences at Louvain – II', *IER* 4:17 (1905), 485–516. Brief sketches of work being carried out at the Higher Institute of Philosophy in Louvain.

1906
6. *The Church and the Working Classes*, CTSI (Dublin, 1906). The content of two lectures given in the Fr Mathew Hall, Dublin.
7. 'Thoughts on philosophy and religion – I', *IER* 4:19 (1906), 193–205.

---

54 For a further discussion of this influence, see K.P. Doran, *Solidarity, a synthesis of personalism and communalism in the thought of Karol Wojtyla / John Paul II* (New York, 1996), which considers the influence of Scheler and Mounier on the thought of Karol Wojtyla regarding the question of solidarity.

8. 'Thoughts on philosophy and religion – II', *IER* 4:19 (1906), 385–402.
   Text of paper delivered to Students' Literary Society in Maynooth College on faith and reason.
9. 'Geometry and philosophy', *IER* 4:20 (1906), 97–116.

1907
10. Maurice De Wulf, *Scholasticism Old and New* (London, 1907). A translation of Maurice De Wulf, *Introduction à la philosophie néo-scolastique* (Paris, 1904). This translation was subsequently reprinted by Kessinger in 2007.
11. 'A new book on Scholastic philosophy', *IER* 4:22 (1907), 357–71. Review of Maurice De Wulf, *Scholasticism Old and New* (London, 1907).

1908
12. 'Subject and knowledge in knowledge and consciousness – I', *IER* 4:23 (1908), 396–414.
13. 'Subject and knowledge in knowledge and consciousness – II', *IER* 4:23 (1908), 481–97.
14. 'Subject and knowledge in knowledge and consciousness – III', *IER* 4:23 (1908), 610–21.
15. '"Appearance" and "reality" – I', *IER* 4:24 (1908), 113–32.
16. '"Appearance" and "reality" – II', *IER* 4:24 (1908), 268–82.

1909
17. 'The new knowledge and its limitations – I', *IER* 4:26 (1909), 337–51.
18. 'The new knowledge and its limitations – II', *IER* 4:26 (1909), 461–74.
19. 'The new knowledge and its limitations – III', *IER* 4:26 (1909), 571–86. Reflections on the philosophical implications of recent discoveries regarding matter and energy.
20. 'Scholasticism and modern thought', *ITQ* 4 (1909), 457–73. A discussion of the importance of the neo-Scholastic movement.
21. Maurice De Wulf, *History of Medieval Philosophy* (London, 1909).
    Translation of Maurice De Wulf, *Histoire de la philosophie médiévale* (Louvain, 1907).

1910
22. 'Historia philosophiae', *ITQ* 5 (1910), 114. Book review of Josepho Kachnik, *Historia philosophiae* (Olomouc [Czechoslovakia], 1909).
23. 'Elementa philosophiae aristotelico-thomisticae', *ITQ* 5 (1910), 114–16. Book review of Joseph Gredt, *Elementa philosophiae aristotelico-thomisticae* (Freiburg).
24. 'Die Ethik des heiligen Augustinus', *ITQ* 5 (1910), 116–17. Book review of Joseph Von Mausbach, *Die Ethik des heiligen Augustinus* (Freiburg).
25. 'Philosophy and sectarianism in Belfast University', *ITQ* 5 (1910), 454–73. A discussion of Presbyterian opposition to the establishment of a lectureship in Scholastic Philosophy in Queen's University, Belfast.
26. 'Genèse et science', *ITQ* 5 (1910), 500–1. Book review of L. Arnaudet, *Genèse et science* (Paris).
27. 'The "new knowledge" and its limitations', *IER* 4:27 (1910), 17–35. Reflections on contemporary ideas on matter and energy.
28. 'The philosophy of energy', *IER* 4:27 (1910), 159–66. A reply to objections made by Walter McDonald to the earlier essay on matter and energy (nos. 17–19 supra).

29. 'Some current phases of physical theories', *IER* 4:27 (1910), 394–412. Final essay in the debate with Walter McDonald, on the proper understanding of kinetic energy. (McDonald was professor of theology in Maynooth from 1881 till his death in 1920.) It appears from McDonald's memoirs that the differences between both men went beyond the strictly academic. See Walter McDonald, *Reminiscences of a Maynooth Professor* (London, 1925), pp 165–6.) The article ends with comment by the editor: 'This controversy may now cease'!

30. 'Some questionable tendencies in the logic of scientific method', *IER* 4:28 (1910), 1–10.

31. 'Some principles underlying "scientific explanation"', *IER* 4:28 (1910), 130–49.

32. 'The principle of the "uniformity of nature": its relation to induction and to deduction', *IER* 4:28 (1910), 228–48.

33. 'Causality, hypothesis and law', *IER* 4:28 (1910), 337–59.

34. *The Inductive Sciences: an inquiry into some of their methods and postulates* (Dublin, 1910). A reprint from *IER* of the four previous articles on the scientific method.

1911

35. 'De qualitatibus sensibilibus et in specie de coloribus et sonis', *ITQ* 6 (1911), 508–10. Book review of Hubertus Gründer, *De qualitatibus sensibilibus et in specie de coloribus et sonis* (Freiburg im Breisgau, 1911).

36. 'Lessons in logic', *ITQ* 6 (1911), 510–11. Book review of William Turner, *Lessons in Logic* (London).

1912

37. 'Reflections on some forms of monism', *ITQ* 7 (1912), 159–79.

38. 'Moralphilosophie', *ITQ* 7 (1912), 238. Book review of Victor Cathrein, *Moralphilosophie* (5th ed., Freiburg im Breisgau, 1911).

39. 'Die Geschichte der scholastischen Methode', *ITQ* 7 (1912), 239. Book review of Martin Grabmann, *Die Geschichte der scholastischen Methode,* 2 vols (Freiburg im Breisgau, 1905–1911).

40. 'Histoire de la philosophie ancienne', *ITQ* 7 (1912), 492–4. Book review of Gaston Sortais, *Histoire de la philosophie ancienne* (Paris, 1912).

41. 'Introductory philosophy', *ITQ* 7 (1912), 491–2. Book review of Charles Dubray, *Introductory Philosophy* (London, 1912).

42. *The Newspaper: its influence for good and for evil* (CTSI, Dublin, 1912). Substance of lectures delivered on the temperance platform.

43. *The Science of Logic: an inquiry into the principle of accurate thought and scientific method,* 2 vols (London, 1912). This work was reprinted by Longmans Green in 1918 and by Peter Smith in 1938.

1913

44. 'The truth about tolerance and intolerance – I', *IER* 5:1 (1913), 337–52.

45. 'The truth about tolerance and intolerance – II', *IER* 5:1 (1913), 609–25. Two articles analyzing A. Vermeersh, *Tolerance* (London).

46. 'Deduction' in C.G. Herbermann et al. (eds), *The Catholic Encyclopedia* (New York, 1913), iv, 265.

47. 'Dialectic' in C.G. Herbermann et al. (eds), *The Catholic Encyclopedia* (New York, 1913), iv, 770–2.

48. 'Gilbert de la Porrée' in C.G. Herbermann et al. (eds), *The Catholic Encyclopedia* (New York, 1913), vi, 555–6.

49. 'Godfrey of Fontaines' in C.G. Herbermann et al. (eds), *The Catholic Encyclopedia* (New York, 1913), vi, 626.

50. 'Henry of Ghent' in C.G. Herbermann et al. (eds), *The Catholic Encyclopedia* (New York, 1913), vii, 235.

51. 'Induction' in C.G. Herbermann et al. (eds), *The Catholic Encyclopedia* (New York, 1913), vii, 779–83.

52. 'John of Salisbury' in C.G. Herbermann et al. (eds), *The Catholic Encyclopedia* (New York, 1913), viii, 478–9.

53. 'A Catholic total abstinence congress', *IER* 5:2 (1913), 337–40. On a national Catholic total abstinence congress planned to take place in Dublin in 1914.

1914
54. *Ontology or the Theory of Being: an introduction to general metaphysics* (London, 1914). This work was reprinted by Longmans Green in 1918 and by Peter Smith in 1948. A facsimile edition was produced by Kessinger in 2007.

1915
55. *Aids and obstacles to Ireland's progress: the enemy within our gates* (Catholic Total Abstinence Federation of Ireland, 1915). No other details of publication.

1916
56. Preface to English ed. of Désiré Mercier, *A Manual of modern Scholastic Philosophy* (London, 1916).

1917
57. *Epistemology or the Theory of Knowledge*, 2 vols (London, 1917). This work was reprinted by Peter Smith in 1985 and a facsimile edition was produced by Kessinger in 2007.

58. 'The people, the state, the drink problem', *Studies* 6:23 (1917), 353–68.

1918
59. 'Conscription menace in Ireland and some issues raised by it', *IER* 5:11 (1918), 484–98. Very sympathetic analysis of the right of Irishmen to avoid conscription by the British government.

60. 'The ethics of total prohibition', *IER* 5:12 (1918), 449–65. Study of the benefits of total prohibition, based largely on the experience in USA.

61. 'Unionism and self-government', *Cath. Bulletin* 8 (1918), 337–44.

62. 'The origins of contemporary psychology', *ITQ* 13 (1918), 355–7. Book review of Désiré Mercier, *The Origins of Contemporary Psychology* (Washbourne, London).

63. 'The beginnings of science', *ITQ* 13 (1918), 381–2. Book review of Edward J. Menge, *The beginnings of science* (Boston).

1919
64. 'Le néo-réalisme Americain', *ITQ* 16 (1921), 82–3. Book review of Réné Kremer, *Le néo-réalisme americain* (Louvain).

1920

65. 'James Connolly's campaign in the light of Catholic teaching – I', *Cath. Bulletin* 10 (1920), 212–24.
66. 'James Connolly's campaign in the light of Catholic teaching – II', *Cath. Bulletin* 10 (1920), 275–9.
67. 'James Connolly's campaign in the light of Catholic teaching – III', *Cath. Bulletin* 10 (1920), 346–54.
68. 'James Connolly's campaign in the light of Catholic teaching – IV', *Cath. Bulletin* 10 (1920), 407–12.
69. 'James Connolly's campaign in the light of Catholic teaching – V', *Cath. Bulletin* 10 (1920), 489–92.
70. *Between Capitalism and Socialism* (CTSI, Dublin, 1920). A new edition of the five *Cath. Bulletin* Connolly articles; later revised and reprinted in the *Irish Messenger*, 1930.
71. *The Social Question in Ireland: some principles and projects of reconstruction* (CTSI, Dublin, 1920). This is a reworking of articles previously published in the *Dublin Leader*, but which I have not been able to locate. This pamphlet was later revised and in part rewritten for printing by the *Irish Messenger* in 1930.

1921

72. 'Two views of ownership', *IER* 5:17 (1921), 126–40. A contrast between pagan and Christian views of ownership.
73. 'Economic ideals and policies for the wage-earning masses', *Cath. Bulletin* 11 (1921), 97–103.
74. 'Tillage versus grazing', *Cath. Bulletin* 11 (1921), 225–9.
75. 'An injustice of the capitalist system' (Jan. 1921). No further details about this article.
76. 'Interest and unearned income' (July 1921). No further details about this article.
77. *An Economic Programme for the Irish Free State* (Dublin, 1922). Written in April or May, 1922 with the *P.H.Pierce* [*sic*] *Study Group* composed of Peter Coffey, Dr Moran, Frank Sweeney, Seamus Hughes, and Fr Joe Flanagan.
78. 'Economic democracy; credit – power and democracy', *ITQ* 16 (1921) 89–90. Book review of two books by C.H. Douglas: *Economic Democracy* (London, 1920) and *Credit: Power and Democracy* (London). These books were to strongly influence Coffey's thought on economics.
79. 'Prices, paper currency and credit – I', *Cath. Bulletin* 11 (1921), 487–93.
80. 'Prices, paper currency and credit – II', *Cath. Bulletin* 11 (1921), 690–4.

1922

81. 'Prices, paper currency and credit – III', *Cath. Bulletin* 12 (1922), 106–11.
82. 'Prices, paper currency and credit – IV', *Cath. Bulletin* 12 (1922), 163–7.
83. 'Prices, paper currency and credit – V', *Cath. Bulletin* 12 (1922), 238–43.
84. 'Prices, paper currency and credit – VI', *Cath. Bulletin* 12 (1922), 370–5.
85. 'Prices, paper currency and credit – VII', *Cath. Bulletin* 12 (1922), 502–8.
86. Article, *Irish Catholic*, Aug. 1922.
87. 'The "just price" in relation to systems of financing industry', *ITQ* 17 (1922), 341–51.
88. 'Capital and labour', *Irish Independent*, 28 & 29 Oct. 1922.

1923

89. 'Post-war finance and industry', articles, *Irish Times*, 23 & 24 Sept. 1923. Two anonymously published articles.
90. 'Irish industries and the social credit system', article, *Irish Independent*, 13 Oct. 1923.
91. Book reviews, *Catholic Times*, 1923–1925. No further details of these publications; it appears that these were reviews of books on economics topics.

1924

92. 'An object lesson in finance: what Guernsey did', *Irish Independent*, 24 Feb. 1924. A letter published under a pen-name.
93. 'Ireland's idle money', letter, *Irish Independent*, 8 May, 1924. A letter published under a pen-name.
94. 'Thoughts on modern war', *Irish Independent*, 20 July, 1924. A letter published under a pen-name.
95. *God's nearness to us in loneliness* (CTSI, Dublin, 1924).
96. 'A plea for Catholic study and action,' *Irish Catholic*, 13 Sept. 1924.
97. 'A modern apostle: Father James A. Cullen SJ', *IER* 5:24 (1924), 233–42. An appreciation of Fr Cullen, a temperance campaigner who died in 1921.
98. *Birth and life: death and after-life* (CTSI, Dublin, 1924).
99. 'Plain talks about money, wealth and debt', articles, *Dublin Leader* (1924–5). No further details about these articles.

1925

100. 'Henry Ford on industry, finance and business', *Dublin Leader* (April–June 1925). A book review. No further details about this article.

1926

101. 'Cardinal Mercier and philosophical studies', *Studies* 15:57 (1926), 95–104. An appreciation of Cardinal Mercier who died on 23 January 1926.

1927

102. *Trials of life* (CTSI, Dublin, 1927).

1930

103. *Between Capitalism and Socialism: some landmarks for the guidance of Irish Catholics* (Irish Messenger, 1930). A reprint of *Between capitalism and socialism* (CTSI, Dublin, 1920).
104. *The Social Question in Ireland: some principles and projects of reconstruction* (Irish Messenger, 1930).
    A reprint of *The Social Question in Ireland: some principles and projects of reconstruction* (CTSI, Dublin, 1920).

1931

105. *The Christian Family and the Higher Idea* (CTSI, Dublin, 1931).
106. 'Capital ownership and credit control', *Clergy Review* (1931), 262–72.

1932

107. 'Christianity and capitalism – I', *Cath. Bulletin* 22 (1932), 551–9.

108. 'Christianity and capitalism – II', *Cath. Bulletin* 22 (1932), 629–35.
109. 'Christianity and capitalism – III', *Cath. Bulletin* 22 (1932), 723–32.
Three articles published under initials PCM (Peter Coffey Maynooth).

1933
110. 'Christianity and capitalism', *New English Weekly* (Jan. 1933). A reprint of the three 1932 *Cath. Bulletin* articles.

1934
111. *The flaw in the money system* (London, 1934). No further details.

1936
112. 'The economic world-crisis: some suggestions towards diagnosis and remedy', *IER* 5:48 (1936), 131–41.
113. 'God or mammon', *The Fig Tree* (Dec. 1936). Reprint of 'The economic world-crisis: some suggestions towards diagnosis and remedy', *IER* 5:48 (1936), 131–41. No further details.
114. 'God or mammon', *Today and Tomorrow. Today and Tomorrow* was a Canadian journal. This article is a reprint of 'The economic world-crisis: some suggestions towards diagnosis and remedy', *IER* 5:48 (1936), 131–41. No further details.

1940
115. 'Capital ownership & credit control', *Hibernia* (1940). A reprint of article of the same title in *Clergy Review* (1931), 262–72.

APPENDIX 2

Peter Coffey's writings rejected by ecclesiastical censors

Many of the details given here are sketchy, coming for the most part from passing references in Coffey's personal 'Narrative' in the Peter Coffey archive, Russell library, Maynooth.

1. *A Catechism of the labour question*. Written for CTSI, 1922 and rejected by diocesan censors.
2. *A Sinn Féin money policy*. Rejected by the Visitors, Maynooth, December 1922.
3. *Between capitalism and socialism: some landmarks for the guidance of Irish Catholics*. A recasting of the *Cath. Bulletin* Connolly articles written for CTSI, 1922. Printed by *Irish Messenger*, 1930.
4. *The social question in Ireland: some principles and projects of reconstruction*. A recasting of the *Cath. Bulletin* Connolly articles written for CTSI, 1922. Printed by *Irish Messenger*, 1930.
5. *James Connolly's campaign against capitalism*. Proposed reprint of 1920 *Cath. Bulletin* articles. Rejected by diocesan censors.
6. *The financing of industry*. Rejected by the Visitors, Maynooth, January 1923 and again in June 1923.

7. *Capital ownership and financial credit control*. Rejected by censor of *IER* 1924 and again in 1940. Published in *Clergy Review*, March 1932 and in *Hibernia*, 1940.
8. *The flaw in the money system*. Written in 1924, and rejected by Sheed & Ward in 1929 and subsequently in 1934 by Burns, Oates & Washbourne.
9. *Essays*. A collection of fourteen previously published articles. Rejected by Visitors Maynooth, Oct. 1929,
10. *The just price*. Written for *ITQ* November 1929.
11. *Christianity and capitalism*. Rejected by *Dublin Review* censor. Published in *Cath. Bulletin*, July, August and September 1932, under the initials PCM, and in *New English Weekly*, January 1933.
12. *Private ownership of real wealth*. No further information.
13. *Control of financial credit*. No further information.
14. *An economic programme for the Irish Free State*. No further information.

The future of Scholastic thought

PHILIPP W. ROSEMANN

Herkunft aber bleibt stets Zukunft, Martin Heidegger once declared, famously, on the subject of the relationship between his own thought and its Catholic roots: 'origin always remains future' or, more etymologically translated, 'where we have come from always continues to head towards us'.[1] What Heidegger meant is that the past does not simply lie behind us, inertly and without relevance, but rather functions as the source of our future projects. Ideas for authentic future developments always originate in a rethinking of the past, a renaissance, or, in Heideggerian terminology, a 'repetition' (*Wiederholung*).[2] Thus, if we forget our past, we remain prisoners of a one-dimensional present, unable to engage in that creative re-appropriation of our history which alone allows us to imagine ourselves differently: hence the importance of keeping knowledge of our cultural heritage alive.

Herkunft bleibt stets Zukunft also implies that it would be ill-judged to try to sketch the future potential of an intellectual movement such as Scholastic thought without a firm grasp of its history; for any such potential can arise only from a re-evaluation of the past in a contemporary perspective. This paper, therefore, falls into two major parts: first, I shall attempt to define what Scholastic thought *was*, historically; following that, I shall proceed to discuss the continuing relevance of Scholastic thought on the basis of its historical reality. In the final section, I shall defend my conception of Scholastic thought against possible objections by clarifying how I understand the relationship between Scholastic Philosophy and Scholastic Theology.

I

So, what was Scholastic thought historically? Twentieth-century historians have essentially offered two types of answer to this question, a doctrinal and a formal one. The Belgian medievalist Maurice De Wulf, one of the pioneers of the Louvain school of neo-Scholasticism, believed it possible to identify a 'doctrinal

---

1 Martin Heidegger, *Unterwegs zur Sprache*, 7th ed. (Pfullingen, 1982), p. 96. 2 For the concept of *Wiederholung*, see Heidegger, *Being and time*, trans. John Macquarrie and Edward Robinson (Oxford, 1978), 74, pp 437–8.

heritage' (*patrimoine doctrinal*) that was shared by all truly Scholastic thinkers.[3] This heritage included, in his opinion, the pluralism of individuals (as opposed to monism or pantheism), the distinction between potency and act, matter-form dualism, the theory of essence versus existence, and moderate realism regarding the nature of universals.[4] Other eminent historians of medieval thought, such as Marie-Dominique Chenu and Étienne Gilson, were quick to draw attention to the problems affecting this approach, which De Wulf implemented, with some modifications, in the successive editions of his *Histoire de la philosophie médiévale*.[5]

For De Wulf, the essence of the Scholastic movement lay in the thirteenth century; indeed, it culminated in the thought of Thomas Aquinas, whose ideas therefore became the yard-stick by which all other thinkers themselves were measured. That De Wulf considered the essence/existence distinction as a defining characteristic of Scholastic Philosophy is telling in this regard. Not surprisingly, this approach led him to the exclusion of some of the most original thinkers of the medieval period. Thus, John Scottus Eriugena found himself marginalized in De Wulf's *Histoire de la philosophie médiévale*: his thought, challenging as it does the dualisms of matter/form and God/creation, diverges too much from the Aristotelico-Thomism which lies at the heart of De Wulf's 'doctrinal heritage'. But is that sufficient reason to declare Eriugena 'anti-Scholastic'? After all, the controversial aspects of his thought are firmly rooted in the tradition of Dionysius the Areopagite and his Greek commentators, whose authority was unquestioned in the Middle Ages. De Wulf's notion of a Scholastic *patrimoine doctrinal*, then, is too narrow: it arbitrarily excludes thinkers whose ideas are firmly embedded in the intellectual universe of the Christian centuries.[6]

A second attempt to define Scholasticism goes back to Martin Grabmann, the German medievalist from Eichstätt. In his magisterial *Geschichte der scholastischen Methode*, Grabmann focused, as the title of his work indicates, on the methodological features of Scholastic thought, arguing that Scholasticism was driven by an impulse to reconcile authority and reason, *auctoritas* and *ratio*.[7]

---

3 See Maurice De Wulf, 'Y eut-il une philosophie scolastique au moyen âge?', *Revue néo-Scolastique de philosophie* 29 (1927), 5–27. The expression 'patrimoine doctrinal' occurs on p. 5. 4 See ibid., 13–18. A somewhat different list appears on p. 24. 5 The essay cited in note 3 is a response to some of these criticisms. 6 For a more recent critique of De Wulf's position, see Riccardo Quinto, *Scolastica. Storia di un concetto* (Padua, 2001), pp 330–9. Rightly, Quinto sees in De Wulf's idea of a Scholastic heritage or synthesis 'a normative term extrinsic to the Middle Ages' unable to do justice to the historical reality of Scholastic Philosophy (p. 338). 7 See Martin Grabmann, *Die Geschichte der scholastischen Methode*, 2 vols. (Freiburg im Breisgau, 1909–11; reprinted, Berlin, 1988). I have commented on the dialectics of *auctoritas* and *ratio* as a leitmotiv of Grabmann's oeuvre in my intellectual biography of Grabmann in Helen Damico (ed.), *Medieval scholarship: biographical studies on the formation of a discipline*, iii, *Philosophy and the Arts* (New York & London, 2000), pp 55–74.

Grabmann traced this impulse to Scripture itself, especially the apostolic letters, which already exhort believers to provide reasons for their faith. Passages such as Titus 1:9, 2 Corinthians 10:4, 1 Peter 3:5, and Acts 17 are examples. Starting from these biblical roots, Grabmann showed how Christian thinkers gradually developed increasingly sophisticated tools to implement the program of penetrating their faith rationally. Since reason abhors contradiction and prizes logical order, such rational penetration required a coherent and systematic articulation of the Christian faith. To this end, tensions both in the revealed texts themselves and, soon, among the commentators of these texts had to be eliminated while the loose narrative presentation of the content of the Christian faith in Scripture needed to be transformed into a doctrinal system. In the latter, the relative place and importance of individual tenets of the faith in the whole of the Christian belief-system had to be determined. Since these tasks exceeded the conceptual resources of the revealed texts, they called for a *Stoffzufuhr*, as Grabmann puts it, that is to say, an influx of concepts and methods from outside the Judaeo-Christian universe. This is why Scholastic thought was from its very beginning characterized by dialogue with non-Christian sources. This dialogue, however, created the further challenge of integrating foreign elements into the edifice of Christian doctrine.[8]

It is not necessary, in the present context, to rehearse Grabmann's presentation of the historical steps in the development of the Scholastic method; his research, brilliant as it was, has been complemented and partially superseded by newer scholarship. Suffice it to say that, in the Latin West, the development of Scholasticism reached a first culmination in the sentence collections of the twelfth century and, in particular, in Peter Lombard's *Book of Sentences*. The Lombard's *Sentences* attempted a systematic and synthetic account of Christian dogma: on the basis of a small number of architectonic principles – such as the Augustinian distinctions between enjoyment and use, things and signs – every aspect of theological doctrine is assigned a logical place in the whole, and the sometimes discordant voices of Scripture, the Fathers and medieval authorities are harmonized by means of the central tool of Scholastic reasoning, the distinction.[9]

While it is not possible, as we have seen, to reduce the diversity of Scholastic thought to a common doctrinal denominator, the key principles of the Scholastic method are at work, in forms corresponding to different stages of technical development, in the works of every thinker of the patristic and medieval periods: in Augustine as much as in Eriugena, Anselm, Bonaventure, Thomas Aquinas,

8 Riccardo Quinto believes that Grabmann's understanding of Scholasticism through the dialectics of *ratio* and *auctoritas* is too theological in its orientation; it does not apply to Scholastic Philosophy (see *Scolastica*, pp 339–49, esp. 348–9). I will return to Quinto's critique in section IV. 9 On the place of Peter Lombard in the Scholastic tradition, see my *Peter Lombard* (Oxford, 2004), as well as *The story of a great medieval book: Peter Lombard's 'Sentences'* (Toronto, 2007).

and Siger of Brabant.[10] Canonists like Ivo of Chartres and Gratian, too, made crucial contributions to the advancement of Scholastic reasoning techniques. Furthermore, after a period of upheaval in the first half of the fourteenth century, even nominalism returned to the concordist inspiration of the Scholastic movement. Thus, we see figures such as Marsilius of Inghen and Gabriel Biel search for ways of reconciling nominalist theories with the older metaphysical tradition.[11] Biel's theological synthesis, the *Collectorium*, draws on Ockham and other nominalists for its first two books but in the last two his main sources are Alexander of Hales, Bonaventure, and especially Thomas Aquinas. Biel, it seems, did not view this eclectic approach as particularly problematic.

Towards the end of the dominance of Scholastic forms of reasoning in the Christian West, we find not only a deliberate and determined attempt to overcome the doctrinal divisions which the rise of nominalism had made impossible to ignore; there was also increasing reflection on the specificity of the intellectual era that was now drawing to a close. Thinkers began to refer to the 'Scholastic' school, 'Scholastic' questions, and the 'Scholastic' manner of proceeding in a way which shows that the Scholastic approach no longer went without question.[12] Furthermore, there were signs of a sense of history, and of an awareness of one's own place within it, which were uncommon during the earlier Middle Ages. This sense of time allowed Denys the Carthusian (1402/3–1471), in the prologue to his monumental *Sentences* commentary, to sketch in a brief outline of the development of Christian thought from biblical times until his own day. The following quotation of the relevant passage will add a medieval voice to our description of Scholasticism, which, so far, has been guided by modern scholarship. Moreover, Denys' text will reveal an aspect of Scholastic thought and its development that neither De Wulf nor Grabmann, nor other modern scholars, have taken sufficiently seriously. Denys writes:

> Yet, although the deficiency, smallness, and paucity of the wisdom of the way [that is, of this life] are enormous by comparison with the wisdom of the Fatherland, nonetheless the wisdom revealed at the time of the evangelical law is very splendid and great. [This wisdom was revealed] first by Christ, then by the mission and inspiration of the Holy Spirit, next by the glorious apostles and evangelists, then by the holy Fathers, and finally by the Catholic and Scholastic doctors, excellently learned not only in the divine Scriptures but also in all philosophy. [This wisdom] powerfully

---

10 Several contributions to this conference, especially those by Liam Chambers and Martin Stone, have drawn attention to the need for broadening our conception of Scholasticism to include the modern period. It would be important to ask, then, to what extent the formal characterization of Scholastic thought that I have just offered applies to modern Scholasticism as well. 11 On Marsilius of Inghen and Gabriel Biel, see *The story of a great medieval book*, pp 127–36 and 161–70, respectively. 12 See ibid., pp 163–5.

exceeds that of the philosophers, but also of the theologians of the Old Testament, and that of the natural law. For – as Gregory testifies – just as wisdom grew in the course of time before the coming of the Saviour, so it also does in the meantime [since his coming]. And most of all from the time when Master Peter Lombard, bishop of Paris, collected his *Book of Sentences*, wisdom appears to have received much and great elucidation, growth, and abundant increase. Which Isaiah once foresaw, saying, 'the earth is filled with the knowledge of the Lord, as the covering waters of the sea' [Is 11:9], that is to say, very abundantly. And those things that were hidden have been brought forth into the light; the difficulties of the Scriptures have been unknotted; and points that can be objected to the Christian faith, and have been objected by the faithless, have been solved outstandingly. Indeed, the aforesaid Master and illustrious learned Scholastics who have written famously on the *Book of Sentences*, have subtly discussed, magisterially clarified, and Catholically treated not only the more difficult places of Scripture, but also the words and writings of the holy Fathers, who have written much that is difficult and obscure in their expositions of the Scriptures and in other treatises.

Since it is known, however, that almost innumerable people have already written upon this *Book of Sentences*, and that moreover even today some are writing [on it] – perhaps even more than is useful, as due to some less illustrious writings of recent people, the more illustrious writings of the older ones are less attended to, read, and investigated – hence it is my intention in this work to prepare a kind of collection of extracts from the commentaries and writings of the most authoritative, famous, and excellent doctors, and to bring the reflection of these doctors back into one volume (*in unum volumen redigere*). For just as the very text of the *Book of Sentences* is gathered from the words and testimonies of the holy Fathers, so this work too is put together from the doctrines and writings of the aforesaid writers upon the *Book of Sentences*.[13]

Denys' conception of the Scholastic tradition contains a number of points that may be surprising to a modern audience. To begin with, Denys does not posit a radical division between the authority of revealed texts and that of commentators upon these texts; rather, the two form part of the single movement in

---

13 D. Dionysii Cartusiani *Commentaria in primum librum Sententiarum*, Doctoris Ecstatici D. Dionysii Cartusiani Opera Omnia 19 (Tournai, 1902), prooemium, p. 36. A parallel text is to be found in the prologue to the *Elementatio theologica*, Opera Omnia 33 (Tournai, 1907), p. 112. For commentary, see *The story of a great medieval book*, pp 149–51 and 191–3. Also see Kent Emery, Jr., 'Denys the Carthusian and the Doxography of Scholastic Theology,' in his *Monastic, scholastic and mystical theologies from the Later Middle Ages*, Variorum Collected Studies Series CS 561 (Aldershot, Hants., 1996), essay IX, esp. pp 332–3.

which God's wisdom reveals itself to humanity. This explains why Denys, and the patristic and medieval periods in general, place such great emphasis on the *auctoritas* of the tradition; why it is inconceivable for them to contradict authors such as Augustine, the Pseudo-Dionysius or, later, Thomas Aquinas, whose ideas must instead be treated respectfully and integrated into each new synthesis. Secondly, a rather dynamic sense of history pervades Denys' text: wisdom was not revealed once and for all in Scripture but develops and grows over time. There is room for the notion of progress here, although Denys does not hold a naïve belief in irreversible intellectual growth. There can be too much theological writing, and writing of inferior quality, so that the insights of previous ages can come to be obscured. (When Denys speaks of the 'less illustrious writings of recent people', he most likely has in mind the *Sentences* commentaries of the nominalists.) Thirdly, anyone who has been raised on the standard fare of contemporary histories of medieval thought may have expected the central figure in Denys' narrative to be a recognized luminary such as Augustine, Thomas Aquinas, or Duns Scotus; instead, Peter Lombard, author of the *Book of Sentences*, plays the role of the linchpin of the Scholastic tradition. It is in the *Sentences*, according to Denys the Carthusian, that the wisdom of the tradition was gathered most effectively; it is the *Sentences* that spawned the remarkable increase in wisdom which came about in the high Middle Ages; and it is the *Sentences* whose approach Denys himself endeavours to emulate in creating a 'collection of extracts from the commentaries and writings of the most authoritative, famous, and excellent doctors, and [in] bring[ing] the reflection of these doctors back into one volume'.

The most significant point in Denys' text, however, and the one most neglected in modern discussions of Scholasticism, is this: Scholastic thought is not anchored in texts, not even the texts of the Christian revelation. If Scholastic thought is essentially characterized by a tension between *auctoritas* and *ratio*, if its mainspring is the impulse to reconcile authorities among themselves and with reason, then this motivation is ultimately due not to respect for texts, for words, but to respect for the Word – the Word Incarnate, that is. Wisdom, Denys the Carthusian writes, was revealed '*first by Christ*, then by the mission and inspiration of the Holy Spirit, next by the glorious apostles and evangelists, then by the holy Fathers, and finally by the Catholic and Scholastic doctors, excellently learned not only in the divine Scriptures but also in all philosophy'. The conviction that all wisdom stems from Christ, the person, and not from some document – even a highly revered one – produces an important corollary: if the authorities who have commented on the words of Christ deserve our respect, it is not least because they were 'holy Fathers', that is to say, because their lives gave personal witness to their faith. It is not an accident that many of the greatest thinkers of the patristic and medieval periods were recognized as saints. Their ideas were considered trustworthy not least because of the fruits that they produced.

II

We post-moderns are reluctant to tie theoretical truth to personal virtue. Indeed, the idea seems vaguely embarrassing, the product of an ideology that would reject Bertrand Russell because he treated his wives badly, or Michel Foucault because of his extreme sexual appetite. Undoubtedly, criticism of a thinker's life can be a facile way to avoid engaging him or her intellectually. Thus, the connection between theory and personal practice does not seem a good starting point to talk about the future of Scholastic thought.

The issue highlighted here, however, is not whether for Scholastic thinkers personal failures served as the ultimate criterion of theoretical truth; clearly, this was not the case. They were interested as much in theoretical cogency as we are; furthermore, thinkers, such as Abelard and Ockham, whose conduct raised eyebrows in the Middle Ages, were nonetheless able to exercise enormous influence on the Scholastic tradition. The crucial point is that, throughout its history, Scholastic thought remained closely tied to its Christian roots. This, in turn, means that Scholasticism is misunderstood outside the context of faith. At the centre of the Scholastic movement – that is the meaning of the passage from Denys the Carthuian which we just read – there is the person of Jesus Christ. Augustine, Eriugena, Anselm, Abelard, Bonaventure, Thomas Aquinas, and, yes, even Ockham, were all fervent Christians. Their intellectual activity is understood only insufficiently as a theoretical project, because what was at stake for each of them in their writing, was a better grasp of the path to salvation.[14]

Again, a contemporary audience may be taken aback. We have come to accept the idea that impersonal objectivity is the hallmark of true knowledge. In mathematics, $2 + 2 = 4$ irrespective of the personal convictions of the mathematician. In linguistics, a grammatical structure or the meaning of a word are not matters whose accurate description is supposed to depend upon the belief-system of the linguist. Even religious studies, the 'scientific' counterpart of theology, in its scholarly study of particular religions abstracts from the truth-claims of these religions. The ideal professor of religious studies, therefore, is not a religious man or woman. But the ideal professor of Scholastic philosophy is. Perhaps, then, Scholastic thought has no future – at least not in modern academe.

But is it true that personal convictions, and personal faith, necessarily stand

---

14 A caveat is in order here: toward the middle of the thirteenth century it became possible to envisage theology as a primarily theoretical enterprise. Thomas Aquinas, for example, defines theology as primarily speculative in character. See *The story of a great medieval book*, p. 77.

in the way of truth? In order to answer this question, a brief genealogy of the scientific paradigm in philosophy, and in the humanities more generally, will be useful. Philosophy sought refuge in scientific methodology out of frustration over the lack of unity in traditional metaphysics. Since Aristotle, consensus has been regarded as an important criterion of truth; in the *Nicomachean Ethics*, the Philosopher stated, 'For we say that that which everyone thinks really is so: and the man who attacks this belief will hardly have anything more credible to maintain instead.'[15] Indeed, which honest and humble thinker is not seriously troubled if it turns out that his or her views are not shared by many other equally or more intelligent people? Kant was thus troubled, and in the *Critique of Pure Reason* he suggested his famous 'Copernican turn' in philosophy in order to overcome the cacophony of metaphysical systems preceding him. If, instead of attempting to investigate the structures of reality, of the things in themselves, philosophy were to focus upon the structures of the human mind, would such an approach not be bound to lead to consensus? For the structures of the human mind are non-empirical and necessary, allowing for synthetic judgments a priori, just like judgments in logic and the mathematical sciences.[16] As we all know, Kant's dream turned out to be an illusion, so that to this day, philosophy has not managed to gain unity. Indeed, in opposition to Kant's move to bring theoretical philosophy closer to the sciences, it has come under attack for being too dry and removed from the flow of life. Nietzsche compared its edifice of concepts to a columbarium, the place where Romans kept the urns with the ashes of their dead.[17] And Husserl believed that the only way to remedy the confusion of rivalling philosophical systems would be a return to the life-world, in which all science and philosophical reflection are ultimately rooted.[18] Yet Husserl's solution, too, has failed to command universal acceptance. Apparently, his account of the 'things themselves' which we encounter pre-theoretically was already too coloured by his own theoretical presuppositions.

Representatives of the Scholastic tradition in the modern university have long had a tendency to accept the scientific paradigm of philosophy, which, as we just saw, was embraced in an attempt to overcome the theoretical discord among

---

15 Aristotle, *Nicomachean Ethics* X.2, 1172b36–1073a2, trans. in W.D. Ross (ed.), *The works of Aristotle translated into English*, ix (Oxford, 1915). On the history of the *consensus omnium* in ancient and patristic thought, see Klaus Oehler, 'Der *Consensus omnium* als Kriterium der Wahrheit in der antiken Philosophie und der Patristik', *Antike und Abendland* 10 (1961), 103–29; reprinted in the same author's *Antike Philosophie und byzantinisches Mittelalter* (Munich, 1969), pp 234–71. **16** See Immanuel Kant, *Critique of pure reason*, trans. Norman Kemp Smith (Boston & New York, 1965), esp. pp 17–37 (Preface to the second edition). **17** See Friedrich Nietzsche, 'On truth and lies in a nonmoral sense', in Daniel Breazeale (trans. and ed.), *Philosophy and truth: selections from Nietzsche's notebooks of the early 1870s* (Atlantic Highlands, NJ & Hassocks, Sussex, 1979), pp 77–97, at pp 84–5. **18** See Edmund Husserl, *The crisis of European sciences and transcendental phenomenology: an introduction to phenomenological philosophy*, trans. David Carr (Evanston, IL, 1970).

traditional systems of metaphysics. Thus, it was claimed that the connection between the Christian faith and Scholastic Philosophy is accidental, and that Christian thinkers as early as Augustine at least implicitly recognized a division between philosophy and faith, or theology.[19] In this way, it was imagined, neo-Scholasticism would be able to meet modern philosophy on the equal playing field of pure reason. One of the main proponents of this position was Fernand Van Steenberghen, of the Louvain school.[20] In insisting strongly on the autonomy of philosophy in relation to theology and faith, Van Steenberghen was one of the Catholic philosophers to give the clearest expression to what appears to be the official position of the magisterium on this topic. Since the First Vatican Council, and most recently in the encyclical *Fides et ratio*, the Church has been eager to distinguish the 'two orders of knowledge' that philosophy and theology represent.[21] Emphasis upon the autonomy of philosophy recurs several times in *Fides et ratio*.[22]

This position, however, appears to be a classical example of what Michel Foucault has termed '"reverse" discourse': an attempt of a marginalized group to overcome its exclusion from the centre by adopting the concepts of the mainstream.[23] In reality, by renouncing or minimizing its connection with Christianity, the Scholastic tradition undermines one of its greatest strengths – and I mean a strength precisely in the context of the contemporary philosophical landscape. Much of contemporary philosophy has well grasped the impossibility of foundationalism, that is to say, of the belief in an autonomous, self-founding rationality. There is no realm of pure reason separate from all historical, social, political, even physical conditions. Rather, the human being is a whole, and as such always reasons from a particular incarnate standpoint. *Fides et ratio* does not deny this fact. The exercise of reason is embedded in, and in a certain sense never leaves behind, truths that are believed on the strength of tradition.[24] *Fides et ratio* even declares, 'Philosophy [...] is the mirror which reflects the culture of

19 That Augustine implicitly recognized the autonomy of philosophy is argued by Fernand Van Steenberghen, *Introduction à l'étude de la philosophie médiévale* (Louvain & Paris, 1974), pp 333–89, esp. p. 351: 'S. Augustin n'ignore pas que sa "vraie philosophie" est *plus et mieux qu'une philosophie* au sens ordinaire du mot; il pose implicitement l'objet et la méthode d'une philosophie proprement dite, non point isolée, mais autonome, quand il affirme la différence essentielle entre la foi et l'évidence, quand il distingue les vérités qu'on ne peut atteindre que sur l'autorité de Dieu et celles dont la raison humaine peut saisir la nécessité intrinsèque.'   20 See, for example, ibid., pp 78–113.   21 *Fides et ratio* quotes the First Vatican Council in affirming, 'There are two orders of knowledge, distinct not only in their point of departure, but also in their object' (*Fides et ratio*, 53, Vatican translation [Boston, 1998]).   22 See, for instance, ibid., 49: 'A philosophy which did not proceed in the light of reason according to its own principles and methods would serve little purpose. At the deepest level, the autonomy which philosophy enjoys is rooted in the fact that reason is by its nature oriented to truth and is equipped moreover with the means necessary to arrive at truth'; 79: 'philosophy must obey its own rules and be based upon its own principles.'   23 Michel Foucault, *History of sexuality*, i: *An Introduction*, trans. Robert Hurley (New York, 1990), p. 101.   24 See *Fides et ratio*, 31–2.

a people.'²⁵ What the encyclical and the magisterium want to avoid at all costs, however, is that the idea of a universal truth, accessible to human beings by means of reason alone, be abandoned because of the recognition of historical and cultural particularity. The task, then, becomes to show 'how one can reconcile the absoluteness and the universality of truth with the unavoidable historical and cultural conditioning of the formulas which express that truth.'²⁶ Contemporary Christian thinkers have taken up that challenge. Alasdair MacIntyre, for example, has convincingly shown that a conception which views reason as constituted by tradition, and indeed indissociable from it, does not have to lead to relativism. The mistake is to assume that the transcendence of rationality vis-à-vis its conditions is built into its constitution as an essential possession; rather, such transcendence is the *telos* of reason, that is to say, the result of a long historical struggle and an almost eschatological end.²⁷

It is alarming that, while the rationalism which characterizes much of modern thought from Descartes through Hegel may have been left behind in contemporary philosophy, contemporary culture is much slower in repudiating it. Thus, our global economy is still predicated on the assumption that there must be unlimited growth: growth not regulated by any *telos* outside the economic and technological system itself – such as the good of human beings – but propelled relentlessly by the self-referentiality of the Enlightenment notion of progress.²⁸

Scholastic thought, as we have discovered it so far in this paper, does not conceive of itself as an expression of universal reason. It has its rule outside of itself, since it is merely the unfolding and expression of divine wisdom in the medium of human rationality. This medium requires the dialectical relationship between *auctoritas* and *ratio*, which therefore lies at the heart of the Scholastic method. For those who may be appalled by such a claim, and who are perhaps afraid that any thought which traces its lineage to God himself must be of the fanatical kind, it is worth emphasizing that there is no way to *prove* – with the validity of universal reason – what Denys the Carthusian says about the place of Scholasticism in the revelation of wisdom. It makes sense only within the Christian tradition. All thought requires roots in a tradition, but not all thought is rooted in the Christian one. There is warranted assertability, as analytic philosophers would put it, in many other traditions.

25 Ibid., 103. **26** Ibid., 95. **27** See Alasdair MacIntyre, *Whose justice? Which rationality?* (Notre Dame, 1988). **28** On progress as the *telos* of human nature, see Immanuel Kant, 'An answer to the question: "What is Enlightenment?"' in Kant, *Political Writings*, ed. Hans Reiss, trans. H.B. Nisbet, 2nd ed. (Cambridge, 1991), pp 54–60, at p. 57: 'One age cannot enter into an alliance or an oath to put the next age in a position where it would be impossible for it to extend and correct its knowledge [...] or to make any progress whatsoever in enlightenment. This would be a crime against human nature, whose original destiny lies precisely in such progress.'

III

Once Scholastic thinkers, recognizing the rationalist mistake that characterized much of neo-Scholasticism, come to acknowledge that their thought is not the authentic expression of pure reason but of the tradition of Christian wisdom, they are in a position to engage fruitfully some of the fundamental issues in contemporary philosophy. These issues are (1) the sectarianism of contemporary philosophy, (2) its historicism, and (3) its relativism, especially in ethical matters.

(1) By the 'sectarianism' of contemporary philosophy I mean that today's philosophical movement has lost any kind of doctrinal unity. There are not only analytic philosophers, continental philosophers, Thomists, process philosophers, Neo-Platonists, and so on and so forth, but any number of sub-sects within each of these groups. The result is an utterly chaotic philosophical landscape, in which the truths held by a particular thinker can easily appear as nothing but the result of subjective preference. Furthermore, contemporary philosophy has lost the concordist impulse which was so strong in the Scholastic period: the desire to move beyond particular views to a synthesis capable of embracing as many of these particular perspectives as possible. The reason why the desideratum of synthesis has been lost is that synthesis requires faith in the unity of truth. Each word is important here: *faith* in the *unity* of *truth*. For the rationalist who is convinced that he or she has *knowledge* of the unity of truth, which is the identity of pure reason with itself, the effort of synthesis becomes unnecessary: any position that does not satisfy the rationalist's criteria is simply nonsense. This is how Descartes and Kant viewed the philosophical tradition. Hegel's approach is more sophisticated, in that for him, knowledge of the unity of truth is the *telos* of a historical process. Stages in the unfolding of Spirit which precede absolute knowledge can therefore be acknowledged in their limited truth; yet once the *telos* is reached (and Hegel regarded it as having been reached in his own thought and in the Prussian state), no further development is possible.

A relativist who believes that there is an irreducible *multiplicity* of truths – for instance, the truths of different systems of historical a prioris, as in Foucault – cannot meaningfully engage in an attempt to synthesize the incommensurable. Only someone who believes that the truth not only is one but that it is also inexhaustible, that he or she has come to grasp only a limited manifestation of it: such a thinker will seek synthesis. This synthesis will not be devoid of presuppositions, but will be guided by the seeker's limited grasp of the truth: thus, there will be criteria for discerning what can find a place in the synthesis and how discordant voices should be harmonized. The result of such a quest will, in the seeker's own understanding, never be *the* truth, but only a finite approximation to it.

This is, I believe, how the Scholastic tradition has always seen its task. It is because of this self-understanding that Scholastic thought created a large array of intellectual practices aimed at synthesis: collections of 'sentences' (*sententiae*, authoritative statements), distinctions in the meaning of words to uncover nuances in the teaching of important texts, disputations and *quaestiones* to allow for the consideration of the different sides of particular issues, concordances and indices to catalogue intellectual material, diagrams to sketch the outline of systems, and *summae* to offer comprehensive doctrinal syntheses. Not all these intellectual practices will play a role in the future of Scholastic thought: *quaestiones* and *summae*, for example, are no longer current as literary genres. In order to remain faithful to its *Herkunft*, however, Scholastic thought will always be animated by the dynamism of synthesis, endeavouring to grow in constructive dialogue with other ways to approach the one truth.

(2) From the concordist aspect of Scholastic thought, it follows immediately that Scholasticism should have a strong sense of history: since there is a difference between finite truth and the truth itself in its fullness – a tension that cannot be completely reconciled in this life – all synthesis always remains perfectible and hence provisional. As Denys the Carthusian saw it in his Neoplatonically-inspired theology of history, the Scholastic tradition moves through periods of unfolding, in which revealed wisdom is expanded upon, and periods of collection or folding-back, in which the fruits of such expansion are critically reviewed and gathered together. Admittedly, Denys is something of an exception in Scholasticism in recognizing so clearly the role of history, or time, in the quest for truth. In fact, many of the greatest Scholastics lack any kind of developed philosophy or theology of history – which is somewhat surprising, to say the least, given the connection between Scholastic thought and the Christian faith. This is not the occasion to enter into a detailed discussion of the reasons for the ahistorical nature of much of Scholastic thought. It makes sense to assume, though, that the influence of the static, essentialist world-view of ancient Greece played a role in this congealing of the intellectual expression of Christianity. Aristotle, in particular, deliberately excluded history from the domain of *episteme*, because for him, science had to deal with necessary causes, not contingent events. Aristotle's world, consequently, was a world of essences which, ultimately, could not change at all: 'a man begets a man'. In the final analysis, any change is a process in which an essential core perpetuates itself.

Scholastic thought, therefore, needs to be saved from itself, as it were, with regard to the question of history, not only because Scholasticism needs the historical dimension in order to be able to function as an authentic expression of the Christian tradition;[29] Scholastic thought must also not close itself off from one of the main insights of modern philosophy since Hegel: the insight that truth is inextricably connected with time. After Hegel, Nietzsche, Heidegger, but especially after Foucault's detailed analyses of the ways in which truth,

---

29 As *Fides et ratio*, 11 declares, 'God's revelation is [...] immersed in time and history'.

reality, and human identity are constituted in different historical epochs – after these developments what its critics now call the 'metaphysics of presence' has lost its credibility.[30] The most compelling contemporary Christian thinkers do not attempt to evade this insight; rather – like Jean-Luc Marion, for instance – they endeavour to revive metaphysical enquiry without recourse to the notions of substance and being, which are so closely connected with the Aristotelian, static vision of reality. The traditions of Christian Neo-Platonism and negative theology appear to be better suited to meet the challenges of our post-metaphysical age.[31]

The reappropriation of Scholastic thought could profit considerably from the insights of a book that is justly acclaimed in medievalist circles but has not enjoyed a broader reception since its publication fifty years ago. In 1959, a young medievalist by the name of Joseph Ratzinger published a study entitled, *The Theology of History in St. Bonaventure*.[32] The study was the author's *Habilitationsschrift*, the second dissertation necessary in Germany to obtain a position as university professor. Yet it is unusually short for a *Habilitationsschrift* – just 163 pages of main text – while its composition shows signs of haste: the book begins with some highly technical chapters whose import becomes fully intelligible only towards the end of the work, where the author finally provides the general context that enables the reader to situate all the details. These problems are not a coincidence: the book was in fact composed in a rush, representing the author's efforts to salvage his academic career with an abridged *Habilitationsschrift* after the original version had been rejected.[33]

Joseph Ratzinger is of course now Pope Benedict XVI, and it may be astonishing to some that this learned and scholarly man experienced such difficulties

30 Such indebtedness to traditional metaphysics may be the reason why the attempts of an earlier generation of Christian thinkers to incorporate modern elements into their thought are no longer attracting much attention – with the exception, perhaps, of Edith Stein. For an impressive overview of this 'older' neo-Scholastic movement in the twentieth century, see Emerich Coreth SJ, Walter M. Neidl, and Georg Pfligersdorffer (eds), *Christliche Philosophie im katholischen Denken des 19. und 20. Jahrhunderts*, ii: *Rückgriff auf scholastisches Erbe* (Graz et al., 1988). I reviewed this book in some detail in *Irish Philosophical Journal* 6:1 (1989), 170–8. Recently, a French selection of some of the most significant chapters has become available: Philibert Secrétan (ed. and trans.), *La philosophie chrétienne d'inspiration catholique: Constats et controverses: Positions actuelles* (Fribourg [Switzerland], 2006).   31 I have sketched a brief introduction to Marion's thought in 'Postmodern philosophy and J.-L. Marion's Eucharistic realism', in Maurice Hogan SSC & James McEvoy (eds), *The mystery of faith: reflections on the encyclical Ecclesia de Eucharistia* (Blackrock, Co. Dublin, 2005), pp 224–44; reprinted in Peter M. Candler, Jr., and Conor Cunningham (eds), *Transcendence and phenomenology* (London, 2007), pp 84–110. 32 See Joseph Ratzinger, *Die Geschichtstheologie des hl. Bonaventura* (Munich, 1959); English translation: *The theology of history in St. Bonaventure*, trans. Zachary Hayes OFM (Chicago, 1971).   33 On the circumstances of Ratzinger's *Habilitation*, see Joseph Ratzinger, *Milestones: memoirs 1927–1977*, trans. Erasmo Leiva-Merikakis (San Francisco, 1998), pp 103–14: 'The drama of my *Habilitation* and the Freising years.'

in his academic career. The truth of the matter, however, is that the pope's *Habilitationsschrift* was too audacious for its principal reader, the conservative theologian Michael Schmaus. For what Ratzinger attempted in this work was to draw conclusions for the life of the Church from a re-examination of the Scholastic theology of history. After Schmaus's rejection, the contemporary portion was omitted, leaving the historical material as a kind of torso. As Ratzinger writes in the foreword to the American edition of the abridged version of the book, he was troubled by the implication that the Catholic tradition was too static, lacking the sense of the value of history and time which must be part of authentic Christianity:

> When I began the preparatory work for this study in the fall of 1953, one of the questions which stood in the foreground of concern within German-speaking, Catholic theological circles was the question of the relation of salvation-history to metaphysics. This was a problem which arose above all from contacts with Protestant theology, which, since the time of Luther, has tended to see in metaphysical thought a departure from the specific claim of the Christian faith, which directs man not simply to the Eternal but to the God who acts in time and history. Here questions of quite diverse character and of different orders arose. [...] Has not the 'Hellenization' of Christianity, which attempted to overcome the scandal of the particular by a blending of faith and metaphysics, led to a development in a false direction? Has it not created a static style of thought which cannot do justice to the dynamism of the biblical style?[34]

Ratzinger's answer to these questions was an attempt to retrieve the authentically Scholastic and unquestionably Catholic theology of history which he found in the writings of St Bonaventure. Ratzinger showed that, if in his later life Bonaventure became increasingly critical of Aristotle's thought, the reason behind this desire to keep a clear distance between the Philosopher and the Christian tradition lay precisely in the theology of history. In Aristotle's doctrine according to which the forms return upon themselves in an eternal circle, the Seraphic Doctor recognized, in Benedict's words, 'the sign of the Beast',[35] 'the very essence of the apocalyptic monster'.[36] Against the Aristotelian error and in line with the historical character of the Christian faith, Bonaventure formulated a theology of history in which time and truth are intimately connected. In this dynamic theology, the meaning of Scripture, for example, 'is advancing in a steady growth through history; and this growth is not yet closed'.[37] Thus, 'the theologian cannot abstract from history in his explanation of Scripture; neither from the past nor from the future'.[38]

34 Ratzinger, *The theology of history*, p. xv. (I have corrected the punctuation in the translation of this passage.) 35 Ibid., p. 147. 36 Ibid., p. 148. 37 Ibid., p. 9 38 Ibid.

Let us remember that Denys the Carthusian has a very similar vision of the nature of the Scholastic tradition. It is important for the future of Scholastic thought to explore the intellectual resources of thinkers such as Bonaventure and Denys. Their ideas enable the Christian tradition to respond meaningfully to the challenges that stem from the philosophies of history which are at the core of the modern and post-modern philosophical projects.[39]

(3) In his last homily before his election to the papacy, delivered to the College of Cardinals on 18 April 2005, the future Pope Benedict identified relativism as one of the gravest dangers to the Christian faith in the modern world. He castigated what he called the 'dictatorship of relativism that does not recognize anything as definitive and whose ultimate goal consists only of one's own ego and desires'.[40] His text includes a familiar expression of despair with the sectarianism of modern thought:

> How many winds of doctrine have we known in recent decades, how many ideological currents, how many ways of thinking? The small boat of the thought of many Christians has often been tossed about by these waves – flung from one extreme to another: from Marxism to liberalism, even to libertinism; from collectivism to radical individualism; from atheism to a vague religious mysticism; from agnosticism to syncretism; and so forth. Every day new sects spring up [...].[41]

As we have seen, this sectarianism is not a problem only for Christian thought, but for modern thought more generally. Various attempts to overcome this problem, such as Kant's 'Copernican turn' or Husserl's return to the life-world, have not proven successful. As a result, much of contemporary thought has capitulated in the face of the multiplicity of irreconcilable claims to truth; some thinkers – Foucault perhaps being the most prominent example – have explicitly embraced the principle of the multiplicity of truths and attempted to justify it philosophically. The fact that such a position is problematic is sometimes less clear on the theoretical plane, but it is always thrown into high relief by the ethical dilemmas to which it gives rise. Foucault was unable and unwilling to pronounce himself on the superiority of modern practices of incarceration over against pre-modern forms of criminal justice, which typically took the form of public torture. Heidegger was not only seduced by Hitler's Nazi ideology but failed to recognize the gravity of his error even decades after the fall of the Nazi regime. His ethics of authenticity, brilliantly as it is presented in *Being and Time*,

---

39 Benedict himself has sketched the outlines of such a response in his recent encyclical, *Saved in hope (Spe salvi)* (Vatican City & San Francisco, 2007), esp. nos. 16–23: "The transformation of Christian faith-hope in the modern age."   40 Joseph Cardinal Ratzinger, "Homily *Pro Eligendo Romano Pontifice*," *Common Knowledge* 13:2–3 (2007), 451–5, at 453.   41 Ibid., 452–3.

apparently failed to furnish him with the kind of ethical compass necessary to recognize evil for what it is.

Nevertheless, Pope Benedict's critique of relativism has elicited a vigorous response in secular academe. The journal *Common Knowledge* devoted the bulk of a double issue to a series of articles defending relativism against the pope's critique.[42] Many of the articles pointed to the virtues of the relativist outlook, especially the fact that it promotes tolerance. Gianni Vattimo, for example, writes, 'To begin a dialogue by acknowledging, "You may be right, I may be wrong, so let's talk", risks a weakening of my identity just far enough to undermine my willingness to die in war or as a martyr, or to kill, or to accept whatever extreme sacrifice may be demanded [...].'[43] It could be argued that relativism is a necessary condition for the existence of our post-modern, multi-cultural societies. Since we no longer live in medieval Christendom, but in the United States or in the Europe of the twenty-first century, we are faced with the task of co-existing in our everyday lives with people from completely different cultural backgrounds and religious faiths. To deny that the world-view of these 'others' could make sense in some way, or from some point of view, does not appear as a recipe for success in promoting mutual understanding and creating peaceful societies. On the other hand, several of the contributors to the relevant issue of *Common Knowledge* also admit that full-blown relativism is a deeply unsatisfactory intellectual position, as well as destroying the basis for any truly meaningful debate. In Jeffrey Stout's words, 'If the truth of all judgments were relative to the opinions of those issuing the judgments, then we would have nothing to argue about.'[44]

Given, therefore, the philosophical as well as socio-political importance of the matter, a nuanced attitude with regard to the relativist challenge must be part of the future of Scholastic thought. As we have already seen in discussing the Scholastic response to the sectarianism of modern thought, the Scholastic tradition possesses the intellectual tools that are necessary to put relativism in its place. Anchored in the Christian faith, which it embraces not as a result of scientific proof but of a contingent personal commitment, Scholastic thought has criteria to judge the claims of other philosophical viewpoints. To the extent that these contain truths compatible with the core of Christianity, they can become part of an open-ended synthesis.

Moreover, there need be no diametrical opposition, it seems to me, between a certain kind of moderate relativism and the Scholastic commitment to absolute truth. In the Scholastic tradition, truth is an analogous term. To be sure, Scholasticism acknowledges *the* truth of divine wisdom, which is absolute. But

---

42 See *Common Knowledge* 13:2–3 (2007), 214–455. **43** Gianni Vattimo, 'A "dictatorship of relativism"?', *Common Knowledge* 13:2–3 (2007), 214–18, at 217. **44** Jeffrey Stout, 'A house founded in the sea: is democracy a dictatorship of relativism?' *Common Knowledge* 13:2–3 (2007), 385–403, at 389.

then there are the limited truths of which the human intellect is capable. What Scholasticism avoids, however, is a chaos of truths competing against each other. It does so through the all-important concept of hierarchy. When Aquinas declares, in the *Quaestiones disputatae de veritate*, that we must distinguish between two truths, the *veritas rerum* and the *veritas praedicationis*, he makes it quite clear that the first applies to God and the second to creatures. There is no confusion about which of the two is primary.[45] When Augustine allows for a multiplicity of meanings in scriptural texts, and even goes so far as to maintain that the commandment to 'increase and multiply' refers to the multiplication of biblical interpretations,[46] he has a standard on the basis of which to judge whether an interpretation is legitimate or not; for all allegorical interpretations are subject to test by passages that have to be taken literally.[47] And when Bonaventure states that there are different forms of knowledge, from the basic arts and crafts to the wisdom of Scripture, he leaves no doubt that the theological way to truth is the highest one.[48] In other words, the Scholastic tradition would be misunderstood if it were considered to be a tradition of rigid uniformity. There is a lot of room for the recognition of various truths at different levels.

IV

Throughout this paper I have treated Scholastic thought as a term covering both philosophy and theology. Insisting that Scholastic thought must be grasped in its historical development as part of the Christian tradition and that, in view of this historical reality, Scholastic thought has a future only if it remains firmly attached to that tradition, I have not made an explicit distinction between Scholastic philosophy and theology. I have quoted a commentary upon Peter Lombard's *Sentences* – a theology textbook – to provide evidence for my interpretation of the nature of Scholastic thought. I have been critical of attempts to dissociate reason from its cultural context (which, in the case of Scholastic rationality, is primarily religious in nature) and so to regard it as autonomous. I have pointed to a certain ambivalence in the Church's teaching on this matter: *Fides et ratio* is, on the one hand, unambiguous in supporting a rigorous distinction between philosophy and theology; on the other hand, the document recognizes that to free philosophy from its cultural circumstances is a task, rather

---

45 See Thomas Aquinas, *Disputed Questions on Truth*, q. 4, art. 6, c. For commentary, see my book, *Omne ens est aliquid. Introduction à la lecture du "système" philosophique de saint Thomas d'Aquin* (Louvain & Paris, 1996), pp 72–93.   46 See Augustine, *Confessions*, Book XIII, chap. xxiv (35–37).   47 See Augustine, *On Christian teaching*, Book II, 15: 'Virtually nothing is unearthed from these obscurities which cannot be found quite plainly expressed somewhere else' (trans. R.P.H. Green [Oxford, 1997], p. 33).   48 See Bonaventure, *On the reduction of the arts to theology*, trans. Zachary Hayes OFM (St Bonaventure, NY, 1996).

than a *fait accompli*, just as 'every truth attained is but a step toward that fullness of truth which will appear with the final revelation of God.'[49]

My positions are not uncontroversial. The Italian medievalist Riccardo Quinto recently criticized me for extending Grabmann's analysis of the Scholastic method to philosophy; such an approach seems to Quinto 'to be irremediably destined to fail'.[50] It is necessary, therefore, that I be clearer on how I see the relationship between philosophy and theology within Scholastic thought.

First, another word about history. In the Scholastic tradition, the distinction between philosophy and theology developed only gradually. In the thirteenth century, the institutional division between the arts and the theology faculties made it possible to identify a thinker for the first time unambiguously as an 'artist' (that is to say, a philosopher) as distinct from a theologian. Some masters at the universities now began to associate themselves deliberately with philosophy over against theology.[51] Disciplines such as logic and speculative grammar grew in importance. Christian thought, however, continued to be primarily the domain of theologians, with few exceptions (Ockham was one of them, never having become a theology master). These theologians saw no reason to distinguish their 'philosophy' neatly from their 'theology' – not even Thomas Aquinas did, though he is often used as the prime example of a Schoolman who exhibited a clear methodological awareness of the difference between the two disciplines. To be sure, Aquinas laid out the theoretical basis for an autonomous philosophy *à la* Aristotle ... only to continue composing theological works and, outside his commentaries on Aristotle, practically no philosophy. My point is this: the notion of a philosophy conceived in harmony with Christian theology, yet completely independent from the latter in its principles and methods, acquired significance only in the modern secular context, in which philosophy defined itself as autonomous rational enquiry freed from the shackles of authority and tradition. To adopt this notion of philosophy carries the risk of importing, unwittingly, profoundly secular conceptions of rationality into the Scholastic tradition.

This is not to say, however, that philosophy and theology are identical, nor that they should be. A Scholastic theologian is a thinker who brings reason (*ratio*) to bear upon the Christian faith, which is defined through the authority (*auctoritas*) of Scripture and the tradition, including the magisterium. The questions which the theologian asks arise fairly directly from the scriptural material: Who is God? What is the relationship between the Old and the New Testaments? What does it mean for the human being to be made in God's

---

49 *Fides et ratio*, 2. **50** Quinto, *Scholastica*, p. 341 n. 30. **51** See, for example, the following book on Siger of Brabant: Ruedi Imbach & François-Xavier Putallaz, *Profession: philosophe. Siger de Brabant* (Paris, 1997).

'image'? What is original sin? What is salvation? What is the meaning of the Incarnation? How should we understand the sacraments? What is the relationship between Scripture and the tradition? And so on and so forth. To address these questions, the Scholastic theologian will draw upon other, non-Christian traditions (such as Greek philosophy or modern history), especially when he or she is faced with what MacIntyre has called an 'epistemological crisis' – a conceptual aporia that cannot be resolved with the intellectual resources of the Christian tradition itself.[52] The Scholastic philosopher, on the other hand, does not reflect upon Scripture; he or she endeavours to apply Christian principles to a philosophical understanding of the world and the self. Like the theologian, the philosopher proceeds by reading and interpreting texts, and understanding reality through them; yet the set of texts is different. In addition to Christian thought as it has unfolded over the centuries, there was a tradition of philosophy before Christianity, and there is a post-Christian tradition of philosophy. All of them need to be taken seriously for the insights that they offer. They compel the Christian thinker to formulate answers to questions that are further removed from Scripture than those of the theologian: What is the structure of the human world? What are the principles which constitute that world: substance and accidents? essence and existence? a priori categories of the human mind? or is it perhaps time that 'gives' being? What, then, is truth? What is the goal of human society, and what kind of government will best ensure that this goal can be reached? But the Christian thinker will go further: How do these questions, and specifically the different answers that can be given to them, relate to the faith? To what extent do particular philosophical positions contradict the principles of the Christian tradition or help refine them? The list is of course open-ended.

My claim, then, is this: the difference between philosophy and theology is not primarily one of principles and methods, but of the constellations of texts ('authorities') on which the two disciplines draw. These different constellations, which have grown historically and continue to develop, suggest different sets of questions for philosophy and theology; they imply different methods as well. The reflections of the Scholastic Philosopher will take place at a greater distance from Scripture because of the role that non-scriptural texts play in the philo-sophical tradition. The Scholastic Philosopher may employ a wide range of different methods, from Platonic and Neoplatonic dialectic through Kantian transcendental deduction to phenomenological reduction. Just like theology, however, philosophy is ultimately founded on the authority of texts and on trust in the people who guarantee the truth of these texts. That is the meaning of tradition. As *Fides et ratio* puts it,

---

52 On the notion of epistemological crisis, see MacIntyre, *Whose justice?*, pp 361–5.

there are in the life of a human being many more truths which are simply believed than truths which are acquired by way of personal verification. [...] This means that the human being – the one who seeks the truth – is also the one who lives by belief. In believing, we entrust ourselves to the knowledge acquired by other people. This suggests an important tension. On the one hand, the knowledge acquired through belief can seem an imperfect form of knowledge, to be perfected gradually through personal accumulation of evidence; on the other hand, belief is often humanly richer than mere evidence, because it involves an interpersonal relationship and brings into play not only a person's capacity to know but also the deeper capacity to entrust oneself to others, to enter into a relationship with them which is intimate and enduring.[53]

The tension of which the encyclical speaks is precisely the tension between *auctoritas* and *ratio*, which pervades, in different ways, both philosophy and theology as long as they are conceived Scholastically.[54]

---

53 *Fides et ratio*, 31–2.   54 This paper has greatly profited from discussions with the participants of the conference on 'The Irish contribution to European Scholastic thought'. I wish to thank, in particular, the Revd Professor James McEvoy and Mr Gaven Kerr.

Values, limits and metaphysics[1]

JAMES McEVOY

I do not suppose it is customary, still less is it obligatory, for an inaugural lecture to begin with a bull; but we are in Ireland, and provided it does not interact too indecorously with the sacred cows we're accused of pasturing, I see no harm in it. Ireland is a land, by no means the only one of its kind, in which there are two of everything, barring nations and the things there are three or more of, such as loyalties, parties and taxes. In our Arts Faculty at Queen's, in true shamrock style, we have a philosophical community of three leaves: Philosophy, Scholastic Philosophy, and, the most recent addition, History and Philosophy of Science. There are of course departments or schools of philosophy in every university throughout the world, and the history and philosophy of science is, thankfully, no longer a rarity, although it is a relative newcomer to the university scene. And it might be added, in institutions of higher learning which do not feel themselves bound as ours apparently does to departmentalize knowledge and research in a way that sets up a series of sovereignties within faculties, philosophical interests and predilections of the most divergent kind exist and subsist under a single roof; I found it so at the university of Munich. But Scholastic Philosophy is, as the title of a university department at any rate, unique in the English-speaking world, and hence in a situation which calls for explanation.

THE DEPARTMENT OF SCHOLASTIC PHILOSOPHY

Now it is not the case that the tradition of philosophical reflection in which my predecessors stood, and in which my colleagues and I were nurtured, is one that was invented in all its parts just for the benefit of Queen's; as an indentifiable set of philosophical interests and tendencies, Scholastic Philosophy is something that possesses a rich intellectual heritage, traceable (although with lengthy inter-ruptions) back to the medieval schools, and in important respects beyond them again, back across the great divide to the ancient world of Greece and Rome. If

1 An Inaugural Lecture delivered before the Queen's University of Belfast on 17 November 1976 and published by QUB in 1977. The text of the lecture is reprinted here with a small number of changes including sub-headings but without the original footnotes. To have carried out a systematic revision of words relating to linguistic gender would have altered the character of the writing and its historicity.

Scholastic Philosophy is unique as the title of a department, that is not because Belfast has shown unusual philosophical fertility and produced a school all of its own, but because Queen's has incorporated a tendency of thought that in certain other lands and in different cultural situations constitutes departments or faculties of philosophy.

Some degree of justification for a department which goes back to within a couple of years of the foundation of this university may fittingly be sought in the attributes and achievements of successive generations of its teachers and students. It is with infinitely more than the customary degree of formal courtesy that I wish to pay tribute to my predecessors. It cannot happen very frequently in the history of university departments that we find three successive generations of heads of department together, as happens this evening at my *Vesperies* to the great joy of all of us; and it is in a spirit of reverence to the generations, and especially the oldest, that I remark that none of the heads in question has balded, bowed or withered. Indeed, there still remains more than a trace of that rusty hue which earned Arthur Ryan his soubriquet among his students. It is an ominous thought for a new appointee that the most signal way in which he might distinguish himself from the tradition of his intellectual forbears would be to lose all his hair before he attains to the age of academic discretion (or, much later, no doubt, ecclesiastical), whenever that fine liminal moment may be. If the value of the philosophical life required a protreptic discourse or a practical exemplification, one would only have to point to the vitality and youthfulness of Arthur Ryan and Theodore Crowley, for both of whom philosophical reflection seems to have discovered the highway to *Tír na nÓg*.

Monsignor Ryan inherited the lecturership in Scholastic Philosophy from its first holder, Denis O'Keeffe, who relinquished it to move to the chair of Ethics and Politics in University College, Dublin in 1925. It is almost a sufficient tribute to his remarkable powers to say that he managed to teach single-handed a course of philosophical studies which included both pass and honours degrees in almost all the branches of the older Scholastic curriculum; yet this is only the heading on his bill of distinction, for during the twenty years of his tenure of the post he travelled widely, lecturing on the most diverse subjects including music and art appreciation, and broadcasting: we are fortunate to have his Radio Eireann lectures on *Perennial Philosophers* preserved in printed form. In his case, it is not too much to say that the man outweighs the parts he has played, for those who are privileged to know him well will agree unanimously that no man carries so many various accomplishments more lightly; his wit, gaiety and kindness are the face of a personality that is quite free from self-importance. Small wonder that he has become a legend for the generation of students whom he held spellbound in the little attic of a Queen's tower, then one of the most atmospheric rooms in the entire Lanyon building.

I turn now to my old master and friend, Professor Emeritus Theodore

Crowley. Coming after Arthur Ryan, he inherited an amount of goodwill within the university even before he had had the opportunity to merit it; twenty-five years later, with the Department expanded in numbers of undergraduates, postgraduates and staff, I realize with admiration just how well my predecessor invested the talent given him. He was fortunate in assuming his post at a time when the university was beginning that spectacular expansion which has only recently slackened; there were during the fifties and sixties resources to hand such as would have been undreamt of in the thirties. He was fortunate too in his colleagues over the years, above all in Dr Cahal Daly, lecturer and later reader in the department, whose wide reading and numerous publications have left such a stamp on its recent history, developing as they did a side of its work that has become well-established, namely an interest in contemporary French thought.

If I paid Professor Crowley the full academic and personal tribute I would like to I should have to use up this entire hour. I trust I shall not embarrass him too much if I underline only three things, and these briefly. He brought with him from Louvain to Queen's the highest standards of academic honesty and objectivity. Unlike a number of academic personalities who seem to exhaust all their rationality within the tiny area of their research, Professor Crowley thought deeply and personally about standards and criteria in university life. His first love was excellence and honesty in scholarship, and he had a spontaneous recognition of these qualities in fields far beyond his own medieval one. He knew the meaning of justice in the university as in life; justice for foe as for friend, and above all justice for the unknown candidate for a post or an award. The university recognized his academic distinction in conferring first a readership on him and then, in 1968, a personal chair, later to become an established chair. But the finest tribute to Professor Crowley is the Department itself, which manifests the influence of a head who spent such a large proportion of his energies in encouraging budding scholars. Each present member of staff in the Department owes at the very least a major portion of his philosophical interests to the guidance of the old master. Theodore encouraged the young partly out of a deep concern for the future of the institution and the society he served, but more so still simply because he loves young people, and because he is just the man he is: generous, confiding, enthusiastic and inspiring. The Department, indeed the Faculty of Arts and the Faculty of Theology on which he served, owe him more than can be said.

Before I end this praise of our famous men, I feel it proper to refer to an aspect of their achievement that belongs indeed principally to them, but in a measure to all who have taught in the Department, and indeed to several generations of its students. It is a matter of historical fact that the two lectureships in Scholastic Philosophy and Celtic were established at Queen's in order to attract the loyalty of the Catholic community in the North to the new institution. The wisdom of that act did not go unquestioned at the outset, for in 1908 the force generated both here and in England by three generations of profound dispute concerning higher education in Ireland was far from being spent; it is only within recent years, indeed one might say months, that a large measure of reorganization of third-level education in Ireland as a whole has become in a measure feasible. However, in the case in point, the counsel that prevailed has proved its wisdom, for Queen's owes it in large measure to these two departments that the community which was to be thrust into a minority situation by the Government of Ireland Act of 1920 nevertheless established and maintained an identification with its local university that was to endure and even strengthen throughout the long political eclipse that awaited it. In retrospect, the destiny of the two departments has been no less than historic, for it has been the signal merit of Queen's to win respect and affection from both northern communities in a measure that no other institution in Northern Ireland can boast.

That being said, it is no less opportune to draw attention to three phases in the evolution of Scholastic Philosophy at Queen's. If the days are long since gone when the students in the Department were mostly aspiring clergymen, the period in which it managed to attract its student population from the minority community alone have likewise happily become a memory, for it now draws its students from three faculties, namely Social Sciences and Theology as well as Arts. I have every confidence that this new, welcome phase will prove to be the most challenging and enriching yet.

THE ORIGINS OF SCHOLASTIC PHILOSOPHY

But what of the subject itself? For a university department is not a piece of social engineering; any value it has to the university world and the life of the human community derives from the intrinsic worth of the academic discipline it pursues and the ideal it aims at embodying; achievements of any other kind can only be of an incidental nature. In a philosophical discipline especially, each succeeding generation must learn to think, and think its own thoughts, if only because the inquiring mind rests ill-content with acquired, habitual understanding and desires to know and to learn, beyond what has been discovered.

How is one to describe the subject of this chair? Of the two words in its title, the second is doubtless the more problematic, for throughout the history of western philosophy many of the most acrimonious disputes and divisions of loyalty among schools can be traced back to a difference about what philosophy is or should be, what sort of problems are real ones and how the philosopher can help to attack them. The adjective 'Scholastic' however, as qualifying 'philosophy', points us in the direction of a school, a tradition of philosophical inquiry, which has grown up around a number of central interests. In answering the question therefore I intend to look in the first place at the historical matrix which germinated the Scholastic movement; and from these observations I shall attempt to draw out a personal view of what this Scholastic style in philosophy, one tradition or school among others both in past and present, seems to me to be.

HISTORIOGRAPHY

The Scholastic movement grew in the nascent universities of medieval Europe as a revival, first of logical questions, then in due course of philosophy as such. If I refer to it as a single movement, I must nevertheless admit that Scholasticism is not easy to delineate, and the closer one comes to it in research the more one hesitates to sketch its nature in a few strokes. A cursory glance at its modern historiography confirms what I say, for several of its historians – and not the least endowed – suggested characterizations which did not answer the case. Prantl, in his *Geschichte der Logik* (1855–70, 4 vols), regarded the philosophical activity of the medieval schools as centering on the problem of universals, but this is taking the part for the whole; though it was influential for several generations, his view was too incomplete to give satisfaction. Franz Ehrle (1845–1934) proposed a thesis of more durable design: Scholastic thought he considered a harmonious synthesis of Aristotelianism and the Christian tradition; its philosophical dimension relied principally on the former and its theological side of course on the latter, although using Aristotle in a purely instrumental way. The value of this view was, however, seriously weakened by Ehrle himself, for he maintained throughout his academic career, well into this century therefore, that the sharpest rivalry in the thirteenth-century schools was between Augustinians and Aristotelians, and he considered Aquinas to be both the leader of the Aristotelian revival and the victor in the dispute. The difficulty can be stated as a dilemma: either Scholastic thought cannot be defined as Aristotelian, or many medieval thinkers cannot be considered Scholastics. So far as I know, Ehrle never succeeded in escaping from this dilemma, which he may not have seen very clearly himself.

In the following generation two of the greatest historians of the medieval period, Ch. Baeumker of Munich (1853–1924) and Maurice De Wulf of Louvain (1867–1947), moved towards a definition of Scholasticism in terms of its content, arguing that the Schoolmen all agreed, at least until 1320 or so, in accepting a considerable number of basic truths, a common patrimony or *Gemeingut* derived from the ancient world and the Christian faith. De Wulf used the idea of a Scholastic synthesis and included in its scope such ideas as the existence of God, his creative action, the worth of human personality, the reality of the supernatural and the objectivity of human knowledge. Once again, the objections were overwhelming and came from different directions; the synthesis outlined by De Wulf is not a Scholastic one merely, but a Christian one that holds true of Christian theology in any period of its history, and even at the present; and even granted that all the Scholastics (save a few whose works were destroyed) believed in the existence of God, not all the medieval doctors accepted that his existence is either self-evident or strictly demonstrable, something that surely indicates a central philosophical disagreement.

The progress of scholarly research over the last forty years or so has demolished the idea that medieval Scholasticism was a monolithic system, by pointing insistently to the diversity of influences, currents and schools within it. Almost all the philosophies of the ancient world contributed to the philosophical thought of the medieval schools. The Greek and Latin Church Fathers were read also, not only for their theological inspiration but for such philosophical ideas and arguments as they had developed or borrowed from Stoic and Neoplatonist sources. The philosophers of Judaism and Islam were known and respected by most medieval thinkers after 1200 or so. The result was a tapestry of currents and ideas in the Latin west, as young masters in the arts faculties applied their minds to problems of logic, of nature, of ethics and metaphysics, while their older colleagues in theology struggled to apply their philosophical grounding in tackling issues like free will, the basis of obligation, certainty, the nature of the soul and its faculties, the provability of God's existence, and the attributes of being. It was among the theologians especially that the most original attempts at weaving philosophical discussions together into a more systematic form were to be found; it is worthy of note that the leading schools of thought from about AD 1280 onwards formed around the memory of the greatest theological figures, Bonaventure, Thomas, Scotus and Occam; and in each case the philosophies on which these schools took their stance were embedded in commentaries on Aristotle or theological works, to a greater extent than in strictly philosophical treatises. The distinction between philosophical and theological method was universally accepted, but in practice and in teaching the Schoolmen, understandably, felt free to interrelate the two disciplines with the greatest freedom.

The word 'Scholasticism', therefore, shares something of the elusiveness of descriptions such as 'romantic', 'liberal' or 'humanistic'; most of us use them confidently enough and feel we know what they mean. They are in that category of words which are frequently employed for effect – and there is always a multitude of people, even some in universities, for whom a little knowledge is a dangerous thing to be without. I think, however, that the character of medieval Scholasticism can be suggested if we place it as a cultural phenomenon within the whole culture of a period, and are prepared to risk a few generalizations and incur consequently a small degree of academic abuse.

LATIN SCHOLASTICISM

Scholasticism as a whole, both the philosophical and the theological sides, was pursued in a single language, medieval Latin, in a small number of university centres of international character, and chiefly in the faculties of arts and theology. Its practitioners shared a language in a broader sense than just the Latin tongue: each could recognize what the other was talking about, he knew where the vocabulary came from and something of how it had developed. They all shared a heritage; each one listened to the past with attention and respect, before explaining just how completely the philosophers of antiquity agreed with himself rather than with certain anonymous dunces in the neighbouring faculty or university. The family of literary forms they used was of limited range: commentaries on ancient texts, treatises on specific problems, or questions within a given area of interest. But above all, the Schoolmen were all Christians. They felt a need to understand how reason and its products stand with reference to Christian truths: granted that human reason is capable of knowing and desires to know concerning the cosmos and man's place in the order of things, does what reason told the Greeks of old, and presumably all men, agree on the whole with God's word? How much of the truth accepted on divine authority does rational, methodical inquiry manage to reach? To what extent can pure reason offer some support to fundamental Christian beliefs? It is evident that thinkers disagreed in the answers they gave to such questions – hence the impossibility of assigning any specific content of truths to Scholastic Philosophy in its medieval development; but they all, whether more intellectualist like Aquinas and Henry of Ghent, or more sceptical, like Scotus and Occam, accepted the fairness of the questions, and even felt their inevitability. I would claim therefore that one dominant characteristic of the medieval period which helps to characterize its philosophies is this non-philosophical or extra-philosophical one: the need felt by its practitioners to relate philosophy to religious belief. And I think it fair to stretch the claim a little farther: as philosophers, these thinkers thought it incumbent upon them to examine with special attention just the sort of questions one would expect any Christian with deep intellectual interests to tackle; and these questions which their culture posed to them in a peculiarly pervasive way tended to come to the forefront of their attention – which is not to say that their answers were all in agreement or were predictable from the outset, nor that they did not feel free to speculate about issues that were quite unrelated to religious belief, out of sheer curiosity and love of intellectual adventure. Historians of science, for instance, have come in recent times to recognize in the speculative play of some notable fourteenth-century minds an important stage in the early preparation of the scientific revolution.

ISLAMIC AND JEWISH SCHOLASTICISMS

It is instructive at this point to permit ourselves a sidelong glance at medieval Islam and Judaism. In both of these cultures recognizable Scholasticisms are to be found that serve as an interesting historical point of comparison for the Latin movement that came in their wake and was under their influence. The *falâsifa* of Islam devoted close and creative study over a period of three centuries to the Greek achievement in physics, mathematics, metaphysics and ethics, and they tried in various ways to base general views of man, matter, spirit and being upon Greek principles. At the same time these Arabic writers felt obliged to relate their philosophical views to the very heart and source of their entire native culture, namely the Koranic revelation. Most of these thinkers faithfully and submissively adhered to their religious faith; some of them, such as Al-Gazzâlî, were philosophers only to the extent of using philosophical concepts and argumentation to expose the errors of the ancients or to 'refute the refutation' of faith proposed by certain dissenters from within Islam itself. But even the latter attached a special importance to issues wherein Aristotle or Plotinus disagreed with Koranic truth, as for instance on the freedom and omnipotence of Allah or the One, the spirituality and immortality of the human soul, the non-eternity of the world, personal identity and responsibility for action; and even Averroës, the most unrepentant rationalist of this tradition, proved eager to demonstrate that philosophical truth is related in a positive fashion to the Koranic faith, as being the abstract truth of which unsophisticated belief is the faithful but too-concrete expression, and theology the symbolic distortion.

Medieval Judaism likewise saw the emergence of a philosophical tradition, and produced two major though unequal figures in Solomon Ibn Gabirol and Rabbi Moses Maimonides. The work of the latter in particular, though it evoked bitter opposition in orthodox circles and was actually delated to the French inquisition by orthodox Jews, is the product of a great philosophical intelligence committed to reflecting upon metaphysical questions of a kind largely prompted by the Jewish faith. As a recognisably Jewish philosopher, Maimonides has not had his equal in history until our own times, which have seen in Martin Buber, and still more perhaps in Emmanuel Levinas, the present head of the Jewish Institute in Paris, an original philosophical contribution deriving its inspiration from central religious themes of Judaism: the infinite and the neighbour, suffering, hope and transcendence.

MONOTHEISM AND METAPHYSICS

These three Scholasticisms, or rather four, for Byzantine culture also produced a flourishing Scholasticism, had only one common point of relationship: each

sprang from the meeting of a strictly monotheistic faith with Greek intellectualism. There was in that meeting a magnetic quality which energized the minds
in which the two things were present and produced a series of novelties, a
genuine growth of culture accompanied by all the pains and crises of true
growth. All the ambivalance of positive and negative attraction came at once into
play, as faith and philosophical understanding approached each other.

To realise how singular this cultural event was, we have only to compare the
Scholastic movements with the fate of the great schools of Hinduism at
something like the same period. The efforts of Shankara and of Ramanuja, to
name only the most famous examples, at producing a single and complete
conspectus of Vedic and Upanishadic thought by reducing the complexities of
tradition to a few basic but architectonic principles, display mental powers no
whit less remarkable than those of the greatest medieval thinkers of Islam,
Judaism and Christianity; yet the resultant discussions remain just as unmistakably Eastern as the writings of the Scholastics are unmistakably Western in
character. Is this simply and solely because the Indian mind made no contact
with Greek intellectualism? That I think is only half the truth; it is equally the
case that the immanent thrust of Hindu belief towards the surpassing of
polytheism and even of theism in the direction of an ultimate monism precluded
the consistent affirmation of monotheistic belief of the Western kind, the kind
namely that felt itself to be irreducible to any of the forms of Greek
metaphysical belief, and was inclined to accept the challenge of the latter and use
against it the weapons of reason and reflection wrested from it. Semitic
monotheism has an innate clarity of outline that impels it towards dialogue with
the products of the mind in its highest application. It is incapable of a purely
passive, inert relationship with genuinely metaphysical thought, by which I
mean any philosophy which aims at representing the totality of being. The
beliefs which monotheistic faiths share lay claim to truth and cannot be regarded
as purely symbolic or mythical utterances transcending the laws of rational
thought and the highest syntheses of reason. They are not themselves the
product of metaphysical speculation, but neither do they belong to a higher level
of truth, that refuge of Shankara, whence logic, living experience and the
wisdom that reflection teaches are all excluded, and where those beliefs must idle
in neutral gear. The great monotheistic faiths claim to deal in reality; that claim
leaves them exposed, often uncomfortably but always healthily, to reason and
experience, as their partners, allies, or enemies. They cannot hide behind the
pseudo–defence of a double truth, a symbolic reduction, or an ultimate
disjunction from human reason.

There is little difficulty I think, in the way of the historian of philosophy who
wishes to show that the Scholastic tradition of metaphysics centres on a
continuous problematic. In the Renaissance period the thought of Nicholas of
Cusa, of Suarez and of Cajetan, for all their individual differences of approach,

evidences a fascination with the enduring problems of the nature of being: the categories of being, the transcendentals, and the analogy of finite and infinite being. In the modern period, the neo-Scholastic movement has been, sometimes too self-consciously, heir to these same problems. The so-called transcendental Thomistic school, whether its members can really be called Thomists or not, are undoubtedly a leading force in contemporary metaphysics; yet for all their modernity and critical awareness they continue to meditate upon the same fundamental problems.

METAPHYSICS AND RELIGION

At this point I wish to enlarge my thesis, which hitherto has asserted an essential link between monotheistic thought, in particular its Christian form, and the Scholastic tradition of metaphysics, and to make the broader claim that Western metaphysics as such, in all its 'revisionary' forms, stands in an essential relationship to religious belief. The nature of the relationship admittedly varies greatly as between, say, Plato and Schopenhauer; but I propose to elucidate it in the following manner. The great metaphysicians of the Western tradition have either aimed to employ philosophical concepts in order to express an under-standing of religious faith (think of St Augustine and St Anselm: '*Fides quaerens intellectum*'), or they have sought to recover in strictly rational terms some of the basic beliefs of their religion (many Christian, Jewish and Islamic Scholastics, but also Plato, Aristotle and Plotinus); or else they have aimed at superseding religious faith by replacing it with pure understanding of the rational structure of reality in the widest sense (Averroës, Spinoza, Hegel, Schopenhauer); or, finally, they have attempted to clear a space in which religious faith may reign, securely removed beyond all apparent challenges of the reason (Kant, Paul Ricoeur). Let me illustrate this thesis before I move on to consider its conse-quences for the fate of metaphysics in our predominantly secular age. I choose my illustrations from the Greek metaphysical tradition and from German idealism.

PLATO

The tenth book of the *Laws*, Plato's last great philosophical dialogue, attempts to give content to the idea of human nature by placing man as microcosm within the political order, and making this in turn the microcosm of the cosmic and divine order, itself the living image of the highest reality. As his discussion of theology develops, Plato inserts numerous clues concerning his purpose. Some are evident and indeed explicit: to uncover the origins of atheism and deism in

the atomism of Democritus and the sophistic thesis that even the divinities exist
ou physei alla tisi nomois that is, as we might render his thought, as products of
culture and traditions *only,* just like moral values. Against such relativistic
hypotheses Plato argues in favour of a series of beliefs concerning the gods: that
they are the source of all order and goodness in the cosmos; are all good and
provident; that they reward and punish justly; in short, he formulates and
defends a canon of all that was best in Greek religious belief and piety, assimi-
lating even the floating and ambiguous popular belief in Destiny (*hEimarmenê*)
into his theology of a beneficient providence. His principal aim, which was to
pitch his exoteric teaching on religion at the level of the Greek common man
whether of city or countryside, is evident from the discussion itself. His other
aim, I suggest, is betrayed somewhat more obliquely; it is to underline the continuity and fidelity of his own thought with the theology of his predecessors and
to establish the unity of theology and belief. The key-words of his discourse
(self-moving soul, mind, justice, logos, order and origin) resonate back along the
Presocratic tradition of thought to Thales' adage, *panta plêrê theôn,* which Plato
introduces at the high point of his discussion. No name of any predecessor is
dropped, yet the Academy cannot have been left in doubt that Plato claimed
Thales, Xenophanes and Anaxagoras, and perhaps even Heraclitus, as his predecessors in rational theology. And it is as true of Plato's own metaphysics as it is
of the early cosomologists, that in their thought *theos* is an attribute of which
kosmos is the appropriate subject; if the cosmos in its entirety bears reference to
the divine, small wonder then that the philosophy of *to ontôs on* culminates in a
theology.

ARISTOTLE

I have made bold to place Aristotle among those metaphysicians whose thought
aimed at a rational interpretation of some beliefs that were basic to the religious
tradition. I think I can justify this bold claim even without resorting to a lengthy
analysis of his book called, variously, First Philosophy, Theology, Wisdom, or, in
the succeeding generation, 'the books after physics', that is, *Metaphysics.* I refer
to the remarkable passage which concludes Lamda viii, the discussion
concerning the number of the eternal moving causes. 'There is a very ancient
tradition in the form of myth', remarks Aristotle, 'that the stars are Gods and
that the divine enfolds the whole of nature' (*physis*). What follows in the text is a
fascinating example of reason demythologizing religious belief in order to create
a new equilibrium among the bearers of human truth: reason, sacred tradition
and culture. Aristotle dismisses as mere stories the popular beliefs concerning
the metamorphoses of the Gods, and regards them as accretions of later ages
consciously invented as a powerful agent of social control and a factor of political

stability. But if philosophical reason must desacralize tradition in the service of truth, still it is no part of Aristotle's intention to dethrone the divine rulers, for he is content to discover behind the myths a truth which he pronounces inspired and which he regards as the crown of all the highest cultures of the immemorial past, namely that the primary instances of being are divine – the very truth that Aristotle himself regarded as the axial affirmation of first philosophy. For him, therefore, just as for his master, the highest dynamism of reason moves towards the primordial affirmation of religion, though with a methodical and self-critical awareness not found, indeed not required, in cult.

GERMAN IDEALISM

In almost the last series of great metaphysical systems which Western philosophy has produced, those known collectively as German Idealism, the relationship established between metaphysics and Christian belief is broadly speaking one of dependence. The dependence of Hegel upon traditional belief is evident, as one by one the great Christian concepts of Trinity, Incarnation, reconciliation and resurrection appear in the pages of his *Encyclopedia;* but each of these beliefs is taken up into the rhythm of dialectical thought which claims to remove them from the domain of faith and posit them as moments in the real and logical self-reflective dialectic of finite spirit in its progressive identity with *Weltgeist* or Absolute Spirit. I should maintain that even if one were disposed to regard Hegel's rationalism as a pure secularization of historical Christian thought, still the essence of his metaphysics remains religious, though its affiliations lie as much with Hellenistic and Hindu religion as with Christianity. So much emerges from the centrality of light-metaphysics in his thought, a factor that relates it in manifold ways to the light-speculation and symbolism of late medieval German mysticism, as also to Scholastic thought; and back through that to Plotinus, Plato and Heraclitus, and even in some measure to the religious thought of all ages and cultures.

For Hegel, finite being is a cosmic light-sphere reflecting the immanent structures of divine Spirit or Logos in its manifestations in nature, history and culture. The highest form of nature is already light, an unreflective sensuously-existing concept constituting the temporal and spatial dimensions of the world and founding the cosmic network of interdependence that mirrors the immanence of all finite relations in the Absolute. Reason in its self-reflective capacity is a light that is the principle of the phenomenological ascent, whose summit is the self-revelation of Absolute Spirit as Light, in religion, art and morality. In this philosophy of the dialectical spiral the phenomenality of experience with reference to the Absolute is expressed in a multiplicity of concepts deriving from aspects of light: *Schein, Erscheinung, Bild, Abbild, Spiegel* and *Vorspiegelung,* as well as *Licht* itself. Hegel's fundamental thought, that reality proceeds as rays of light unfolding themselves into a multitude of finite things that absorb and reflect the creative Light, is a reminiscence of a religious belief that recurs across many cultures. His basic metaphysical thought is a derivative of religion.

SECULARIZATION AND THE DECLINE OF METAPHYSICS

If the thesis I have defended is broadly true, then the decline of metaphysical thought in our predominantly secular age is intelligible. There have indeed been some great recent philosophers who have interested themselves in metaphysical questions, but such figures as Collingwood, Jaspers and Heidegger stand outside the mainstream of contemporary philosophy in the measure that they developed their thought in dialogue with the classical metaphysicians of the past, indeed the remote past of the earliest Greek philosophers in Heidegger's case. If their thought was original, the questions that were their starting-points were often quite perennial; think for example of the question Heidegger puts at the start of his *Introduction to Metaphysics*: 'Why are there beings rather than nothing?' The age of secularism has produced no characteristic metaphysical thought, and metaphysics today, where it is pursued at all, seems to come out of an atmosphere that is somehow not quite modern, but austere, venerable and even a little antiquated. The recent revival of metaphysics in Anglo–Saxon philosophy gives the impression that it originates from a rather bad conscience about the excessive purges associated with the philosophical revolution of the positivist phase, and it carries alongside the white flag of truce a standard reassuringly proclaiming its non-revisionary zeal.

The most characteristically modern philosophies, when judged from a metaphysical standpoint, manifest certain common features. Marx, Nietzsche and various forms of pragmatism and utilitarianism attempt to place man within a social and historical framework of meaning which orientates him towards a future that will be more meaningful than his present state. The philosophical prophet of the modern age undertakes within this framework of historical dynamism to specify the conditions by which historical progress will lead human beings towards a fullness of humanity experienced as shared and liberated. A quantitative, even a qualitative, leap forward is possible for society *if*, and the individual philosopher enjoins his own particular oracle: if the proletariat will take history at its flood and change the relationship of man to fellowman, to the earth and the fruits of labour; or if man can be persuaded to abandon the prison-house of sacral morality and assume a terrible but fascinating freedom as *Uebermensch;* or if the democratic, liberal state can maximize individual freedom and thus release human potential for the good of society. In any case, secular philosophies posit an understanding of man – surely a truly philosophical enterprise – but do so in terms of society and history alone. The individual consciousness is pointed towards freedom as its essential dignity, and invited to see the fullest meaning of that freedom through an historical and social consciousness that makes man a cultural being in the deepest sense, vowed to the products of human culture, the enlightenment offered by its secular achievements, and the future that these postulate and assure for humanity. Our age is historically conscious to a degree that is unprecedented. We are curious about the origins and early history of every aspect of man, from language to science to charitable institutions, and we feel that to replace a human phenomenon in time and to follow its evolution is to have acquired an understanding of its essence. And, of course, it is not contradictory to be at once turned towards the human future and interested in the past, for the two concerns are profoundly complementary. Beneath both, however, lies a desire to understand human nature by placing man within time, society and culture as ultimate horizons of his being; and so, it is not very surprising if the characteristically modern philosophies are in the last analysis philosophies of culture and of history in the most all-embracing sense of these words; they make of culture and time the ultimate terms of reference of human Nature, at once the matrix of the comprehension of man and the reality to which the individual human being is referred in his search for meaning and truth.

The natural and biological sciences partly escape from this generalization, but only partly, I think. In the measure that the scientific mind investigates nature, it's study is of the non-human reality of *physis,* and not of *nomos* nor of *techné,* cultural and human values. The sciences add in some way to our knowledge of life, of the earth, and of the cosmos – all of them realities which culture and history presuppose as the physical environment of man. However, we have long been banished from the Eden of scientific innocence where the scientist pursued the truth of nature for the satisfaction of knowing her. He has taught the rest of us only enough to convince us that we laymen should leave the game to the experts and not expect to learn from them how to behave to each other and to the world. More ominously still, scientific knowledge has come to be more valued by society as a powerful instrument of change and as practically the same thing as technology. In itself an achievement of human culture, science, it is felt, will enable us to exploit nature and assure the future of historical and social goals that we choose to affirm.

In other words, of the four great categories of early Greek metaphysics our age and its philosophies have largely dethroned the divine, left *physis* to the scientist, and retained only culture and civilization, *nomos* and *techné,* as the terms of reference in which human nature is to be understood. Retaining these anthropological categories, we have infused into them a future orientation: values posed by the collective will and realized by technological power, nourished by a hope that is secular and immanentist – such seems to be the sum of being, the lived ontology of the present age.

OVERCOMING ANTHROPOCENTRISM

A view of reality which seeks to understand man's existence in the light of anthropological categories alone must lead to anthropocentrism and to the sophistical conclusion that 'man is the measure of all things, of the reality of what is and the unreality of what is not' (Plato, *Theaetetus*). It will be forced to conclude that human values cannot be derived from reality or facts, and to identify human freedom with sheer spontaneity of a more or less heroic existentialist kind, in which man creates himself at each moment out of nothing at all.

There is, however, in the eyes of the metaphysician, a Nemesis that is visited upon every neglect of reality, and a limit upon consciousness and freedom, even though denied, does not cease for all that to operate upon us. Nature, for so long a mere presupposition of human construction, of *homo faber*, has clearly threatened to impose a limit on history and the technological goals which progress has made appear obligatory and inevitable. We stammer a new language as our advanced technological societies begin to measure their utopian aspirations against the materials available for their realization; and behind all that language of ecology, environment, energy, atmosphere, conservation and natural resources, a simple substitution discovers fire, air, water and earth, the cosmic elements of which man is the microcosm. Our stammering has not yet reached the elements as realities; it is still too anthropomorphic, since after all we mean by atmosphere what humans breathe, by energy what they burn, etc.; but that we are on the way towards the reality underlying our requirements is signified by the sudden reappearance of the word cosmos to denote our environment of earth and heavens. In the measure that this usage is not a purely cosmetic one, if the pun may be pardoned, it suggests the surpassing of the eighteenth-century idea of nature and the universe, the Newtonian machine of colourless dead matter in clockwork motion, in a thought-vector that moves away from purely scientific reason towards the valuational and symbolical appraisal that acknowledges the presence of goodness and dignity in the world that supports our life, in its rhythm, harmony and balance of elements. We are caught up for the moment in the exciting discovery that value and obligation have an ecology, so to speak, not in our subjectivity and liberty alone, not even in the recognition of the neighbour and his rights as limiting our freedom, but in the primordial meeting of the human race and the natural world. Just as surely as the *ancien régime* was summoned to renounce domination and exploitation of the disenfranchized, man is required to relate anew to the earth he had thought subdued to his service. New values and a new behaviour before nature are required of him: respect, reverence and love are the indispensable basis of a new relationship. We have begun to codify these values, and to set up a pale of legislation forbidding pollution, governing waste-disposal, providing for conservation, resisting encroachment. As we seek to demarcate urban civilization and prevent its encroaching upon the natural environment we unconsciously mime the actions of our ancestors, who jealously guarded the zone of the sacred and forbade its pollution by the profane. In all that we do in this regard we are acknowledging our past failure to see in nature anything more than a storehouse of goods for human use. Now, the defeat of our former exploitative attitude contains within it a metaphysical moment: the spontaneous recognition of nature's goodness. Not for us now nor for our children's sake merely do we respect and conserve our environment, but for what it is in itself. In every species, even the cruellest and most repulsive, there is a basic value: its reality, as sharing in being in its own particular way. We are beginning to acknowledge, as men have done from time immemorial, that there are a priori limits upon the individual and collective will of humans, and to recognize that some of the natural-order limits will, if contravened by human action, exact a just retribution upon us.

It emerges from such considerations as these that man's environment enters into the very definition of human nature; human existence presupposes its environment. The uniqueness of man among natural beings is, however, that alone among animal species his habits, his life, his consciousness, cannot be defined by a restricted environment or habitat representing the sum or totality of the biological conditions allowing survival. It is a fundamental insight of Scholastic metaphysics that the environment of man admits of no a priori restriction; save at the biological level, man has no fixed habitat. Already at the perceptual level; his consciousness is geared to the assimilation of wholes, *Gestalten*, and it searches naturally for higher and higher syntheses and unities. The natural environment of the mind is not limited to the earth, nor to history or culture merely; it is not only nature and the solar system that supports the conditions of life on our planet, it is not merely the tiny part of the cosmos that we can glimpse from the earth's surface: it is the aim at all of these and their relativization in function of a beyond that defines the human mind, by attesting its lack of a priori limitations. The mind only is what it is because it knows realities in the light of what they are not: the totality, or being, on the one hand, and nothingness. Just as the eye selects form against field, so the mind grasps the reality of each thing against a cognitional field that is potentially unrestricted. The human mind steers its way, not by gazing at the waves but by looking to the horizon and the sky for its orientation. Neither man nor any individual thing, not nature nor even the cosmos, is the measure of all things; but being enfolds all the things that *phyein*, that is, that come to be and pass away. Things participate in being, and therefore symbolize it to the mind, which samples it in its individual instances, whether of matter, life, mind or spirit. But it is only in thought that bends itself to uncover the totality which is the a priori of all our knowing, that we learn to search out the interweaving of the highest forms, the *symplokê eidôn:* nature, knowledge, will, action, self and other, society and history; and to recognize the limits placed on each and all of these.

THE HUMAN MICROCOSM AS ETHICAL SUBJECT

The Scholastic metaphysics of the participation of existence in being, which I have adumbrated here, yields a vision of the human condition. Man's situation before and within being summons him to live in a conscious finitude as the microcosm of all that is. His truest freedom occurs in the practical recognition of limits that *can* but *may not* be transgressed. I speak, having in mind the ethical limits which the value of the human person imposes upon us, and which true culture and education endeavour to sustain. We are all conscious of the extent to which moral restraints have been broken down these last few years, and how one by one we have seen ethical values and the limits they impose upon our action replaced by physical barriers between communities. We have learned with dismay, first that armed combatants might be liable to be killed, then that the civilian is not safe, nor the woman, nor the child, nor the aged, nor the sick. We have learned that the citizen is not protected by the law from torture, nor by innocence from the fury of the diseased but technologically ingenious, militaristic mind. Our students at Queen's have not been spared: one was shot in his home on the way to his brother's wedding, another was picked up on the road and murdered, two more killed on their way out of church. Progressively, the only limits the killer respects are physical ones, which, being physical, are not optional. There are fewer and fewer things he cannot bring himself to do, so that it is impossible for the rest of us to understand his mind, since one cannot any longer perceive the apparent good that draws him to the evil. None of us can be in any doubt that there are in this society killers whose only regret is that there exists a physical limit to the torture their victims can suffer before they finally succumb.

CIVILIZATION AND CULTURAL-
EDUCATIONAL RESPONSIBILITY

The educator in Queen's speaks to an audience that is already awakened to the great human issues. His privileged task is to nourish the appetite for truth unrestrictedly, and to educate in himself and in his students a freedom that recognizes and affirms the reality of limits upon the will – a freedom that is innocent, not through ignorance of what is happening and being done around us, but which, through knowledge of the best and the worst that men are capable of, sets itself to live out the best and accept the consequences. Anyone who wishes to research and teach in our situation assumes a colossal responsibility, if he is to develop and hand on what he considers to be the highest values of human culture, values that are capable of surviving even the decline or collapse of civilization itself, because they are not, like civilization, a possession that submits the environment to our control but *are* that humanity itself. Civilization may give us power over external forces, but only a high human culture promises us a beginning of order and mastery within ourselves; the one is a means, the other an end and part of the Kingdom of Ends. Civilization with all its technical instrumentation can be implanted, transplanted and conveyed from one society to another – though not necessarily nor always to the latter's good; whereas culture, since it is what we are, must be elaborated by the sublimation of the instinctual energies it is meant to transfigure into value and truth. We must learn how to acquire and form in our students a sense of the self that crystallizes around those transcendent values which reason and philosophy can only adumbrate: compassion and love, the highest lessons of all religions that do not disfigure and exhaust themselves in ideology.

Twentieth-century Irish Scholasticism: a survey of publications (1900–75)

ÉAMONN GAINES

This paper is a survey of philosophy in Ireland carried on in the Scholastic tradition between approximately 1900 and 1975. It is divided into two main sections, the first of which deals with some notable figures in Irish Scholasticism, specifically in terms of their published work. The second section covers Scholastic philosophical publications in Ireland both in terms of publishers and periodicals. In each of these sections the sample treated is indicative and representative rather than exhaustive. The conclusion will take the form of a brief sketch of current work in the Scholastic tradition in Ireland and the prospects for its continuance.

SOME NOTABLE IRISH SCHOLASTIC THINKERS, 1900–1975

The Scholastic tradition in Ireland in the twentieth century can be generally although not exclusively identified with a particular set of philosophical questions and methods, as well as a concentration on certain landmark authors and texts. Thus the use of traditional Aristotelian logic, a general preference for Aristotelian metaphysics as mediated by Aquinas and a concentration on metaphysics and natural theology are all characteristic of this period in Irish thought. Different university departments of philosophy had their own preferences in that University College, Galway had for some years a significant Franciscan (OFM) complement while University College, Cork was home to various Capuchins; these naturally led to some attention being given to typically Franciscan figures such as Duns Scotus or Roger Bacon.[1] In addition to the Universities, there were the various philosophical and theological houses of

---

1 The varieties of Franciscan life can be confusing; briefly, the Conventual Order of Friars Minor (OFM Conv.) was not present in Ireland between the Reformation and the 1970s. The Order of Friars Minor of the Leonine Union was created by order of Pope Leo XIII out of a variety of Franciscan communities – they use the postnominals OFM without any addition. The Friars Minor of the Capuchin Reform (OFM Cap.) are historically a more rigorous community that is quite distinct from each of the other two.

formation belonging to twenty-six dioceses and the many religious orders and communities. What was common to them all, during our period, was the presence and even the predominance of the clergy, at least during the first half of the twentieth century. This section will be devoted to a brief treatment of some notable figures from this period. The formation they enjoyed was broadly Thomistic, although some space was given to alternative figures such as Bonaventure and Duns Scotus. Each of the thinkers covered here had strong theological commitments which were evident in, but not I think determinative of, their philosophical orientation. Many of them also displayed a broadly synthetic methodology, somewhat in the manner of Aquinas himself.

The following selection is intended to indicate only *some* of the researchers active in this field during our period and to discuss only some of their work. A more complete treatment would require far greater length than a single article.

James Desmond Bastable

Any treatment of Irish Philosophy would be incomplete without considering the career of James Desmond Bastable (1916–2000). A priest of the Dublin diocese and successively professor of philosophy at St Patrick's College, Maynooth and lecturer at University College, Dublin, he was responsible for the creation and maintenance of *Philosophical Studies* which was for many years the only professional philosophical journal on the island. Bastable in the latter stages of his career developed an interest in John Henry Newman, and edited a collection entitled *Newman and Gladstone: centennial essays* (Dublin, 1978). A survey of his work with *Philosophical Studies* is essayed below.

Patrick Bastable

Patrick Bastable (1918–91) was the brother of J.D. Bastable and like him worked in University College, Dublin. His career was more varied however, in that he worked in a range of European and American universities. He also had an active career in psychology and was a founder member of the Irish Psychological Society. His published work spans almost half a century and included traditional Thomistic concerns like natural theology, in *Desire for God* (London, 1947). He also produced a masterly text, *Logic: depth grammar of rationality* (Dublin, 1975). This was both a practical text book as well as a theoretical foundation for the discipline. One of his most significant works was also one of his shortest. *The Person of Conscience* (Dublin, 1983) was a reflection inspired by John Henry Newman on the experience of human autonomy and affectivity in the light of philosophical reflection and of theological revelation. It concludes with two rather unusual sections, one of personal reflection on the formation of the author's own conscience on the issue of *in vitro* fertilization and the other on the kinship of conscientiousness with music. Despite being only 47 pages long, it makes a profound impression. Patrick Bastable's last published work was a study of the theological dimension of St Patrick's letters. A joint publication with Fr Daniel Conneely, a Colomban Father, it appeared posthumously in 1993.

Desmond Connell

Desmond Connell was born in Dublin in 1926 and studied at Holy Cross College, Clonliffe, University College, Dublin, St Patrick's College, Maynooth and the Université catholique de Louvain. After completing his doctorate he returned to Ireland in 1953 and took up a teaching post at the department of metaphysics at UCD. His scholarly contribution was for the most part by way of occasional but masterly periodical articles. His most significant single work was based on his doctoral thesis and is entitled *The Vision in God: Malebranche's Scholastic sources* (Louvain, 1967). It remains a standard work in the study of Malebranche.

Theodore Crowley

Theodore Crowley OFM (1910–90) was for many years lecturer, reader and finally professor of Scholastic Philosophy in the Queen's University of Belfast. As a Franciscan his research interests naturally moved toward John Duns Scotus, St Bonaventure and Roger Bacon. The latter formed the topic of his book *Roger Bacon: the problem of the soul in his philosophical commentaries.*[2] His article 'Humani generis and philosophy',[3] published in 1952, attempted to give a programmatic account of what Scholastic Philosophy should look like by placing the principles of finality, causality and sufficient reason at the centre of a realist metaphysics. In this vein he had little hesitation in joining battle with analytic philosophy in defence of metaphysics generally in his article 'Metaphysics and Professor A.J. Ayer.'[4]

Arthur Little

Arthur Little SJ (1879–1949) was a Jesuit priest who taught philosophy at their college at Tullabeg, Co. Offaly. His contribution to Irish Scholastic Philosophy was wide-ranging and stretched from popular works such as *Philosophy without Tears*[5] to *The Shield of Pallas: or the Nature of Art.*[6] His most philosophically significant work was *The Platonic Heritage of Thomism.*[7] He meant this to be a corrective to the view that Aquinas was an exclusively Aristotelian thinker. Little wanted to propose a Platonic basis for much of Aquinas' thought and of course saw the concept of participation as central to St Thomas' intellectual project. Little's aesthetic was principally concerned with clarifying the nature of aesthetic experience while simultaneously ensuring its conceptual separation from mystical

---

2 Louvain: Institut Supérieur de Philosophie, 1950. 3 *Irish Theological Quarterly* 19 (1952), 25–32. 4 *Philosophical Studies* 3 (1953), 83–99. 5 Dublin, Clonmore & Reynolds, 1946. 6 New York, NY: Longmans, 1946. 7 Dublin, Golden Eagle Books, 1949.

or religious experience. It is worth noting that Little himself was an accomplished musician and a published poet; thus his aesthetic judgements had the authority of personal experience as well as the force of his own arguments.[8] His major work on Platonism and Thomism was published shortly after his death. Most of the rest of his periodical contributions appeared in *Studies*, the Irish Jesuit journal, and covered such diverse subjects as philosophy of science, Leibniz, Descartes, Existentialism, Neoplatonism and a headline article in a symposium entitled 'The case for Philosophy in secondary education.'[9]

Colmán Ó hUallacháin

Colmán Ó hUallacháin OFM (1922–79) was active in Franciscan studies in the 1940s and published on Duns Scotus. His subsequent interests developed in the direction of linguistics and he spent the last years of his career at the University of Ulster as lecturer in Modern Languages (Irish). His principal contribution to Irish Philosophy was his reconstruction, often from manuscript sources, of a technical vocabulary for philosophy *as Gaeilge*, in the Irish language. The preface to this eccentric but very thorough work was contributed by Louis de Raeymaeker, himself a native Flemish speaker who offered a spirited defence of the use of minority languages in philosophical practice. It is doubtful whether Ó hUallacháin had extensive experience of actual use of this terminology in philosophical writing or debate. It seems more likely that he collated and organized it to facilitate subsequent use. What is not in doubt is the sheer scale of the achievement and its comprehensiveness. Some terms are simply given their ordinary language equivalents, thus *visio* becomes *radharc*, mind or *mens* becomes *intinn*, as they would in non-philosophical usage. He also makes extensive use of transliteration or loan words, particularly those where there were existing parallels, thus giving *subaíocht* for subject and *feineaméin* for phenomenon. Thanks to the subsidy received by An Gúm, his *Foclóir Fealsaimh* or Philosophical Dictionary is still in print and readily available.

Feichín O'Doherty

Eamonn Feichín O'Doherty (1918–98) is described by J. Christopher Jones, on his personal website, in the following terms: 'Priest, theologian, student of Frederick Bartlett in experimental psychology, student of both of Jungian and Freudian psychologies and clinical psychologist himself, student of Jan Lukasiewicz in logic, theorist of creativity in art.'[10] O'Doherty had an enormously varied career in which his principal contributions were in psychological theory and practice. Sexton and Hogan point out that he pioneered professional psychological formation in the Irish Republic.[11] O'Doherty also

8 I am grateful to Fr Little's pupil and confrère Fr Francis Finnegan SJ for this insight. 9 *Studies* 27 (1938), 529–55. 10 Retrieved on 19 August 2008. 11 Virginia Staudt Sexton

combined his professional work as a psychologist with his theological and pastoral reflection as a priest. Thus his book *Religion and Personality Problems*[12] covered questions such as adolescent development and the Oedipus complex but also ranged over the potential connections between psychopathology and mystical phenomena, as well as treatment of practical questions about the emotional health of seminarians.

Walter MacDonald

It is worth noting that even among the Catholic clerical community the Scholastic approach was not necessarily unanimously supported. A case in point was Walter MacDonald (1854–1920) who was appointed prefect of the Dunboyne Establishment (that is, head of postgraduate theology) at Maynooth in 1888. His book *Motion: its origin and conservation* was published in London in 1898 and led almost immediately to controversy. McDonald's aim was to propose a theory of motion that would supplant Aristotelian ideas and replace them with the then current version of the kinetic theory. More strikingly, he claimed in the preface to his work that 'it is impossible to err in Physics without proportionate error in Metaphysics and Theology. Hence we may be sure that every advance in physical science will lead to proportionate development in Metaphysics and Theology.'[13] This rather subservient role for theology led rapidly to condemnation from Church authorities in Rome, and indeed his views did not garner widespread interest or support. He published three books subsequently, one a fairly straightforward ethics textbook *The Principles of Moral Science* (1903) and his final work *Some Ethical Questions of Peace and War, with special reference to Ireland.* (1920). This last stirred controversy again, as it argued against the movement toward political independence for Ireland. There is a sense in which MacDonald's *Reminiscences of a Maynooth Professor*, which was published posthumously, comes across as a settling of old scores, as he re-fights the battles to which his idiosyncratic views had led him.

IRISH PUBLISHERS IN THE SCHOLASTIC TRADITION

During the period under consideration the only significant means of disseminating widely the results of philosophical research was by way of books or periodicals. While some Irish authors were published overseas, for example, Patrick Bastable's 1947 book *Desire for God* was brought out by Burns & Oates in London, many authors chose to stay closer to home. Two of the more likely

& John D. Hogan, *International Psychology: views from around the world* (Lincoln, NE, 1992), p. 230. 12 Dublin, Clonmore & Reynolds, 1964. 13 *Motion: its origin and conservation* (Dublin: Browne & Nolan, 1898), ix.

destinations for aspiring Scholastic authors were Cork University Press on the one hand and Clonmore & Reynolds on the other.

Cork University Press

Cork University Press[14] is of course associated with University College, Cork, and dates back to 1925. It is the oldest Irish university press to have survived down to the present day and during its first forty years made occasional forays into Scholastic thought. Almost all of these were examples of applied philosophy, that is to say that they were concerned with the implementation of moral, philosophical principles in practical questions. This is particularly true of the 'University and Labour Series' which ran to ten separate monographs published between 1938 and 1951. The first three publications in the series covered *Reform or Revolution* (James O'Mahony), *Modern democracy* (James Hogan) and *Economics and the Worker* (W. Pascal Larkin). Subsequently a significant proportion of them were the work of the Cork polymath Alfred O'Rahilly and ranged over widely varying topics from *Money* (1941) to *Aquinas versus Marx* (1948) and *Moral Principles* and *Social Principles* (1948). This more theoretical focus was balanced by the practicality of the non-philosophical publications in the same series in which issues in child care as well as the cost of living index were covered. The latter topic was the last in the series.

Even after the end of the 'University and Labour' series, the applied Scholastic theme was continued by publications such as Jeremiah Newman's 1954 book-length study on *Thomism and Justice*. Unusually for Cork University Press there was a publication of a purely theoretical kind in 1950 with the appearance of Peter Dempsey's *The Psychology of Sartre*. This was an attempt to subject Sartre to a twofold critique, from a philosophical viewpoint and from Dempsey's experience as a clinician and psychologist. It met with a broadly appreciative critical reception, with even the critic for *Mind* giving it a guarded welcome as 'an important sourcebook.'[15]

The years 1960–1 saw the last Scholastic publications by Cork University Press in the shape of two guest lectures by Joseph Costanzo SJ sponsored by the US State Department, as well as a text on *The Church of England and the Ecumenical Movement* by then professor of theology at UCC, Fr James Good. Although Cork University Press has very occasionally ventured into philosophy since then, the early 1960s can reasonably be said to have seen the end of their engagement with the Irish Scholastic tradition.

14 I am grateful to Catherine Coughlan of Cork University Press for providing a complete catalogue of their publications for this period. 15 C.A. Mace, 'Critical Notice', *Mind* 62 (1953), 253.

Clonmore & Reynolds (1946–68)

The other principal locus for Scholastic publication was the idiosyncratic Dublin firm of Clonmore & Reynolds. The 'Clonmore' element of the partnership was an erstwhile clergyman of the Church of England who converted to Catholicism in 1932 and began to engage in apologetics for his faith after military service in the Second World War. As heir to the earldom of Wicklow, his courtesy title was Lord Clonmore; his partner was Paddy Reynolds, a well-known figure in the Dublin book trade.[16] Their catalogue ranged far and wide and included *inter alia* convert stories, spiritual treatises, history, apologetics and translations (usually by Lord Wicklow himself) from the French Catholic intellectual milieu of the day.

Their contribution to philosophical publication was, as one would expect from a Catholic firm of that era, almost entirely Scholastic, or more precisely Thomistic. Unfortunately there is no complete catalogue of Clonmore & Reynolds publications but what can be surmised from the catalogues of the National Library of Ireland, the British National Catholic Library and the Library of Trinity College, Dublin is that philosophy formed only a small part of their overall output. Their principal focus was on apologetics, devotional literature and specifically religious texts such as liturgical manuals or biblical commentary. The philosophical material they did produce included a pamphlet by P.J. McLaughlin, then professor of physics in Maynooth College, on the topic of *Modern Science and God* (1952); in addition they published in 1965 McLaughlin's *Nicholas Callan: priest-scientist, 1799–1864*.

Somewhat surprisingly for a Dublin-based firm, their most frequently published philosophical author was an Englishman, albeit one of obviously Irish descent. Martin D'Arcy was an English Jesuit, born in 1888; he was successively master of Campion Hall and then head of the English Jesuit province. Following his dismissal from that post he worked as a lecturer and preacher until his death in 1976. His publications with Clonmore & Reynolds were jointly published with Burns, Oates and Washbourne, so it is difficult to say who commissioned the works. Two of the the three books he published with this Dublin-London partnership cover familiar territory in natural theology and the philosophy of religion; these are *The Nature of Belief* (1958) and *Of God and Man: thoughts on faith and morals* (1964). His third text was an anthology entitled simply *Thomas Aquinas* (1953), in which D'Arcy took a selection of Aquinas' texts in translation and attempted to knit them into a thematic unity. Interestingly, it is the only Clonmore & Reynolds title still in print, even if only as a reprint with a Catholic publishing company in Colorado.

16 My grateful thanks to Nick Lowry of the *Brandsma Review,* Jeremy Addis of *Books Ireland* and to Michael Gill of Gill & Macmillan for information on the genesis and demise of Clonmore & Reynolds.

Besides a small pamphlet by a Cork-based Dominican, Aegidius Doolan, entitled *The Revival of Thomism* (1951) the only other philosophical work to come from Clonmore & Reynolds seems to have been Cahal Daly's book length critique of Glanville Williams' *The Sanctity of Life and the Criminal Law.* Entitled *Morals, Law and Life* it was intended to counter Williams' permissive positions on contraception, abortion, sterilization, artificial insemination and euthanasia. This work is of a piece with the then Dr (now Cardinal) Daly's concern for an intellectually well-grounded Christian public discourse.

Having appeared in partnership quite suddenly in 1946, Lord Wicklow and Mr Reynolds disappeared equally suddenly in 1967 or thereabouts. At any rate, they do not appear to have published anything later than that date. Neither M.H. Gill nor Burns, Oates and Washbourne acquired their remaining stock or back catalogue. Paddy Reynolds died in the mid-1970s while Lord Wicklow lived on until 1978; their firm seems to have disappeared without trace, except, that is, for the eclectic list of titles they published.

PERIODICALS

Studies: An Irish Quarterly Review (1912–)

While Scholastic Philosophers working in Ireland had to wait until 1951 for a home-grown specialist periodical in which to publish their work, an opportunity to publish in a more general review was offered by the Irish Jesuit journal *Studies.* Subtitled 'An Irish Quarterly Review,' its role was that of a general cultural discussion forum. While it did not aim for the level of abstraction or special-ization of a journal like *The Thomist,* for example, it provided (then, as now) a resource for the serious general reader who was eager to be informed about contemporary Christian culture. A cursory glance at the cumulative index of the 1912–61 period shows, for example, no fewer than seven articles on various aspects of Aristotle's philosophy. Even a small sampling of the authors featured in its pages shows Peter Coffey, Frederick Copleston, Michael Bertram Crowe, Jeremiah Newman, E.F. O'Doherty, Denis O'Keeffe and Alfred O'Rahilly. In addition to the kind of articles one might expect from a Jesuit journal of that era (for example, criticism of Bertrand Russell or analysis of contemporary British philosophy from a Thomistic standpoint) there is also a fascinating symposium on the place that philosophy ought to have in secondary education. The lead article was penned by Arthur Little SJ and there were various responses to it from educationalists and scholars such as Alfred O'Rahilly and Michael Tierney.

Philosophical Studies (1951–92)

While *Studies* was a welcome outlet for Irish philosophers in this period, what was really required was a specialist journal that would cater primarily for the philosopher, even if it had room for other disciplines. That lacuna was to be filled by the most influential forum for philosophical exchange within and beyond the Scholastic-Thomistic nexus, the journal *Philosophical Studies*. Founded in 1951, it was, in many ways, the personal project of James Desmond Bastable, its editor. Although he shared the editorship for a few years with Patrick McLaughlin and had an editorial board that usually had between three and five members, his presence was the one constant factor over most of the forty years of its existence.

At its foundation, Bastable was professor of philosophy at Maynooth College. The programmatic statement attached to the journal at this stage made clear its scope and approach when it spoke of having 'for its aim the development and diffusion of Christian philosophy by way of exact analysis and specialised study'. This basic approach was of course particularly receptive to researchers working in a Scholastic vein. The other principal features of *Philosophical Studies* were an attentiveness to 'contemporary problems and movements' as well as the provision 'of a forum for discussion for the young graduate as well as the more practised writer'.

At least during the earlier years its denominational Catholic identity was obvious, given that the ecclesiastical censor's permission to publish was prominently displayed on the title pages, or subsequently on the copyright page of every issue from the first to the twentieth. Appropriately enough it was only with the 21st annual issue that the journal was published with purely academic rather than ecclesiastical oversight.

These factors did not prevent it from having a catholic rather than exclusively Roman Catholic reach. Its early issues were generally but not exclusively concerned with familiar problems in Scholastic thought, and indeed Thomistic issues. Thus Volume Two had an article on the proof for the existence of God as well a historical treatment by Professor Theodore Crowley of Roger Bacon and Avicenna. It would be a serious mistake however to imagine that this approach indicated an insular mentality. In the first four volumes, theoretical and experimental psychology were represented by E.F. O'Doherty, and lively challenges to Russell, Ayer and the British anti-metaphysical approach to philosophy were forthcoming from John Burnham, Ephrem McCarthy and, in a memorable neo–Platonic dialogue, from Theodore Crowley.

The approach to philosophical writing in *Philosophical Studies* was to solicit articles and to engage in book reviews, as one might expect. Bastable and his collaborators had a third option, in addition, that of the Critical Notice. Rather than a simple summary and qualitative critique of the book review *simpliciter* this was intended to provide an opportunity for a more extended debate with a significant author or text. Thus in Volume Two one can find a trenchant debate with Heisenberg's *Philosophic Problems of Nuclear Science*, and in the subsequent volume there is an extended and broadly sympathetic treatment of a prominent Catholic critic of Thomism, Gabriel Marcel.

This general pattern of historical material, dialogue with contemporary approaches, especially Analytic ones, and the lengthy critical notices continued for most of the rest of *Philosophical Studies'* existence. Thus the thirteenth volume in the series (1964) had material on Boolean logic, Aristotelian and Thomistic metaphysics as well as C.L. Stevenson's ethics and Wittgenstein's *Weltanschauung*. In addition to ten full articles there were critical notices on Thomas Kuhn's *The Structure of Scientific Revolutions* and Anthony Kenny's *Action, Emotion and Will*, as well as *inter alia* a volume of John Henry Newman's letters and diaries.

The intellectual and social context in which *Philosophical Studies* existed was changing by this time, and the changes were far-reaching. The generally accepted approach to philosophy for many in Ireland had been broadly Thomistic, and the philosophy departments in which they learned this approach had been Catholic and clerical in their make-up. With major shifts in the culture of the Catholic Church in Europe following the Second Vatican Council, this Thomistic consensus was being challenged. Bastable believed that his project could survive and even thrive in this new environment. In a rare editorial, in the 25th edition, he celebrated the move to 'rediscover [...] the personal reality of the human being who directs his life with moral respect for others and who asserts the superiority of his living mind over its creations.' He also welcomed what he perceived as a 'new openness to non-Materialist viewpoints', and a search for 'a wisdom which values personal subjectivity in knowledge and choice without devaluing objectivity in truth and goodness.' He concluded by noting that 'we have sown some seed; the plant has survived and should grow further.' This optimism was not as well-founded as it may have seemed at the time.

Coupled with the intellectual move away from a broadly Scholastic-Thomistic intellectual culture, a gradual but increasing fall in the numbers of men going to seminaries and being ordained was noticeable. Neither the basic rationale nor the personnel required for the old system were present any longer. This was reflected in the striking revision to the programmatic statement of *Philosophical Studies*. In Volume 31, the journal was claiming for its aim 'the development and diffusion of philosophy by way of specialised study without excluding theological, social or scientific reflection.' The specific reference to 'Christian philosophy' was gone, and its absence marked a decisive move away from its original founding vision. Volume 31 was a bumper edition, with twenty articles, thirteen critical notices and numerous book reviews filling more than 550 pages. Although it had something of the old Scholastic style about it with articles such as 'The religious dimension of human reason' by James McEvoy or F.J. Fitzpatrick's 'Aristotle, Aquinas and Ryle: thought processes and judgment', these were in the minority. There was a great deal on Plato, as well as J. H. Newman, Eric Voegelin, Karl Jaspers and Alasdair MacIntyre. Christian philosophy was certainly still present but it was an altogether more diffuse even fragmented thing. This was the last issue to be edited by the founder of *Philosophical Studies*, J.D. Bastable. Volume 32 was due to appear in 1988 but was held over until 1991 when it appeared under a new editor, Professor Dermot Moran; he announced subsequently that Volume 33 would be the last in the series as the journal was to be re-launched under a new title and as part of the philosophy portfolio of what was Routledge (now Taylor & Francis). Bastable's journal made a significant contribution at a time when no-one else in Ireland did; it survived for most of its thirty-five years by dint of his hard work and dedication (to say nothing of financial support until the NUI agreed to offer a grant). However this personal element also meant that it could not survive its original editor's retirement and so it metamorphosed into the *International Journal of Philosophical Studies* which continues a not wholly dissimilar mission, albeit with a strong Analytic focus in recent years.

CONCLUSION: CURRENT WORK IN THE SCHOLASTIC IDIOM IN
IRELAND AND THE PROSPECTS FOR ITS CONTINUANCE

There was undoubtedly a conscious reaction against the perceived Thomistic dominance in most Irish philosophy departments during the 1970s and until at least the 1990s. Some institutions moved from a broadly Scholastic approach to one of the two chief competing schools internationally, i.e. the Continental-Phenomenological and the Analytic or Anglo-American. The continuing stable presence of some philosophers working in this historically rooted, metaphysically open-minded tradition was until recently guaranteed by the presence of a denominated Scholastic Philosophy department in Belfast and a broad but open Scholastic orientation in NUI Maynooth. Organizational changes have removed almost all of the institutional Scholastic presence in Queen's Belfast, and despite a thriving third-level Catholic University College in the west of the city no alternative provision has been made. Maynooth has traditionally been a welcoming place for Scholastic Philosophy, and this was especially true under the tutelage of Professors James McEvoy and latterly Thomas A.F. Kelly. The sudden and tragic death of Professor Kelly deprived Ireland of a distinguished philosophical mind.

Given that there is no guarantee of an institutional university presence, we can at least say that there are some individuals working in this philosophical idiom. To take only a random sample, there is first-class work being done on Irish medieval thinkers such as Richard FitzRalph. Analytic engagement with Aquinas is on offer in Trinity College, Dublin, and if University College, Dublin is no longer the home of a Thomistic school of thought, it has at least room for it at the table, so to speak. More encouraging, however, is the project originated by the late Thomas Kelly of Cáirde Thomáis Naofa or Irish Friends of St

Thomas. This was envisioned as a meeting place for Thomistic-Scholastic thinkers and those of an Analytic bent; the hope is to allow a fruitful collaboration between these very different traditions. With the rigour and conceptual clarity of the one and the historical depth and sapiential dimension of the other it is hoped that a renewed and deepened sort of philosophizing might emerge.

In the final analysis, though, the strength of the Scholastic tradition in Ireland depends on the perennial value of the questions it poses and the historically grounded, philosophically rigorous way in which it poses them. If these fundamental values of historical awareness, philosophical seriousness and a synthetic impulse are maintained and developed then there is no reason why Irish Scholastic thought – in whatever institutional form – may not see another hundred years or more.

Prosopography

JAMES McEVOY

In these pages the careers of the first four appointees to the Department of Scholastic Philosophy are summarized and a bibliographical note is added regarding each one.[1]

DENIS O'KEEFFE, 1882–1952

Born at Fairview in Dublin on 16 July 1882, Denis Joseph O'Keeffe attended CBS Marino. Entering Clonliffe College in 1899, he became an MA in Philosophy of the Royal University in 1904. He studied Theology at Maynooth and was ordained a priest in 1908. Appointed in 1909 to the newly-established lectureship in Scholastic Philosophy at Queen's University, Belfast, he had to ride out two appeals made against the post to the Irish Universities Committee of the privy council in Dublin. The appeals were dismissed, and O'Keeffe was to remain at Queen's until his appointment in 1925 to the chair of Ethics and Politics at UCD. He died suddenly on 21 April 1952. His acknowledged gifts of scholarship, tact and *savoir-faire* won over his colleagues at Belfast.

There, he lectured principally on Scholastic metaphysics, logic and ethics, while developing wide interests in the German idealists and the contemporary figures of Nietzsche and Bergson, whom he studied in the original languages. He had a keenly-developed literary sense and was a devoted reader of Dante, on whom he published an article. He became dean of the Faculty of Philosophy at UCD, and he served for three terms on the Senate of NUI. In 1950 he was appointed chairman of the newly-established national Council of Education. His published output was small by comparison with the esteem in which he was held by his contemporaries for his learning, and also that 'dignity and fun, wisdom and charm, which endeared him to all who knew him' (Ryan, 1952, p. 316).

Frequently his publications began as book reviews (for example, his study of Dante, 1924, and of Duns Scotus, 1927). His opinions on the books in question were liable to be trenchantly expressed, in a way that would not be acceptable

---

1 Entries (by J. McEvoy) on D. O'Keeffe, A.H. Ryan and T. Crowley appeared in T. Duddy (ed.), *Dictionary of Irish philosophers A–Z* (London, 2004).

nowadays. His political judgments were both acute and realistic. Writing in 1938 on the nazi movement in Germany he denounced a principle which its apologists seemed to share with communism: 'the materialistic concept of history [...], a principle which enables the communist to explain everything and understand nothing [...]. Historical causation is too manifold for any simple formula' (p. 2); 'the totalitarian idea, apart altogether from the pagan movements [associated with National Socialism] involves of necessity a conflict with Christianity', he argued (p. 3). Racism, in his view, inevitably resulted in the active persecution of the Jews, and it led directly to what he called 'an aristocracy of the strong'. He opposed to this evil of totalitarianism in Germany two doctrines: 'the assertion of the dignity and value of human personality and the theory of natural rights', both of them developments owed to Christianity (p. 9). Incidentally, he wrote as a self-professed Germanophile. Writing on democracy (1939) and equality (1941) during the early years of the war he defended both political ideals, and pleaded that 'Unless there are individual family and group rights independent of the State, it seems impossible to escape from the multiform tyrannies with which modern man is threatened. This is the Catholic philosophy of organised society' ('Equality', p. 172).

O'Keeffe also tackled questions that were actual in Ireland. In 1936 he discussed the pros and cons of second chambers in democratic constitutions – an issue which was live, and little less than explosive, in the wake of the abolition of the Irish Senate. The following year (1937) he reviewed recent French and German works relative to vocational organization within the political, economic and social order. He firmly opposed the notion of a bureaucratic, corporatist system imposed upon society from above, seeing therein the ideology of the totalitarian, authoritarian state. He supported the Catholic ideal of voluntary vocational organization.

A man of great industry, his consistent aim was to inculcate 'a critical, scholarly, philosophical attitude that would enable [his students] to grapple with any problem in any terminology' (Ryan, p. 313).

Bibliography
'Ethical problems of the future', *Irish Ecclesiastical Record* 28 (1910) 573–89; 29
   (1911) 14–28; 146–62.
'Henri Bergson's critical philosophy', *Irish Theological Quarterly* (April 1913),
   178–89.
'Philosophy and life', *Maynooth Union*, 1914.
'Dante's theory of creation', *Revue Néo-Scolastique de Philosophie*, February
   1924.

Published in *Studies* [Dublin]:
'John Duns Scotus', 16 (1927), 564–78.
'The problem of the Senate', 25 (1936), 204–14.

'Co-operative organisation of society', 26 (1937), 177–89.
'The Nazi movement in Germany', 27 (1938), 1–11.
'Democracy: an analysis', 28 (1939), 185–94.
'Liberty and law', 29 (1940), 187–96.
'Equality', 30 (1941), 161–72.
'Catholic political theory', 30 (1941), 481–7.
'The law and the universities', 38 (1949), 270–2. (A symposium comment on an
    article by D.A. Binchy published in the same number, pp 257–65.)

The above list may be incomplete; it is taken from the tribute written by his
friend A.H. Ryan: 'Denis O'Keeffe', published in *Studies* 41 (1952) 309–16.

ARTHUR RYAN, 1897–1982

Arthur Haydn Ryan was born on the Falls Road, Belfast on 1 January 1897, the
son of a policeman. He was a clever and studious boy and won exhibitions in the
junior, intermediate and senior grades while a pupil at St Malachy's College. In
1914 he matriculated at Queen's University with an entrance scholarship. He
graduated three years later with first class honours in classics. In 1917 he
enrolled in theology at the Urban College of Propaganda (Rome), from which
he was in due course to graduate with doctorates in philosophy and theology. He
was ordained priest from the Irish College in 1921. After teaching classics at St
Malachy's he was appointed to lecture in fundamental theology at St Patrick's
College, Maynooth. In 1925 he moved to Queen's University as lecturer in
Scholastic Philosophy, in succession to Denis O'Keeffe. In 1946 he was
promoted to a readership. Two years later he became parish priest of St Brigid's,
Belfast, where he remained until his death, which took place on 16 June 1982.
He was a member of the QUB Senate, and at the time of his death was the senior
pro-chancellor of the University, which had conferred an honorary DD on him
in 1958.

    A fine example of Ryan's thought and style may be found in a public lecture
on 'The Church and civil governments', delivered in Dublin (*Studies*, 1952).
The speaker voiced the 'instinctive suspicion that there is something dangerous
about a theory which claims either absolute authority or universal competence
for a political power' (p. 1). Continuing, he unfolded a critique, conducted in the
light of Catholic social principles, of the European phenomenon of totalitarianism during the previous thirty years, and focused especially on Stalinism.

    The broadcast lecture was a feature of the pre-television age, and Ryan
mastered the art. His book, *Perennial Philosophers*, gathered his radio talks on St
Augustine, Boethius, Abelard, St Thomas Aquinas, the origins of philosophy and
the ideals of the neo-Scholastic movement – ideals which he promoted in practice

through his courses. In these lectures he depicted the personalities of his subjects against a skillfully-painted historical background. His formation as a classicist made up the indispensable background to his writing on patristic and Scholastic authors. A second book, *Legionaries of Christ*, also had radio origins. In it Ryan studied the Christian writers of the post-Apostolic age: Ignatius of Antioch, Polycarp of Smyrna, the Epistle to Diognetus, Justin Martyr and Irenaeus.

Publications

Perennial Philosophers, Dublin (Clonmore & Reynolds), 1946.

Legionaries of Christ, Dublin (Clonmore & Reynolds), 1947.

The Church of Christ, Dublin (Clonmore & Reynolds), 1948. (A work of apologetics.)

'The Church and civil governments', *Studies* 41 (1952), 151–62.

'The early story of the Department of Scholastic Philosophy', in James McEvoy (ed.), *Philosophy and Totality*, Belfast (Queen's University), 1977, pp 7–21.

Ryan wrote numerous articles and occasional pieces in *Studies*, the *Capuchin Annual*, the *Irish News* and *The Collegian* (the St Malachy's College annual). A representative selection of these was edited after his death: Arthur H. Ryan, *Mirroring Christ's splendour*, ed. Ambrose Macaulay, Dublin (Four Courts Press), 1984. This collection of articles and addresses on religious themes, as well as occasional sermons, includes tributes by the late Bishop William J. Philbin (Down and Connor) and Dr Peter Froggatt (vice-chancellor emeritus, QUB), as well as by the editor of the book. The Mgr Arthur Ryan Prize is awarded annually to the best student in philosophy (formerly in Scholastic Philosophy) at QUB.

THEODORE CROWLEY OFM, 1910–90

Cornelius Crowley was born near Fenit, Co. Kerry, on 14 September 1910. He was raised by an uncle who sent him to the Christian Brothers grammar school at Tralee. At the age of sixteen he was enrolled at the Franciscan College at Multyfarnham, and the following year he received the habit in the novitiate at Killarney, becoming Br Theodore. In 1928 he was sent to the Catholic University of Louvain, where he was awarded the *Baccalauréat en philosophie* (1930). He pursued studies in theology at the Antonianum University at Rome, where he was ordained a priest at the exceptionally early age of twenty-two. His superiors sent him back to Louvain, first to complete his theology course at the Jesuit Faculty at Egenhoven (1933–4), then to study successively for the *Licence en philosophie* (1935) and the *Licence en sciences historiques* (1937). In 1939 he was awarded (*summa cum laude*) the degree of *Docteur en philosophie* for a thesis on the psychology of Roger Bacon. He spent the war years lecturing in theology to Franciscan students at Galway. In 1946 he was entrusted with the task of re-possessing St Anthony's College, Louvain on behalf of the Irish Franciscan Province. He combined his duties with research under Professor Fernand Van Steenberghen at the Institut supérieur de philosophie, and on 18 December 1949 he publicly defended his thesis for the higher doctorate, becoming *Maître agrégé en philosophie*. Within a short time (1950) this thesis appeared as a book.

Crowley applied for the lectureship in Scholastic Philosophy at Queen's University, Belfast and was appointed, in 1951. He was duly promoted Reader (1954), and in 1968 he was awarded a personal chair in his subject. He retired in 1975. Moving to England in 1978 he became chaplain to an orphanage adminis-tered by the Daughters of Charity at Gravesend. In 1986 he moved back to Belfast where he continued to live up to the time of his death (13 February 1990). His remains were interred in the Franciscan plot at Glasnevin in Dublin. A window dedicated to his memory can be seen in St Brigid's Church, Belfast.

In 1960, when the crisis in the Belgian Congo was at its height, the independence of the young Lovanium University was threatened. The academic authorities at Louvain deputed Crowley to go the Congo as vice-rector *pro tem.* of the university, placing reliance on his independence of mind, his fluency in French and his Irish passport. He met many of the leading personalities at the diplomatic end of the conflict. As things turned out, the rector of the institution was not targeted politically, so that the crisis passed and Crowley was able to return to Belgium and Ireland, with new African interests and a fund of stories about his experience.

In his specialized publications Crowley explored historically the reception of Aristotelian philosophy by Scholastic authors of the thirteenth and fourteenth centuries. His formation in historical method enabled him to make expert employment of the primary sources in this field, including manuscripts witnessing texts by Roger Bacon. His efforts at reassessing the chronology of St Bonaventure (1974) have won widespread approval among scholars. He argued against the ontologist interpretation of Bonaventure's theory of knowledge, and maintained that the latter's views concerning divine illumination were in fact close to those professed by Thomas Aquinas in his teaching concerning the *lumen naturale*, or the created mind whose activity depends intimately upon the uncreated light of truth.

Though he had a good knowledge of Descartes he was firmly opposed to the notion that the *tabula rasa* of methodic doubt could produce a uniquely-valid starting-point for philosophy. In the same spirit he opposed the efforts of Père Maréchal to bring the Kantian transcendental problematic into the centre of neo-Scholastic method, believing as he did that critical realism is a chimera. He pursued a similar line of criticism against the *Cartesian meditations* of Husserl.

In a printed symposium on the encyclical *Humani generis* published in 1952

Crowley set out the nature of Scholastic Philosophy as he saw it. He placed the principles of finality, causality and sufficient reason at the centre of a realist metaphysics as opposed to an idealist approach. Reviewing some issues that concern philosophy as well as faith and theology, and writing on the relations of reason to faith in the context of the recent encyclical letter, he argued that 'It is only by being true to itself, by respecting its [own] fundamental principles, that philosophy can advance.'

Publications

Roger Bacon: the problem of the soul in his philosophical commentaries, with a Preface by Fernand Van Steenberghen (Louvain and Dublin, 1950).

E. Lousse, *The Catholic University of Louvain during the Second World War*, translated by Theodore Crowley (Bruges, 1946).

Hidden God. By Fernand Van Steenberghen, translated by Theodore Crowley (Louvain, 1966): a translation of *Dieu caché. Comment savons-nous que Dieu existe?* Essais philosophiques, 8 (Louvain and Paris, 1961).

Published minor theses for the degree of Maître agrégé en philosophie (UCL): Theses quas cum dissertatione cui titulus 'Roger Bacon's Aristotelian and Pseudo-Aristotelian Commentaries' [...] publice propugnabit Theodorus Crowley, presbyter ordinis Fratrum Minorum [...] Universitas Catholica Lovaniensis in oppido Lovaniensi, divi Thomae Aquinatis Schola. No. XXIII, 12 pp. (The fifty minor theses in this publication formed part of Crowley's public *soutenance de thèse* [Louvain, 19 December 1949] in view of the higher doctorate in philosophy. Mgr Van Waeyenbergh, Rector magnificus of the Universitas Catholica Lovaniensis, presided at the session, with Prof. Louis de Raeymaeker chairing the *jury d'examen*.)

'John Peckham OFM, Archbishop of Canterbury, versus the New Aristotelianism', *Bulletin of the John Rylands Library* 33.2 (1951), 242–55.

'Roger Bacon: the problem of universals in his philosophical commentaries', *Bulletin of the John Rylands Library* 34.2 (1952), 264–75.

'Roger Bacon and Avicenna', *Philosophical Studies* 2 (1952), 82–8.

'*Humani Generis* and philosophy', *Irish Theological Quarterly* 19 (1952), 25–32.

'Metaphysics and Professor A.J. Ayer', *Philosophical Studies* 3 (1953), 83–99.

Preface to Fernand Van Steenberghen, *The philosophical movement in the thirteenth century* (Edinburgh, 1955).

'The Non Christian in a Scotist setting', in *De Doctrina Ioannis Duns Scoti*, Acta Congressus Scotistici Internationalis Oxonii et Edimburgi 11–17 Sept. 1966 Celebrati, vol. III: Problemata Theologica. Cura Commissionis Scotisticae (Rome, 1968), pp 757–66.

Transcendence. An Inaugural Lecture delivered before the Queen's University of Belfast on 25 February 1970 by Theodore Crowley OFM, professor of Scholastic Philosophy, New Lecture Series no. 53 (Belfast, 1970).

'Illumination and Certitude', in *S. Bonaventura 1274–1974*. Volumen
Commemorativum Anni Septies Centenarii a Morte S. Bonaventurae
Doctoris Seraphici. Cura et Studio Commissionis Internationalis
Bonaventurianae, Grottaferrata (Roma), 1973, pp 431–48.
'Bacon, Roger', in *Encyclopaedia Britannica*, 15th ed., 1974, pp 567–8.
'St Bonaventure chronology reappraisal', *Franziskanische Studien* 56 (1974),
310–22.
'St Bonaventure of Bagnoregio O.Min., 1221–1274', *Capuchin Annual* (1975),
56–63.
'Medieval Franciscan Ideology', in James McEvoy (ed.), *Philosophy and Totality*.
Lectures delivered under the auspices of the Department of Scholastic
Philosophy (Belfast, 1977), pp 23–32.
Eighteen articles appeared under Crowley's name in the *New Catholic
Encyclopaedia* (see vol. XV: Index, 1967). These included contributions on
minor figures of medieval times, and medieval historians (Reginald Lane
Poole, Alfred Plummer).
An appreciation of him has been published: James McEvoy, *Heart in Pilgrimage:
sermons and meditations* (Belfast, 1996), pp 98–105.

The following poem was written after his death by his QUB colleague, Professor
G. Singh, who occupied the chair of Italian Language and Literature at QUB.

In memory of Father Theodore Crowley

'Benigno a' suoi ed a' nemici crudo'
Dante on Bonaventura (Paradiso, XII, 57)

As you walked laboriously along
Malone Road, carrying the burden
of your years and ailments, they
somehow seemed alien to you,
like a stranger you had casually met
on the road. As if what was real
and lively about you had
nothing to do with them.

Cars passed you by – and often
so did I,
as your solemn, dignified figure
walked its measured steps –
we heading off as if escaping
ourselves, and you
slowly returning home.

CAHAL BRENDAN DALY, 1917–

The future Cardinal Daly was born on 1 October 1917 at Loughguile, Co. Antrim, where his father was the schoolmaster. As a boarder at St Malachy's College during the 1930s he came under the influence of the Revd John McMullan, an excellent teacher of Greek and Latin in the tradition of that institution. Cahal Daly studied classics at Queen's University, graduating with first class honours in 1937. At the same time he read Scholastic Philosophy for two years under Arthur Ryan. In the same year he proceeded to the study of theology at St Patrick's College and the Pontifical University, Maynooth. The degree of MA (in classics) was awarded him by QUB in 1938. The study of Greek and Latin grammar and literature have shaped his mind and lent it that analytical and historicizing cast which has been apparent in much of his published output. Ordained priest at Maynooth (1941), he was awarded the DD of the Pontifical University in 1944. Two years later he received a junior appointment in the Department of Scholastic Philosophy, QUB, following a short period spent as a Classics teacher at his old college in Belfast.

A twenty-year academic career is much shorter than the average, but C.B. Daly filled those years with labour and learning, the fruits of which showed themselves regularly. As a lecturer he was always well-prepared, dictating (as was then the manner) material that appeared to be fully written out in his very shapely longhand. Some of the material he taught, in ethics principally, had by 1960 found its way into print; he found an outlet for some of his work in the Irish journal, *Philosophical Studies*, to which he was practically an annual contributor over a considerable period. Keeping up his interest in theology, he also wrote and reviewed with some frequency in the *Irish Theological Quarterly*. Some of his published philosophical work has recently appeared in two collected volumes (1996 and 2007).

There can be no doubt that the course of Cahal Daly's thought and the motivation for much of this academic output came not only from France, a country and a culture he has loved all his life (he is an admirer of the philosophical Personalists, the late Emmanuel Mounier and the late Maurice Nédoncelle), but from the group of Catholic philosophers, Thomists like himself for the most part, which met annually for many years at the English Dominican retreat, Spode House. Their leading light, intellectually speaking, was incontestably the late Elizabeth Anscombe. With her Dr Daly formed a friendship that was to last until her death in 2001. Her husband, Peter Geach, who has survived her, was also an enthusiastic member of the Spode House philosophical group.[2]

---

2 Cardinal Daly paid a personal tribute to the couple in the Foreword he wrote for the volume honouring them: Luke Gormally (ed.), *Moral truth and moral tradition: essays in honour of Peter Geach and Elizabeth Anscombe* (Dublin, 1994), pp vii–ix.

In 1967 Dr Daly was appointed bishop of Ardagh & Clonmacnois. Virtually from that moment onwards he became a dynamic force within the Irish Episcopal Conference. His scholarly reputation, when combined with his energy, meant that his fellow bishops often looked to him to provide leadership in terms of ideas, and in particular to interpret the post-conciliar developments in the church on the European mainland. Bishop Daly was translated to the diocese of Down & Connor in September 1982 and remained there until 1990, when he acceded to the archbishopric of Armagh and thus became Primate of All Ireland, and cardinal shortly afterwards. An ecclesiastical history specialist has recently commented that just as William Walsh was the outstanding Catholic bishop in Ireland during the first half of the twentieth century, so Cahal Daly has proved to be in the second half. Scholarship has lent depth to his perceptions and blended into a unique set of talents and personal gifts. Queen's University made him a Reader in Scholastic Philosophy (1965) in acknowledgement of the value of his publications, and conferred an honorary DD upon him during his episcopal years in Belfast. His involvement in academic research and teaching have meant that C.B. Daly moves at ease within university circles, where he enjoys respect as a scholar. In his academic role he dialogued with philosophers of all hues, and proved unafraid of any fair challenge in conversation, in print or in broadcast discussions.

Publications
No list has been made of C.B. Daly's publications, but the following is a complete list of his books and monographs. Throughout his long life he has been a prolific author. Part of his output derives from the years he spent in academic life but much of it stems from his episcopal activities, taking the form of sermons, pastoral letters, memoranda, public addresses and occasional writings.

Morals, Law and Life (Clonmore & Reynolds, Dublin, 1961).
Natural Law Morality Today (Clonmore & Reynolds, Dublin, 1965).
Violence in Ireland and Christian Conscience (Veritas Publications, Dublin, 1973).
Peace, the Work of Justice (Veritas Publications, Dublin, 1979).
The Price of Peace (The Blackstaff Press Ltd., Belfast, 1991).
Peace: Now is the Time (Veritas Publications, Dublin, 1993).
Law and Morals (Four Courts Press, Dublin, 1993).
Tertullian the Puritan and His Influence (Four Courts Press, Dublin, 1993).
Moral Philosophy in Britain from Bradley to Wittgenstein (Four Courts Press, Dublin, 1996).
The Minding of Planet Earth (Veritas, Dublin, 2004).
Philosophical Papers (Four Courts Press, Dublin, 2007).
The Breaking of Bread: Biblical Reflections on the Eucharist (Veritas, Dublin, 2008).

War: The Morality, the Reality, the Myth. A Lecture in Memory of Monsignor Arthur H. Ryan given at the Queen's University of Belfast on 2 February 1984 (QUB, 1984).

Appendix: List of staff in the Department of Scholastic Philosophy, 1909–2009

Denis O'Keeffe (1909–25)
Arthur H. Ryan (1925–49)
Robert Murphy (1941–2)[1]
Cahal Brendan Daly (1948–67)[2]
Theodore Crowley (1950–75)
James P. Mackey (1960–6)
Dennis Hickey (1961–2)
John Dowling (1967–8)[3]
Henry C. McCauley (1968–75)

Philip Pettit (1967–8)[4]
Hugh Bredin (1966–2004)
James Daly (1968–2002)
James McEvoy (1971; 1974–88; 2004–9)[5]
Timothy Lynch (1975–2004)
Bernard Cullen (1976–)
Dermot Moran (1979–82)

Contract and part-time appointments, 1987–

Aidan Donaldson (1987–9)
Deirdre Carabine (1988–9)
Philipp Rosemann (1989–90)
Alan Gabbey (1990–1)
Eoin Cassidy (Metaphysics 1987–2003)

Colin Harper (Ethics 1994–5; 2001–2)
Ian Leask (1998–2000)
Michael Dunne (Scholastic Metaphysics 2002–9)
Éamonn Gaines (Scholastic Ethics 2002–)

---

1 Replaced A.H. Ryan for two lengthy periods of the latter's sabbatical leave.   2 In 1986 QUB awarded Bishop Cahal Daly (Down and Connor as he then was) the degree of DD *honoris causa*. 3 John Dowling and Philip Pettit were each appointed to a half-lectureship in the year between James Daly's appointment to a lectureship in 1967 and his taking up the position in 1968. Both were temporary and part-time.   4 QUB awarded Professor Pettit (Princeton) the degree of D. Litt. h.c. in July 2007.   5 1971–2: Temporary assistant lecturer in Scholastic Philosophy; 1974–5: Assistant lecturer; 1976–88: professor of Scholastic Philosophy; appointed external examiner in Scholastic Philosophy, 2000–4; reappointed to the chair of Scholastic Philosophy, 2004–9 (part-time).

Index